The Captain and "the Cannibal"

NEW DIRECTIONS IN NARRATIVE HISTORY

John Demos and Aaron Sachs, Series Editors

The New Directions in Narrative History series includes original works of creative nonfiction across the many fields of history and related disciplines. Based on new research, the books in this series offer significant scholarly contributions while also embracing stylistic innovation as well as the classic techniques of storytelling. The works of the New Directions in Narrative History series, intended for the broadest general readership, speak to deeply human concerns about the past, present, and future of our world and its people.

The Captain and "the Cannibal"

An Epic Story of Exploration, Kidnapping, and the Broadway Stage

ഗ

JAMES FAIRHEAD

Yale UNIVERSITY PRESS

New Haven & London

Published with assistance from the Louis Stern Memorial Fund.

Yale University Press books may be purchased in quantity for educational, business, or promotional use. For information, please e-mail sales.press@yale.edu (U.S. office) or sales@yaleup.co.uk (U.K. office).

Designed by James J. Johnson and set in Bembo type by Westchester Book Group. Printed in the United States of America.

Library of Congress Cataloging-in-Publication Data

Fairhead, James, 1962–

The captain and "the cannibal" : an epic story of exploration, kidnapping, and the Broadway stage / James Fairhead.

pages cm — (New directions in narrative history)

Includes bibliographical references and index.

ISBN 978-0-300-19877-5 (hardback)

1. Morrell, Benjamin, 1795–1839. 2. Morrell, Benjamin, 1795–1839—Travel—Papua New Guinea. 3. Dako. 4. Papua New Guinea—Description and travel. 5. Papua New Guinea—Discovery and exploration. 6. Ship captains—Connecticut—Biography. 7. Indigenous peoples—Papua New Guinea—Biography. 8. First contact of aboriginal peoples with Westerners—Papua New Guinea—History—19th century. 9. Kidnapping—Papua New Guinea—History—19th century. 10. Sideshows—New York (State)—New York—History—19th century. I. Title.

DU740.6.F35 2015

995.7′1—dc23   2014029610

A catalogue record for this book is available from the British Library.

This paper meets the requirements of ANSI/NISO Z39.48–1992 (Permanence of Paper).

10 9 8 7 6 5 4 3 2 1

To the memory of Dako and "Monday"

ಠಃ

Contents

ฬ

Acknowledgments

I should like to thank the two people who have been fundamental in helping me develop this work: Jennifer Blythe and Sally Holloway. Without Jennifer this would be a half-told tale, and without Sally, a badly told one. Jennifer Blythe has shared so generously her extraordinarily detailed anthropological research from Uneapa and Garove Islands in 1975–76 and 1986. She has been a wonderful correspondent, helping to resolve the enigmas that this story has thrown up and to correct my often untutored deductions. Sally Holloway, at Felicity Bryan Associates, saw a potential in this story early on, but her insights on narrative have also provided analytical inspiration and enhanced the work's rigor. I am hugely grateful to others, too, who have advised so superbly on style, structure, and content, including George Lucas at Inkwell, Chris Rogers and Susan Laity at Yale University Press, and an anonymous reviewer. I should like to thank, too, Bill Nelson for drawing the maps, Alexa Selph for creating the index, and designer James J. Johnson and assistant editor Erica Hanson at Yale University Press, who helped prepare the book for press. Chris Ballard's incisive comments on a very early draft helped give impetus and shape to the work. To all, I apologize for not always following advice. Responsibility for errors of fact or interpretation must remain mine and mine alone.

Many other people have advised or helped on the Pacific dimension to this work, some perhaps even without realizing it, including

Liza Bailey, Joshua Bell, Bob Blust, Robert and Salme Bugenhagen, Sarah Byrne, Ann Chowning, Dorothy and David Counts, Simon Day, Chris Gosden, Rick Goulden, Rowena Hill, Rebecca Jewell, Ray Johnston, Steven Keu, Ian Lilly, Naomi McPherson, Mary Mennis, Michael Musgrave, Alice Pomponio, Malcolm Ross, Marshall Sahlins, Hiroko Sato, Michael Scott, Gunter Senft, Marilyn Strathern, Alice Street, Nicholas Thomas, and Bil Thurston. I am deeply thankful for advice concerning the Madagascan dimension to this story from Gwyn Campbell, Patrick Harries, Alison Jolly, and Pierre Van Den Boogaerde, and for advice concerning the French dimensions and especially the La Pérouse mystery from Jean Guillou, Samuel Houssou, and Jacques Lavo.

For advice and assistance in hunting manuscripts concerning the American dimension I would like to thank Terry Barnhart, Derrick Beard, Kristin Johnson, Gay and Charlie Lord, and Herschel Parker. And my thanks, too, go to Wendy Schnur and Charlotte Walker-Said, who both gave hands-on assistance at Mystic and Yale libraries.

In researching this work, I have a developed a huge respect for the hospitality-at-a-distance and helpfulness of librarians and archivists across the United States and beyond. Works such as this depend on their goodwill, and I have never had anything but a warm reception for my mails out of the blue. Among those who have been particularly helpful are Liz Farrell of the Brooklyn Historical Society; Dorothy Woodson, Judith Schiff, Graham Sherriff, and Diane E. Kaplan at Yale University Libraries; Alison Moore at the California Historical Society; Tracy Potter of the Massachusetts Historical Society; Megan O'Shea and Thomas Lannon of the New York Public Library; Leanda Gahegan and Daisy Njoku of the National Anthropological Archives at the Smithsonian Institution; Earle Havens of the Sheridan Libraries at Johns Hopkins University; Cliff McCarthy at the Stone House Museum; Barbara E. Austen at the Connecticut Historical Society; Carol Ganz at the Connecticut State Library; Jasmine Jordan of the Royal Botanic Gardens, Sydney, Australia; Ian Tattersall and Paul F. Beelitz of the American Museum of Natural History; Irene Axelrod of the Peabody Essex Museum; Margaret Downs Hrabe of the

University of Virginia Library; Linda S. Ford at the Museum of Comparative Zoology, Harvard University; Jeanne Solensky at the Winterthur Library; Anne Thacher of the Stonington Historical Society and Museum; Kelly Drake at Mystic Seaport's Museum of America and the Sea; Laura O'Keefe of the New York Society Library; Michael Yockey and Carol Odhner of the Swedenborgian House of Studies, Berkeley, California; and Betty J. Duggan and Craig Williams of the New York State Museum, Albany. I am fearful that I may have forgotten others in the intervening years, and if so I apologize and thank you in equal measure.

I would particularly like to thank the Huntington Library in San Marino, California, and Olga Tsapina, curator of the Woodworth family papers. This archive became crucial to the story and the history. I am extremely grateful for your help in making this archive available.

I am extremely grateful, too, to my colleagues at Sussex, including Jeremy Reffin, whose wizardry in informatics revealed the plagiarists of old; members of our experimental "hybrid ethnography" reading group, including Alex Aisher, Raminder Kaur, Katy Gardner, and Andrea Cornwall; and our library staff, which has never backed off from tracking down some of the most obscure works on which this volume depends.

Finally, I thank my family. They have put up wonderfully with an obsessed father, son, son-in-law, and husband, and have helped enormously in reading and discussing the work. Thanks to Cassie, Rory, Xanthe, and Francesca; to Jane Fairhead and Penny Leach; and most of all to Melissa—whose patience and partnership mean all.

The Captain and "the Cannibal"

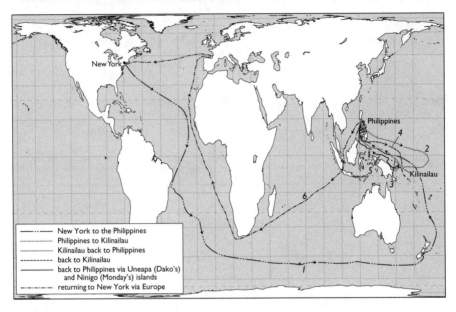

Voyage of the *Antarctic*, 1829–1831 (map by Bill Nelson)

Prologue

ℒℚℒ

B y dusk on Friday, February 22, 1833, the 101st anniversary of
George Washington's birth, the New York sky had finally
cleared, ending a winter's siege of cloud and storm. There
was no sign of the daylong pomp and pageantry that had accompanied the centennial the previous year. This February's celebrations
would be confined to a special evening of festivity.

For many people, the events began on Broadway, where customers shelled out 25 cents at the American Museum to experience
the brilliant new illumination and wonder at the latest in gas lamps
throwing their novel light over a hundred thousand curiosities. Rev-
elers entered the vast marble halls to mingle with a crowd of life-
sized wax figures, the likes of King Herod, Cupid, and Sleeping
Beauty among them. And together they faced an amassed multitude
of stuffed beasts, ranging from cougars to condors and chimpanzees,
all in a "perfectly natural state of preservation." This was the private
collection of the late Mr. John Scudder and the largest scientific collection in America. It exhibited exotic live animals—alligators, turtles, snakes, and even the occasional kangaroo—alongside the dead:
Egyptian and Native American mummies, mammoth tusks, and puz-
zlingly huge antediluvian fossils. In these pre-photography days, a hall
upstairs enticed visitors to peer into endless optic boxes and for the
first time be drawn into perspectival paintings that conveyed them to

the "most remarkable places in the world." All in all, it was a quarter well spent.

As the evening progressed, grandees with five dollars to spare were dropped off by carriage at the Military and Civic Ball at the Park Theater. The more frugal strolled under the freezing night sky and crescent moon to cheaper options at the Masonic Hall, the Military Hall, and the Concert Hall, or ventured into the fancy-dress version at the City Saloon on Broadway, sporting costumes both "splendid and grotesque." For others it was the theater. And the savvy ticket tonight was a new show at the Bowery, *The Cannibals; or, Massacre Islands.*

The reviews had not been great, but the audiences were loving it and the show tonight promised to be extraordinary. On this night, and for one night only, the Cannibal himself would take the stage. The piece was written by the renowned poet Samuel Woodworth, whose "Ode to George Washington" had been sung at the centennial. This year, his offering related the recent true-life adventures of a daring sea captain whose crew had almost all been massacred and eaten on a distant Pacific island, and of one crew member who had been captured and would have suffered a similar terrible fate had he not been heroically rescued by his captain. The reviewers had applauded the dream sequences and premonitions, but professed disappointment with the less-than-convincing savages. These were white actors whom the director had dressed in calico dresses and green jackets, not even blacking their faces. The audiences deserved more, felt the reviewers; more perfect savages, "wild, uncultivated islanders" of a "dark mulatto or copper color," like "the two specimens brought to this country." And so on this, the third night, in honor of the Founding Father, Dako, then known as "Sunday" and one of the very "specimens" of which the critics spoke, was to join the performance, play himself, and demonstrate his mighty power with the javelin.

Other later commentators who have stumbled on the improbable performances by Dako have dismissed him as a "faux cannibal," a "domesticated Pacific Islander or African American impersonator posing as a savage." I could have drawn the same conclusion myself had I simply read the news coverage, but I chanced upon him rather differ-

ently. Being an anthropologist with a particular interest in the lega-
cies of past land use on modern African landscapes, I had been searching
for early descriptions of West Africa that several slaves had reputedly
recalled to researchers in America. Churning through the archives
and publications of the emerging science of anthropology, I stumbled
upon the lives of a few other people whom fate had also pulled to
New York from the farthest reaches of the world and who, like these
slaves, had been singled out for interview. As the "faux cannibal" was
among this select group of key informants, his story was not to be
dismissed so easily. And as with the others, his life had been documented in rare detail. It was riveting, and I was gripped.

The anthropologist who had taken it upon himself to meet the
captive "cannibal" in New York and document his language and life
was Theodore Dwight, Jr., who doubled as a crusading journalist
expounding on the injustices of the world. He befriended the islander, and throughout the winter of 1832 and into the next spring
the two could be seen regularly traipsing the docks and factories of
New York Harbor, visiting the schools and shops of the city, learning
of each other's worlds.

As I followed their traces from archive to archive, I began to
realize that neither Dwight nor his new friend knew the precise
whereabouts of Dako's home island. In order to locate it, I showed
Dwight's transcriptions of the captive's language to a modern linguist, who quickly pinpointed its origins to a small island off New
Guinea named Uneapa. This intrigued me. This island and its region
had supposedly not been "contacted" by the Western world until the
1870s, forty years later. What was going on? How had this captive
ended up at the Bowery Theatre lobbing javelins? And what had
become of him? Since he didn't even know where his native island
was, could he ever have returned? The fates had delivered me half of
his story like a ripped banknote and began taunting me to find the
other half. Here was a man who had starred at one of New York's
most notorious theaters and enthralled the city's nascent intelligen-
tsia but whose very existence now seemed so improbable that it had
been airbrushed away.

So I returned to the archives to recover his life. Immediately, I stumbled on a second, equally improbable, epic tale: that of his captor, the celebrated American sea captain Benjamin Morrell, whose own life, I discovered, was every bit as mysterious as that of his captive. And as I soon found out, their intertwined odysseys had not stopped at the mischievous theatrical scene of 1830s New York. They led me to the banks and backstreets of America, to its muses and museums, and then back across the world, from Stonington, Connecticut, to the South Seas—to Mozambique, Madagascar, Canton (Guangzhou), and Cuba. Intellectually, they led me into the altogether more dangerous debates that raged both in America and on the Pacific Islands at the time concerning who, exactly, was fully human—or indeed fully alive. This was not just a story of adventure on the high seas. I found I had strong anthropological reasons to persist.

Initially I was interested in these events for what they said about America and the Western world. But thumbing through the archives and reading between the lines, I found this new impetus unsettling. Should I inquire only into what the "informant" meant to "us"? Or might that simply be piling fresh injustices upon old? After all, this man had been ripped violently from his world, so by looking at him from a one-sided perspective, wasn't I doing further disservice to his memory? Perhaps the story could be told the other way round, and I could explore what he made of his abductors and of the "anthropologists" who befriended him and of their worlds. Ask not only what his life meant for "our past," I decided, but also what our past meant for him, for his "anthropology," in whatever form it took.

This was a big task, and much easier to envisage than to achieve, especially regarding a man whose life began two hundred years ago on an island that scholars still assert would wait more than his lifetime to be visited by anyone in the Western world. Such "reverse anthropology," as some have called it, would also require me first to grasp how this exile interpreted the world around him, and then what he made of the novel events, encounters, and emotions as he lived them. In short, it required me to narrate his story. Serendipitously, the archives delivered.

But there were problems. First, this was fast becoming the kind of narrative history that stands accused by a host of historians of being unsuitable for the very thing I was now trying to achieve. To make the past familiar enough to carry Dako's story, and to establish enough empathy to drive it forward, would I not have to paste over the radically different worldviews with which all works of history—but especially this one—must grapple? Could I resolve the tension between accuracy and empathy when narrating the life stories of a captain and his captive, neither of whom initially regarded the other as entirely human?

Second, I wondered about my own interest in relating the story. Was I not merely snatching a few more guilty pleasures from these events and from the clichés of first contact and their parodies? Was I behaving as a voyeur even as I denounced Dako's predicament? It is a danger signaled in this book's very title, *The Captain and "the Cannibal,"* which rehearses old prejudices only thinly veiled by a pair of quotation marks. This is dangerous territory for any author to venture into, let alone a twenty-first-century anthropologist whose whole academic pursuit has been to confront such bigotry. But histories can and must be told. Pleasures can be taken. Indulge in irony, I decided, and feel the guilt.

Third, given the sheer scope of a story that tacks round all seven seas and as many continents, I would inevitably make mistakes. But in this ambition I drew inspiration from many modern writers who, even as they try to delimit their work when probing "American" history or "English" literature, for example, realize that they too must highlight the global exchanges that shape them. There is no alternative to placing history in its global context, even though it is a colossal task. One tactic taken, for instance, by writers on the "Black Atlantic" or "The Pacific" is to switch analytical focus from nations to oceans and trace the connections across them. Another way of tackling this impossible vastness is to see the world through the proverbial grain of sand—so long as that grain encompasses the globe. This usually means following something—a person, an object, the money, or even a metaphor—wherever it goes and untangling their new experiences.

Thankfully, in the era I was exploring, the 1830s, all these could only travel by sea, so if I followed the voyage, I'd be doing well. Voyages can become veritable microscopes for the study of global history. Not only do they convey us to an array of contact zones, but the ships became multicultural melting pots—unwitting laboratories exposing social and national frictions as the world expanded (or contracted). Moreover, voyagers shipped their results back home—so in our case, not only did the captain bring his captive home to display, but he and his crew wrote of their adventures; publishers and playwrights brought the stories to print and stage; preachers and scientists argued their implications; and novelists probed their eternal truths. The effects would run deep. Voyages did not end at the harbor.

The telling of the interlaced odysseys of the captain and Dako is a work of history, and I have been as constrained as enabled by the myriad sources that have made it possible and that I hold to. As the sources themselves—many of questionable reliability—are so much a part of the story, I would beg the reader to bear with me when considering whether I have read them critically enough. These sources include the mass of disparate documentation through which this story reverberated around America and the world, ranging from three full-length books to manuscript logbooks, journals (often ciphered), sketches, memoirs, legal protests, pamphlets, business prospectuses, newspapers, and magazines, but extending also to oral recollections from Dako's own island. I have been careful to retain the language of the original material, especially when it conveys the complex characters of those involved, either by holding to turns of phrase or by using explicit quotations. Sharing the many powerful characters in this book as they have emerged from the hard rock of history has not been easy: writers develop friendships with those whom they breathe new life into, but dead friends can be as fickle as the living. Now that the story is written, I have the uncanny sense that I have not been its author at all. It has been lying dormant for nearly two centuries, awaiting its moment. The story spins us, not us the story.

CHAPTER I

The Island

ෆᏊ

T he smoke cloud diffused gently across the surface of the sea, where it had lingered after the broadside of cannon, swivel guns, and muskets had been unleashed from the merchant schooner. Echoes of their blasts had long since returned from the island's mountainous backdrop, leaving a percussive silence and eerie expectation on board the ship. As the view cleared, it became apparent that the water was "literally covered with dead bodies and fragments of canoes"—at least according to twenty-year-old Oscar Sturtevant, who was one of "several young gentlemen of a romantic turn of mind" who had joined the ship's crew in search of adventure on the South Seas. Decades later, he would recall the horror of that Sunday morning, November 14, 1830, as the brilliant blue waters turned red with slaughter.

Most of the American crew aboard the *Antarctic* were as young as Sturtevant, if not younger. The navigator, John Keeler, had only just turned sixteen. In the calm later that evening he diligently updated the ship's log, setting down in this book of truth what had happened that day: how a large number of canoes from the island had approached—some of them carrying, he claimed, upward of fifty or sixty men. Then, as the islanders closed in under the stern with their slingshots prepared and their spears at the ready, "we fired a volley into them."

The previous day, the twin-masted schooner—supposedly the fastest her country had ever built—had dropped her anchors half a mile off the southern shore of the island, where they held fast to the barrier reef, shimmering at a safe depth some five or ten yards below the water. Her crew had spotted a gap in the shallow fringing reef that otherwise encircled the island nearer to the shore. This promised a rich harvest of sea cucumbers and pearls—if only the men could be left alone to gather them.

A week earlier, the Americans had been forced for the second time to abandon similar reefs five hundred miles away off the island they had previously dubbed "Massacre Island" after the inhabitants had killed thirteen of the crew. So now, as the canoes approached the ship off this new island, the captain prepared his cannons, each loaded with canisters holding two or three hundred musket balls or with the double-headed shot linked by chains that whistled as they spun to shred their marks.

As the flotilla of war canoes neared, it became clear to the Americans that they were not manned by the stunted and feeble Harafora people that their *Universal Geography* had led them to expect. Instead, many of those standing on the canoe platforms holding their laboriously crafted javelins, slingshots, and war clubs were nearly six feet or even taller, dwarfing the ill-nourished crew members, few of whom stood more than five feet five. The same authority had cast these islanders as "doomed to perpetual misery, and incapable of rising from the very bottom of the scale of humanity, or of acquiring the habits and feelings of civilized beings." But its pronouncements rang hollow as the canoes closed in on the schooner, revealing the classical physiques and proud stances of their occupants, whose naked bodies were enhanced with delicate necklaces, armbands, and earrings. Some had back-combed their black hair to curl it more tightly and bulk it up enough to hold daggers crafted from the leg bones of the flightless cassowary, or to decorate with brightly colored parrot feathers.

The cacophony began long before the cannon erupted. The captain of the *Antarctic* had had to holler his commands through a brass speaking trumpet in order to assert order amid the disorienting blare of shell horns pulsating from every direction. With operatic effect the islanders spun further confusion by chanting a chorus to merge with the rhythms they struck with their paddle blades.

After the cannon had blasted through it all, and while both the vessel and the sea were still shrouded in acrid, sulfurous smoke, the crew were not immediately sure what damage they had done. A few coughs broke the stillness. Then the groans and gurgling of the mortally wounded reached them from the water. Survivors took cover behind the remains of their shattered canoes, then tentatively made their way back to shore, unmolested.

In the aftermath, one man remained clinging to the *Antarctic*'s rudder pole. A rowboat was lowered to recover him, and the stunned islander was dragged aboard, as eventually were three canoes and some beautifully crafted spears and slingshots floating limply among the bodies. These would make good money as curiosities back home.

The crew jokingly named their captive "Sunday," after the day of his "rescue." Standing on the prow of the lead canoe, he had escaped the full force of the fusillade only because he had leapt onto the ship's rudder just as the shots had exploded above his head.

Naked and "dark copper" in complexion, he had a handsome face, "African" hair, and, according to those more used to assessing slaves at market, teeth that "were very regular and sound." The captain's wife was impressed. Just twenty-two, she was herself strikingly beautiful, with her dark eyes, rounded face, and delicate mouth. As she eventually related in her best-selling account of the voyage, their new captive was a stout, well-made man of five feet eleven, weighing about two hundred pounds and "remarkably strong and active." He bore himself bravely, she thought, and "No one on board our vessel possessed equal muscular power." His powerful arms and shoulders, his chest, and his legs were all tattooed with geometric devices. His ears too were works of art. Their slit lobes hung heavily down the side of his neck, distended to accommodate delicately crafted shell earrings like the ones the oarsmen were now busy removing from the bobbing bodies. In the coming days and years, he would leave his lobes empty, hooked up over his ears to keep both them and the memories out of the way.

At this precise instant, though, the man the sailors called Sunday was simply terrified.

The creatures that had hauled him from the ship's rudder had weird flapping skin that was oddly striped over their torsos and white down the legs, though there were recognizable feet sticking out at the bottom. As another "first contact" from the highlands of the New Guinea mainland (some three hundred miles from the island) recalled over a century later: "The face was like a human's, but the body kept changing its skin. The skin had holes in it, which they could put things in, and then take them out again. They could put things inside their neck at the front and then take them out again."

Precisely where these strange beings came from Sunday had no idea, but he could speculate. His geography envisaged the sky as an upturned bowl that met the horizon at the end of the world. This included the neighboring island of Naraga, a day's paddle to the north, and other islets of his archipelago, including Garove, an equivalent distance to the northeast, as well as the shores of Bariai, known now as New Britain, a long day's journey to the south. Through travel or hearsay, he probably also knew that the mainland of New Guinea lay to the west, though we don't know what he called it. Farther east, his known world may have included what is today New Ireland, and to the north, the Manus (or Admiralty) Islands. But his captors certainly did not look like the real, mortal inhabitants of any of these places.

The man knew that other beings did sometimes appear from the parallel world of the dead, but they were glimpsed only occasionally—and even then usually as animals, birds, fish, or stones. These were the *vuvumu;* the original beings who had given rise to humankind but who since that time had lived increasingly separate from the human dimension. As a child, the man had listened in the cool calm of evening to his elders as they recounted stories about vuvumu. He had grown up knowing the wooded groves and rock outcrops where they lived, occasionally even spotting their pigs as they scuttled away disguised as common rats.

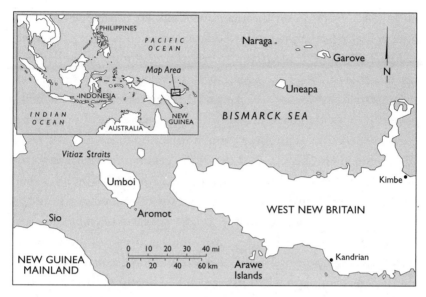

Location of Uneapa Island (map by Bill Nelson)

Only the most powerful vuvumu, he knew, could take on human form, but they were also the most capricious. One such was Mataluangi, who was human above the waist and a snake below. His asexual being tormented him in marriage, but secured him a potency and power over life's nonsexual regenerative forces. It was Mataluangi who enabled yams to spring from yam cuttings, fruit from fruit trees, and long boats from short sticks. Most potently, though, it was he who provided new bodies for the dead that were suitable for the new dimension to which they were destined. Were these hideous new creatures with their humanoid heads, sheddable skins, and lack of visible penises or anuses in some way connected to Mataluangi?

Like his fellow islanders, the man had heard stories of other massive ships passing by, commanded by another vuvumu spirit, Pango. Pango's force was second only to that of Manaka, the ultimate Creator. Whereas the Creator controlled the human world and viewed it through the sun, Pango presided over the parallel world of the dead and was manifest in the moon. His netherworld was seismic and capable of terrible destruction. Long ago he had had a hand in the cataclysmic eruption on the island of Arop, far to the west, and the time of darkness that had followed it. More recently Pango's presence had been felt on Garove Island, where strange forces had killed dozens of people in a series of thunderous explosions. These had been accompanied by massive rocks and fire ejected with incalculable power, along with a dark and sulfurous ash plume that shot high into the upturned bowl with force enough to perforate it.

Tales had also been passed down the generations that Pango had once left on the island of Naraga an unnaturally heavy black ball, which was now kept in a special cave. Stories of the apparition that had left it and the damage that it could inflict had been passed along the islanders' social networks across the sea. But the most disconcerting recollection of Pango's destructive force concerned a time many generations ago when fishermen had begun to disappear, then people on shore. As Pango's depredations become worse, the islanders had attacked him, but their flotilla had been annihilated, leaving a lone survivor as witness. The entire population had had to abandon the island until, eventually, a brave pair of twins had managed to slay this incarnation of the spirit, paving the way for the islanders' return.

When the *Antarctic,* with its two huge masts, each carrying three billowing sails, had come to its unnatural stop on the barrier reef the day before, the men from the shore-side settlements had convened on the beach to deliberate. Pango was back. That first evening his ship had launched a second, smaller sailboat from its stern. Hoping that a show of strength might intimidate him into leaving, they had crammed into their canoes en masse with their weapons and paddled upshore. Several of their canoes were equipped with sturdy single outrigger floats and platforms slung across their midships to accommodate more people. As they glided close to shore in the evening calm, their brightly colored prows had glinted in the fading light, while the lowering sun had picked out the palm-thatched houses that stood back from the shore. Children sitting with their mothers and elders looked anxiously out at the apparition of which they had heard so much spoken, but had never seen.

Two views of the schooner *Antarctic,* from Jack Halliard (pseud.), *Voyages and Adventures of Jack Halliard, with Captain Morrell* (1833), 24, 117

There had been no violence that evening. John Keeler had noted in his log that about fifty canoes were launched, with more venturing offshore, but they did not attack. "Expect some vessel has gave them a lesson," he recorded.

It was only the next morning, after the apparition had maintained its uncannily fixed position on the barrier reef, that the islanders had resolved to attack. The men had fetched their weapons and shunted their canoes back down into the water to board for battle. Now, an hour or so later, the survivors, many nursing wounds from the small but mysteriously heavy balls projected by the sulfurous puff of Pango, emerged from the surf to bring accounts of death, defeat, and dejection.

The man who had led them—the man whom the Americans had dragged out of the water and were now calling Sunday—was Dako, the son of the political leader of the southwest of the island. Descriptions of Dako rarely moved beyond his mesmerizing physique: "remarkably well formed"; the shape of a "warrior and a general." He was also tremendously strong. The American sailors who eventually learned to challenge him playfully at wrestling found to their cost that he would simply "smile pleasantly and open his arms," then clasp them "like a bear, and, with one tender hug, lay them sprawling on the deck." But in time those who would come to know him better began to comment on much more than his strength—on his friendliness, his inquisitive intelligence, his smile, and his mellow, even obliging air.

For the moment, though, he presented none of these traits. Bound and below deck, he was trying to work out why he had been taken, by whom, and where they were going. He could soon discount the hand of Mataluangi. His abductors had forced him into strange flapping skins just like their own, and although on first sight they had appeared to lack organs for sex and shitting, it rapidly became obvious in the confinement of the ship that crew and captain had penis and anus alike. So his speculations, he later confided, fixed more firmly on Pango and his parallel world of the dead. This, he said, was because their white complexions resembled something from the spirit world; a world in which all was "white, nearest to what is invisible." Though dressed in white and stripes, not all the *Antarctic*'s crew were otherwise particularly "white" in complexion: on board were several African Americans and sixty Filipinos, and after over a year at sea, even the dozen or so "white" sailors were weathered, tanned, and bearded.

But there were other reasons for Dako to think that he had been captured by the dead. He knew that after death humans entered the freer existence of the netherworld: the lands beyond the horizon, the underground and the moon. The portals that led from the mortal world to this other dimension were the stuff of legend. As Dako eventually revealed to an inquisitive interviewer, there was a famous cave portal on the nearby island of Garove which led to this other world where the "good go after death." In this world, said Dako, the spirits were invisible even to one another, only distinguishing them-selves through sound. Wonderful plants, flowers, and animals also flour-ished here, all white and nearly invisible, too. It was a world of voice and music. Long ago—presumably when he was in a more affable mood—Pango had offered to the living the flutes, pipes, and reeds that they now used to communicate with their dead.

According to Dako, the entrance to this cavern portal was guarded by two men, who were also white. Many stories circulated about the portal and the world beyond. In one, a survivor of a tsunami which had swept the island had glimpsed the spirit of a drowned person dis-appearing into the cave and decided to follow it. They had both emerged on top of a reef in the land of the dead, where the spirits welcomed their living visitor and provided him with food and gifts. Not only did he return to the human world laden with food and trea-sures, but the path to the spirit world remained open for him, and he visited regularly for the miraculous provisions that kept his fellow survivors alive. In another story the spirits had been less welcoming and chased a living intruder out. This man had managed to flee, but the aggrieved spirits had been so angered at being outdone by him that they had blocked the path down from the cavern, making it im-possible for the living ever again to enter their world that way. None-theless, every islander knew that the man had gone to the reef, come back, and survived.

There were other portals, though. On Dako's own island were three situated on the sheer, inaccessible rock face of Mount Tamongone through which members of prominent families passed when they died. Such portals and the spirit world beyond them were not just destinations for the dead. They were also the source of all bounty. All invention and inspiration for the living came from there—all musical instruments, artistic designs, ideas, and dreams. Dako had probably laughed at the story of a trickster called Dau, who had deceived the spirits into revealing their artistic designs at one of the Tamongone cliff portals. To do this he had pretended to be dead, persuading some accomplices to prepare his body the way they would a corpse and then wail over him in mock mourning. Mimicking the gait of the dead, Dau had then approached the portal and hailed the spirits, demanding that they open up. Fooled, the dead had let down the decorated ladder. That was enough for the artist: he took a good look at the ladder and the designs of the world within, and then hotfooted it back to the village with his valuable secrets.

The most famous portals, however, took the form of two enormous ships. These were the ships of the dead that came to take new recruits to their world. Was Dako in one of these now? Like others from his island, he had surely seen their distant forms occasionally shimmering on the horizon—or indeed some degrees above it, as a mirage might—at sunrise or sunset, before they suddenly vanished. One of the ships was said to be black and the other decked, but both were crewed by the dead and presided over by Pango. A sighting of either was a terrible portent for anyone at death's door. Many of the newly dead would follow a well-trodden path down to a shoreline cove, where the vuvumu Mataluangi first provided them with a new body, then they boarded the ship that would convey them beyond the horizon to the other dimension.

Finding himself aboard such a ship did not bode well for Dako. But at least he was alive, and the accounts of others who had returned from such portals perhaps offered him some hope. His fate might well depend on whether these spirits were his relatives: unrelated forebears were more usually destructive, even cannibalistic, and dead sorcerers were to be especially feared, streaking like meteorites across the sky, sinking canoes at whim. Dead relatives, by contrast, were generally more helpful. And as the dead were also the source of all creativity and invention, life among them could perhaps even be a blessing. If there were deceased relatives among his captors, might they ultimately bring him good fortune? Was this perhaps a new opportunity? Dako could have conceivably reasoned his way from panic to calculation and deflected despair into the determination to return to his own world that many observers later discerned in him.

For eight hours after the battle, and despite the onshore winds, the *Antarctic* remained motionless, floating above the barrier reef and the world of the dead. Among the unknown number of survivors who made it back to the beach was Dako's half-brother, Pongaracoopo, who had been badly wounded in one eye. He brought the news ashore that Dako had been captured and taken into the bowels of the ship. Many years later, when Pongaracoopo himself descended below the decks of a similar ship, he became visibly terrified at the thought of entering a bottomless vessel that led directly to the spirit world.

One of those looking on from the beach was Dako's father, Tupi, the leader of this part of the island. Dako was his eldest child and in line to inherit his ceremonial drum, and with it the title of Tumbuku. Today had been a mighty setback. Those watching the stationary ship from onshore must have recalled with trepidation how when Pango had last destroyed an attacking flotilla, the whole island had been forced to decamp. But as evening fell again and as the winds swung offshore, the ship's sails billowed out. She turned west-southwest and silently disappeared over the horizon.

If the ship's departure was a relief for some, it was not for Dako's favorite wife, Vakale. She and their young son, Tupi—whom they had named after his grandfather—could not be consoled. Her sorrow was so profound that it is still recalled on the island today:

> Oh how that woman cried over her husband that the white men had captured. His wife was grief-stricken over him. She didn't know whether he would come back or whether he was lost. She really didn't know, poor creature, and she and the child were very unhappy. The woman went and stayed

on an island and gazed across the water because she believed that they had taken her husband in that direction. She wondered if they would bring him back. She didn't work. She just sat there doing nothing. She couldn't see her husband and she was full of sorrow. She painted herself with black paint according to our custom because she thought he was dead and would not come back.

Back aboard the *Antarctic* in his new white skin, Dako, too, was in despair. The crew had had to tie him up below decks; otherwise, as an American newspaper later reported, he would without doubt have "jumped overboard at a great distance from the shore, had the opportunity offered, being very dexterous in the water, sometimes swimming two or three miles without the slightest appearance of fatigue." Dako had many reasons to return. What his captors could not know was that not only had they parted Dako from his devoted wife and family, but his island was in turmoil and his home community in danger.

Dako called his island Uneapa. It is just six miles across, formed from the crater of an ancient exploded volcano out of which three younger volcanic cones have pushed themselves up, producing a trio of mountainous humps on the skyline. As these eroded, they left precipitous cliffs and jagged lava flows, enwrapped, to the untrained eye of the Americans, in virgin forest. For the islanders, however, there was nothing virgin about these forests. Nudging this tropical island's natural exuberance into a more productive form had been the stuff of their lives for generations, enriching the forests with the useful species that bore them fruits, nuts, and medicines, or which they could carve into massive trading canoes. Each year the islanders staved off hunger by harvesting trees such as mango, breadfruit, and Java almonds before their gardens full of yams, taro, and greens finally matured. Their ancestors had enriched their lands with sago palms for their thatching fronds, areca palms for construction timber and betel nuts, and coconut palms for the milk on which their cuisine depended.

Although small, the island was divided politically into two alliances that were not always at peace. Dako's people lived in the lower

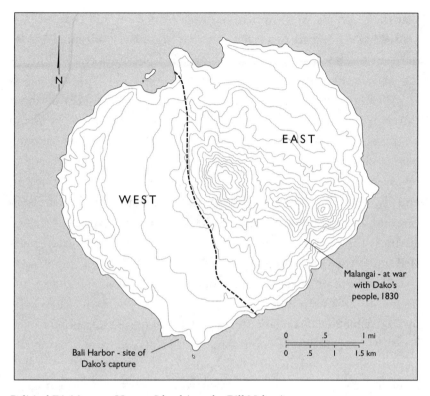

Political Divisions on Uneapa Island (map by Bill Nelson)

lands of the west; their rivals in the more mountainous east. The two
groups spoke with distinctive accents, narrated different histories, and
nurtured different links across the sea. Easterners traded with Garove
and with the volcanic "Bay of Fire" (Barentuno Bay) on the mainland, whereas Dako's people had links with his mother's island of
Naraga, and the more westerly reaches of the New Britain coast.

The rivalry between the two sides could be playful: the launching of a new trading canoe would hardly be complete without one
side challenging the other to a race—even though the celebrations
might well degenerate into a fight. Sometimes, however, young men
from one side acted more provocatively, perhaps conspiring to capture an attractive young woman from the other to take as a wife to
one of them—making the women living in the borderlands understandably reluctant to garden far from home. The abductors knew

that their actions would provoke bitter retaliation and that revenge battles would be called. Played out on one of the traditional battlefields in the borderlands, these skirmishes sometimes resulted in injury, but hardly ever death.

With a population of around five thousand in an area of about thirty square miles, it was inevitable that most people on the island would be in some way related, especially if they calculated back ten generations or more, as was the norm. A lot of everyday life therefore revolved around finessing competing allegiances among relatives or, equally, cementing kinship through helping out favored relatives in ceremonies or everyday work. In the long run, people strengthened alliances through marriages, and by ensuring that only cousins married down the generations.

The occasional abduction, elopement, or love tryst across the border also sometimes turned rivals into relatives. As it was wholly unacceptable to kill a relation, descendants of these cross-border marriages had the benefit of being somewhat protected from fighting and so were often called upon to broker peace. So forbidden was it to kill a relative that, when sparring, men would shout out the names of their ancestors as a form of self-defense. Relatives would back off.

Dako himself had this kind of mixed ancestry. Although a westerner, his ancestry on his father's side could be traced back to a revered member of a leading family of the east, Vaharee. One of his many-great-grandmothers, Peepe, had eloped with Vaharee and borne him twins, though she was later jilted and abandoned by him.

Right now, though, the usual checks and balances between rivalry and relatedness that helped keep peace had failed, pitching Dako's people into a deadly confrontation with the easterners. The trouble had started when a "young shark" from the east named Pilapila had seduced—or perhaps raped—his own sister-in-law, a neighbor. The shark's father, Vorai, was so ashamed of his son's behavior and concerned that the girl's relatives would exact revenge that he had sent the youth, under the escort of his other sons, across the sea to live with relatives in New Britain. Denied the chance to punish the shark, the aggrieved girl's family had hired an assassin to kill the father and, adding to the aggression, torch the magnificently decorated "house-of-respect" that had been lovingly carved and painted in his honor. So when the other sons returned from dropping off their brother in Bariai, they found their father dead and his ritual house reduced to ashes. The violence escalated rapidly. With the support of their father's friends, the brothers rallied their relatives across the island to attack the girl's settlement, completely destroying it and killing everyone and everything. This massacre stands out in the island's history for its exceptional ferocity. Villagers still point to stone figures they say were carved to commemorate it.

Usually, those like Dako, who had relatives on both sides of the east-west divide, were reluctant to take sides, but in this instance the violence was such that they were forced to. The murdered man had been a prominent eastern leader, while his assassin, a man named Puto, was from the west. Thus a family feud in one village had escalated into an island-wide war. As a relative of the assassin and leader of a key western territory, Dako's father had been drawn into the conflict, his territories open to attack.

The lethal cannon of the *Antarctic* had decimated the young men of Dako's community just at the time when they were most needed to defend it against the east. Now Dako, the rising leader, had been spirited away. What effect might his abduction have on the balance of power on the island? His family—his aging father, his wife, their young son, and his two other, unnamed wives—had never been so vulnerable. Bound up in the dark belly of this ship of the dead, powered by the weight of his responsibilities, Dako strained his muscular frame against the ropes that held him, but in vain. Instead he was impelled to reflect on the practical realities of switching realms and suddenly finding himself living a myth.

CHAPTER 2

The Captain

ନ୍ତ୍ର

The forces that had spun the thread of Captain Benjamin Morrell's life and led him to the reefs off Uneapa had not been kind. Morrell was a veteran sailor of thirty-six when he had set sail as commander of this, his fourth voyage. Clean-shaven and confident, he stood neither particularly tall nor particularly powerful. His heavy eyebrows and large Roman nose were somewhat top-heavy for his small mouth, rounded jowls, and cleft chin. He was a distinctive if not exactly handsome man, but a man with presence. His air of authority lay partly in his coif and dress, in the force of his curly dark sideburns and silk top hat; but it lay primarily in the captain's tailcoat which covered his improbably spotless white cotton waistcoat and trousers and which conformed so closely to the contours of his body that it was an essential part of him.

His character was more difficult to pin down—as many of those who were to be deceived by it were to find. What can be said, however, is that he was more of the commanding than the conversing or confiding kind—at least according to his wife, Abby. As she said, he "remained silent to her on most subjects of the voyage"—and voyages were his life. This reticence, though, perhaps simply reflected his way with women. Aboard the *Antarctic* he kept a tight ship, but with his infectious optimism and obvious seafaring skills he was popular with the crew. There are no records of any of his crew deserting, which is

Captain Benjamin Morrell in 1832. Engraving by Gimber and Dick after painting by "Sloan," from Benjamin Morrell, *A Narrative of Four Voyages, to the South Sea, North and South Pacific Ocean, Chinese Sea, Ethiopic and Southern Atlantic Ocean, Indian and Antarctic Ocean* (1832), frontispiece extremely unusual for the era, and many of those who sailed with him chose to do so again—and again. Several spoke well of him even when they need not. When well-educated young men from prosperous New York families sought out the romance of the sea, signing on to sail as green-hand crew before the mast, they (or their parents) seemed happy to place their trust in Morrell. Trusting Morrell, however, was usually a mistake.

Morrell's checkered rise to captaincy encapsulates the wider story of America's encounters with the Pacific. Since the 1600s the British East India Company had been exporting China teas to the new colonies in America, and later it supplied them with other luxuries from Canton (or Cathay, as it was then known). As the main ports of Boston, New York, and Philadelphia grew, it had initially been British traders who had unloaded the cherished Chinese porcelain vases and ornamental bowls; lacquerware, ivories, and jade; silks, cottons, and tapestries; scrolls, screens, and intricately woven carpets. But the Revolutionary War of 1775–83 had interrupted this traffic, and immediately afterward America's newly independent merchants and shipbuilders took over the trade. The United States was then composed of little more than a strip of seaports, farms, plantations, and inland market towns stretching down the eastern seaboard from New Hampshire to Georgia, but to a great extent it was shipping which was now transforming the country—bringing in immigrants and slaves, books and silks, while at the same time exporting cotton and flour to the European markets.

Initially the American ships plying the Cathay trade took the long route east to Canton: tracking south and east across the Atlantic, doubling South Africa's Cape of Good Hope, crossing the Indian Ocean, and then pushing on into the western Pacific through the Sunda Strait between Java and Sumatra. These trader ships were soon joined by the whalers and sealers which supplied the oil that kept America's growing towns lit in winter and the pelts that kept its people warm. As their prey became depleted, both the whalers and the sealers were obliged to explore beyond their original hunting grounds in the Atlantic, pushing the limits of seafaring south toward the Antarctic.

By 1800, the most courageous of them were also sailing westward around the much more dangerous Cape Horn at the southern tip of South America, leading directly into the Pacific. American seafarers were "going west" into the Pacific Ocean five decades before overland migrants established the West Coast states of California and Oregon and drew those territories into the union.

The American traders in the eastern and central Pacific had to compete with British and French merchants both for their cargoes and for the political influence they needed in the Polynesian world if they were to secure those cargoes. By the time of Morrell's voyage in 1830 more than a hundred American ships were visiting Hawaii each year, and navigating round Cape Horn and trading with Polynesia had become almost routine. It was another thing entirely, however, to cross to the western Pacific halfway round the world again and enter the seas off New Guinea. This was the farthest reach of the world from New York, equidistant from the city whether one sailed west or east.

Very few vessels had dared visit Dako's region. Indeed, no American ship had even entered this most ill-charted reach of the South Pacific before, while only two European vessels were known to have neared Dako's island—and neither had made contact. One was captained by the Dutch navigator Abel Tasman, who had passed by almost two centuries earlier on his epic 1643 voyage, during which he had left his calling card many times on the emerging maps of the world. The other visit, a full century and a half later, in July 1793, was by a French naval flotilla commanded by a nobleman from Aix-en-Provence named Antoine Bruni d'Entrecasteaux. He had been sent to look for the wrecks of an extravagant French scientific and exploring expedition commanded by one of King Louis XVI's favorites, the comte de La Pérouse, whose ships had gone missing during the French Revolution with many of France's top scientists aboard. Whether for global science or national pride, the revolutionary French National Assembly had ordered Bruni d'Entrecasteaux to find them, and he set sail with a fleet manned by a mixture of royalist officers and republican crew. On July 1 this flotilla reached Dako's island, which Bruni d'Entrecasteaux charted and named Merité after one of his officers. (This officer was later discovered to have secreted his lover onboard disguised as a man, making Abby Morrell the second Western woman to see the island.) Bruni d'Entrecasteaux himself died of scurvy within days of sighting Uneapa, and his expedition then fell apart in Java, when news arrived that the French king had finally been executed. The royalists on board split from the republicans, but the charts they had drawn up together were kept, and after many an adventure these were eventually copied into the commercial navigation charts published by the famous British cartographer Aaron Arrowsmith in 1808. It was a copy of these charts which lay on the table in the captain's cabin below deck on the schooner *Antarctic*. No one had had cause to consult this corner of the world for a very long time.

When accounts of Bruni d'Entrecasteaux's expedition appeared in English in 1796, the descriptions of the northern coast of New Britain were not encouraging. This region, one officer bragged, was extremely dangerous: for 1,200 leagues—some 3,600 miles—there was nothing but a line of dangerous reefs beneath shallow water. Racism further deterred Western visitors. A French explorer named Jules Dumont d'Urville, who was at this time working up a Pacific geography, inscribed race into the region's very name, placing its seas within what he coined Melanesia ("the islands of the black-skinned people"). The "Melanesians" were, he pronounced, "disagreeable" and "generally very inferior" to the "copper-colored race" of "Polynesians." This racism had another effect: when European vessels did reach "Melanesian" shores, the crew often acted violently toward the inhabitants, who learned to reciprocate, further fueling the Europeans' disrespect, which in turn became amplified in the yarns spun by sailors about the "cannibals" who lived there.

The most significant problem for traders in this region, however, was the impossibility of speaking with the indigenous peoples. In the central Pacific, it was usual for traders to hire or capture linguists to translate for them—islanders in the region, even those separated by huge distances, spoke closely related languages. Around New Guinea, by contrast, the sheer profusion of languages rendered the translators' skills nearly useless—just where traders needed them most to smooth their way through increasingly aggressive welcomes. Most traders soon decided they could make a better living elsewhere. Following Benjamin Morrell's expedition, significant European-American encounters with the region's people would not occur for another forty years.

Back in New York, the owners of the *Antarctic* had no idea that their ship would be sailing in the central South Pacific, let alone in its most ill-charted reaches. They thought that they had funded a sealing voyage to the stormier seas of the Antarctic Ocean farther south. Thirty years previously, a sealing captain from Morrell's home port of Stonington, Connecticut, about 150 miles up the coast from New York, had turned an investment of eight thousand dollars into a profit of fifty-two thousand in a single expedition. This was Captain Edmund Fanning, whose astonishingly lucrative voyage had sparked an investment boom at Stonington, which had then prospered as a sealing capital—at the expense of the seal populations of the known islands of the Antarctic. The next generation of sealers, which included Morrell, was forced to explore deeper into southern latitudes and search for new islands and new sealing grounds. Sealing soon became synonymous with exploration—except that, unlike explorers, sealers tried to keep their discoveries secret.

Stonington's population of three thousand was distributed over a large area. The port's gently undulating hinterland was a thickly strewn chaos of rocks and stones, and the New Englanders had broken many a spade prying them out of the ground to build foundations for their clapboard houses and drystone walls. The stones found their way to the lighthouse that protected their ships; the bank that protected their money; and to the Presbyterian and Baptist churches that protected their souls. Until the sealing boom, this had been a world of cod, cheese, and cider. Now the stones were used to build wharfs to accommodate the small, nimble sealing ships.

Stonington's early English settlers had massacred or subjected the indigenous Pequot people in the 1630s, but nevertheless a community had survived in a reservation atop a bleak hill six miles inland, where they lived in wigwams or poor cottages. When Morrell was growing up he had labored alongside the Pequot, but in a world that treated them with contempt. When the president of Yale, Timothy Dwight, visited Stonington in the 1820s he proclaimed: "The former proud, heroic spirit of the Pequod, . . . [is] shrunk into the tameness and torpor of reasoning brutism." The Pequot, he stated after a day or two's research, were lazy, insolvent, untrustworthy, thieving liars who neglected marriage and the true religion and in their vice "doze away life in uniform sloth and stupidity." Nevertheless the settlers depended on those they despised, using them as laborers, nannies, and maids. Such work was civilizing, they reasoned. There was no nobility to unguided savagery. Without employment and religion the Pequot led "the life not of a man, but of a snail," more "a moving vegetable than a rational being." It was this attitude to Native Americans that would sweep Andrew Jackson to the presidency in 1829 on the back of his cleansing policy to remove native peoples from the United States; an attitude that Morrell and many on board American ships took global.

Seafaring had become the path to prosperity for many of New England's youth and an alternative to heading west. Benjamin's father, also called Benjamin, had trained in Rye, New York, as a carpenter, but in 1796, at the age of thirty, he had moved his young family to Stonington to build ships just as the sealing boom took off. He quickly established a good reputation for his shipyard, located four miles away, down by the narrows in the deep harbor of the Mystic River. Several leading merchants and captains commissioned him, including the famous Fanning. Benjamin Jr., his firstborn, was only a year old when the family moved; afterward his wife was to bear him another three sons, among them Jeremiah, the brother to whom Benjamin became closest. Such was Benjamin Sr.'s reputation as a carpenter that in his early years in Stonington, a sea captain named George Howe hired him as an officer for three years on the sealing schooner *Oneco.* This ship's unfortunate voyage ended in Peru, where the captain was forced to sell his ship, was defrauded of the revenues, and died. How his crew returned home remains unrecorded, but on his return Morrell Sr. regaled his sons with tales of the hardships, haz-

ards, and privations during this "disagreeable" time. From then on he
stuck to shipbuilding.

When Benjamin Jr. was just eight or nine, he and his brothers lost
their mother, then within a year or two their first stepmother, Abigail, who died at age nineteen. When Benjamin's father married for a
third time, it was to Betsy, the granddaughter of one of the old Stonington families, the Burrows. By 1810 the fifteen-year-old Benjamin
had three half-sisters: Abigail, an unknown other, and the youngest,
Eliza. Theirs was a large family, and one that was to face many a setback.

As Stonington expanded around sealing, young Benjamin's future as a sailor, sealer, and carpenter became all but inevitable, and he
was impatient to begin. In 1812, aged seventeen, he ran away to New
York and the sea, to find work as a green hand on the schooner *Enterprise*. She was shipping a cargo of flour to Cádiz to profit from the
hunger created on the Iberian Peninsula by the Napoleonic Wars.
But Morrell's impatience served him ill when he found that he had
unwittingly stepped into a new war between Britain and the United
States. America had thrown off British authority at the end of the
Revolutionary War in 1789, but by 1812 Britain was putting new pressure on its erstwhile colonies to stop trading with France during the
Napoleonic Wars. France, however, was America's revolutionary ally.
Not only that but the Royal Navy had taken to capturing American
sailors and forcing them to crew its own ships, which rankled. More
galling still, the British were lending their support to Native Americans in America's Northwest Territory and undermining the former
colony's own expansionist ambitions. Angered on all three counts,
the United States declared war on Britain on June 12, 1812—a war
that was to be fought mainly at sea. Warships and private vessels from
both sides preyed on one another's merchant shipping up and down
the Atlantic seaboard. The British blockaded what coastal ports they
could, bombarded many (including Stonington) and burned down
towns and cities, including the newly built Washington, D.C., and its
new presidential residence, the White House.

On the return voyage from Cádiz, Morrell was captured by a
British vessel and detained for the next eight months on a prison ship

in the colony of Newfoundland. When the British released him, he returned briefly to Stonington to be reunited with his relieved and forgiving family. But he soon went back to sea, in 1813 joining the crew of a Baltimore-based privateer. He was promptly captured again. This time his British captors took him across the Atlantic to the no-torious Dartmoor prison, set among the bogs and fogs of the high moors of England's southwest. The new prison had initially been built to house French prisoners, but it was suitable for American cap-tives as well. Morrell and his fellow Americans languished there until a truce brought the war to a close in 1815.

Morrell was not a lucky man. By the time he was twenty, his planned seafaring career had had two faltering starts. Once he was freed from Dartmoor, he managed to visit home briefly and took a short passage on a European voyage. But when he returned from this, he found that his stepmother, sister, cousin, and grandmother had all been drowned during a freak hurricane, which had smashed into Stonington in mid-September 1815 and swept away their shore-side house. Benjamin's father had been out helping neighbors when the storm surge had snatched their timber home from its foundations. The house had floated off to sea with the family still inside, pounded to death by the waves. Then, a few months later, two of Morrell's brothers were also drowned at sea. His prosperous family now all but destroyed, Benjamin's father was a broken man. Benjamin and his one surviving brother, Jeremiah, again took to sea, this time as car-penter crew. If there was one bright spot among this series of disasters it was the sympathy shown to the family by the good people of Ston-ington and the kindness of the Baptist minister, Benjamin's stepmoth-er's uncle, the Reverend Silas Burrows. Burrows encouraged his own son Enoch, a wealthy shipping merchant, to adopt Benjamin's two surviving younger sisters and treat them as his own. Their adoptive brother Silas E. Burrows, Jr., was later to shape both Benjamin's and Dako's lives.

Within a few years, Benjamin and Jeremiah had both managed to work their way up from crew to captain. Benjamin's own break came during an 1818 voyage commanded by a family friend, Josiah Macy, who was shipping silks and sugar from Calcutta. Macy offered Benjamin a position as mate, the first rung on the ladder to captaincy. It was a rung on the social ladder, too, as it enabled Benjamin to marry a sea captain's daughter, a Miss T. A. Bishop of Wilmington, North Carolina, in April 1820. Meanwhile, Jeremiah had sailed as carpenter on the highly profitable sealing expedition that discovered Antarctica for America in 1820. In June 1821, Benjamin and Jeremiah were reunited as first and second officer, respectively, on a follow-up sealing expedition on board the *Wasp,* whose captain eventually offered Benjamin the command of the companion vessel home. On its safe arrival, Morrell was rewarded with the full command of the *Wasp* itself. Benjamin Morrell was now a sea captain. He sailed her back to the Antarctic on a sealing cruise in 1822. Soon Jeremiah also became master of a sealing schooner, the *Chile,* which was owned by Silas E. Burrows. Life was looking up.

Many years later, when he was famous, Morrell claimed that his first voyage as master of the *Wasp* not only turned its owners a good profit but also made navigation history by sailing deep into the Antarctic Circle, descending to latitudes of more than 70° south. Neither boast was true, and his accounts from the time of the voyage tell an entirely different story. Morrell gave a newspaper interview directly on his return to New York in May 1824 in which, after twenty months away, he described how he had literally sailed the seven seas, covering 82,000 miles "without making any valuable discoveries." He had made it to 66° south, but no farther, and even then "at a cost of tremendous suffering to both crew and officers in the vast fields of broken ice." The only claim he made then—and he was not one to shy away from claims—was that after he had sold the *Wasp* for his owners in Chile, he earned a lift home by piloting a ship called the *Endeavour* through the Magellan Straits, thereby becoming the first American to navigate them. His claim was not contested.

Returning to Stonington after his first captaincy, Morrell found that jinxes continued to follow him. His wife and both his tiny children had died. Nothing more is known of this first family beyond its tragedy. "A speedy second marriage," his father advised, "would restore happiness." And within weeks Benjamin Sr. had arranged for his son to remarry, this time to his first cousin Abby. Somewhat improbably, the marriage was a success.

When they married in the summer of 1824, Benjamin was twenty-nine and Abby was only fifteen and therefore under age. They had met just once before, when she was five and he was recently returned from Dartmoor. Abby was to become a "very pretty American girl," and the engraving on the frontispiece of the narrative she published of her travels conveys her as a well-clad Venus, with serenely smooth skin and an ample neck, her hair heaped into an elaborate pompadour and her body swamped (though subtly enhanced) by a billowing dress. With her youthfully rounded cheeks, small mouth, and wide-set eyes, she must surely have appeared more child than adult. As to her character at that time, little can be said save that it was forged without the luxuries of childhood, marked by the assistance she was required to give her struggling mother when her well-to-do family fell into poverty.

Abby's marriage had a dynastic quality. Her mother was Benjamin Sr.'s sister, who had married a sea captain, John Wood. He had died at sea in 1811 when Abby was two. In the ensuing settlements Abby's mother had been disinherited by the Woods and left destitute, creating a rift between the families. Three years later Abby's mother had remarried, this time to a widower, Burritt Keeler, whom Abby and her younger sister came to consider their real father. The following year the new couple had a child, John, Abby's half-brother. So by marrying Benjamin, Abby had not only "done well" for herself by getting a sea captain for her husband, but perhaps more important, she had done well for both the Morrell and Wood families by drawing them together again. Abby and her mother were back in the fold, and Abby's nine-year-old half-brother, John Keeler, would now have the chance to secure a nautical future. He was sent to study navigation at Mr. Nash's Nautical School in the Bowery in New York City before joining Morrell as navigator on the *Antarctic,* where he documented Dako's capture. The downside of the marriage, for Abby at least, was that she found herself wedded to a man she hardly knew, in a marriage

Abby Jane Morrell in 1832. Engraving by Gimber and Dick after painting by "Sloan," from Abby Jane Morrell, *Narrative of a Voyage to the Ethiopic and South Atlantic Ocean, Indian Ocean, Chinese Sea, North and South Pacific Ocean, in the Years 1829, 1830, 1831* (1833), frontispiece

that could be consummated only when she reached an acceptable age and after her husband returned from his next voyage.

This was another sealing expedition, which in 1825 took Morrell round Cape Horn, up America's western seaboard to the Galápagos

Islands, past the future California to the future Oregon, and then west across the Pacific to the future Hawaii. When he returned twelve months later, in May 1826, it was with an insignificant cargo of seal-skins, much to the anger and despair of his investors. With two unsuccessful voyages behind him, Morrell now struggled to find a new command that had the potential to make good money. For two years he was reduced to captaining trading vessels toiling over to Europe and back—which was perhaps a blessing for Abby, who by now had produced their first son, William, born in 1827.

Eventually Morrell managed to link up with an old acquaintance in New York, a merchant named William Skiddy. During the war with Britain these two had been imprisoned together in Newfoundland and, being much the same age, had become close friends. Since then, Skiddy had gone on to become a far more successful captain than Morrell, amassing enough capital to switch from financed to financier. Morrell had already worked for eighteen months as first officer under Skiddy. Now Skiddy was looking to invest in a new ship, and he wanted Morrell to captain it.

Skiddy partnered with a New York shipbuilder, Christian Bergh, whose yards had been turning out some of America's swiftest vessels since the late 1790s. Together with another investor, the New York Democratic Party politician Charles Livingston, they sank twenty thousand dollars (equivalent to half a million today) into building and fitting out a new sealing schooner. This ship was conceived to be America's fastest clipper. Morrell took a hand in the schooner's design and was as proud of the vessel as were her owners. She was built to turn in an instant—as sealing demanded. She could also carry 170 tons of cargo, and was about 90 feet in length and so large enough to ride out storms, but with a shallow enough draft to navigate close to shore.

The departure of the *Antarctic* on her maiden voyage in June 1828 was lodged in the memory of all who saw it. As was the custom, the harbor pilot from New York was at the helm, and on board were not only the crew but also the captain's family and the ship's owners, who all took a ride as far as Sandy Hook at the harbor entrance. When family and friends finally took their leave and transferred with the pilot to his yacht, the *Antarctic*'s owners wagered him a case of champagne that he couldn't outstrip their ship. The New York pilots' racing yachts were reputed to be the fastest in the land, so this was quite a gamble. The race that ensued was to be recalled decades later: under full sail, the *Antarctic* simply pulled away.

The problem which had dogged Morrell's earlier voyages was that the seal population on the islands of the South Seas had already collapsed. In a single year following the sealers' discovery of the South Shetland Islands in 1820, for example, forty or more ships had been dispatched there and had slaughtered and skinned more than half a million seals. Within the decade, both seals and unexplored islands were scarce even at extreme southern latitudes. No longer could a sealer discover a new island, plunder its pelts, and keep the location a secret. On Morrell's maiden voyage with the *Antarctic,* he found hardly any seals at all. After he had been away for a year, searching down the west coast of Africa, he was wary of returning empty-handed and so turned his attention to other trading opportunities. On one island he discovered a huge guano deposit—ancient piles of bird droppings that could be mined for fertilizer. He also prospected ranching cattle for export in what is today Namibia. But commercial potential was not what his investors required; they wanted short-term profit. And when Morrell returned, he returned without it. This was Morrell's third failure. His investors deliberated on whether to give him another chance. As Skiddy recalled, "Mr. Bergh asked my opinion. I told him it was hard to abandon a man because he had been unfortunate and if he had no objection we would let him try again." Morrell had never in his life turned in a good profit, but he knew the language of optimism. Moreover, his investors were oblivious to the effects their voracious plundering could have on the seal populations, and believed that simple profits were still there to be made. They agreed to finance a fourth voyage.

After a turnaround of only three months, the *Antarctic* was ready to set sail again, this time to the sealing grounds of the South Shetlands, which lie off the southern tip of South America. Morrell was to have provisions for three years. This prospect, however, was too much for Abby. Life over the previous year with a small baby and no husband had been difficult and lonely enough. Now with a three-year voyage in the planning, she was desperate. She begged Benjamin to let her sail with him, making "earnest and unceasing solicitation."

It was very rare for a woman to sail with her husband at this time, but a forthright woman from Nantucket, Mary Hayden Russell, had set a precedent some six years earlier, enabling women like Abby to dream. Some crew also found that they preferred to sail with the captain's wife on board, as a master was rarely as brutal to them in his wife's company as he would otherwise be—and usually provided better food. Some commanding couples voyaged with their young children, who provided a doting audience for the sailors' yarns. Benjamin initially refused to let Abby come with him, but she persisted, so he took the question to his investors. They refused categorically, "considering it a voyage quite unfit for a female." The usual argument was that if a captain were allowed to bring his wife along, he would take fewer risks and so make smaller profits. By way of recompense the investors offered to loan Morrell a 10 percent stake in the voyage, which would make his family rich if it proved successful. But Abby was still not to be moved—indeed, she threatened to leave Benjamin if he did not relent. So Benjamin was caught between his wife's ultimatum and his investors' offer—and decided to have it both ways. As the ship departed, Abby was hidden away in a ship's locker. This meant she had had to leave her two-year-old son behind in New York with his grandmother, something that was not uncommon. And just as well, given what was to follow.

Morrell's was to be a temperance ship, so he had advertised for crew who would eschew "ardent spirits." Curiously, those who signed up were largely British sailors, not American. Among them were men who had long ago absconded from the British naval vessels that had press-ganged them. Francis Patterson was one such veteran tar who had followed the seas for fifty-five years and seen many naval engagements. Others had their own reasons for being in the United States or on the high seas, but kept those reasons to themselves.

Among those applying to join the ship, however, were also an entirely different kind of seaman. Highly educated young men from New York's middle or upper classes saw in whaling, sealing, and trading vessels an opportunity to see the world and break the family bond. Among those who took a year or two off in this rather fashionable way were several future writers whose work would be defined by the experience, including Richard Henry Dana, Herman Melville, and James Fenimore Cooper. For some, like the Harvard-educated Nathaniel Ames, life before the mast was to become more than a youthful adventure. But not all those seeking this freedom had aspirations to write. Others went on to become professionals—lawyers and politicians. Morrell's reputation as a fair, humane, yet nonetheless adventurous captain made him attractive to this group. As the *Antarctic* sailed, there were at least two highly educated New Yorkers aboard: Oscar Sturtevant and William Vanduzer, both scions of the city's prosperous old Dutch families and friends of the ship's owners.

The first and second officers were two Americans, Moses Hunt and Henry Wiley of Charlestown, but the third officer was a Scot named Scott, originally from Bo'ness near Edinburgh and more latterly of the Isle of Man. He had sailed with Morrell on the *Antarctic*'s maiden voyage and had become intensely loyal to him. Also sharing the officers' cabins were John Keeler, the navigator, and another young apprentice navigator named Samuel Geery. He was the son of a New York merchant and related to the ship's owner, Christian Bergh. According to Benjamin's eventual account of the voyage, he was also the lover of Abby's sister.

Soon after sailing, many on board fell ill with a high fever. Samuel Geery died, and Abby was close to death for several days. It was an inauspicious beginning. Nor did they find any seals. By January 1830, after four months of futile prospecting, Morrell anchored with an empty hold at the fledgling mission settlement on New Zealand's Bay of Islands. He was again facing financial disaster for himself and his owners. An alternative to sealing had to be found. Morrell decided to stray from his owners' remit by making for Manila in the Philippines, where he hoped to find a commercial cargo to take to

Europe or America. It would be better than returning with an empty hold. Morrell's main investor and friend Skiddy recalled later that Morrell proved to be a visionary character, who instead of complying with his instructions, set off on a voyage of discovery. But Skiddy's retrospective interpretation of events hardly did Morrell justice. This change in plans, which would eventually lead to Morrell's entering uncharted waters, was a direct result of the environmental catastrophe wrought in the southern ocean by the generation of sealers before him.

Manila itself was set in a vast bay, but the outline of distant hills and mountains sweeping round it produced the effect of a giant lake. The city, colonized by the Spanish in the 1560s, was the hub of a booming trade among the Americas, the Pacific islands, and the coasts of Asia, China, and, increasingly, the new British colonies of Australia and Tasmania. Merchant adventurers with well-armed and well-manned vessels could take on brandy, rum, wines, tea, sugar, iron tools and all kinds of hardware, clothing, gold, and silver from the main ports, and then trade these for arrowroot, coconuts, sugar, pearls, dried sea cucumbers, dyewoods, tortoiseshell, cured fish, and the like from Pacific islands, or furs and maize from the American seaboard. It was a rough world in which many vessels crisscrossed the ocean for years in a variety of profitable permutations, and with little allegiance to anyone except themselves and their own gain. Hundreds of merchants from across the world had congregated in Manila to profit from this trade.

When Morrell arrived, he found a fortified city enclosed by a massive, dark, mossy stone wall that screened everything from the outside world, bar the red-tiled roofs, and the towers and domes of its cathedral and churches. A broad moat around the wall was joined to a river and added to the defenses. Only a single bridge led across to the gate and the city. Inside, its streets were narrow and gloomy, as the houses, churches, and monastic buildings had been built with thick walls to withstand earthquakes or attack. For the same reason the huge domed cathedral of Saint Peter lacked elegance from the outside, but inside it glimmered with gilt, its altar overhung by a canopy of crimson silk. While its pungent atmosphere of echo and incense drew visitors into a different world, the deep tone of its vesper bell brought the busy city streets to a standstill from time to time as the inhabitants were for a few moments transformed into solemnity by the muttering of prayers. Manila was a magnificent city. The houses were on two levels, laid out in quadrangles with inner courtyards. Covered balconies on the second story faced out sociably over the street, and their large windows could be thrown open to bring in what little breeze there was. These were glazed not with glass but with the translucent inner shells of mussels; a surface that reflected luminosity rather than light and left the streets dusted by a white talc in dry periods. Several of the streets were devoted to shops kept principally by speakers of Hokkien Chinese who had inherited a trading tradition that long predated the Spanish. They offered a huge variety of goods, luring in customers with offers of cigars and betel, but they had taken up the southern European habit of closing for siesta. Outside the main city, the more populous suburbs could be found over the bridge to the north, where a mass of bamboo and reed huts, raised from the ground on piles and shaded by towering trees and bamboo, extended up into the foothills of the surrounding mountains.

When he arrived in March 1830, Morrell could find no worthwhile cargo to ship back to America. There was, however, a promising alternative in dried sea cucumbers—a Chinese culinary delicacy. Known around the Pacific as *Bêche-de-mer,* these abounded on the reefs and sands of Pacific islands, where they were harvested by hand from flat-bottomed boats. Once dried, they preserved well and could be rehydrated by boiling and soaking them to restore their slippery texture. They went well in soup and stir fries with winter melon, dried scallops, Shiitake mushrooms, and the like. Their value, however, was not limited to dietary enhancement. In China and across southeast Asia they had acquired a reputation for promoting penis enlargement, partly because of their look and feel. When grabbed from the reef these phallic creatures would stiffen and ejaculate a jet of fluid in defense. Some five to eighteen inches long, they fed on the coral of the reefs, creeping into the shallows whenever they were exposed to the sun at low tide. They looked a little less symbolic when they were dried, having been slit at one end and squeezed of their entrails. Washed and boiled, they would next be buried in the ground for four hours and then boiled again before being heated under the sun or over a fire.

It happened that Morrell dropped anchor in Manila just when two other American vessels had arrived from Fiji with full cargoes of dried sea cucumbers. After off-loading them in China, where they were worth a fortune, the captains intended to return with silks and teas, covering tens of thousands of miles in pursuit of Pacific profit. The *Antarctic*'s owners had a commercial agent living in Manila, George William Hubbell, who for a decade or so had doubled as the American consul. Hubbell now wanted to take on sea cucumbers, so the arrival of Morrell and the *Antarctic* was wonderful luck. In broaching the sea cucumber plan to Morrell, however, he also encountered the beautiful Abby, and soon appeared to be planning to take on her as well.

Though lucrative, the sea cucumber trade was particularly dangerous, as it brought trading ships into direct contact with the islanders whose reefs they sought to harvest—who did not take kindly to intruders plundering their shores. The *Antarctic,* however, was well suited to the task as she was quick and heavily armed. Indeed, her arrival in Manila had already frightened local traders. Rumors were circulating that the superb ship, with her disciplined and battle-ready crew, was actually a pirate vessel that had ventured into port to acquire intelligence so that she could prey on commercial ships more effectively. The authorities in Manila wanted to see the back of her.

Hubbell knew that, apart from an armed ship, the other ingredient for success in collecting and preserving sea cucumbers was a skilled director of operations who could manage relations with islanders. The success of the two recent American voyages had depended on a former English sea captain who had subsequently settled in Fiji and learned the language. Hubbell naturally sought to employ him, but found that his price had become exorbitant; instead, he and Morrell employed another Englishman, John Wallace. Hubbell helped Morrell equip for the expedition and sold him all the powder and guns he needed from the store in the government magazines. But just as Morrell was preparing to sail, Hubbell refused to allow Abby to rejoin the ship.

The scandal that unfolded was to alter everyone's destiny. Explanations of what happened differ. Hubbell was thirty-four—slightly younger than Morrell—and, as depicted by Philippine artists of the time, much better looking. He epitomized the vanity of wealthy men of his era, dressed in starched collar and exuberant dark suit and sporting a well-groomed forelock and sideburns, his dark hair falling in curls upon his collar. His father had been a successful sea captain and a pioneer of American trade in the Pacific, and he and his family still traded around the world, especially throughout America, Europe, the Philippines, and Canton. Having established his own trading house in Manila in the early 1820s, Hubbell was rich, single, handsome, and lonely. A French trader, Monsieur Lafond de Lurcy, who happened to be in Manila at the time and followed the affair, suggested that it was Benjamin Morrell who had wanted to leave Abby in Manila, as it would have been improper for her to sail on a ship that would regularly take on board naked islanders. Abby, however, provided a very different reading of events in her later memoir of the voyage.

According to Abby, the consul was initially extremely respectful toward her, but Benjamin, presumably suspecting Hubbell's interest, was fast becoming moody, if not morose. A few days before they were due to sail, Hubbell told Morrell that the Spanish governor of Manila was opposed to Abby's departure. Abby was not the kind of woman to accept such an order easily, but she trusted her husband when he said that it was the governor, not he, who sought to detain her. Yet soon Abby suspected the consul had other motives. In Abby's words: "All was as plain as day to me, though I dared not express myself freely to my husband, for fear of the consequences from his quick sense of injury, and his high spirit as a brave man." Abby continued, rather unconvincingly, that after the consul's advances she did not trust her own interpretation: "My youth and ignorance of the world made me fear that I had put a wrong construction upon the

Consul's demeanor." Could she really have been so naive? It is hard to discern the truth, as both Abby's and Benjamin's published accounts of events in Manila were written for public consumption, are one-sided, and appeared after the death of Hubbell. What is certain, however, is that something was going on between the consul and Abby.

Abby pretended to accede to the request that she stay, but rather than lodge with the American consul, as would have been the norm, she arranged to stay with the British consul. Secretly, however, Abby still plotted to leave—or at least Benjamin plotted to take her.

On the eve of the *Antarctic*'s departure, Abby's half-brother, young John Keeler, smuggled her on board ship. But not secretly enough. The plan was foiled. Hubbell was rowed out to the schooner in a harbor boat along with a delegation of two American captains, a British captain, and the port and customs officers. They boarded and revealed that they knew Abby was aboard, again appealing to Benjamin to leave his wife in Manila. This time the consul claimed that he had pledged to the Spanish government not to let her sail and that if Abby did not return, then as agent of the ship's owners, he would relieve Morrell of his command—as he was empowered to do. Benjamin had no option but to acquiesce and order Abby to be sent ashore to stay with the British consul's family. Thereafter, by her account, she ignored the American consul—but later found that there had been no directive by the Spanish governor to force her to stay.

What had so far already been a disastrous voyage now became calamitous. Sailing without Abby, Morrell first headed southeast to the Micronesian islands on his way to Fiji some forty-five hundred miles away, but met countercurrents and winds that hindered his progress. After some unproductive prospecting for sea cucumbers, pearl, and shell in Micronesia, he was forced by winds and currents to give up on Fiji and turned southwest instead, toward the Solomon Islands. On his way he came upon the tiny, low-lying Carteret Islands, a circular atoll enclosing a lagoon ten miles across, though with only perhaps a third of a square mile of inhabitable land. The British explorer Philip Carteret's own "discovery" of this atoll in 1767 had ended

Captain Morrell siezing a Savage by the throat.

Benjamin Morrell at Kilinailau ("Massacre Island"), from Halliard (pseud.), *Voyages and Adventures of Jack Halliard, with Captain Morrell,* 104

in violence when he had looted an islander's shell-inlaid canoe and its cargo of coconuts, and it seems that other visitors had followed suit.

New York newspapers later reported that the crew of the *Antarctic* had received a portent of impending disaster—and portents mattered for seamen of the era: "'A little bird, as black as ink' came on board the schooner, and could not be induced to leave her. Some of the men, with the credulity common to seamen, thinking it was a bird of ill omen, wanted to kill it, but the captain, pleased with its perfect tameness, determined on preserving its life. On the following day the islands to which the name of Massacre Islands was afterwards given, were discovered and the little bird immediately flew to the land."

The Carteret Islands' reefs were enticingly rich in sea cucumbers. Morrell landed on the main island as if he owned it and immediately instructed his director of operations, Wallace, and twenty-five men to clear land, build a curing factory for boiling and drying the sea cucumbers, and plant a garden. The reaction of the inhabitants of this minute but hugely populous island to the invasion goes unrecorded, but as there would not have been a twig untreasured, it would inevitably have been hostile. The next day, when the ship's armorer fired up his iron forge on land, it drew a large crowd of locals, and a number of tools went missing. The inhabitants had no metal, and imported iron was extremely valuable to them. Nor had they seen a forge before, or the manipulation of red-hot metal. On the third day the landing party again lost some equipment. When he found out, Morrell—who usually stayed aboard the *Antarctic*—was furious. He went ashore with six armed men to threaten the chief, only to be confronted, to his apparent surprise, by several hundred equally angry islanders armed with spears and bows and arrows. In the ensuing stand-off, Morrell managed to take one of the leaders hostage, forcing the islanders to disarm before he retreated to the beach. He also made five senior islanders accompany him back to the *Antarctic*. Later, Morrell claimed that he treated them to food and a dance, but according to the ship's log, one of those detained must not have appreciated the hospitality, as he jumped ship and swam ashore.

Whatever the case, the next morning Morrell blindly imagined that all was well. He returned the remaining chiefs to the island, and sent twenty or more crew with them to continue building the cucumber-curing factory. Later that morning, the islanders attacked and fourteen crew were lost, among them Wallace and Second Officer Henry Wiley. Others narrowly escaped, rescued from the battle by a relief boat sent from the *Antarctic*. The schooner itself escaped the approaching canoes of the enraged islanders only by cutting anchor and leaving a great deal of equipment behind.

Only nineteen crew survived, forcing Morrell to return directly to Manila, again empty-handed, where he was reunited with Abby. But he was still angry, and he decided to prepare a retaliatory expedition, which he also hoped would turn a good profit. For labor, he persuaded the governor to relax the rule of allowing only a third of any one ship's crew to be composed of locals and permit him to hire as many "Manila men" as he needed. Shipowners and captains generally distrusted Manila men, who were mostly of mixed Spanish and local heritage and whom they considered to be a mutinous bunch. Morrell, however, now recruited sixty-six Manilans to join his nineteen Americans, which was a huge proportion—and indeed, a huge number for the ninety-foot *Antarctic,* which had only one level below deck.

The American consul, Hubbell, remained at odds with Morrell and refused to finance his punitive expedition—perhaps because of its unlikely profitability, or the unconventionality of its crew, but most probably because by now he had fallen out with both Benjamin and Abby. However, Morrell managed to secure a twelve-thousand-dollar loan from the British consul, who had been a close friend of John Wallace and so was equally keen on revenge. With these funds, Morrell adapted the *Antarctic* for battle, fitting her out with high bulwarks to protect those on deck, fixing swivel guns atop, and introducing further gun ports for the new heavy cannon he took on.

In an effort to reduce the risk and increase the likely profit from the sea cucumbers, Morrell also sought a new collaboration with Captain Gabriel Lafond de Lurcy, who was again in port. "We could," Morrell apparently suggested to Lafond de Lurcy, "do a good operation in bringing a large number of Manila men to fish sea cucumber and the two teams could defend each other in these inhospitable islands, and could perhaps force the natives to work for us." Lafond de Lurcy declined.

Morrell now "made a declaration of war on his own responsibility" on the Carteret Islands. This was the first in a series of extremely violent engagements on which Morrell, now with Abby at his side, decided to embark. Predictably, as soon as the *Antarctic* arrived at the Carteret Islands, the islanders organized an attack. Morrell responded with a full ten minutes of cannon fire. He then turned his guns on the beachside villages. The numbers killed can only be imagined.

During this attack a canoe in which sat a solitary figure pulled off from the island and made for the ship. As it neared, the Americans recognized one of their former crew, Leonard Shaw, whom they had long presumed dead, but whom in fact the islanders had captured and kept alive to teach then ironworking. Faced with the cannon

The Ship firing upon the Savages.

"The ship firing upon the savages," from Halliard (pseud.), *Voyages and Adventures of Jack Halliard, with Captain Morrell*, 112

fire, the islanders had released him to sue for peace. Shaw had learned a little of their language and could interpret for them, which helped. The next day, Morrell "negotiated" a peace with the islanders and took control of one of their uninhabited smaller islets, paying for it "in cutlery, trinkets, axes, hatchets, adzes, chisels, plane-irons, gimlets, spoke-shaves, knives, scissors, razors, looking-glasses, and beads of different kinds."

Having taken their revenge, the American crew and Manila men now set up a base, this time building a treehouse fortress and a vast drying room in which they could cure sea cucumbers on an industrial scale. Intending to stay for some months, they also felled and cleared all the trees around their buildings to give a clear line of fire in case of attack. Nevertheless, the islanders put up continued resistance, harassing the Americans at every opportunity, on the seas, on the reefs, on the beaches. After many a pitched battle, the islanders eventually forced Morrell to give up his hopes of harvesting sea cucumbers there, and he left. When, later that year, an Australian whaling captain visited the island, he confirmed the destruction of its vegetation, and found remnants of the tree castle and building. He also found incised in the tree that held the castle the initials A[bby] B[enjamin]—with a heart and the two crossed arrows of love.

There were two ways back to Manila from the Carteret Islands: a direct route around the eastern end of New Ireland or a less direct one to its west, through the narrow Saint George's Channel between New Ireland and New Britain. Morrell was in the rare position of having a vessel suitable for the notoriously dangerous westerly route; she was also now well armed and well defended. He opted to sail through the channel and prospect for trade along the northern coast of New Britain, which was still largely uncharted.

By now Morrell had not only failed to make money for his investors, he had also acquired an enormous personal debt. He was ever more desperate to turn a profit on this voyage, or it could well be his last. He needed to find locations rich in sea cucumbers, tortoiseshell, and pearls, and he now realized that he needed translators from the islands to act as intermediaries. Kidnapping was the obvious solution. He planned to take captives from promising islands and sail with them to Manila. Sea captains had long since learned that if they treated a traumatized captive well, "protected" him from other hostile crew, and exposed him to the magnificence of cities such as Manila, the captive would often develop a paradoxical empathy and allegiance to them—and work gratefully as a trading intermediary when taken home. Morrell would treat his captives well and impress them with Manila's modernity, then reequip and return with gifts for the captives and for trade. Acquiring intermediaries was crucial not only for the expedition itself but also for resolving the problem of securing the loan in Manila that he would need to finance it. Financiers realized well enough that a pliant intermediary would take the risk out of what would otherwise be a reckless gamble.

So it was a desperate and indebted Morrell who, on his way back to Manila, anchored his ship in the only natural harbor on the southern shore of the island of Uneapa. Under his command was probably the fastest and most maneuverable ship in the Pacific. It was also extra-ordinarily well armed and carried a huge and angry crew who had been denied their bonuses at "Massacre Island" after being harried for weeks by its inhabitants. As Dako's people approached its bulk in their war canoes, they were not to know the explosive danger they were putting themselves in.

CHAPTER 3

At Sea

ॐ

Dako was not the first man Benjamin Morrell kidnapped on that voyage. A week before, at the Carteret Islands, he had abducted a man during the final battle. Badly wounded, the man had died on board six days later—the day before the *Antarctic* arrived at Uneapa. The young navigator John Keeler entered in the ship's log that at one o'clock the crew "hove his body overboard."

Nor was Dako the last captive to be taken on the voyage. After leaving Uneapa, Morrell sailed westward along the coast of New Britain, north along the coast of New Guinea, and then east toward the low-lying islands, sandbanks, and lagoons that were marked on his maps as the "Chess Board" Islands, now the Ninigo Islands. The *Antarctic* arrived there on Monday, November 22, and the crew leveled their cannon at yet another flotilla of approaching canoes. In the ensuing battle they captured a man whom they imaginatively named "Monday." The pages of the ship's log concerning this encounter were removed to conceal the island's location, but several other accounts relate the events.

In her memoir of the voyage, Abby describes how, when the *Antarctic* arrived off the island—which was extremely rich in sea cucumbers, pearls, tortoises, and oysters—an enormous number of canoes approached the ship in a bid to capture her and drag her onto a reef. In a pamphlet eventually published by John Keeler, he claims that the approaching force numbered "near two thousand warriors"—which seems hardly likely given the relatively small population of the islands. Abby goes on to describe how, this time, Morrell let the islanders attach their canoes to the schooner in order to try and drag her ashore, but then broke their lines by offering a little sail to the brisk wind. Once the lines parted, noted Abby, the islanders shot arrows at the schooner in a rage. She also describes the captain firing a few cannon shots over their heads to frighten them. She continues: "The report of the cannon astounded them, and many leaped into the sea for safety. We had already had enough of blood, and were unwilling to shed it. A boat was lowered while they were in confusion, and one of the natives picked up." Abby's account was directed at an audience of American women whose sense of righteousness might have been offended by the truth. But the editors slipped up, for it was later revealed in a contradictory account in the same book. "Monday," it says there, was "picked up from the water: the canoe in which he was being destroyed by the cannon-shot, he took to the water, and being wounded, was taken in by our boat's crew sent for that purpose."

"Monday," as he shall always have to be called since his birth name goes unrecorded, was younger and shorter than Dako, but nevertheless powerful and agile. Those who vividly described his "savage," determined countenance and lively, brilliant eyes failed to acknowledge, however, the look of ceaseless terror that filled them. Instead they spoke of his silky hair, fine nose, and well-proportioned forehead, of how "nature ha[d] given every indication that she cast him in one of her most exquisite moulds."

Previously Monday's world had been one of long-distance trading voyages in the huge sailing canoes for which his islands were famous, to the New Guinea mainland three hundred miles to the west and the Admiralty (Manus) Islands a hundred miles east. But the two captives now bound together below decks in the *Antarctic* did not share a common language, and so had no way of understanding each other beyond looks exchanged and signs of sympathy offered. Unlike Dako, Monday at this stage made no attempt to escape. Instead, according to Abby, when he was allowed on deck he would sit and look steadfastly upon the ocean toward a point on the horizon for hours at a time. Later, in New York, journalists picked up on the different characters of the two captives, contrasting Dako's escape bids at sea with Monday's apparent docility—and somehow deducing from this that Monday must have been a criminal or slave in his native land.

Abby must have realized that Monday was petrified, but for the large readership of literate American ladies she described instead how well he was treated: "Every kindness was shown him; he ate what he pleased, and when, and not a blow was ever given him by any one; the sailors having strict orders not to disturb him nor his companion." She went on: "He wandered about the deck, and showed at length some marks of interest in things around him." When the newspapers later described the islanders' experience aboard, however, they gave a very different account, presumably gleaned from the crew who took pleasure in terrorizing them. The *Nantucket Inquirer* reported: "They are extremely timid, and when given to understand by the sailors that they would be eaten alive on their arrival here, they exhibited much agitation; and at other times would tremble with fear." Dako truly feared that he might be killed and eaten: the torment handed out to him and Monday by the sailors dovetailed with the legends of Pango. Nor was the idea of cannibalism alien to him. On Uneapa, it was acceptable for a person who was killed in combat to be eaten—although never by relatives. The bodies of those so killed could be sent to nonrelatives, who were later required to return the favor.

On board, the two captives may have been allowed to eat when and what they liked, as Abby claimed, but they were still limited to a sailor's fare, which was far from anything they would have previously tasted. Instead of fish with yams cooked with coconut milk and assorted greens, their diet was now dominated by ship's biscuit, or hardtack, which was a dry, compacted wheat-flour cracker that had been baked four times to help it last in the tropics for years—even if it was infested with weevils. On very rare occasions, sailors enjoyed a salt pork or beef stew known as salt horse, but otherwise their staple diet was lobscouse—in which the cook added to the ship's biscuit some of the fat liberated in the boiling of salt horse, and stewed the mix in molasses and water. Occasionally the cook also threw in some potatoes or sweet potatoes to turn this mix into the more luxurious potato scouse, but that was the limit of his creativity. For a festivity, though, he might make a dessert of plum duff: flour, lard, yeast, and dried fruit boiled together, hard. Fresh vegetables, fruit, pork, and chicken were taken on board whenever possible, but these perished in the heat, so had to be eaten immediately. There was no space for live animals. When the crew caught a large shark one day and landed it on deck, Dako was quick to seize it even while it was still thrashing around. He then surprised them by eating a part of it—probably the oily liver—while it was still alive, apparently with "great satisfaction."

Although they were not to know it, the two captives had now become the cornerstones of Morrell's future. The captain tasked Leonard Shaw, the sailor who had been held prisoner on the Carteret Islands, to look after them since he had acquired some understanding of one of the local languages (though not either of theirs). Dako and Monday were therefore lodged with Shaw and the common crew before the mast, probably toward the middle of the ship in steerage rather than in the forecastle, which was reserved for more trusted crew members, who preferred to keep as far away as possible from the eye of the officers in the aft. Sailors in steerage had fewer chances to dance, sing, play cards, smoke, or complain than those quartered toward the bow, living under the close observation of the steward, who was perceived as an officers' man. Many of the "untrustworthy" Manila men were also probably quartered in steerage, along with the better-paid artisans—the cook, the carpenter, the gun keeper, and the sailmaker—who all worked by day but were not required to keep watch. Both steerage and forecastle offered unpleasant accommodation at the best of times. The forecastle was perhaps three yards by three, dark, lacking in ventilation, and most likely had shelf berths for sixteen men, sleeping in two shifts. Steerage was a little bigger, but had to berth twenty-five or more in each twelve-hour shift. There was no escape from the wet, the heat, and the stench of close-packed humanity. Rats and cockroaches reigned. In the heat and humidity, iron soon turned to

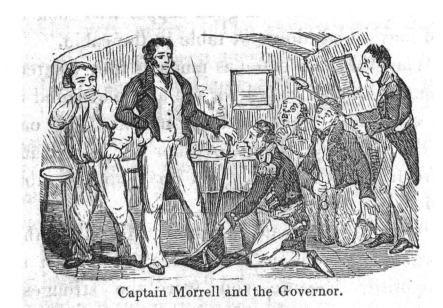

Captain Morrell and the Governor.

Benjamin Morrell (middle, standing) in cabin of the *Antarctic,* from Halliard (pseud.),
Voyages and Adventures of Jack Halliard, with Captain Morrell, 88

rust, and leather and paper to mold. The South Seas had a climate that
ridiculed most of the trappings of the temperate world. The sailors
might not have been allowed to dispense with their uniform of striped
cotton shirts and white pantaloons, but the improbability of wearing
shoes was accepted, and they were left to rot deep in the hold while
their owners went about the decks barefoot.

Neither the captives nor the ordinary crew members were permitted access to the officers' quarters. Life there for Abby and the
captain was cramped but somewhat exclusive. His transom, or after
cabin, with its windows overlooking the stern, was their refuge. Its
comforts extended to a large upholstered sofa under the window, a
barometer, a thermometer, a mirror, and perhaps even a painting fixed
to one of its walls, as well as the chart table with its instruments. This
refuge, however, served also as reception room, sitting room, parlor,
office, director's room, jury room, and Supreme Court. The monotony of its wood echoed the watery monotony of the sea: wood floors,
wood-paneled walls with wooden lockers, and wooden doors with

slats let into them for ventilation. A wooden hatch was set into the wooden ceiling that could be opened to let daylight in. In a lockable case were, among other books, the twenty volumes of Captain Cook's and George Vancouver's voyages round the world, loaned to Morrell by the ship's owner, Skiddy—and never given back.

A door opened into Benjamin and Abby's stateroom, which was hardly any bigger than the after cabin, with a simple berth for a bed. With Abby aboard, the captain had probably ordered the ship's carpenter to make their bed somewhat more comfortable by building in a canvas mattress, albeit at the risk of introducing a cockroach refuge. Aside from these two private rooms and the water closet, however, Abby had access only to the eating cabin—perhaps eight feet by ten— which she shared with her husband, her brother John, and all the other ship's officers. This was a genteel if cramped room where they ate off porcelain, the raised ridges of the table preventing the screwing motion of the ship from tipping everything onto the floor. Next to the eating cabin were the officers' own tiny cabins, also shared, the wooden bunk berths serving as their only personal refuge.

Decorum forbade Abby from venturing forward. As she had had to join the *Antarctic* secretly, too, the ship had left port without any of the adaptations that were sometimes made when a captain's wife was aboard. Presumably, though, Morrell had later ordered the carpenter to make her the usual six-by-six-foot refuge on deck so she could take the air in the kind of privacy a captain's wife would require. This and their two private rooms were the areas that Abby could make homely, perhaps with a carpet and a curtain below or a few potted plants above. Yet despite their cramped quarters, Abby and Benjamin certainly had a little privacy: within two weeks of the naked brutality of Monday's capture, they had conceived their next child.

The ruthless hierarchy of the *Antarctic* must have been evident to the captives. Even before breakfast, the crew cleaned the decks for two hours under the supervision of officers. The sailors were kept at work incessantly and in silence for the rest of the day, whether mending and storing the rigging or climbing aloft to shape the sails to the wind. The first officer's job was to implement the captain's orders and take charge of the cargo's storage and safekeeping, while the lower-order officers ensured that the crew had the equipment they needed. This rhythm of permanent work, which was usual on all ships, was designed to stifle mutiny. It was broken only on Sundays, when the officers slackened their demands and the sailors tried to dress up and were permitted to read, talk, smoke, or simply relax on deck.

Morrell was particularly convinced of the cleansing power of vinegar. Teeth were to be washed in vinegar daily, and it was doled out with the food three times a day. It was also added to drinking water for purification and to enhance perspiration. Foul parts of the ship were washed and sprinkled with it, rather than the more usual concentrate of urine. In the battle against scurvy and fever Morrell had brought dried apples aboard for the crew to eat three times a week, collected wild celery where he could, and forbade seamen to sleep in wet clothes or on deck when it was either very hot or very cold. He also obliged them to change and wash their clothes twice a week—moderating, perhaps, but not eradicating their odors.

Where the *Antarctic* diverged from sailing custom was in its drinking policy. Morrell kept his ship free of all "ardent spirits"—that is, the gin, rum, and whiskey that usually were an integral component of a crew's life at this time. His was a temperance ship and a moral ship, at least as understood by the resurgent Protestant ethic of New York and New England. Newspapers had carried stories about Morrell's unusual restrictions before the *Antarctic* set sail and eulogized them on his return. The crew instead found their spirit in music: in fiddles and fifes and probably guitars and banjos, which could strike up the dancing styles of New York or the folk styles of the Appalachian Mountains or, for the British on board, the sea chanteys of Cornwall and Clydeside. Dako was more accustomed to drums for dance and the ethereal music of panpipes for music. What he and Monday made of the sailors' music goes unrecorded.

Sagas on the island of Umboi, lying in the straits between New Britain and New Guinea, reveal that there was once an enormous Malaz tree. It had all sorts of wealth in its branches: cockatoos,

cassowaries, birds of paradise, black ochre, clay pots, pigs, dogs, wooden
bowls, black beads, "and—oh boy! everything you could possibly
imagine of any worth." The tree grew near the village of Barik. One
day, the village men gathered beneath it noticed an old man hobbling
toward them. This was the heroic Ambogim, a rogue, wanderer, and
creator of wealth and custom now disguised in the flayed skin of his
father. He had just seduced one of the men's wives during her men-
strual cycle and another who should have been in seclusion after giving birth. The disguised Ambogim offered to help the young men at
their work, but they suggested he sit with the elders. Instead, he made
the sky pour with rain, and while the men were distracted heading
for shelter, he climbed the Malaz tree, where he shed his disguise and
stopped the rain. One of the women he had seduced now arrived on
the scene, and the men looked up to see the spectacularly handsome
Ambogim dressed in his feasting finery. Angry at being fooled, the
men hacked at the tree to fell it and kill him. As the huge tree began
to sway, Ambogim merely rocked it farther so that it swooped over
the New Guinea coast to the southwest. The open clay pot, a cockatoo, and the wooden bowls fell out there. Now it swayed back to the
north, and bows and arrows, black clay pots, wide-mouthed pots,
another cockatoo, a cassowary, a bird of paradise, and the black ochre
fell out over a different part of the coast. Next it swayed east over New
Britain, where the short-tailed pigs, hairless pigs, spears, tapa cloth,
and boar tusks dropped out, with obsidian falling only on the island
of Garua. Then it arced once more toward the western tip of New
Britain and snapped. Out fell a third cockatoo, a cassowary, and black
beads—and Ambogim, who escaped. So it was that when this wondrous tree finally fell down, all the most valued goods in the region
were distributed, but Umboi and the islands nearby were left empty.
Eventually, Ambogim became contrite at the sterility his play and
sexual transgressions had brought to the island and made good by
providing it with a monopoly on the large sailing boats that hence-
forth traded between New Britain and New Guinea.

If the tree had swept over Uneapa distributing its less than natural
endowments, it must have dropped the pigs, dogs, yams, red paint,

and woven arm and leg bands for which the island was known. Yet Dako, like all Uneapa islanders, also needed or cherished all those other items the tree of wealth and plenty had distributed elsewhere in the known world. And, like everyone else, he nurtured friendship networks far and wide in order to get hold of these things. It was these networks linking his island with the rest of the upturned bowl that now carried the story of his capture far beyond the shores of Uneapa.

In particular, Dako and his powerful father had a trading partner who lived directly south across the sea on one of the islets set among the reefs a couple of miles off the New Britain coast. Those living on these tiny islands had to paddle to the mainland to tend their crops in gardens back of the mangrove-fringed shore. They had to bring their water and wood from there, too, but it was a small price to pay for the security of a two-mile moat, for the breeze and sandy beaches, and for the freedom from snakes, spiders, and mosquitoes it secured. Dako's family friend seems to have been a powerful but elderly man named Tantargeely, who presided over the islet of Samilani. This was about a quarter of a mile around and so crammed with stilted houses that there was space for only seven or eight coconut palms. Tantargeely spoke a different language from Dako, known locally as Kove, yet many Kove people were used to staying at Dako's harbor and had learned the language of Uneapa, while among Dako's people there were many who had learned to speak Kove in the same way. The lives of the people from these two shores were intertwined.

It was the custom for Uneapa men like Dako and his father to exchange gifts with their established partners in among the Kove islands. And it was from Tantargeely or similar partners that Dako's family had received items such as the leg bones and feather ribs of the large and flightless cassowary which the Kove people hunted. Uneapa's people treasured these bird parts as a kind of currency, and Dako used them to tip his javelin and make his delicate earrings. Tantargeely also supplied him with the hand drums, *pandanus* (screwpine) mats, and woven plates his people made, and could procure as well items such as carved wooden bowls, stone axes, and pottery that the Kove did not make themselves but could acquire in turn from their other gifting partners to the west. Coveted objects passed through many hands as they traveled along the gifting networks that stretched from as far afield as the New Guinea mainland about two hundred miles away. From the east Tantargeely could also lay his hands on strings of shells, razor-sharp obsidian, and red paint, some of which he would pass along to Dako.

When Tantargeely visited Uneapa, Dako's family would have presented him with the bounty of Uneapa, such as pigs, dogs, yams, paints, and practical items like baskets and fire tongs. Dako and Vakale would have produced some of these themselves, but they would also have acquired items from friends whose boats perhaps Dako had helped to build or paint. Some of the baskets and armbands that Dako gifted to Kove may have originated from other islands. Everyone in the region was adept at balancing the giving and taking of presents, but it was Kove like Tantargeely who had the strongest reputation for negotiating the gifting networks best in order to accumulate the shell strings that they, at least, treasured beyond all else.

These networks crisscrossed the entire region, and it would have been through these that news of the battle at Uneapa and of Dako's abduction would have passed. News of similar incidents had probably reached Uneapa from islands in the straits between New Guinea and New Britain which were more familiar with apparitions like the *Antarctic*—Australian trading ships often passed that way when the winds were favorable, as did the occasional whaler. Directly after Dako's capture, and on his way to Monday's island, Morrell had sailed across these straits and managed to swap iron for fresh food while Dako was secured below decks. So once news of the events on Uneapa had passed down the coast to the straits, everyone would have been able to relate it to sightings of the strange ship.

Despite the distances, trading voyages to Garove, the Kove islets, and mainland New Britain had been a regular feature of Dako's life. The Americans had arrived just when the notoriously rough waters of the Bidera (Bismarck) Sea were entering one of the two, short, calmer seasons that enabled islanders to paddle the forty miles to the mainland. These were the slack seasons when the prevailing winds were changing, as the northwesterlies that blew from January to March oscillated with the southeasterly winds that blew from May to November. Even these slack seasons, though, had their dangers, as strong winds could still come up suddenly and change directions dangerously many times a day.

Gifting friendships endured down the generations, and it sometimes happened that the families intermarried. Dako's father, Tupi, would eventually confer his gifting friendship to Dako, his firstborn, and Tantargeely would pass the responsibility down to his firstborn—whether a son or daughter (firstborn girls delegated the traveling to their brothers or husbands). Several families from Dako's island cherished their own particular friendships with Kove people and guarded these jealously down the generations from any usurper who might think to wrest them away. For only through such personal relations could islanders participate in the wider world, and to have their names passed along the network to people as yet unmet was an honor that many strived for. People took pleasure in their connections beyond their particular area. "They may never see my face, but they know my name!"

Thanks to his father, Dako's name was probably already well known, but he had also worked hard to build up respect and a reputation for leadership. One of the strongest memories Dako would have taken with him aboard the *Antarctic* would have been of the celebration of his first sea voyage across to Tantargeely's islet in the company of his father. Uneapa's parents honored their firstborn children with a sequence of ceremonies and festivities that celebrated various milestones: the first haircut or ear piercing; the first fish catch. Parents arranged for these privileged youth to be introduced formally and festively to the various spirits associated with their land and with the offshore reefs. Each festivity gave the children a leg up the social ladder which would become more important as they got older. The ultimate gesture parents could make for their first child was to arrange for the community to build a house-of-respect in the child's name. These were small hangar-like constructions, built around two main upright posts with a ridgepole slung between them, carved and painted to resemble a barracuda. Their delicate roofs splayed out on either side to rest on smaller supports, and projected far enough to shelter the exterior walls, which artists painted in a baffling array of black, white, yellow, and red ochre triangles. Men stored their musical instruments and other ceremonial objects in the gloom within, and behind them met in exclusive privacy. It mattered little whether a firstborn was a girl or a boy, as firstborn daughters of leading families were as entitled to inherit the ceremonial drum of office and have a house named for them as were firstborn boys. Either would have to go through the heavy schedule of ceremonies, and both earned respect and privileges and—depending on their personalities—authority. Girls also had to learn, like boys, their genealogies and details of everyone's land rights, in case they were consulted over disputes.

Dako's first sea trip to Kove and the festival that surrounded it was, then, a rite of passage that ushered him into the adult world of travel. Until then, he might have visited his mother's island of Naraga, but otherwise he would have been effectively grounded in his village, watching his similarly aged mates with some envy as they led lives less constrained by such formalities. The buildup to the trip would have involved an extravagant exchange of gifts, and on arrival at Kove, all those accompanying Dako would have made directly for Tantargeely's islet, where they would be greeted with a feast and dancing. And on his return to Uneapa as a man of the world, Dako would surely have glided back into harbor standing as proudly on the prow of his canoe as he did during the attack on the *Antarctic*.

When, in turn, Tantargeely and his companions crossed over to Uneapa, Dako's father would have plied them with tobacco, betel nuts, and coconuts, and dropped everything to gossip, relax, and sport on the shore before putting on a dance in the evening. Men would have been put up in the houses-of-respect, while the women, if they accompanied them, would have stayed with female relatives.

Now, almost a generation on from his own initiation into this world, if he had not been snatched away Dako would have been starting to plan for one of these firstborn ceremonies for his own firstborn, Tupi. Vakale would have been spending her days in their yam gardens storing up surpluses, or shinnying up the palms in their plantation to collect extra betel nuts or coconuts. When she took a canoe out with her friends to dive for shellfish or hook fish for the evening meal, she would, with luck, have a surplus there, too. During the busy seasons, even in her more relaxing moments by the house there would still have been baskets to be woven or the small grass panels to be made that she and the other women wore for modesty front and back in an otherwise naked world. But as the seasons cycled so there was more time for dance and festivities, when Vakale could decorate herself with more than just a flower in her hair or a shell bangle. Then she would whiten her hair with lime powder, don her necklaces, armbands, and a fresh grass panel, as well as a mix of scented leaves, in the hope that Dako—and her friends—might notice. Dako and Vakale would have gardened and built up the family reputation through the ceremonies of their firstborn as a joint endeavor. But now Dako was lost and Vakale was inconsolable.

It was mid-December 1830 when Morrell arrived back in Manila Bay with his captives. On this occasion they had to anchor some eight miles from the city in the sheltered Cavite harbor, a dilapidated place whose amenities included a dockyard, an arsenal, numerous churches, a hospital and barracks, and a telegraph station that communicated with the capital by semaphore. Morrell and his crew took the large outrigger canoe service into Manila city, passing a forest of masts that must have truly astonished the two captives when Morrell brought them into town later. Having reached the main landing place, protected by a circular gun battery, Morrell made straight for the British consul's residence, where he could count on a welcome.

When Morrell brought Dako and Monday ashore a few days later, he found that the townspeople were so interested in them that he could hire a room and display them for good money. The show was overseen by Leonard Shaw, whose own capture, release, and reappearance made a powerful story. Nothing is known of this show except that according to Morrell, it drew large crowds of "citizens of all classes." The captives themselves would certainly have been amazed at the sight of their first city—precisely as Morrell intended. He and Shaw would have taken Dako and Monday on a city tour in one of the cheap taxi carriages drawn by a pair of ponies—all entirely new to them. In the evening they would surely have gone for a promenade along the magnificent tree-lined boulevard outside the city wall known as the Calzada. This was a world of fashion. Manila men dressed in striped calico trousers and shirts made of a supple pineapple-leaf fiber; a thin, richly embroidered gauze that enhanced their physique. Women wore light muslin tops and brightly colored calico wraps around the waist, set off by jewelry and lace turbans. The only blemishes to the locals' beauty, to American minds, were their red lips and blackened teeth, acquired from chewing betel nuts, the local stimulant of choice.

It was the custom for the governor to appear on the promenade in his coach and four, attended by his ornately dressed cavalry bodyguard. Two thousand uniformed armed troops drilled there each evening, too—accompanied by two full brass bands. But this was pomp with a purpose. Spain's colonies were in political turmoil. The Bolivarian revolutions in the first part of the century against the empire's authority in South America had already destroyed its global power— with much support from republican Americans. The foster brother of Morrell's sisters, Silas Burrows, was at this very time dispatching a ship commanded by Stonington's other hero, Nathaniel Palmer, to run guns and soldiers to the revolutionary leader Simón Bolívar in Venezuela. Unsurprisingly, Americans like Morrell were viewed suspiciously in Manila and checked rigorously for the trappings of sedition, including books by Rousseau, Voltaire, and others. If caught in possession of such revolutionary tracts they would have faced the death penalty.

Now that Morrell had his captives, he presumed that he would be able to secure further credit from the American consul, Hubbell, in order to return to their islands and trade. It had, after all, been the consul's own idea to go into the sea cucumber business. But Hubbell refused. Morrell was furious. As he later wrote: "The importance of my new discoveries was universally acknowledged," claiming, "Had it not been for the envy and perfidy of some of my own country-men, I should have succeeded in raising funds to fit out the Antarctic in such a manner as immediately to realize a portion of the immense profits which still await a well-conducted expedition." Abby was equally aggrieved. According to her version of events: "On our arrival at Manilla, as I apprehended, we found that our evils were not at an end. Our English and Spanish friends were as kind as people could be; still the Consul continued his persecutions." Perhaps because Abby refused to sleep with him; perhaps because he considered him-self dishonored by her suspicions; or perhaps because he believed it to be commercial madness to back the serially unsuccessful Morrell, Hubbell continued his "perfidious machinations." These, combined with Morrell's lack of credit elsewhere, forced Morrell to abandon his plan to return to the Bismarck Sea. Instead he was obliged to return to the United States, and en route try to defray his losses by drop-ping off a cargo at Cádiz.

This voyage was turning out to be a financial disaster for both Morrell and his investors. It would also destroy once and for all his reputation as a merchant captain. The two islanders offered him his only lifeline: the possibility of convincing New York investors that he not only knew where a fortune in sea cucumbers and shells was to be had, but that he also possessed the interpreters to make such an expedition a commercial success. As Morrell's only tickets back to the region, he would have to take Dako and Monday with him to New York to show to his investors. He would also have to keep them in good health while guarding the exact locations of their islands, pre-tending that they were his own discovery and shrouding them in mystery in every subsequent conversation and publication. This was usual practice for a sealer used to protecting his commercial secrets. Morrell even tore out the pages of the ship's log that concerned the capture of Monday despite this document rightfully belonging to the *Antarctic*'s owners, financiers, and insurers. His secret, however, was that he had no secret, as the islands were marked on every mod-ern chart.

The captain paid off his Manila men, sold off the rest of his trading cargo, took on a cargo of "China goods" for Cádiz and shell for
America, and set sail. Manila was no longer a place to linger, as a global
cholera epidemic had recently reached the city, turning its vivacity
into social insularity. The *Antarctic* weighed anchor on January 13,
1831. The cholera would eventually follow Morrell to Europe and
New York, but by the time he reached them, it had already claimed
the one American Morrell probably hoped it would: the consul, Hubbell, who died in March. Hubbell would never be able to tell his version of his fraught relationship with the Morrells, which gave them a
free hand over the story.

It was a very long voyage home. Abby and Benjamin knew that
the popular interest the captives commanded in Manila would be just
as keen in America, so during the long days on board they began to
write up their story. With John Keeler as clerk they prepared an account of their voyage and of Leonard Shaw's experiences as a captive
on "Massacre Island."

Abby, meanwhile, was in the latter stages of her pregnancy, and it
was touch and go whether she would reach New York in time for the
birth. When the *Antarctic* arrived in Cádiz, the authorities, aware that
the ship could be carrying cholera, imposed a forty-day quarantine.
The Morrells did not have forty days to spare. Caught between the
pressures of the looming birth and the quarantine, and with the chance
of making at least some money, Morrell sailed on without off-loading
the cargo and instead traveled to Bordeaux, where he arrived on June
20, escaped quarantine, and delivered the freight destined for Cádiz.

The day after the *Antarctic* anchored in Bordeaux Harbor (which
was still a slaving port), word reached journalists in town that she had
two "cannibals" aboard. Dako and Monday, by now recovered, had
not been making life easy for the crew. The rumor reaching the reporters was that during the passage the crew could "preserve themselves from the fury of the savages with difficulty." In search of a story,
a French journalist visited the schooner and began to examine the captives "closely." According to the journalist, one of them threw himself
at him, then the other joined the fight. Whether provoked by the jour-

nalist or driven by fear, Dako and Monday were clearly desperate. Apparently only a customhouse officer aboard managed to separate them, and even then, so the rattled reporter wrote, only "at the sacrifice of his dog to their appetite." The journalist interpreted the attack as due to the captives' cannibal impulse, writing that it showed "unequivocal indications of a desire to devour him." What Dako and Monday made of the encounter again goes unrecorded.

Morrell was financially desperate. By delivering freight to the wrong port, he forced the shipowners to forfeit their transport commission, and they would also have to pay a penalty for inaccurate delivery. All he had to show for the entire voyage was debt. Moreover, he had stopped at Singapore on the way back and sold off part of the cargo without accounting for it—possibly pocketing the money. Nevertheless, as his own debts had yet to catch up with him, he found that in Bordeaux he was still creditworthy, so, before sailing, he borrowed another four thousand dollars from local banks on his own account. With this cash in hand and his two captives aboard, he sailed directly for New York.

CHAPTER 4

The "Cannibal Show"

෨෨

T he *Antarctic* navigated the narrows between Staten Island and
Long Island into New York Harbor on the late summer evening of August 27, 1831, watched over like every incoming
vessel by the three tiers of cannon that guarded the city in the massive
fortresses on each shore. Morrell ordered the anchors to be dropped
next to the shipyards of the East River, and brought the *Antarctic* to
her final halt between the city on Manhattan Island and the town of
Brooklyn to the southeast.

New York at this time was America's largest city by far, but its
population of about two hundred thousand was crammed into the
southern three miles of Manhattan. Greenwich Village was still a
leafy suburb, and the hamlet of Harlem lay six miles away, across
fields and woodland. Yet the city had already begun its extraordinary expansion. Once the Erie Canal had connected New York
with the vast interior farming regions of the American Great Lakes
in 1825, the small port funneled its commerce with Europe and
grew rapidly on its shipping to become the metropolis and cultural
melting pot of America. English, German, and French were common languages on the streets, and about fourteen thousand free African Americans lived there, as did many descendants of Native
Americans. The city also had a small but growing Jewish population, and a surge of new arrivals from across Europe had begun,

including increasing numbers of destitute Irish fleeing British colonial rule.

The old wooden houses of the original Dutch settlement were victims of this new prosperity, pulled down and replaced with modern brick. In 1811, the state legislature had decreed a grid of spacious streets and avenues to cover farmland to the north of the city, anticipating the builders who were now enticing the wealthy out of the cramped old town to elegant new addresses in Lafayette Place, Bond Street, and Bleecker Street. The old boulevard of Broadway held this grid together, feeding the heart of the city from the north and inheriting its grand width from the horses, traps, and coaches and four that had veered ever more widely over the ages to escape one another's ruts. Downtown, this space had produced a commercial center where owners of the remaining two- or three-story timber houses that flanked the thoroughfare felt taunted by the four- and even five-story redbrick buildings thrown up alongside them. The charm of the old market town was still there, though, in the odd surviving poplar that punctuated the pavement, and in the church spires and Liberty pole that still overlooked most houses. Shop fronts along Broadway promoted their fashions through as many panes of glass as could be spliced together—which threw back a moving staccato of disjointed reflections to the passersby. Cobblers, firewood vendors, and flower sellers chanted out their wares from the sidewalks as if they could not be seen, and carts pulled up peddling glasses of water or even ice that had been cut from winter ponds and stored against the summer heat. Off Broadway, the bankers had their offices in Wall Street, the wholesalers had colonized South Street, and the dry-goods merchants were building new warehouses in Pearl Street. With trade booming, some of these warehouses were now being built of sturdy granite, or even with facades of fashionable marble. While the streets inland were locked into the mercantile force of Broadway, those nearer the shoreline were configured by the greater gravity of the Hudson and East Rivers. Here parallel streets led down past warehouses to the slips and jetties where traders and ferries moored, and to the incessant to-ing and fro-ing of people, carts, and cargo.

The *Antarctic* had moored at Christian Bergh's shipyard at the foot of Scammel Street on the Lower East Side. This was the sordid end of the city. Just to its east was the bend in the river known as Corlears Hook that lent its name to the down-market "hookers" who frequented it, with their short dresses, tinsel, and brass jewelry, who made their living from a constant traffic of seamen.

Abby's mother (who was also Benjamin's aunt) was at the dock to greet them and had brought with her the Morrells' three-year-old son, William. Hardly surprisingly, young William was reticent, greeting his mother almost as a stranger, "as one from a far distant country." If there had been any letters home, they could only have been sporadic, dependent as they were on chance encounters with homeward-bound vessels and the fate of seafaring. Childhood can be harsh: nine days later William was again to be displaced from the lap of his recently returned mother when Abby gave birth to a new baby son, whom the Morrells named John Burritt. She had only just made it back in time. Her mother had also brought bad news to the dockside: the only father that Abby knew, her stepfather, Burritt Keeler, had recently succumbed to tuberculosis, or "consumption," which was then taking a fifth of all New Yorkers to their graves.

But the *Antarctic*'s return was not just a family affair. It made news citywide. Splashed across the following morning's *New York Gazette* ran the headline "Massacre in the South Pacific on Newly Discovered Island." The article reported the loss of nineteen men, including the thirteen killed on "Massacre Island," and eight wounded. As ever, the paper printed a roll call of the dead, among whom six were American, eleven British, and two from Manila. The element of the story that proved most intriguing for its readers, though, was that Morrell had taken two "cannibals" prisoner and they were now in New York.

The Morrells had planted the story. Their debts now amounted to at least sixteen thousand dollars—four hundred thousand or more in today's money—and payment was going to be demanded soon. Their story of the massacre and the *Antarctic*'s revenge, along with the rescue of Leonard Shaw, was thrilling enough, but the arrival of the two "cannibals," the first "Melanesians" in New York, had the potential to develop into a media storm. The difficulty the Morrells faced was to turn fame into profit. Initial news reports cast the captives as "objects of much curiosity" and incorrectly ascribed them as coming from "Massacre Island"—mistakes the Morrells did nothing to correct. Instead, they concentrated on feeding the papers with an acceptable narrative to justify the abduction of the men to a nation that had outlawed the capture and import of slaves in 1807, and to a city and state that had outlawed slavery itself just four years previously, in 1827. Morrell therefore made out that it was his intention to return the islanders "to their homes, when he hopes that the treatment they have received at his hands will ensure him a better reception from their countrymen, and that the knowledge they will have acquired here, will be the means of introducing amongst them some of the advantages of civilization."

The ship had docked on a Saturday, and by the next morning word had circulated that the fate of its crew would be revealed after the Sunday sermon at the Mariners' Church down near the wharfs on Roosevelt Street. This was a nondenominational church devoted to the souls of all seamen, with a mission to usher in "a new era in the history of Christian effort against sin"—in this case mainly against typical mariners' drinking and sexual exploits. Morrell was welcomed as a favorite of the church, having set a moral example by commanding a temperance ship. The church was packed. Some relatives of the dead came but also a huge audience of seamen and others, drawn by the allure of cannibal talk. The pastor that day was the church's charismatic founding preacher, the Rev. Henry Chase, famed for directing his temper at intemperance—and, more lucratively, for performing more marriages than any of his rivals. His sermon covered the inevitable ills of alcohol and praised the upstanding Morrell, but after the service, he added a long account of the massacre, pre-prepared by the Morrells, which gave "a relation to the bloody transaction which precipitated thirteen men into eternity."

Intense rivalry among New York's newspapers ensured that the story spread, and fast. A few days later, the leading paper, the *Courier and Enquirer,* decided not to contain the story within the usual shipping-news section, as the "circumstances attending to the voyage of this vessel are of too remarkable a character." It carried a full eighteen-hundred-word account of the voyage, the massacre, Morrell's revenge, and Shaw's experiences on the island. But the story abruptly stopped short with the suggestion that Morrell tell his own story and for his own profit: "Capt Morrell still prosecuted his voyage and made many other important discoveries, they are, however, his property, and we therefore abstain from noticing them in the hope that he will at another day reap that advantage from them which during this voyage has been denied him."

Morrell hardly needed encouragement to cash in on his adventures, but the article certainly helped. It was republished across America and then around the world. He was famous. The editor of the *Courier and Enquirer,* and the sympathetic writer of the article that propelled Morrell to fame, was an old acquaintance of his, the playwright Mordecai Noah. The two had been captured together during the war with England in 1813—although they had suffered very different fates. Whereas Morrell had been sent to Dartmoor, Noah, as the U.S. envoy to Tunis, had been able to claim diplomatic immunity and was released.

Benjamin and Abby quickly rented a house at 140 Canal Street, just east of the Bowery Theatre, and Dako and Monday lodged with them under the continued supervision of Leonard Shaw and John Keeler. But Benjamin also needed to secure a venue where he could display his captives as he had done in Manila. Benjamin's journalist friend Noah had previously led the political machine that controlled New York's Democratic Party, the Tammany Society, and his paper was its official organ. The Society's headquarters was in the newly built Tammany Hall, on East 14th Street, and it had a large, unfurnished meeting room available. Morrell was well connected among the city's Democrats: one of his investors, Charles Livingston—who had perhaps not yet realized the scale of his losses—was a state assemblyman, and his sister's foster brother, the wealthy merchant Silas Burrows, could also pull party strings. And so it was that, within four days of setting foot in America, Dako and Monday were starring in their own show at Tammany Hall, billed as "Two Cannibals of the Islands of the South Pacific." They were not the first Pacific Islanders to reach the United States—several had enrolled as crew on ships crossing the Pacific—but they were the first "Melanesians" from the region of Papua New Guinea.

The Morrells printed up a pamphlet to accompany the show, written by Keeler, which gave an extended account of the *Antarctic*'s voyage and of Shaw's capture. The "cannibal" hook certainly helped to draw the crowds, but Americans' interest in global humanity went beyond the sensational. Attitudes to race divided Americans as nothing else did. Were Africans, Native Americans—and now these Pacific Islanders—equal in the sight of God? Even noble? Or were they lesser peoples to be exploited? Were Pacific Islanders related to Native Americans and among the lost tribes of Israel, or were they a separate and inferior species—one of God's less successful creations? These were the questions that white Americans agonized over. Instead of touting the two captives simply as cannibals in a freak show, Morrell set about promoting them by stoking the crossfire of creationism. His brochure depicted the islanders as a superior sort of "savage" and exquisite exemplars of humanity. In a text that anticipated the prejudices of the audience as much as it confirmed those of the writer, it used the captives to denigrate others from around the world:

The South Sea Islanders

The two south sea islanders, who were brought to this country by Captain Morrell, in the schooner Antarctic, are really interesting objects of curiosity. Judging from the portraits which voyagers have exhibited of the copper colored race in that area of the globe, an unfavorable opinion has generally been adopted of their form and faces. We find nothing agreeable in the dull, snub nosed idolaters of the Sandwich groupe, or in the shrunken and misshaped cannibals of New Zealand. But in the pleasing and intelligent countenances of SUNDAY and MONDAY—by which names Capt. Morrell's protegees are called—there are lineaments well worthy of contemplation. Most of our readers have seen in the streets of our city, Chinese men and women with their long tails and silly looks, from the Celestial Empire; and have occasionally met with Indians of the Osage, Meneminee and Wyandott tribes, with their calumets, silver rings, and uncouth features, from the far West of our own republican land. But we assure them, that to these, in form and feature, the dark strangers from an unknown and distant region, of whom we have made mention, are infinitely superior. . . .

We have only to add, that they are perfectly docile, and behave with propriety. Nothing indecent or offensive appears in their persons or deportment. They now wear clothes similar to those of the colored men of this country, and appear to be very much gratified with being arrayed in this fashion. They still keep their war implements, such as bows and arrows, spears and war clubs, and their fishing geer; together with their ornaments and former articles of dress of their own manufacture, for the examination of the public. It is understood that all their lines and habiliments are made of the bark of a tree, and their fish hooks are made of the mother of pearl and tortoise shell.

Leonard Shaw was the show's compere, enthralling his audience with the story of his own captivity and release as well as his version of the cannibal ways of the islanders who had killed so many of his companions. Although Shaw did not speak either of the captives' languages, he was still advertised as a kind of interpreter, and he left many of those who saw the show thinking that Dako and Monday were from "Massacre Island." One visitor noted that the captives "have no idea of a Supreme Being, are ignorant of every form of worship, and kill all the children except those of their chiefs to make room for their overgrown population. Although inhabiting adjoining islands their languages are not understood by each other."

Some journalists described Dako and Monday and their attire in a little more detail. They wore linen trousers, wrote one, "and large shawls of their own domestic manufacture"—which is curious since such shawls were as alien to their world as other clothes. The captives also wore headbands to which plumes of red feathers had been attached, while Dako had an earring made of a large drop of jasper—which Americans would have interpreted as a sign of rank, although again this was not from Dako's world. Both men also wore shell necklaces and armlets, breast armor and shields, and were allowed to hold impressive javelins, war clubs, axes, and daggers, all of which amazed the New Yorkers. As another report commented, these items were manufactured "in a style that many artisans in civilized countries would in vain attempt to excel." The two also appeared to have acquired a fine array of fishing tackle. When they captured Dako and Monday, Morrell's sailors may have skimmed some weapons from the sea, but it is improbable that there was fishing gear among the trophies. It seems far more likely that the two islanders were sporting weaponry, jewelry, and other ethnographic objects picked up from all over the Pacific—the shawl was most likely from Manila. But the audience would have been none the wiser. In general, it was the captives themselves, not their gear, which attracted attention. One journalist commented that "the clear large fierce eyes, in particular, of our savage Othello will attract notice," and went on to note that they had "a supreme contempt for shoes and hats."

The newspapers that reported the show usually reproduced the text in Keeler's brochure, but others adapted it to their own ends in ways that reflected different perspectives on diversity. Mordecai Noah, for example, writing in the relatively liberal-minded *Courier and Enquirer,* expressly did not describe Monday as "savage and determined," but instead suggested that there was something "noble" in his physiognomy. Also, instead of describing Dako as "much better shaped for a warrior and a general" and "not like . . . a negro," he suggested that Dako's body was "not so well favoured" and that "though there is no known affinity between him and the African race, he yet bears a resemblance to some of the handsome black men in the United States."

The pair did not just capture the popular imagination; they also attracted attention from the world of science. A well-known New

York doctor, Felix Pascalis, was dispatched to examine them for the *Evening Post*. After a close inspection, he pronounced authoritatively that on the basis of their skin color, hair, feet, and scent, these New Guineans had their ancestral origin in Africa:

> Of these antipodean human beings we doubt not but their natural descent is from the African race, perhaps very anciently transplanted into the boundaries of the Pacific Ocean, or at least, to the land of New Guinea. We have long ago assigned the characteristic and exclusive attributes of the black race; the first is their color, the second the crisped hair, and the third the insertion of the leg nearly into the middle of the foot, which is thereby flat and supports the body better on sandy grounds, than if it was arched as in our own forms; and consequently leaves behind a much protruding heel, a malconformation never to be seen in the white races. . . .
>
> The present savages, however, are not so intensely black as our Atlantic black races, the unmixed generations of which among us, makes them, in the course of time, clearer by paler and lighter shades than their original color. As for the crisped hair of our visitors, it is unquestionably an entire and genuine characteristic, especially in these two savages. The older body of the two has teeth very regular and sound, and a muscular form, of remarkable perfection and portly aspect. By these, as much as by his numerous tatooings on the limbs, chest, and shoulders, by his various ornaments on the arm, wrist and ears, of rings of bones, shells and metals, he most probably appertains to a commanding rank and authority among his natives.

The only known image of Dako was captured in that room in Tammany Hall. It shows him holding a javelin and decked out in the shawl, feather headband, jade earring, and shell necklace that the newspapers describe. But when the young artist who drew it showed Dako the finished sketch, Dako examined it for a moment, seemed "wonderfully affected," turned pale, sank back in a chair, and "gave signs of the wildest terror and amazement."

The detailed execution of the sketch in itself would have astonished Dako. As an artist himself, he was accustomed to using twigs to paint, not fine brushes, and his palette was restricted mainly to the reds, browns, blacks, and whites of local colored earths, plants, and powdered lime, though once in a while he might have acquired specialist reds from the mainland. But his evident terror at the sketch stemmed from something else: his very concept of what art meant. Dako's art—consisting of patterns and designs and stylized representations of what he saw around him—was sometimes based on nature and sometimes inspired by dreams derived from the spirit world. Some of the patterns he drew depicted fish, yams, turtles, butterflies, shells, ferns, trees, or, more abstractly, sunlight on water. But for Dako, just as nature drew its patterns from the parallel spirit world that infused it, so the simple suggestion of that natural form could evoke its spirit being. His was a recursive world in which paints and carving could turn mundane and inanimate objects into the most powerful and dangerous, or the most beguiling and sensual, of creations. Paints could literally breathe life into the world and so were not to be treated lightly.

Dako's painting needed neither canvas nor paper. Drums, combs, musical instruments, or paddles might be painted, or more powerful objects such as masks, canoes, houses-of-respect, and even bodies. The depictions could hail into being feelings and forces much as medieval reliquaries were thought to, or be combined with scenery, movement, rhythm, music, and words to provide performances of extraordinary emotive force. Dako had thus been unnerved by the power that the artist who sketched him had displayed. To him this drawing was not a simple sketch but an element in a wider performance of which he, Dako, was a part, whose totality he did not understand. But whatever the picture represented, it was imminent and it was frightening.

Fifty years later, when European-Americans again "discovered" Dako's region, many would be fascinated by the sculpture, designs, and other arts they encountered there and collected for display. These

A South-Sea Islander.

Dako as depicted in the only known picture of him, in *Parleys Magazine* (1833), 24

pieces would be labeled according to location and perhaps function, though not performative force. It was only after the objects found their way in the early twentieth century into the flea markets and museums of Paris, where they were discovered by modernist artists, that their animation and evocation were reconjured: Picasso, Braque, and the cubists re-created their evocations in dislocated forms; the surrealists discerned their trancelike qualities; and even graphic modernists discovered the baffling but beautiful geometries of the shield patterns which were meant to confuse and irritate opponents. Dako's panic was, then, both modernist and medieval.

But the captives' terror had only just begun. After a week of performances at Tammany Hall, Morrell found that the "Cannibal Show" had proved so popular that he was able to switch venues to the more central, prestigious, and lucrative Peale's Museum. This was New York's foremost museum, located on Broadway opposite a small triangular plot of grass optimistically called the Park.

Peale's Museum was designed to lure the crowds off New York's muddy and chaotic main street with the offer of shelter and a range of novelties from antiquities to the supermodern. This was an altogether different experience for the captives from the empty rooms at Tammany Hall. Rubens Peale, the owner, had built his huge museum only six years earlier, and designed it around four cavernous halls. The first was dedicated to natural history and the skills of the taxidermists who gave life to all kinds of stuffed animals. The second was a picture gallery with portraits as well as massive perspectival scenes that drew the onlooker into the great landscapes and cities of the world. The third embraced an eclectic collection of curiosities which at this time included an Egyptian mummy, the dried tattooed head of a New Zealand chief, a living anaconda, several full-size waxwork figures, and some dinosaur fossils. The fourth hall was reserved for the traveling lectures and shows that circulated the country, and was well adapted for the "Cannibal Show."

Museums ran in the Peale family. Rubens's father, Charles Willson Peale, was a celebrated artist, naturalist, and American revolutionary who had built America's first museum in Philadelphia in 1786, and then set his children up with the names of Old Masters and museums of their own. Rubens Peale and his brother Rembrandt had taken over the running of their father's museum, but each also had a new one for himself in another city—Rembrandt's in Baltimore and Rubens's in New York. Their formula was simple and profitable: combine a large basic collection with touring exhibits and lectures that would keep regulars coming through the door at twenty-five cents a time, half price for children. Exhibits had to be crowd-pleasers to entice visitors to return, but they were balanced by educational exhibits that played to the self-improvement ethos of the era. Ideal exhibits combined the two: for example, the hugely successful skeleton of a mammoth-like mastodon fossil that the family acquired. As there were no national museums or collections at the time (the Smithsonian was founded fifteen years later, and New York's Museum of Natural History in 1869), these private museums became the places for America to display the new finds that its expanding borders were turning up. They were also the venues where the latest scientific discoveries were demonstrated, among them new electrical phenomena and photography. Yet the Peales shunned pure spectacle. They did not stoop to the endless sequence of freaks and frauds to which many other private New York museums were eventually to succumb.

Rubens Peale's was the most prestigious of the New York venues, and success there for Morrell would ensure a profitable tour to the other private museums on the American city circuit. And the "Cannibal Show" easily outdid the competition in New York—its only rival being Scudder's American Museum, soon to be taken over by that ultimate showman, P. T. Barnum. "Cannibals" were such a crowd puller at this time that when the wax sculptor at the Cincinnati Museum, Hiram Powers, fused together various body parts from the wax figures of several degenerating dusty Americans in the 1830s to produce an "actual embalmed body of a South Sea Man-eater secured at great expense," it helped save the museum. Dako and Monday, however, were the real deal. Advertisements appeared in New York papers informing the public that "an arrangement has been effected with the two South Pacific Islanders for their exhibition in Peale's

Museum . . . from 9 in the morning until 10 in the evening." And that "one of the schooner's crew who was wounded and taken prisoner by them will give any information required by the company."

During their first few days in New York, the captives had become relatively used to walking every morning from Canal Street to Tammany Hall on the edge of the city dressed in their "Melanesian" costumes and enduring the leers of the crowds that followed their every move. Unsurprisingly, though, they still "evinced signs of great timidity." Then, on the morning of Tuesday, September 6, they were escorted to the vast halls of Peale's Museum, filled with over three thousand curiosities. The huge living "anaconda" (actually a boa that had just shed its skin) they could perhaps make some sense of, but what of the stuffed Bengal tiger or the grizzly bear? Or the full-sized waxwork figures? In Dako's world, the most powerfully efficacious objects were usually stored in special elaborately carved and painted houses-of-respect, or they were destroyed. To him, this was a special place, filled with objects that were not wondrous and curious but terrifyingly powerful.

Some sense of what Dako and Monday must have made of the museum can be gained from the circumstances that led to Monday's escape that evening. News accounts of events are fairly consistent. The moment the captives entered the museum, they became alarmed. Apparently it was the wax figures that they found the most unsettling. Eyewitnesses deduced that the two were worried that either they were about to be turned into wax themselves or they were to be killed and put into one of the museum's glass cases. Realizing their mounting anxiety, Morrell called over Peale, who thought it might help if he showed the captives how waxworks were made. He melted a new block of wax and went through the various stages of wax carving from the lump to the unfinished wax head, and then painted it in their presence. By one account this calmed them a little, but by another it did no such thing.

Then, by chance, a company of soldiers who were parading on Broadway with their muskets thought to drop into the museum. The sight of soldiers with guns transformed Monday's previous unease into panic. He seized his war club to defend himself, showing "a determination to fight or die like a warrior." Eventually he was pacified, but when he and Dako were dismissed later that evening, Monday became "sulky and sad"—apparently still convinced that he was being prepared for a strange and most unsettling kind of death and afterlife.

There are no records of Monday's ever having spoken to his captors, or indeed anyone else. However, having by now spent ten months almost exclusively in each other's company, he and Dako could apparently communicate a little to each other. The papers reported that Monday had discussed his plans for escape with Dako, proposing that they should seize the canoe which Morrell had plundered from Dako's island, put to sea, and make for home. Dako refused. So at about one o'clock in the morning, after the regular nighttime patrol had passed by the captain's house, Monday prepared to leave alone. Dressed in his sailor's jacket and trousers, he left the attic room he shared with Dako and Leonard Shaw and crept downstairs past the door behind which slept Benjamin and Abby Morrell. Another flight of stairs and he entered the cold kitchen, let himself into the backyard, and vaulted the fence to the liberty of a pitch-dark New York night.

As Monday was clad in the sailors' gear that many African American crewmen wore, he had the perfect disguise for a city in which thousands of African Americans roamed freely. At 2:00 A.M., most quarters of the city were more or less still and the streets vacant, but not Canal Street. Only a few decades earlier, this quarter had been the epitome of gentility; now it was anything but. From their attic window just around the corner from the licentious Bowery Theatre, the captives would have had a prime view of the carnal showcase of the Western world, including the most famous sexual slum of all: Five Points, so called because of its intersecting roads. Here, nearly every house had a groggery below and a brothel above; the rest were gambling dens, lottery offices, pawnbrokers, and junk shops. This was one of the poorest neighborhoods in Manhattan, where laborers and immigrants slept many to a room on rags, straw, and shavings, and where houses "ready to tumble together in a vast heap" were arranged in medievally crooked streets and threateningly dark alleys.

Had Monday headed in the direction from which the noise was coming, he would have found himself amid streets overflowing with women in assorted states of undress, mingling with their customers and controllers. He would have passed doorways framing bare-breasted hookers on the prowl, and uncurtained windows framing men and women at sexual acts. During the day, respectable New Yorkers walked many blocks out of their way simply to avoid this area "where black and white promiscuously mingle and nightly celebrate disgusting orgies." Yet in the evening many of these same self-righteous citizens were to be found here, living the lie. Monday's first taste of freedom was in a part of the city so disreputable that it had become a required attraction for tourists from Europe who came to judge it against similar neighborhoods back home. Some of the more up-market addresses drew the lust of the wealthy and fashionable, although they were forced to queue alongside the rest, from office clerks to the inhabitants of virtuous villages taking time out in town. One such establishment was Mrs. Collins's at 123 Canal Street, just a few doors along from the Morrells' lodgings. Expensive carriages lined up nightly as each client waited his turn, though the queues moved fast—one agent of morality observed twenty-eight clients passing in and out in half an hour.

This immoral economy was maintained through racketeering and a gang culture, and by a mutually determining mix of male sexual frustration and the destitution that many young girls and women found themselves in. A full tenth of women living in New York had at some time in their life sold their bodies. Among them were those who had been born poor, but there were others who had been more haphazardly tossed into the trade after a death or illness in the family. Among the women, too, like the men, were those of a more respectable but adventurous kind, drawn to this archipelago of pleasures with its havens of exoticism in the very heart of their world. This same "immoral" economy melted racial divisions, too. Some establishments were run by African American proprietors, among whom were those who dealt exclusively with African American customers. Other establishments, under assorted owners, offered more equal opportunities, where women worked in racially mixed houses for racially mixed customers. Such equality raised the ire of white moralists, who denounced interracial sex, or "amalgamation," as it was termed, in the city newspapers as "worse, by far, than sodomy."

Monday may have lingered in these streets, but it is more likely that he avoided the crowds and sought the quiet of the night. Here and there, lamps that had been given too much oil might have been throwing disturbing shadows, and the new gas lamps on the steamboat docks marked direction and distance, but otherwise the streets would have been dark. Yet the city was asleep and silent for only a short time. Theaters closed at midnight, and polite guests had usually left fashionable parties by one. Carriages would rumble home for an hour or so after that, until finally the horses were stabled. A brief period of silence would follow, but then, long before daybreak had been saluted by a cannon shot from Governors Island, laborers would start walking in from the upper wards down to the city. Lines of carts would rattle in from the north as well, laden with milk, bread, meat, and drinking water. Poorer commuters would gather at the steam ferries from Long Island and New Jersey heading to Manhattan. Soon after sunrise—an event usually obscured by the dense haze of chimney smoke—a larger flood of commuters would walk into the city, meeting at Broadway and Canal Street before descending to the wharves, mechanics' shops, and construction sites, swinging tin kettles containing their lunch and a stove with which to heat it. Office workers would arrive a little later, and after another hour or so, their employers. Fourteen thousand children attended primary school, which began at nine. This reverberation of the city stirring into motion could even be heard across the water in Brooklyn Heights, where, by some accounts, the sound of economy on cobbles reached a crescendo akin to the roar of Niagara Falls.

New York was a city of pedestrians, but in good weather, and even more in bad, wealthier commuters had taken to the new horse-drawn buses or sleighs that made the streets so dangerous in the rush hours. Pedestrians who were caught in a shower of rain were welcome to step into shops for shelter and conversation. Lawyers made for City

Hall, and medics headed for Barclay Street. By the time midday approached, the apple women and orange men who hawked on Broadway were serving an altogether more affluent crowd of fashionable promenaders and shoppers. This city's elite were reputedly oblivious to the extreme poverty and squalor to be found just off its main streets, or to the narrow passages stuffed with barrels, packing boxes, and wheelbarrows and garbage rifled by wandering pigs.

Monday escaped on a Tuesday night, and was still missing that Friday. New York's fledgling police force was put on the lookout for him, as was the night watch, but little intelligence was forthcoming on his movements. The *Commercial Advertiser* reported that some boys, presumably street children who eked out a living selling newspapers, had seen him on Chatham Street in the Five Points area and had followed him, but to no avail. Since arriving in New York, Dako and Monday had apparently shown every desire to return home on board the *Antarctic,* so the concern was that Monday would attempt to secret himself on a ship moored in the harbor in the hope that it might take him back to the South Seas.

On Friday, the *New York Commercial Advertiser* ran the story under the headline "Fugitive," though it did not state which law he had broken. Monday was definitely a fugitive from Morrell, despite the latter's claims to be the prisoners' savior. Morrell was now becoming increasingly concerned that one of his return tickets to the Pacific—and half of the attraction that was paying off his debts—was on the run. He informed the papers that he intended to take the two back to the South Seas, and that "it is to be hoped that the runaway will not escape; as the probability is that he would fall into bad hands, or perish from not being properly taken care of." Rumors began to circulate that Monday might fall into the hands of kidnappers, who would carry him to Georgia as a slave and that, not knowing English, he would be unable to protest. Faced with such a prospect, Mordecai Noah's *Courier and Enquirer* reported that it would be "an act of humanity to restore him to Captain Morrell, whose object is to undertake another voyage to the Pacific, and return with these men to their country."

Monday did not get far. He was eventually discovered on Sunday afternoon in Greenwich Village only a couple of miles away. Conspicuous for not wearing a hat and for eating an apple plucked from a tree, he was spotted stalking the gardens belonging to Alderman Henry Meigs. It was the good alderman himself who captured him: "I hailed him. No answer. I walked after him, and held him readily by the arm. He then uttered some unintelligible words. He was known to me instantly—it was the young cannibal savage from the new islands of the Pacific, whom I had seen very kindly treated when I first saw him at Tammany Hall." Meigs gave Monday a meal to quell his hunger, and his wife and daughter "made him various presents to inspire him with confidence." Meanwhile Meigs sent a carriage to fetch Monday's "keeper," Morrell, who arrived within the hour. Meigs discerned in Monday's timidity a terror that he was to be eaten, and noticed him secreting a knife in his shirt, which he gave up without resistance. The next day the papers reported that Monday had been hiding in the rough woodland between New York and Harlem (now Central Park) and that only hunger and the temptation of the apples had drawn him back to the city. They speculated too on his fears: "He still appears sulkily impressed with apprehensions that he is to be sacrificed." Some papers postulated that his fear reflected badly on his island's customs: "He seems to think that he is to be sacrificed according to the manner in which his countrymen treat their prisoners." Other comments, though, were more sympathetic. "We are glad that he is found. Continued kindness will soon restore the tranquility to Sunday and Monday (for so these poor fellows are called) and they will be in a condition to show what measure of docility they possess."

The "Cannibal Show" was reduced to a solo affair during Monday's weeklong absence, but now Morrell pressed the two islanders straight back to work from nine in the morning until ten at night: "Any gentlemen or ladies who desire to see how people look who eat each other up when they have a chance will now have an opportunity of gratifying their curiosity by going to Peale's Museum where two of these interesting people from the south seas are exhibiting in all their unseemly loveliness and horrible beauty."

Not all New Yorkers were happy with the way the captives were being treated. The events surrounding Monday's escape and capture were evidence enough that the two were not performing in New York voluntarily. A letter published in the morning papers the day after Monday's capture voiced these concerns: "If it is intended to make a fair experiment of taming the two wild men from the Pacific, now exhibited at the Museum, they should be withdrawn from it as soon as general curiosity is satisfied and not carried through the country for similar purposes." The letter's author knew full well that Morrell now intended to tour the show, and to discourage this he offered a veiled threat against Morrell by suggesting that "the case of the Esquimaux, many years ago, was a painful one to every benevolent mind."

He was referring to a show in which a sealer by the name of Captain Hadlock had displayed three "Esquimaux" in New York in 1821 in much the same way as Morrell was now doing with Dako and Monday. An Inuit man, Niakungitok, a woman, Tonnojuack, and her ten-month-old son, Erelow, were all dressed in sealskins and displayed with a sealskin canoe, sledge, and team of Huskies—"part wolf, part fox." After it turned out that they had been taken from different parts of the Davis Straits (between the Labrador coast of Canada and Greenland), and that Niakungitok could not only read and write his own language but speak English, New Yorkers felt somewhat deceived. Then, when the child died, the city turned on Hadlock and had him arrested for kidnapping and cast into prison. Therein lay the veiled threat for Morrell. Hadlock was eventually released, but only on the testimony of Niakungitok, who had agreed to take part in the show for ten months on the advice of his mother, who had been paid with flour, bread, pork, and molasses. Morrell would have been unable to secure any such testimony from Dako or Monday. By Hadlock's agreement with Niakungitok's mother, the three Inuits should have been returned home within the year, but after his release Hadlock instead went to London, where in 1823 the "Esquimaux" were to be found performing at the aquatic theater of Sadler's Wells, and for royalty at London's aristocratic masked balls. By 1826, the Inuit couple and their new children had all died during tours in Europe.

Alderman Meigs, who had recaptured Monday, was a popular New York politician, and Morrell nurtured him as a powerful ally, paying him a visit of thanks two weeks later, this time accompanied by not just Monday but also the more equable Dako. Meigs commented in his diary: "They are losing their fear of being devoured and gaining a knowledge of our language."

Toward the end of September, audiences in New York were tailing off. Morrell ignored the risk and continued to plan a tour, first to Albany, and then south to Philadelphia, Baltimore, and Washington. When they took to the road (and boat) they were quite a troupe: Benjamin and the captives accompanied as ever by log keeper John Keeler, chaperone Leonard Shaw—and trunkloads of equipment. Abby was set to join them in Baltimore with two-month-old John Burritt and young William. The captives were about to see the grandest cities of America—and experience its cruel winter.

CHAPTER 5

The Tour

ཉཉ

Early in October, the entourage boarded one of the two side-wheel paddle steamers that plied passengers up the Hudson River from New York to Albany, churning out thick black smoke from their chimney stacks as they paddled the 150 miles in just over half a day, overtaking the myriad of small trading ships that also traveled upriver. Albany was the third-largest city in the state, with a population of about twenty thousand. As a provincial center it provided a contrast with cosmopolitan New York. It was a city of crooked streets and wooden houses, although State Street, which led half a mile up the hill to Grand Central Square, was a broad avenue and the square itself was dominated by the massive white marble Capitol, or State House—something of an architectural mix, with its massive classical portico and dome somewhat eclipsed by a bank of huge chimneys.

The low-key private Albany Museum had been recently installed in a suite of rooms above the post office in a new marble building on the central square at the corner of State Street. It was not doing well. Indeed, it was lucky to have more than a few visitors a day coming to see its permanent collection of stuffed quadrupeds, birds and reptiles, fossils, "Indian curiosities," and wax figures. So the desperate proprietor was always looking for traveling attractions, whether it be a Tyrolean singer or a ventriloquist act. The arrival of the "Cannibal

Show" on October 10 would therefore have been something of a sensation. That the show had run at Peale's Museum for several weeks was recommendation enough, but the advertisement that heralded it also described how thirteen of the schooner's crew had been murdered and eaten on "Massacre Island," and how the skulls of the dead had hung at the door of their chief while Leonard Shaw had secreted himself for fifteen days and witnessed it all. Shaw, the advertisement assured readers, would narrate the show himself. Morrell was exhibiting his "protégés" to "make good the immense losses he had sustained in his voyage of discovery, in an unknown country, and among savages." To help pull in visitors at twenty-five cents a ticket, the owner of the museum included in the advertisement that he had also just added a fine musical clock from Germany to his collection as well as a camera obscura.

The Albany show was relatively short-lived, though most of the town would have attended, especially those with relatives working as crew on the whaling ships frequenting the Pacific. Among such visitors was probably an impressionable twelve-year-old schoolboy named Herman Melville, who many years later was to inscribe a version of Dako into the American psyche when he used him as a model for his harpooner Queequeg in *Moby-Dick*.

Little more is known of the Albany show, except that Morrell left a few Pacific artifacts with the museum. After backtracking by paddle steamer to New York, the party immediately set off for Philadelphia. As they journeyed through the fiery colors of the fall, for Dako and Monday, whose trees at home never faltered, these trunks slowly losing their leaves and grasping at the sky, as well as the blood-red sunsets, must have spoken of death and the aftermath of catastrophe. And as fall ceded to the rigors of a Mid-Atlantic winter, black clouds brought sleet, driving rain, and snow, to be followed soon by clear skies, frost, and ice, which could shut down river transport. The white snow, white river ice, and penetrating cold of the wind surely contributed to the sense of otherworldliness, but what Dako and Monday made of the gradually deepening winter can only be imagined. Certainly it made travel hard. The journey from New York to Philadelphia would have begun well enough, with a short, early-morning steam-boat ride from the quay at New York Harbor to the small port of South Amboy. Here, however, the travelers picked up a stagecoach for the more punishing fifty-mile ride to the Delaware River. (The British actress Fanny Kemble described the same road the following winter as "unspeakable." She could not sit for two minutes without being catapulted across to the lap of a neighbor, she claimed, or, presumably, receiving a similarly flung visitor.) The captives, the captain, and their entourage must have come to know one another fairly well.

Thankfully a boat was waiting on the Delaware to take the travelers comfortably down to Philadelphia, where they arrived late in the evening of Tuesday, November 1. Philadelphia was a magnificent city. The huge white marble fronts of the civic buildings downtown dazzled in the sun and glowed with the moon. The columned facade of the Bank of America had been modeled on Rome's Pantheon, and architectural rivalry between the United States Mint and other banks had produced a profusion of marble columns which tested Philadelphians on their knowledge of Doric, Ionic, and Corinthian styles. Whereas New York's streets were still largely mud, Philadelphia's were paved in stone.

When the troupe arrived, they had no particular venue booked, but Morrell got the publicity machine going straight away. Venues were hard to come by. The Peale's Museum in town had been pre-booked with a steam train display, and the arrival of the "cannibals" also coincided with that of the first living orangutan to reach America, on view at the grand saloon of Washington Hall on South Third Street. This creature, which had been shipped in from Borneo, became quite a hit. Gentle, docile, and fully clothed, she astonished visitors by drinking from a tumbler, eating with a spoon, and tucking herself up with a blanket when she needed a rest, all "with human composure and nonchalance."

Morrell eventually settled for the Old Masonic Hall on Chestnut Street. This was a popular multipurpose venue, housing everything from horticultural exhibitions to wine sales, Democratic Party dinners to exhibitions of traveling paintings—whether huge canvasses such as Benjamin West's *Christ Rejected,* or panoramas of Niagara Falls.

Philadelphia was a center of American scholarship, home to universities and academic societies and the most prestigious medical school in the country. Once the show was up and running, it drew, among others, eminent doctors puzzled by human diversity. One such was Charles Pickering, the librarian of the Academy of Natural Sciences and a member of the American Philosophical Society. Many years later he himself voyaged to the Pacific, and published his book *The Races of Man and Their Geographical Distribution,* in which he recollected seeing Dako and Monday during their tour. Dako, he recalled, "belonged to the Papuan race." He went on: "I think I can recall in some measure his features, which were rather good-humoured than impressive." Monday, he thought, belonged to the "Malay race"; but in place of the "openness and simplicity of the Polynesians," he possessed "rather the East Indian temperament." Monday was also, reflected Pickering, unacquainted with the proper manner of holding a knife. Such was the stuff of science.

The journey down to Baltimore could be done in a day, but it was another hard one. Having taken the steamer from one of the Philadelphia wharves on the Delaware, which was about a mile wide at this point, the group would have disembarked to cross the narrow neck of land that divides the Delaware from the Chesapeake River. A canal and railway were both being built to help travelers across, but in the winter of 1831 the only option was again the terrible horse-drawn carriage. Once on the Chesapeake, though, the troupe would have returned to the relative calm of the steamboats. Abby and the children, who had caught up with the travelers in Philadelphia, would have been able to sit separately in the ladies' cabin.

After New York, Baltimore was the second-largest city in the union and growing rapidly. Fifty years earlier it had been a tiny harbor town in the hills north of the Patapsco River in Chesapeake Bay. Then all the logics of commerce had focused in on the harbor: the trade in tobacco, cotton, and flour, and in the slaves who might produce them; the watermills that could process them; and the shippers and shipbuilders who could move them. One consequence was that the prosperity vainly planned for the nearby capital city of Washington, D.C., had flowed into Baltimore instead. Baltimore's Catholics had built a new, massive cathedral styled on a Roman temple, with a pillared portico and a dome, whereas the Unitarians had favored the domed cube of the Pantheon for their church. The huge new corn exchange glorified the logic of commerce over the logic of politicians and, as if to spite the city of Washington, Baltimore's citizens had just built their own vast memorial to Washington, the man: a singular white marble Doric column that towered over all else in the city.

The harbor was crowded with shipping, and the travelers from Philadelphia drew up alongside the wharf under some rather dingy warehouses. The city's shipbuilders were famous for their rakish, fast clippers and the city for its equally rakish captains of ambiguous character, "something between pirate, smuggler and wrecker." One such was Matthew Kelly, with whom Morrell had sailed during the War of 1812. Now a prosperous merchant and shipbroker, Kelly still derived some of his prosperity from the Cuban slave trade. Baltimore clippers had been the fastest in the world until the New York pilot boats took the mantle, and Kelly had a fleet of them. Morrell, it seems, now reforged his ties with his former cabinmate and most likely lodged with him, too.

The Peale's Museum in this town was available, and Morrell managed to book it from November 22 for a couple of weeks. Dako and Monday again worked each day for a full twelve hours, from 10:00 A.M. until 10:00 P.M. For the first time, however, Morrell had found a venue large enough and empty enough to let the captives demonstrate their javelin technique, and by now he was sufficiently confident of them to let them throw at a target. Dako would balance and poise his javelin with care, then hurl it forward with precise aim and "such fearful velocity that it would shatter into fragments a one inch and a half board at a distance of seventy feet." Morrell immediately realized that he had been missing a trick and altered the show accordingly: "The cannibals will throw their spears at 11 o'clock, A.M., 3

P.M. and in the evening. It is astonishing with what power and accuracy they can throw them."

With this new attraction, Morrell became more adventurous but also less scrupulous. He now managed to secure the lucrative top slot at the evening circus as well. Circus had been a permanent and popular feature of Baltimore life since the early 1800s, but an "equestrian marvel," William Blanchard, had recently galvanized investors to finance a vast new permanent circus building in the old town, at the corner of Front and Low Streets. It boasted the largest pit of any theater in the United States; it alone could hold a thousand spectators, and its seats could be removed for indoor equestrian events—or the new "Cannibal Show."

Also in town was a Scotsman known only as "Mr. Frimble," or the "living statue." Rivaled apparently only by Michelangelo's David as a body beautiful—the flexing of which he combined with an ability to switch position "mechanically"—Mr. Frimble even fell over like a statue. He had with him a painted classical backdrop against which he shifted among thirteen Grecian and gladiatorial poses in a show that had previously enraptured audiences at New York's Bowery Theatre.

Morrell linked up with Mr. Frimble and the circus owner, Blanchard, to develop a program of wide-ranging entertainment. The show kicked off, as Blanchard circuses usually did, with a grand parade of Turkish horses, the epitome of obedience, and some comic horsemanship by a family named Whittaker. Then Mr. Frimble ran through his repertoire, followed by the star attractions, Dako and Monday. Dako's javelin throwing was the centerpiece of the show, but later this developed into a "trial of skill"—basically wrestling and a fistfight into which the whole company, including Mr. Frimble, Leonard Shaw, and John Keeler, pitched themselves that in some way reenacted the "Massacre Island" encounter. This was also an opportunity to show off Dako's muscularity against Mr. Frimble's—pitting the black Odysseus against the white. The evening was rounded off by a little nautical entertainment further provided by the Frimble family: a hornpipe and a yarn spun by "Black Eyed Susan" (Mrs. Frimble) concerning Chessie, the fabled sea monster of Chesapeake

THEATRE AND CIRCUS.

FRONT STREET OLD TOWN.

BOX 50 CENTS.—PIT 25—GALLERY 25.

☞The doors will be opened in future at half past FIVE, and the performance commence at half past s x o'clock precisely.

FOR THE BENEFIT OF

SUNDAY AND MONDAY.

IN CONSEQUENCE of the unbounded applause bestowed on the first representation of a "*Safe return to America*" in which SUNDAY and MONDAY, Savages of the South Sea Islands, made their first appearance, and several applications having been made to witness their astonishing performance with the Spear, the public is respectfully informed an arrangement has been made with Capt. MORRELL for them to perform This Evening for his Benefit. Mr. FRIMBLEY, the Living Statue, has in the kindest manner volunteered his services, and will appear in the nautical interlude of "*A Safe return to America*"—the 'Statues'—and Crack in the Turnpike Gate. Captain MORRELL, with his Lady, who shared with him the voyage, the first American female that ever circumnavigated the Globe, together with his brother JOHN, and SHAW the sailor will appear.

THIS EVENING, December 3,

The performances will commence in the circle with

A Grand Entree, by Ten Horses.

Battoute Leaps by the whole company.

Mr. FRIMBLEY, will represent as the Gladiator, an entire new Tableu, entitled Grecian Sculpture. In the course of the evening a nautical interlude, written expressly for the occasion, called

A Safe Return to America.

Jack Junk, Mr. FRIMBLEY, in which character he will dance his celebrated 'Sailors' Hornpipe.' SHAW and JOHN, by the originals who escaped in the battle, and who will appear with SUNDAY and MONDAY, the original South Sea Indians, who will throw the Spear &c. &c.

Mr. Bancker will introduce the wonderful Horse

NAPOLEON.

Horsemanship by Master ROGERS.

Mr S. P. STICKNEY will appear in the circle, and introduce his pleasing performance on 3 horses.

To conclude with the laughable Farce of the

TURNPIKE GATE.

Crack, - - - - - - Mr. FRIMBLEY.

☞Mr. LAMB'S BENEFIT on Monday.

Boxes 50 cents—Pit 25—Gallery for coloured persons 25. Tickets to be had, and seats secured at the Box-Office during the day and at H. W. Bool's, 60 Baltimore street.   dec 3

Advertisement for a "benefit" for Dako and Monday at the Baltimore circus, *Baltimore Patriot and Mercantile Advertiser* (December 3, 1831), 3

Bay. Abby played her part, too. Her box was lit up for all to see, and she was advertised as "the first American female who ever circumnavigated the globe."

The circus program was an astonishing success. The takings from each evening were far greater than those from the museum, and were each night directed to the benefit of different performers: the Morrells, the Frimbles, and, on the extra night of December 3 to meet audience demand, Dako and Monday—although their money presumably went to Morrell.

From Baltimore, the "Cannibal Show" moved on to its final venue of the tour, the capital of the republic, Washington, D.C. But Benjamin Morrell had another reason to go to Washington. Not only did he need a fresh audience, he intended to lobby the federal government for funding for his next voyage. The troupe arrived one afternoon in December after being thrown about again in a stage coach that had left at dawn. Morrell could find only a small venue, but at least it was centrally located. This was the grandly named National Museum: another private enterprise which some investors had recently put together at the Rotundo, where Thirteenth Street met Pennsylvania Avenue. Washington was a young city, which could hardly support even one theater, and the Rotundo was also far too small for javelin throwing, so Dako and Monday found themselves posing among yet another collection of stuffed curiosities: a camel, a bear, a Bengal tiger (strangely denoted as "from Africa"), a kangaroo, an ostrich, three monkeys, nine dirty wax figures, and a collection of clams and mussels. Like the Peale museums, the National Museum also doubled as an art gallery, exhibiting large painted cosmoramas of European cities and a collection of "Old Masters" of dubious provenance.

As a city, Washington did not yet have the feeling of a metropolis. The grids of magnificent wide boulevards suggested aspiration, but little had been accomplished. Nevertheless, Dako and Monday were performing at the very heart of the nation. Looking one way down Pennsylvania Avenue they would have seen the White House, newly restored after the fire in 1814, while if they turned the other way, less than a mile up the avenue loomed the magnificent marble Capitol building. Both buildings appeared all the more miraculous given the muddy mess of miserable untidy hovels that made up the residential part of town, and the scattered building sites out of which a painted red-brick city was slowly being born.

Whether the president, Andrew Jackson, ever wandered the quarter-mile or so from his front door to see Dako and Monday is unknown, although his policy, then in full swing, to relocate all Na-

tive Americans to the west of the Mississippi River suggests little interest in wider humanity. Yet as this was almost the only show in
town, many senators and representatives surely took the opportunity
to visit. By the time the tour was over, a goodly proportion of Americans had seen Dako and Monday, while these two had seen much of
the country—and more than enough of its museums.

Morrell had always had a hard time finding the best word to describe the islanders. Americans in New York had no right to take
prisoners or captives as slaves; theirs was the land of the free. Thus,
although the first news reports described the men as prisoners, by the
time they were on show in Albany, Morrell had begun to call them
his "protégés." Throughout the tour, he encouraged visitors and reporters to assume that the captives were performing of their own free
will, despite the obvious fact that early on it was almost impossible to
communicate with them, and that Monday, at least, had sought desperately to escape. Morrell also promised that part of the proceeds
from Dako and Monday's exhibition would be channeled toward the
islanders' education and own civilization, and to a voyage that would
take them home the following summer "somewhat enlightened and
improved."

The public display of the world's people as human zoos became
more widespread as the century moved on, and was transformed from
the ad hoc presentation of those, like Dako and Monday, who had
arrived somewhat accidentally or through the entrepreneurial whim
of a lone trader as in the case of the "Esquimaux," to the larger recruitment of global exemplars for commercial circuses and imperial
fairs later in the nineteenth century. Yet the practice dates back in
Europe to the time of Columbus, or earlier. The great explorer had
returned from the Americas with captives, whom he put on display.
In Tudor England and Medici Italy, shows of people arriving from
distant shores attracted large audiences. These are not well captured
by the catchall phrase of "freak shows." To be sure, shows displaying
abnormally proportioned people, conjoined twins, and the like had
begun to do the circuit at this time, but so had traveling shows of
novel animals such as the orangutan and electric eel, and of ingenious

apparatus to demonstrate newly discovered electrical forces. Dako and Monday were regarded as interesting but not necessarily freakish. The publicity Morrell put about for his protégés reveals unresolved ambiguities in what they were meant to display. While he touted the two as "Cannibals" and "Savages"—concepts which at this time peppered newspaper accounts of the dangerous world outside America—he also boasted of their physical perfection and strength, good temperament, and convivial conversation. Ambiguity was inevitable as Morrell balanced the exigency of making a profit with criticism from sections of the paying public who were questioning the morality, even the legality, of the show. And so Dako and Monday had to be seen as performing "for their own benefit." Even as the show indulged its audience's taste for the erotic, the grotesque, and the ethnographic, it did so while also suggesting that these baser interests were somehow already consigned to the past.

Whether money was spent on their "enlightenment" or "improvement" remains unclear, but Morrell was certainly planning to take Dako and Monday back to their islands in the Pacific in June 1832. He needed to set out for the southerly seas at that time to catch their summer months later in the year.

Now that he was in Washington, Morrell lobbied the U.S. Congress for funds. The Petition Clause in the First Amendment to the Constitution guaranteed any citizen the right "to petition the Government for a redress of grievances," and Morrell had managed to convince himself that he had a grievance—the cost of looking after Dako and Monday. Initially, he simply solicited Congress to repay the expenses he had incurred in bringing the two islanders to the United States. To present his case to the House of Representatives he petitioned the New York representative, Gulian Verplanck, who was then a solid supporter of President Jackson. The argument Morrell presented was that during his voyage he had discovered several populous islands that would be commercially valuable, but in order to overcome the hostility of the inhabitants, to "conciliate" their feelings toward all Americans, and to "induce a future commercial intercourse with its inhabitants," he had brought with him "two natives of one of those Islands, which he intended to return to their homes the ensuing summer"; he therefore requested that he "be reimbursed such expenses as he has, and may incur, in consequence thereof." Whether the House of Representatives considered Morrell to be the aggrieved party or Dako and Monday remains unrecorded. Formally, however, the request was passed by the House over to the Committee on Naval Affairs.

On the back of his growing fame, Morrell was also becoming far more ambitious. He soon lobbied the federal government not only to fund his return voyage but to include in it an attempt to reach the South Pole. There had been a growing movement in the United States for an exploration to the Pole, as well as for a U.S. presence in the Pacific in support of American merchants. This lobbying came from several quarters, but its most indefatigable proponent was a charismatic newspaper editor named Jeremiah Reynolds, who had been taken with the idea that the earth was both hollow and habitable within, and that it consisted of a number of concentric spheres, one within the other, which opened at the South Pole. He had picked up this idea from a former U.S. infantry captain, John Symmes, who argued, quite convincingly, that concentric spheres and holes in the poles made sense of magnetism, volcanism, and a lot more besides. Reynolds had spent the late 1820s trying to secure federal financing for an expedition to the Antarctic to discover more, but also arguing that scientific exploration would dovetail with the interests of American whalers and sealers. He and his allies maintained that the United States was squandering the enormous navigational knowledge amassed by its merchant whalers, sealers, and traders and that it risked being outdone by the Europeans in scientific and commercial developments. Reynolds had taken his lobbying to the lecture circuit and had eventually managed to generate a little money and enough interest to build an alliance across the scientific and merchant community to convince Congress to appropriate fifty thousand dollars from the navy's 1828 budget to finance the expedition. Only Jackson's victory in that year's election had scuppered the funding, but Reynolds nevertheless had managed to embark with some sealers—sponsored by Captain Fanning, the Stonington sealer who had made a fortune at the turn of the century.

Morrell picked up where Reynolds had been rejected. By the middle of January 1832 he had worked up a memorial inviting Congress to stump up a mere $30,000 for an "Expedition to the South Pole." His memorial immodestly sketched both the importance of his previous voyages and discoveries, and the commercial benefits that would derive from them and from the fruits of a new exploring expedition. He was the man for the job, too, having sailed to 67° south, farther than any other American. Morrell presumably reasoned that simply petitioning for funding would provide him with further legitimacy. Just in case the full $30,000 might not be forthcoming, though, he again slipped in the claim for reimbursement of the $350 that he had already spent on Dako and Monday.

In making an appeal for government funding, Morrell was putting himself up as a rival to Jeremiah Reynolds. But Reynolds, despite his lengthy lobbying, was not a ship's captain. Morrell was, and by now he was also a famous one. Newspapers in Philadelphia and Baltimore that had reported on Dako and Monday had learned of Morrell's plans, and lent him their editorial support. Boston followed suit, as did the Washington papers, the *Telegraph* and the *Daily National Intelligencer.* Morrell, it was reported, was stimulated both by a conviction that there was more to be discovered in the southern ocean and by a desire to "register his name among the greatest navigators of the world." They also backed his character: "We have seen and conversed with Captain M, we find him to be enthusiastic and intelligent, and we presume him to be eminently qualified for such an enterprise," wrote the *Globe.* The *Intelligencer,* backing Morrell as "one of the finest as well as the ablest of navigators," voiced the hope that his petition would receive the early attention of Congress. Morrell also received the endorsement of the *Sailors Magazine and Naval Journal* for the full thirty thousand on condition that he "confine the objects of his voyage entirely to discovery." It argued that, with the national treasury overflowing, the proposed voyage would seem an object worthy of consideration and patronage. This journal had long solicited federal money for expeditions, but always on condition that the venture be restricted to exploration, not trade. In the view of the editors, government financing should not confer an unfair commercial advantage on its recipients.

Morrell hankered for government support, but he was not going to rely on it. He would also try to appeal to regular merchants. His problem was, though, that the losses he had brought upon his recent investors made attracting commercial financing something of a challenge. Even Morrell admitted that his previous voyage was "a total failure" financially. The owners of the vessel, Skiddy, Bergh, and Livingston, had been in New York to greet the *Antarctic* and learned rapidly of their massive losses. Skiddy, unable to admit the catastrophic decline in seals and distrustful of the circumstances reported in which his own agent had instigated Morrell's switch of focus, had been horrified to find that the captain had not persisted with sealing. He personally lost ten thousand dollars and vowed never to put money into such voyages again. He was to vent his fury on Morrell years later in his unpublished memoirs, in which he suggested that Morrell was "famous for going on an altogether different voyage from the one he was commissioned for, proving him unworthy of trust and devoid of every principle of honour and honesty." Skiddy likened Morrell's mix of confidence and ineptitude to that of Don Quixote. The investors were forced to put the *Antarctic* up for sale to recuperate their losses. Morrell had borrowed two thousand dollars from the owners in return for a 10 percent stake in the ship's profits (never repaid), but this also made him liable for 10 percent of the investors' losses in addition to the sixteen thousand he already owed in Manila and Bordeaux.

So if Morrell's reputation among New York merchant financiers had been paper thin before his recent voyage, it was now shredded. He would need to attract completely new backers if he was ever to return to the South Seas. In Morrell's favor, however, was his long experience in the Pacific, his growing national fame, his trading secrets, and above all Dako and Monday, whose presence as intermediaries became essential to selling the new venture, as well as to turning trade in this difficult region into profit.

By the end of December 1831 or early January 1832, the "Canni-bal Show" had run its course. Since Morrell had by this time pre-sented his memorial to Congress, he and the captives returned to New York, where Dako and Monday again found themselves per-forming at Peale's Museum, with the added novelty of Dako's throw-ing his javelin with "wonderful dexterity" to lure customers back through the door. Morrell, however, had stopped off in Baltimore en route to whip up the interest of commercial investors. He printed a small prospectus to solicit financing from Boston merchants, and ap-pended a reprint of his memorial to the U.S. Senate in a document he titled "To Commercial Men: An Important Enterprise!" Morrell was never one to understate his case. Just as his memorial presented him as an American Captain Cook—though marginally more successful—so the financial prospectus advertised the proposed voyage in glow-ing terms:

> Capt. Benjamin Morrell, Jr. late of the Schooner Antarctic from a Voyage to the South Pacific Ocean, takes the liberty of laying his views before the commercial and other citizens of this city. Trusting that a perusal of it will serve to elucidate such facts as to elicit the necessary aid to get up an operation, which from its character may be considered one of the most important and if successful one of the most valuable ever made from this or any other country. . . .
>
> The undersigned is the first discoverer of certain Islands in the South Pacific only known to himself and probably more valuable in certain products which are fully specified hereaf-ter, than any other part of the world; in as much as the hand of civilized man has never been there—and consequently the respective value of products refered to, not having been known, they are now in profusion having as supposed layed for ages undisturbed; and they consist of Bush Le Mar [sea cucumber], Pearl Shell, Pearls, Ambergrease [ambergris], Birds of Paradise, the Edible Birds Nest, (so highly prized in China;) Sandall, Sappan, and Ebony Woods; with probably the greatest quan-

tity of the best quality Tortoise Shell ever found in any Group of Islands: the whole of which can be collected with the greatest facility, particularly now as the two Prisoners taken during the last operation say [*sic*] "Sunday" and "Monday," are or will be acquainted with the English Language, and being much attached to the undersigned, and appear to enter into the spirit of Civilization with a considerable zeal and fervor—and their services may be depended on, as they will accompany the operation.

Morrell attached to the prospectus an outline of the voyage, which he estimated would take just under two years to complete. He budgeted thirty thousand dollars, hoping to sell thirty shares of a thousand dollars each in a joint stock company. The cost of the vessel he estimated at ten thousand, the outfitting, crew, and provisions at eight thousand, and the trading cargo at twelve thousand. The proposed voyage would take them around the Bismarck Sea, visiting Dako and Monday's islands and then presumably any others for which he could inveigle an introduction, at each location proffering gifts and promising to return in a few months. If during this time the islanders could build a cargo of tortoiseshell, pearl shell (mother of pearl), and pearls, he would deliver a cargo of American goods in return. In the meantime, he would have a team drying sea cucumbers and collecting edible birds' nests of the swiftlet. He anticipated taking two such cargoes to China while the other cargoes were being collected.

To his potential investors Morrell promised a spectacular return. The Chinese sales would net some $160,000. From the islands he anticipated a vast cargo of about 10,000 pounds of tortoiseshell, valued at $120,000, and 250 tons of pearl shell, worth $50,000. He promised $20,000-worth of pearls, 5,000 pounds of ambergris (a perfume ingredient taken from sperm whales) worth $5,000, and 5,000 birds of paradise that could net an extra $25,000. In all, this would total $390,000 (more than $10 million today). And, said Morrell, he was so confident of the venture's success that he would require no other remuneration than 10 percent of the net proceeds of the voyage. There was one qualification. These figures were, he maintained, a fair estimate, but doubters could reduce them by 75 percent, and see that what he was presenting was still a first-rate investment.

Morrell's capacity to make good on such strong claims as an explorer and as a trader was backed up in his prospectus by sixteen references. Those named first were the main shipping magnates of Baltimore and New York: Captain Kelly of Baltimore, with whom Morrell was probably now staying; the sea captain and merchant Nathaniel Silsbee, who had become a U.S. senator for Massachusetts; and Charles L. Livingston, speaker of the New York Senate, who, despite his losses as one of the owners of the *Antarctic,* must have decided to back Morrell again. A second group of endorsers included six well-known shipping merchants from New York City, among them Morrell's foster brother, Silas E. Burrows, and the owners of three other shipping lines. Morrell also claimed the support of some veteran sea captain explorers, including Edmund Fanning, who only three years previously had been very close himself to securing government backing for Reynolds's exploring expedition. The merchants whose fortunes had been most dented by his previous expedition—Skiddy and Bergh—were notably absent from Morrell's list.

The claims in Morrell's prospectus were also supported by the fame he was acquiring around the country with the "Cannibal Show," which was now beginning to eclipse his appalling financial track record. But everything rested on Dako and Monday's acting as intermediaries. Even if they did not realize it themselves, the enormity of their value to the new expedition was now becoming clear to Morrell. These "cannibals" were worth hundreds of thousands of dollars.

Dako and Monday themselves fared very differently during their first few months in America. Monday, who still never spoke a word to anyone except perhaps Dako, remained suspicious, moody, and determined to escape. When Thomas Jefferson Jacobs, a New Yorker who eventually came to know Dako and Morrell well, reflected back on Monday's experience at this time, he captured his bleak desolation: "No kindness could win his confidence, nor could anything

banish from his mind a notion that he had conceived, that they intended to kill him and devour him. He hated the confinement of
dress and the restraints of orderly and civilized life, and often wept in
bitter agony, shedding tears and wringing his hands in grief for the
country of his birth."

By contrast, by the time they had arrived in Baltimore, Dako
could speak English "tolerably well" and appeared cheerful and com-
municative to the American visitors who questioned him about his
life on the island. Most accounts suggest he was gentle, affectionate,
inquiring, and intelligent.

But a very different insight into Dako's experiences in those early
weeks emerges from a letter which appeared in the New York newspapers in March 1832. It not only revealed his name for the first time,
but was apparently signed by him, giving his full name as Terrumbumbyandarko. In this curious letter, despite his wobbly grasp of English, not only does Dako apparently allude to the canon of English
and American literature laid down over the ages which rails against
unjust captivity, but he also uses the epistolary form: a literary device
then unknown in the South Seas in which a letter ostensibly addressed to one recipient ("Pomingo," his beloved wife back home)
actually addresses a wider audience.

"I write from a great city in this new world," the letter began,
"where, since my arrival, I have been shut up the greater part of the
time, and made the sport and gazing stock of the people." The letter
initially relates Dako's capture and confinement—ambiguous in all
details—and how their mutual sufferings have made him and Monday good friends despite the language barrier. Dako then reflects on
who his captors are:

> Whence did they come? Wither were they going? And what
> were their intentions to do with me? Did they descend from
> the clouds, or had they habitations in the water? Were they
> children of the sun or of the moon? It was evident they were
> a moon-faced people, endowed with superior wisdom. Their
> customs were strange and new; though sometimes ridiculous.

They wore garments on their whole person, excepting the face and hands—their feet were enveloped in a covering. . . . They dressed us in garments of a similar description with their own;—which was to us a most painful operation, for with our legs swathed round with cloth it was at first difficult to walk.

Dako, "annihilated with terror," deduced that he was being fattened as a present to a king or to furnish a feast for his warriors and so "resolved not to gratify them" by abstaining from food, taking only sufficient "to keep the flesh from dripping from my bones." He refused presents, too: "The son of a great warrior is not a woman to be enticed by trinkets."

In recounting his arrival in New York, the letter makes much of the noble savage at the heart of the metropole:

I sometimes even doubt my existence, and seriously ask myself if it is really Terrumbumbyandarko, that sees all these sights and hears all these sounds which he thinks he sees and hears. Before us lay the land of the moonfaces—not covered with rocks and woods—not shaded by the broad spreading palm-tree, nor enriched by the fruit of the coconut. It was one thick mass of houses constructed of red stone, and built so high in the air as to suggest many fears in my mind lest they would fall to the ground whilst I was gazing at them. A great noise like an earthquake, with a thick cloud of smoke, rose constantly from the houses before us—ah, thought I, our doom is now approaching—that noise is the rejoicing of the people at the arrival of their prisoners, and the thick smoke that we see rises from the funeral pile prepared for our sacrifice.

We were shortly taken on shore and thrust into a small house on wheels, drawn by two animals such as I had never before seen. . . . Wherever we passed, we beheld them in crowds staring at us with looks of ferocious satisfaction—nay they even followed in our path, shouting and gesticulating as if they would instantly seize upon our persons and thus anticipate their king in the feast of his prisoners.

At length we reached in safety the palace of the king which is splendid and magnificent beyond description. We were carried through rooms after rooms, all decorated in the most gorgeous manner, with every kind of ornaments imaginable.—Pictures of men, women and children were suspended on all sides—beasts, birds, fish, insects of all varieties were there. There were animals there larger than twenty canoes—birds taller than men—snakes longer than twenty men—but what filled me with the greatest horror was the bodies of some of our own tribes placed here with their bows and arrows, such as they were wont to use. Ah! What dreadful thoughts rushed through my mind on perceiving these unknown persons, who had been taken like myself, perhaps prisoners in war, and after their flesh was devoured, their skins had been stuffed and their forms are thus exposed to the cruel gaze of their enemies. Such alas! thought I, is to be my fate! I shall thus for ages be the sad spectacle of triumph to these odious people!

This letter first appeared in the *New York Constellation*—a newspaper edited by one of New York's more flamboyant humorists, Dr. Asa Greene, who regularly published spoof letters that offered his readers edgy entertainment. Exactly who wrote the letter, and whether it derives directly from a conversation with Dako or simply from the poetic deduction of someone who met him briefly, may never be known. If Dako's own voice was ever in the letter, it was drowned out completely. Factual details concerning his island are supplanted by general observations of places elsewhere in the Pacific so vague that it is more than possible that Dako had no hand in the letter at all. Much of the content is wrong, too: it alludes to bows and arrows, which were unknown on his island, and is addressed to "Pomingo," who was not Dako's wife but a chief of the Native American Chickasaw Nation, "Mountain Leader," whose people were then facing "removal."

If this letter had not truly given Dako a say, it nevertheless transformed him for an instant from a museum curiosity to be gawped at and speculated over to a persecuted and aggrieved man violated by those who had captured him and by the thousands of upstanding citizens who had visited him—Asa Greene's readership. The humor lies in Dako's baffling encounters with America, but again the edge is there. Readers are made to realize afresh the savagery that their countrymen have unleashed upon the world and the barbarity of their museum exhibits. Morrell was not without his critics.

CHAPTER 6

The Books

ᜒᜒ

Back in New York, Morrell's attention now turned to publishing a book about his voyages. He was introduced to two young printers, James and John Harper, who in 1817 had formed their own publishing company and had recently built up quite a business supplying the affordable nonfiction classics that every educated American needed for the "Family Library." Harper and Brothers offered Shakespeare, Walter Scott, Edward Gibbon, and "Modern American Cookery" to boot. Americans' interest in travel and voyages at the time was also huge. This was an era of "discovery," and books of nautical exploration and adventure such as those by James Cook in the Pacific and Mungo Park in Africa had become enormously popular. The Harper brothers realized that the Morrells' fame, the massacre, the harrowing story of Leonard Shaw's capture and release, and the capture of Dako and Monday provided a thoroughly marketable story. Benjamin Morrell's petitions to Congress and his bold claims of navigational prowess had been widely reported and added to his allure. For Benjamin, a book devoted to his voyages had the potential not only to make money but to transform him from a minor figure on the American museum circuit into the kind of global celebrity the most adventurous navigators could then become. And it would be a book rather than a new voyage that would transform him into the "American Captain Cook"—a promising but vacant niche. If a book could establish his preeminence as a sea captain, it would surely also generate the publicity he needed to secure backing for his return voyage to the South Seas—whether from Congress or private investors. The only problem—and one which Morrell shared with Captain James Cook—was his complete lack of writing skill. But that was a problem that could be easily solved.

Only a year previously Morrell's foster brother, Silas E. Burrows, had commissioned New York's most famous poet and playwright, Samuel Woodworth, to write a song commemorating the last words of the Latin American revolutionary Simón Bolívar. Venezuelan tradition variously records Bolívar's final words as: "Damn it! How will I ever get out of this labyrinth?" or "Fetch the luggage, they do not want us here," but Burrows had apparently been blessed by a letter written from the Liberator's deathbed in which his dying words were recorded as "I pity and forgive"—and he wanted all New York to know about it. Woodworth's setting of these words to the Funeral March of Beethoven's Third Symphony, the *Eroica,* had proved a popular choice. So most probably it was Burrows who put Morrell in contact with Woodworth, but if it were not, other paths led to his door. Woodworth was a friend of Morrell's old acquaintance Mordecai Noah. He was also well regarded by the Harper brothers. Indeed, he had just completed another commission for them, compiling what was known of the "festivals, games, and amusements" of Native Americans, European-Americans, and slaves for an Americanization of a popular British book of that title that had outlined the entertainments of old Europe: the classical Olympics, gladiatorial sports, and the dramas of antiquity; the jugglers, Morris dances, and card games of more recent times.

Samuel Woodworth's strong track record therefore made him the obvious choice to ghost Morrell's memoirs—but ghosts can have a powerful and unexpected effect on their subject's life, as the ensuing years would prove. Morrell, with all his bravado and tales of high adventure, would have been regarded by sophisticated New Yorkers as a brash New England Yankee—and, as it happened, a few years earlier Woodworth had written New York's first real hit musical, *The Forest Rose,* in which he had introduced the cocky yet sympathetic

Yankee character to the American stage. In *The Forest Rose*—which played for forty years and toured Europe as well as America—the Yankee in question was a character named Jonathan Ploughboy, whose naïveté and brash ineptitude in love and life epitomized the Yankees' supposed virtues and excesses. Woodworth had gently mocked Plough-boy's country accent, but at the same time managed to hail those qualities that captured the essence of American life and manners: ideals of mutual oversight of moral behavior and of civic virtue that developed from their rural roots in New England. His feel-good musical—in which the laughs that established Ploughboy's humanity were made at the expense of a black servant named Rose—also felt good in racist America. By choosing Woodworth to ghostwrite for Morrell, the Harpers could be sure that the captain would be cast as a sympathetic, quintessentially American hero.

The Harper brothers were not only interested in signing Benja-min Morrell; there was, they reasoned, a strong untapped market for travel writing among America's increasingly literate female audience, and a companion work by Abby should sell well, too. Although the Morrells' claim during the "Cannibal" tour that Abby was "the first American woman to circumnavigate the globe" was not entirely true, a woman's perspective on seafaring was overdue. But Abby was no writer either, so the Harpers enlisted a second ghost to help, the political biog-rapher Colonel Samuel Lorenzo Knapp. It might seem to be a curious choice to have a military man ghost a woman's book, but Knapp had just completed a study, *Female Biography,* which set out to offer a more appreciative representation of women in American history and biogra-phy. He had also worked as a Washington-based journalist and politi-cal speechwriter, and so easily adapted to any commission—another of his recent works was a biography of the conservative presidential hope-ful Daniel Webster. He was a pro.

Benjamin and Abby signed contracts with the Harper brothers on March 7, 1832. Woodworth was to produce an authoritative account of all four of Benjamin's voyages, while Knapp was to produce a lighter volume on Abby's behalf which would be published just after her husband's and would use Abby's feminine touch to campaign for improved conditions for American seamen. Until this time, the only printed material concerning Morrell's voyage had been the brief pamphlet to support the Cannibal Show written by Keeler; the derivative newspaper articles that appeared as a result of this; and Morrell's memorials to Congress. Benjamin's contract with the Harpers stipulated that Woodworth was to take Morrell's notes and memoranda and his memorials to Congress and "make a valuable book of four or five hundred octavo pages." In return the Harpers would pay Woodworth a flat fee and recuperate their costs from the first printing of three thousand copies—then pay Morrell $250 for every additional thousand copies printed. The Harpers struck similar terms with Abby and Knapp. On this basis the publishers and the Morrell family had the same concern: that their books would sell.

The two ghostwriters were part of New York's early vibrant literary scene, in which novelists, poets, and playwrights found a common spirit as a loose-knit group of patriotic writers known as the Knickerbockers. European authors had long dominated American literary culture, and for most of America's colonial history, publishers had largely supplied local readers with pirated editions of European works. But everything had changed in early 1809, when Washington Irving published his *History of New York from the Beginning of the World to the End of the Dutch Dynasty, . . . by Diedrich Knickerbocker.* This was a book by an American for Americans that impelled readers to laugh at the absurdities of the New York political scene. To add to its satirical humor, Irving had initially popularized his book through a type of hoax that has since been copied many times and which got American literature off to a mischievous start. Irving placed a missing-person advertisement in New York newspapers for the author, Diedrich Knickerbocker, who, it was claimed, had disappeared from his hotel:

> Distressing
>
> Left his lodgings some time since, and has not been heard of, a small elderly gentleman, dressed in an old black coat and cocked hat, by the name of Knickerbocker. As there are some

reasons for believing he is not entirely in his right mind, and as great anxiety is entertained about him any information concerning him left either at the Columbian Hotel, Mulberry street or at the office of this paper will be thankfully received. PS. Printers of Newspapers would be aiding the cause of humanity in giving an insertion to the above.

Newspapers around America complied, circulating reports of the missing Knickerbocker. Then, when the book came out under Knickerbocker's name, Irving followed up with advertisements to the effect that the author had never been found; rather that the hotelier had published the manuscript, which he found in Knickerbocker's room, to settle the missing man's bill. Irving continued the gag in further letters, stirring up controversy around the author's identity—and, consequently, interest in his book. This was the nineteenth-century equivalent of viral marketing. The book transformed the perception of American literature in Europe, too, proving an equal success there. Diedrich Knickerbocker had finally put American authors on the global literary map and inspired other Americans to try to live by the pen. Soon Irving's fellow New Yorkers, such as Samuel Woodworth, who felt that Americans could write as well as Europeans, identified themselves as Knickerbockers. The war with Britain in 1812 further consolidated their patriotism around a truly American literature, as it prevented literary imports and stoked literary nationalism. Self-consciously, Knickerbocker writers took to using Americanisms and American allusions, taking inspiration, vocabularies, and metaphors not from the classics of European culture but from the towns, farms, wagon trails, and wigwams of frontier America.

Woodworth was a lynchpin to the social scene of boozy creatives who energized New York's burgeoning cultural life. Washington Irving himself had moved to Europe, but in his absence other aspiring authors, artists, and thinkers practiced their wit on each other over drinks in the city's downtown restaurants, clubs, and bars. Among those at the table were novelists such as James Fenimore Cooper, author of *The Last of the Mohicans,* and James Kirk Paulding, author of

Samuel Woodworth, c. 1814, by Robert Fulton (reproduced by permission of the
New-York Historical Society, bequest of Randall J. Le Boeuf, Jr., 1976)

Westward Ho!; poets such as Fitz-Greene Halleck and William Cullen
Bryant; and friends passing through, including the bird artist John
James Audubon. By the mid-1820s their most popular haunt was the
City Hotel, where Wall Street ran into Broadway. The printer and
publisher Charles Wiley had his bookshop just around the corner,
where he also kept a smoky room at the back known to all as the Literary Den. Here they retired after dinner to mull over the works of
colleagues and rivals until late into the night.

On one such evening in 1823, Samuel Woodworth and his friend George Pope Morris, an apprentice, devised a weekly arts and literature magazine they were to call the *New York Mirror*. This magazine rapidly became the principal focus for writers of the Knickerbocker group, and the dominant voice in a new literary criticism designed to perfect American writing through ridicule of imitation and complacency. The Knickerbockers had assorted other venues—the Old Shakespeare Tavern, Fraunces Tavern, the Café Français, John Bartlett's bookshop, and Bixby's Hotel to list but a few, all fumigated by their smoke of rough pipe tobacco from the American South. Woodworth's own homes, first in Duane Street and later in Pearl Street, were also popular meeting places, while his wife and muse, Lydia, proved a charismatic hostess.

Nearing fifty by the time he came to write Morrell's memoirs, Woodworth was a well-groomed, swarthy man with powerful features and dark eyes, his curly hair sporting a fashionable forelock—and he was never seen without his pipe. By reputation he was wholly devoted to Lydia and their ten children, whom the couple drew into the literary world. Theirs was a house full of art, poetry, and music—Samuel played the flute and guitar, and his children an assortment of other instruments. Their welcome extended to poets such as the American Byron, Fitz-Greene Halleck, more famous for his celebration of male love than of female romance, who nonetheless managed to pen one of his most celebrated poems, "To a Poet's Daughter," for Woodworth's second daughter, Harriet.

Woodworth used to joke with his friends that his religious beliefs had always been a little peculiar, or "as some think, fanatical, not to say fantastical." As a young man he had adopted the prophetic teaching of the eighteenth-century Swedish mystic Emanuel Swedenborg, whose theology more closely resembled Dako's than that of most New Yorkers. Swedenborg had written on scientific themes until 1743, when he discovered he could enter trances through which were revealed to him a spirit world in which he could converse with the dead. Before the dead move on to heaven or hell, Swedenborg found, they initially inhabited a domain in which they could still associate with living people. Like Swedenborg, Woodworth realized that although his thoughts and emotions might seem to be his own, they actually derived from the particular assortment of spirits who associated with him. All his thoughts and desires, all his poetry and prose, and all his devotion to his wife ultimately derived from these spirits. It was as if without this company of spirits, he would be void. People attracted the spirits they deserved: a covetous, selfish, and vengeful person would attract covetous, selfish, and vengeful spirits. To lead a good life, Woodworth knew, he needed to attract equally good spirits; then at death, too, his own spirit would become an angelic one, destined for heaven, rather than the infernal type, en route to hell.

Swedenborg had published some of his works in London in order to avoid the censors, and while he himself had no intention of starting a religion, several of those who read his revelations thought fit to form book groups which in the 1780s evolved into the New Church. One British follower, John Glen, had sailed to Philadelphia in 1784 to lecture on the reality of the spiritual world, and through him Swedenborg's books became popular in America. Reading groups appeared in the major cities, and genial figures such as John Chapman ("Johnny Appleseed") spread the word—and in his case, apple trees as well—across rural America.

To promote Swedenborg's take on spirituality Woodworth had published a monthly magazine, and he soon became vice president of the New York Swedenborgian society: the Association of the City of New York for the Dissemination of the Doctrines of the New Jerusalem. Being highly attentive to the society of spirits that associated with him, he regularly reported on his encounters to his literary friends, who, if not utterly convinced, were usually prepared to forgive this endearing eccentricity.

Swedenborgians preached religious tolerance in a world not known for it. Anyone who did good, according to their religious principles, was sure to secure a passage to heaven. (Although Swedenborg does not appear to have encountered New Guineans, he was known to appreciate African religious practices and considered Africans to have been particularly privileged by God in their ability to discern a spirit world in a way that European-Americans had generally become blind to.) Woodworth thought that some of the spirits that particularly associated with him also associated with others, accounting for the strong empathy he felt toward his friends. Spirits that associated with him might equally associate with Native Americans too—or indeed with Dako, whom he was to meet at Morrell's house. Moreover, Woodworth was attentive to the possibility that he himself might actually be influenced by the good spirits of "other" peoples. This was a radically different perspective on the integration of humanity to that which dominated in New York at this time. His first novel in the wake of the British war, *The Champions of Freedom,* turned on a scene in which the revolutionary voice of George Washington could be heard speaking through a mysterious Native American chief, producing a unified national identity in a Swedenborgian fusion. In Woodworth's imagination there would be a new America in which European-Americans and Native Americans would find a common future.

Of the Knickerbocker authors, only the most celebrated, such as Cooper and Irving, had managed to live well by their writing. The others had to make money either through taking on commissions like the Morrells', editing newspapers, or working as politicians or merchants—and no fine line could be drawn between these professions.

New Yorkers loved their newspapers: in 1830 there were ten dailies, seven twice-weeklies, and sixteen weeklies. Most were run on a shoestring, their editors writing any original text themselves and pirating the rest from other sources. Half the Knickerbocker writers edited newspapers; indeed, Woodworth himself had started life as an apprentice printer in Boston before switching to editing and printing literary magazines for children and women, and then, during the war with Britain, a popular newspaper aptly titled *The War.* Here he fought the British with pen and print—and neither Woodworth nor his closest Knickerbocker friends, such as George Pope Morris and James Kirk Paulding, ever ceased their "paper war" against monarchy. But Woodworth was not good with money and fell so much into debt with the paper that after it folded he had to work his way back up the ladder again, starting as foreman of the *Republican Chronicle* in 1818 before eventually becoming its editor.

Although newspapers were themselves financially precarious, they provided editors with potentially lucrative political patronage. Politicians liked to pay editors retainers to secure their support, and editors could count on subscriptions and advertising revenue from members of their political faction. An editor who backed the right candidate might even expect a political appointment. When Andrew Jackson was swept to the presidency after the election of 1828, he gave profitable government positions to the seventy newspaper editors who had supported him—propelling a number of Knickerbocker writers into the heart of government. Several of Woodworth's writer friends did particularly well. Moredecai Noah had such a success with his Democratic paper the *Courier and Enquirer* that President Jackson appointed him surveyor and inspector of the Port of New York, one of the most remunerative positions in town. Woodworth, however, abhorred Jackson, whose policy of Indian Removal contrasted starkly with his spirit of inclusion. Somehow Woodworth always seemed to back the wrong party.

Editing newspapers was also tiring work, requiring long and unsociable hours that did not fit well with a family of twelve. Before the 1820s, Woodworth had established his reputation as *the* (more or less only) American poet, although he was soon to be eclipsed by many better hands. Only his most famous poem, "The Old Oaken Bucket," has endured. He did not care to write for the literary and social elite but for everyday Americans, crafting his work more as an artisan than an artist. Sometimes his inclusive humanism and sympathy for the weak, underprivileged, and persecuted produced writing that was overly sentimental, moralistic, and instructive. At other times he traded his principles for money. And so, in 1832, Woodworth, broke as usual and desperate for the money, undertook the Morrell contract.

From March 1832 until the end of the year Woodworth worked with Morrell, setting down the captain's early life and accounts of his four main voyages. To generate the five hundred or so pages commissioned, Woodworth visited libraries and read through a wide range of published sources that contextualized Morrell's "discoveries"—and would help him to embellish them, mixing the dry descriptive narratives of "authentic" exploration with more effusive and poetic depictions. And when the crew was threatened or death struck, the prose he laid down veered into the melodrama of adventure fiction.

Woodworth offered up Captain Morrell as a man of estimable character who kept his crew healthy and sober. In Woodworth's hand, Morrell became an American hero—even in his flaws. To square the captain's heroic status with the capture and enslavement of Dako and Monday, Woodworth adapted an argument being made at the time to justify deporting slaves: freed slaves would become the prime force to bring "civilization" back to their homelands in their recolonization of Africa through the bridgehead of the American colony of Liberia. Across America, white elites were forming colonization societies to support the cause. Abolitionists' qualms about their slaveholding ancestors were soothed by the realization that slaves, once educated, Christianized, and freed, could complete the larger mission from God to evangelize their continent. So Woodworth played up the capture of Dako and Monday as a way to help bring civilization to their islands—rather than just trading profits for the Morrells—although in New York at this time *trade* and *civilization* were synonymous.

Morrell needed the book to be not just an account of his voyages but also a support for his petition to Congress and his appeal to commercial backers. For Congress in particular, he had to present himself as the leading American explorer in the South Polar latitudes. Many American sealers had sailed to the Arctic Circle at 66° south, as he had done in the *Wasp* in 1823, but none had made it farther. With Woodworth's help, Morrell was able to travel a fictive four degrees more, to reach 70° south. Such southerly latitudes had been attained only by Captain Cook; a Baltic German officer in the Imperial Russian Navy, Fabian von Bellingshausen; and a British sealer named James Weddell. Weddell seems to have reached 74° south the same year Morrell was sailing in the *Wasp*. Woodworth drew on Weddell's recently published *Voyage Towards the South Pole* and his startling observation that once ships sailed below the ice fields between 60° and 65°, the sea actually became warmer and clearer of ice, opening up the opportunity for them to sail even to the South Pole itself. So Woodworth not only sent Morrell as far south as 70°; he made out that Morrell had turned back in the clear seas he found there only for want of fuel, water, instruments, and scientists. Woodworth was not to know that he had placed Morrell not in deep water but on land (now called Enderby Land), and that where he dreamed up a land mass that Morrell claimed to have discovered and called New South Greenland, there was actually nothing but water. No one else was any the wiser, so it hardly mattered. Woodworth also supplied the rhetoric necessary to support Morrell's petition for an American expedition to the South Pole. After he had about turned back at 70° south, Woodworth wrote in Morrell's voice:

> The anguish of my regret was much alleviated by the hope that on my return to the United States, an appeal to the government of my country for countenance and assistance in this (if successful) magnificent enterprise would not be made in vain. To the only free nation on earth should belong the glory of exploring a spot on the globe which is the ne plus ultra of latitude, where all the degrees of longitude are merged into a single point, and where the sun appears to revolve in a horizontal circle. But this splendid hope has since been lost in the gloom of disappointment! The Vassals of some petty despot may one day place their precious jewel of discovery in the diadem of their royal master. Would to heaven it might be set among the stars of our national banner!

Since Morrell also needed the book to attract commercial investors, Woodworth transformed him into a skillful trader, adept at overcoming potentially hostile islanders and attentive to the importance of intermediaries—hence the capture of Dako and Monday. A return voyage would bring investors immense wealth in both this world and the next—in cash profits and in the souls to be saved from missionizing the islands:

If there be sufficient commercial enterprise in the United States to fit out an expedition to these islands, and thus enable me to restore these civilized cannibals to their own islands, the stockholders of the concern would not only realize incalculable profits by the first voyage, but might monopolize the invaluable trade as long as they please; because I alone know where these islands are situated.

If these two natives are enabled to return, they will also be prepared to instruct their countrymen in the art of agriculture, of which they are now entirely ignorant. By this means thousands of infants would be preserved, which are now doomed to perish, lest the population of these islands become too great for their means of sustenance. Was their rich, mellow, luxuriant soil only partially cultivated, it would produce sufficient for ten times the population which now occupies it. These two natives, whom I call "Sunday" and "Monday" will also prepare the minds of their countrymen to receive and protect missionaries; they will report how kindly and tenderly they have been treated here; how much more comfortably we live than they can without some of the same means; and how pleasant it is to attend the worship of the Great Spirit in a Christian temple, where his praises are chanted by hundreds of sweet voices, borne to heaven on the breath of the pealing organ!

Woodworth's Morrell both enticed his supporters and flattered them. The captain had voyaged with up-to-date charts which named all the islands he had visited, but his book made out that he had discovered several of them, as well as many bays and rivers, which he named strategically. His main financiers, Skiddy, Bergh, and Livingston, all had islands named after them, while the sitting secretary of the navy, Levi Woodbury—to whom Morrell's petitions had been directed and to whom he also dedicated the book—got a bay.

As this was Morrell's book, not his, Woodworth was not in a position to push his own agendas. Morrell had killed Pacific Islanders, and when Woodworth narrated these deeds there was no shame or re-morse. Islanders' customs were noteworthy, their crafts were interest-ing curiosities, but their lives meant nothing. And yet the book was inconsistent in its racism. In Woodworth's world, this could be trumped by republicanism. So when Morrell observed the British treating South Africans inhumanely, or when he met with slavers off the coast of Africa, in Woodworth's hands he berated their inhumanity and found common spirit with the people of the Kalahari against their colonial oppressors.

Morrell provided a great deal of original geographical data for the work, but Woodworth did not stop with these observations. He transposed vibrant tropical forests onto bleak treeless shores and lo-cated massive ancient ruins where only huts had been. Perhaps he was expanding Morrell's romantic hunches into the kind of full-blown hoaxes that Knickerbocker writers so enjoyed, or perhaps he was sim-ply adding romance and significance to what had actually been, in the main, four rather ordinary voyages.

Abby Morrell's book, much shorter than Benjamin's weightier work, shaped up very differently under the authorship of Colo-nel Knapp. Despite having risen to the rank of colonel in the militia during the war with Britain, Knapp sometimes attracted criticism from literary purists, who found much of his writing "unpatriotic": he was part of the old guard who drew heavily on the Greek, Roman, and modern European classics. One scathing reviewer of a work of literary criticism Knapp had recently published even cast him as an embarrass-ment to America's struggles to cast off foreign literary domination. Having praised him faintly as a "ready sketcher of brief biographies, customs and manners" and "a sprightly conversationist and conviv-ial companion," the reviewer complained that his literary work "of-ten soars beyond his strength—expatiates on things above his ability or knowledge . . . his eloquence is dogmatism and his argument, assertion."

Knapp, however, could shoulder such attacks: he was one of Amer-ica's foremost Freemasons, and it was the Masonic traditions from the ancient world that tempered his patriotism and shaped his opinions. At this time Freemasonry was both very popular and a very popular target for criticism. Righteous Christians had taken to attending anti-Masonic conventions, subscribing to anti-Masonic journals, buying anti-Masonic books, and voting for anti-Masonic candidates. The extent of the anti-Masonic industry in itself gives some idea of the importance of Freemasonry in American society; Knapp himself, just before writing Abby's book, had been commissioned to write an authoritative defense of the cult, *The Genius of Masonry.*

Knapp was particularly obsessed by a Masonic kind of feminism. Although only men could be Masons, he argued, everything men do in the name of chivalry, love, and valor was done for women. Women, he maintained, were the guardians of morality and of the next generation. Knapp was in the middle of developing a massive study of female biography to drive this view home when he started work on Abby Morrell's memoir. So although Abby's narrative, as written by Knapp, affirmed the wonderful moral qualities of her husband and, indeed, of the missionaries they encountered around the world, she was portrayed above all as a moral woman who, aloof from political or commercial interest, could harangue politicians, sea captains, and ship owners about the appalling conditions to which they subjected ordinary sailors. Without improved conditions there could be no effective reform of the degenerate drinking habits and sexual exploits of seamen.

If reform of conditions aboard ships were really Abby's cause, it is curious that she never spoke about it outside her ghostwritten book. Any sense of the everyday experience of a woman on board a ship is also entirely absent from her book, another indication that she had little input into her own story. Ousted from the narrative, too, is the Abby who carved a love heart at the scene where the *Antarctic*'s cannon fired on the islanders' bamboo village, or who watched "the roar of the guns, and the unexpected effect which our star and double-headed shot produced upon their light habitations."

Colonel Knapp was a close friend of Samuel Woodworth's from when they had been printers together in Boston. They shared in the struggle to live by the pen, and Woodworth's Swedenborgian mysticism was not so far from Knapp's Masonic order. The two certainly consulted during the development of the two books, which were composed to interlock like husband and wife. When Knapp eventually published his massive work on female biography, he acknowledged his debt to Woodworth, too, prefacing it not with a verse by a female poet but with one of Woodworth's which invoked women's hidden power over men's politics.

By June 1832, Morrell's original plan to return to Dako's island that year was looking improbable. Congress had not stumped up the cash to support the captives' expenses, let alone the voyage, and although Morrell was attracting investors, the deadline for the summer sailing season was too close. More important, perhaps, his original plans for a return voyage had been made at a time when he thought that it would be simply another commercial journey, albeit intended to dig him out of debt. Now Morrell found that he had become a celebrity. He would gather greater fame and fortune by supplementing his previous voyages with a little fiction. It was an impossible task too for Woodworth to put together five hundred pages in three months. The return voyage would have to wait a year.

This delay was surely a disappointment for Dako, who knew enough English by this time to realize that he would return home only when circumstances would permit. Knapp cast him in Abby's story as trustworthy, open, generous, and helpful. During the year, the Morrells had learned a little more about him, too, including that he had three wives and was the son of the "king of the islands." Not only that but they had apparently secured a promise from him to "make them all do right" on his return—a phrase which has often come to haunt those who use it. As a prince, Dako would presumably be powerful enough to keep that promise. Meanwhile, both books hinted that all was not well with Monday. Knapp managed to find an optimistic form of words, but he had clearly struggled. Monday was, he wrote,

> rather sullen in his temper, but has never appeared vindictive
> to us. He is ingenious, and very imitative. At first he seemed

to wish to remain in ignorance, but after a while came to a better disposition, and was desirous, in some measure, to oblige. His countenance is that of a savage in every respect: he has the Indian high cheek-bones and the dark humours of the eye. He is not of a strong constitution, seeming rather inclined to consumption; but how any being could have that complaint who was born and lived in the climate he did I cannot tell. Perhaps the thoughts of being a prisoner preyed on his mind, and the sickness of his heart was taken for that of another kind.

In their writings, the Morrells and their ghosts were keen to present their captives' transformation from savages to civilized beings, from antagonists to accomplices. Their books noted that when captured they were "ferocious savages, and, as they now confess with horror, even CANNIBALS!" Yet by 1832 Dako and Monday had become "civilized, intelligent men, well fitted for becoming proper agents, or interpreters and missionaries to open an intercourse with their native isles." Benjamin asserted that this transformation "would result in immense commercial advantages to the United States, and also incalculable civil and moral blessings to a portion of mankind never before known or heard of by the civilized world." This was a tall order for the two captives, whose imprisonment in a New York house had just been extended for another year. Now they were worth an even greater fortune.

CHAPTER 7

Dako, God, and Humanity

ᨠᨿ

I n the fall of 1832, a journalist, travel writer, and linguist named
Theodore Dwight, Jr., called at the Morrell family home seeking
to speak with the captives. Presumably having seen them at the
museum and read about them in the New York papers, he had taken
the steam-ferry to Manhattan from his quiet home across the East River
in the village of Brooklyn. Theodore Dwight cut a slight but stylish
figure. At thirty-six he wore his sideburns long and bushy, as was the
fashion, and his wavy hair was capped with the popular forelock. Dwight,
however, was not a vain man. He was an inquisitive and impassioned
scholar devoted to social justice. From one of New England's most respected and austere families, he had briefly studied theology at Yale,
where his uncle Timothy Dwight was president, but had renounced
his studies for travel, journalism, and activism. His father was a popular lawyer and writer who as a member of the House of Representatives had led the Federalist Party in its vision for the new nation built
on federal institutions, such as a national bank; tariffs; and good relations with Britain. Before sending his son out into the world, Dwight
Sr. had armed him with shorthand note-taking and typesetting skills
and a hyper-Protestant ethic.

Set loose on the world in the early 1820s, Dwight had first crisscrossed Europe, acquiring languages as he went, adding to his Latin
and ancient Greek fluency in modern Greek, French, Spanish, Ital-

ian, and German. Raised a radical republican, he gradually became even more revolutionary. In Italy he fell in with students in Genoa much his own age whose uprising was then being crushed by Catholic Royalists, and over the next decades he was to organize charitable financial support for Italian republican leaders such as Giuseppe Mazzini and Giuseppe Garibaldi—the latter eventually entrusting Dwight to translate his autobiography.

Returning to New York in 1823, Dwight worked for similar causes in America, in particular the Lyceum movement, dedicated to adult education and "self-improvement," where he lobbied for a system of universal education funded through taxation—a strategy then opposed by America's conservative and Catholic interests. The Lyceum movement also allied itself with the American Mechanics Societies, which promoted the interests, rights, and social advancement of the laboring class "against the bonds of caste and the barriers of prejudice." Together the two organizations campaigned not only against class injustice but also against slavery and the removal of Native Americans from their lands. With a passion, Dwight and several colleagues in these movements developed interests in the ways of life of those they supported, publishing scholarly works on their languages and cultures in the journal of the Lyceum's proceedings, the *American Annals of Education*. Eventually, in the 1840s, this group went on to found the American Ethnological Society, which was to become by some margin the most politically liberal society in New York and eventually the institutional home of modern anthropology.

Being a vehement campaigner against slavery, Dwight was fascinated to find that among the slaves from West Africa were many highly educated Muslims who were literate in Arabic. He made contact with several of these, including in particular "Lahmen Kibby," or "Old Paul" as some called him. Dwight interviewed Kibby over several months in 1833, during which Kibby described in detail the scholarly and educational practices of his homeland—and much more besides. As vehemently opposed to the new national policy of Indian Removal as he was to slavery, Dwight also met with leading Native American campaigners, sharing his disgust at the policy with others in the

Knickerbocker set, including Samuel Woodworth and the playwright
and actor John Howard Payne, who was even arrested for his militancy.

According to one friend, Dwight was "quiveringly sensitive to
the varnished evils of caste, still cherished in Europe, where Royal
dynasties, landed aristocracies, and privileged orders are maintained
by the impoverishment and degradation of those who would supply
the necessaries, the conveniences, the elegancies and the luxuries of
life, and without whom there could be no commerce—classes, the
fruits of whose industry are largely absorbed by institutions and
standing armies to keep them at the foot of the ladder." But Dwight's
radicalism was firmly rooted in his evangelical Protestantism, and his
anger was primarily directed at European Catholicism, which he had
experienced supporting its aristocracies—and which he endeavored
to undermine at every opportunity.

Such was the man now on Morrell's doorstep. Morrell was happy
to let him in, and under his auspices Dwight was to talk with Dako
not only on that day but on many subsequent occasions. Indeed, the
two became close friends. Dwight later reflected on this friendship,
noting that it was strange "to feel such a kind of friendship towards an
ignorant savage as I acquired for Daco." Yet, he went on, "one's attachment for such an individual may be as sincere, and productive of
more real gratification, than we sometimes find among the children
of art, the eons of luxury and vice around us; and I have the pleasure
of thinking that my feelings were reciprocated, which is more gratifying than a whole volume of false professions of friendship."

Although curious enough to turn up unannounced at their doorstep, initially Dwight had been suspicious of both Morrell and Dako.
Some people clearly distrusted Morrell (with reason) and questioned
Dako's authenticity, thinking him perhaps an African American im-
postor. Yet Dwight quickly came to like Morrell, too, and was impressed by his apparent intelligence, modesty, and philanthropic
sentiments. Dwight was not so bedazzled by Morrell's charm, however, that he did not also check what he learned from Dako with such
published works as were available on the Pacific. Eventually he came
to the conclusion that "if deception has been practiced in relation to

Theodore Dwight, by John Trumbull, 1828 (reproduced by permission of the
New-York Historical Society)

the Uniapa Islands, (a thing certainly supposable,) the native must have
been unusually guarded, or he would have betrayed himself in some
way or another."

By now Dako had acquired sufficient English to teach Dwight
about his language and islands. Besides their discussions at Morrell's
house, the two took to walking around town together, visiting schools
and other places. Morrell was beginning to trust Dako enough to

allow him to go out alone on these outings, and this helped Dako gain the confidence to visit factories and workshops in New York by himself, as he was later to do "with the inquisitive eye of a philosopher." As a boat builder and craftsman at home, Dako was particularly interested in shipbuilding and the mechanical arts: forging and working iron, and the use of machinery and edge tools. He was apparently "never satisfied until the use and principle of every operation [had] been explained to him." He also began making rough sketches, presumably to record the things he saw so that he could explain them or reproduce them back home. Meanwhile, Dwight was beginning to speak Uneapa and to write it down. Their long and involved conversations continued month after month, walk after walk.

For Benjamin Morrell, Dako was the key to a fortune, but for Theodore Dwight he provided a key to something much greater: an understanding of God's creation. Were people around the globe all born of Adam and Eve, or had God made several attempts at human creation? Americans at the time were not just interested in the question of human origins, they were impassioned about it.

Once the Erie Canal opened in 1825 connecting New York with the hinterland, the small port rapidly grew into a cultural melting pot of Europeans, Native Americans, and Africans, and attitudes toward race divided Americans as had nothing else. The dominant white Americans debated how to treat minorities: Were Africans, Native Americans—and now Pacific Islanders—equal in the sight of God or lesser peoples to be exploited? In these years, over two decades before Darwin published *On the Origin of Species,* most Americans were creationists—but fascinated by how to account for human diversity. Had God created only one human species, or several, as he had apparently done with finches, monkeys, and snakes? The question was not just an issue for specialists; accounts of peoples from across the world were now filling the pages of many popular newspapers and magazines. Magazines diffusing "useful knowledge" had become profitable, feeding the self-education, self-improvement ethic of the time. When the doors at Tammany Hall and the Peale Museum had opened the year before for the "Cannibal Show," the advertising had surely played to Americans' fantasies about the Pacific, but visitors to the "Cannibal Show" also speculated about how Dako and Monday, as the first "Melanesians" in New York, fit into God's scheme.

The creation question was even being posed in children's magazines. In 1832, the children's writer "Peter Parley"—the pseudonym taken by another Knickerbocker writer, Samuel Griswold Goodrich—put it to the young audience of his *Children's Annual.* After sketching out the salient characteristics of the diverse peoples of the world, he encouraged his readers to reflect:

> My young friends, observing this great Difference between different races of mankind, will of course be likely to inquire whence the difference. This is a question very easily proposed, but very difficult to answer. Did the Divine Creator of man make a common race from which all others descended? Or did he make a black pair and a white pair from which all the great varieties arose? Does heat of climate make white people black? Does difference of climate alter the shape of the head, the jaws, and the bones? What effect has food in causing an alteration? These and such questions are continually arising in the mind.

Since it was the parents who purchased his magazines, Parley found it prudent to support their primarily Protestant morality, and literate middle-class America still strongly upheld a single creation. As he put it:

> We know that light and air, food, climate, occupation, and situation, have all a great effect upon the human species; and, although there are many difficulties on these points, yet, upon the whole, every circumstance concurs in proving that mankind are not composed of species essentially different from each other; that, on the contrary, there is but one species, which, after multiplying and spreading over the whole surface of the

earth, has undergone various changes by the influence of climate, modes of living, epidemic diseases, and mixture of
dissimilar individuals; that at first these changes were not so
conspicuous, and produced only individual varieties; that these
varieties became afterwards more specific, because they were
rendered more general, more strongly marked, and more permanent, by the continued action of the same causes; that they
are transmitted from generation to generation as deformity or
disease pass from parents to children.

By such reasoning, Parley could conclude for his young audience that
"God formed all the nations of the Earth of one blood, and that,
however much they might be separated by climate, by distance, by
language, by color, by religion, or by stature, they are still Brothers,
before God the universal Father." By no means were all Americans of
this accord, however, and their debates over racial diversity were not
just academic or moral. The clash of opinions was becoming ever
more political.

The dominant theory of God's single creation had not prevented
either slavery or Native American genocide, but it did lend support to
the abolitionists' cause, and now even this was under attack. Slaveholders had been able to square their practice with the prevailing view
of a single creation by casting their possessions as the descendants of
the biblical Ham, the cursed son of Noah. Pious slave traders felt free
to lever open slaves' mouths to check their teeth, squeeze their mus-
cles in the market, and even heave them overboard to drown on the
passage to America, all on the basis that the apical African ancestor,
Ham, had apparently sodomized or castrated Noah. As God had
cursed Ham's descendants eternally for this act, slave owners could
despise, patronize, rape, and whip their possessions without religious
anxiety. They could separate children from their parents without disturbing their own Sundays. As for Native Americans, it was considered irrelevant whether sin or environmental degeneration had reduced
them to savagery: they were savages nonetheless. Some white Americans advocated their extermination, and many imagined this would

be their destiny anyway: Jackson had won the 1828 presidential election in part on the back of Indian Removal.

Now, however, many Americans began to question the single creation. Archaeologists and Egyptologists were revealing that there had been insufficient time since God's creation (or at least since the biblical flood) to account for the diversity of humanity. Owing to the calculations of Archbishop Ussher in the seventeenth century, creation was known to have happened in 4004 B.C.E. or thereabouts, and it was becoming increasingly difficult to argue, as Parley did, that all the "races" Americans were now encountering had acquired their modern traits since that time simply through gradual adaptation to their physical environments. The new findings from Egypt especially were showing that physical diversity was apparent among the world's peoples as far back as the flood. Theorists faced a stark choice: either the date of the single creation was wrong—which was hardly something that could be admitted publicly—or God must have created several humanities.

The possibility of multiple creations had major implications for how the white majority imagined their global neighbors and slaves. A single creation implied that "degenerate savages" could at least profit from education, religious instruction, or an improved environment. But had God actually created a more fixed inferiority? If the character and intelligence of peoples across the world came about as an act of separate creation, did that make education of the "inferior races" a vain hope? This would seem to explain the recalcitrance that Native American "savages" were then showing toward the philanthropic attempts to civilize them. A further quandary vexing the white Americans who thought about it was that if the savagery of Native Americans could be attributed to their environment—as eminent, if condescending, European writers had suggested—then what did that say about their beautiful country and their own future? Were white Americans also now on the inevitable path of degeneracy? The idea of multiple creations solved this quandary and made white America beautiful again—and theirs for the taking.

Not everyone embracing the multiple creation theory supported slavery. It was possible to argue that people should not be enslaved merely by dint of being inferior. Yet how much easier might slavery lie on a slaveholder's conscience if Africans, Native Americans, and "Melanesians" really were different species. This was an argument that, if won, would stop the abolitionists in their tracks and make the expansion of the United States across the North American continent inevitable—even divinely ordained.

By contrast, the idea of a single creation was fundamental to the abolitionist cause. With it, African Americans, Native Americans, and their supporters had a case for equality. The abolitionist movement had managed to put an end to slavery in New York State in 1827, and the black community was organizing across the North to claim further rights and establish schools, literary societies, newspapers, and orphanages. But although the city itself was a hub of interracial abolitionist agitation, many New Yorkers were still bitterly opposed to abolition. If anything, tensions were mounting. Newly arrived desperately poor Irish and other European migrants found that they were competing with American-born free black people for menial work as cleaners, cooks, shit haulers, and sweeps. And these immigrants had allies for their cause in the many wealthy New York merchants who were making good money from the trade in southern cotton and tobacco and the slavery that upheld it. With newfound strength, anti-abolitionists rioted throughout the 1830s, attacking the homes, stores, and churches of blacks and abolitionists alike, while New York's newspapers fueled passions on both sides.

Meanwhile, as the 1820s turned into the 1830s, medical doctors, archaeologists, missionaries, and others interested in answering the questions of creation were beginning to marshal their historical evidence, but took two starkly different approaches. A contingent of natural historians emerged that attempted to resolve the question through comparative anatomy, in particular the study of dead skulls in a science they called craniology. Another faction preferred to trace human history by comparing languages and customs, for which they needed living informants like Dako.

Skulls had acquired super-significance in European and American science because a theory had recently become fashionable that human character could be discerned from their shape and size. Specialists had identified the seat of thirty-seven human characteristics in different parts of the brain and reasoned that their exact nature was perceptible in the shape of a skull. It was an Austrian, Franz Gall, who had first put forward the theory in the 1790s in a science he called phrenology. Since then it had become widely accepted. British and American phrenologists charged high fees to read the character of clients from the contours of their skulls. It had become prudent and fashionable to check out the cranial contours of a potential spouse, for example, to ensure compatibility before wedlock. Skull readers could make a good living, and phrenological societies proliferated, conferring even greater authority on the freelancing practitioners.

Some phrenologists thought they could discern racial as well as psychological traits from skull types. A German, Johann Spurzheim, claimed that "the foreheads of negroes, for instance, are very narrow, and their talents of music and mathematics are in general very limited," while a particularly influential Scotsman, George Combe, proclaimed that the Australian Aboriginal's skull was a little better than that of the "Charib" (Caribbean), despite a "lamentable deficiency in the regions of the intellectual and moral organs."

Now that the skull was deemed crucial to forming character, comparative anatomists reasoned that the best way to discern the history of humanity was through the comparison of skulls. Simply put (and it was put simply), God's creative choice would become clear if scientists compared skulls from around the world with one another, and modern skulls with the ancient specimens that archaeologists were beginning to recover from excavations in Egypt, the Americas, and elsewhere. What were needed in order to do this were skulls, ancient and modern—and lots of them.

A Philadelphian doctor and phrenologist named Samuel Morton became preeminent in the field of comparative craniology. In 1830 he was putting together a lecture on the "different forms of skull as exhibited in the five races of men" when he realized that if he could acquire the largest, most comprehensive collection of heads from around the world, his would become the authoritative voice on creation. He quickly became America's most ardent skull collector, and used his collection to argue in favor of multiple creations. He surely had attended Dako and Monday's "Cannibal Show" at Philadelphia's Old Masonic Hall in November 1831, and presumably had taken a good look at their skulls. Two months later, he placed an appeal for skulls in America's foremost scholarly journals. Eventually Morton managed to procure almost a thousand skulls.

With skulls holding the key to personal and racial characteristics, and now even God's intention, global demand escalated, and a highly lucrative market developed that propelled American and European head-hunters across the world. Skulls were collected from the battlefields and burial grounds of South Africa, Afghanistan, Sarawak, and the South Seas; from the prisons and hospitals of India and China; and from hanged pirates wherever they might be. Others were taken from cemeteries and sanctuaries, then boiled and brought to Europe and America. But acquiring heads was not always easy. Native Americans were more than a little resentful of "Americans who now robbed graves for the heads of their recently deceased relatives." Such was the demand for skulls in the southern oceans that by April 1834 New Zealander heads were being sold in Sydney at around twenty-five dollars a piece. There was competition: traders paying chiefs to tattoo and kill slaves for the New South Wales curiosity market ignited conflicts to ensure a supply. As one of the main beneficiaries of this chaotic global head-hunt, Samuel Morton was devoted to his accumulating collection, to the intricate instruments of cranial measurement, and to a meticulous bookkeeping of God's account.

Those studying skulls tended to fall in the multiple-creations camp, scorning their opponents for holding outdated religious and moral convictions which were now being surpassed by the rigors of modern science. Yet those arguing for a singular humanity had their own methods. By studying the relation of the languages and customs of the world's peoples to one another, they could discern exactly how Adam and Eve's children had diffused across the globe. For them it was the languages and customs of the living, not the skulls of the dead, that held the key to God's creative intent. Linguists had long studied languages to answer other questions: whether there was a universal language which mirrored the mind, for example; or whether ancient, original, or primitive languages might illuminate the nature of reason itself. Now, however, the stakes had been raised beyond philosophy. Would the study of language and customs reveal human unity?

The "South Sea Islands" (modern Oceania) became a central theater of battle in America's creation wars. Who had first peopled America? Had God created Native Americans independently and, if not, who were they and where did they come from? One view held that Native Americans derived from the South Sea Islands. This was most cogently set out in 1834 by John Lang in his *View of the Origin and Migrations of the Polynesian Nation,* using linguistic and cultural evidence as support. Samuel Morton and the craniologists begged to differ. Morton considered Native Americans a distinct family of the human race; a separate creation. When Morton's teacher George Combe eventually visited America later in the 1830s, he reviewed the debate, arguing that if ancient skulls resembling those of South Sea Islanders should ultimately be found in America it would strongly corroborate Lang's opinion; but until such time, evidence from the skulls of existing tribes favored Morton. The trouble was that crania were hard to acquire, and those from the South Seas were the most difficult. When Combe's nephew, the phrenologist Robert Cox, solicited skulls in 1834, he noted, "Any from the South Sea Islands would be especially acceptable."

The question of Native American origins dug deeper still into American politics, as it was important to claims of "being American" put forth by other peoples, in particular the growing American Jewish community. In the 1820s, Samuel Woodworth's friend, the leading Jewish intellectual Mordecai Noah, popularized the idea first aired in the sixteenth century that Native Americans were one of the lost ten tribes of Israel. Noah was countering anti-Semitic arguments in favor of regulating Jewish immigration. As Semitic peoples had long been present in the New World, he argued, they had a modern right to it. Noah looked for—and found—traces of Hebrew origins in Native Americans' beliefs: in their idea of a singular God; in their lunar calendar and ceremonies; in their seasonal festivals; in their temples, covenants, and altars; in their laws of sacrifice, ablution, and marriage; in their food prohibitions; and in their language, history, character, and appearance. For Noah and many American Jews, therefore, Native Americans were not a separate creation but shared a common origin. Woodworth himself made the same argument when he described Native American festivals—first fruits celebrations, hunters' feasts, and so on—as deriving ultimately from Jewish customs.

The idea that Native Americans might be a lost tribe of Israel was equally important for the more millennially minded Protestant evangelists. Many God-fearing Americans at this time imagined that the massive religious revival of which they were now part, known as the Second Great Awakening, would usher in the rapture—paradise on earth and the last judgment—and sooner rather than later. Biblical prophecy made the question of Native American origins particularly important. Preachers realized that the literal restoration of the descendants of the Hebrews to the land of their fathers, Palestine, was overdue. The ten lost tribes needed to return home immediately. Anyone impeding their return would suffer the wrath of God in the last judgment. Identifying the lost tribes, and helping them return home, was thus a question of national salvation.

America was awash with anxious interpretations of millenarian prophecies. Would the day of judgment be brought forward by allowing Jews to spread unmolested across the world? Would the conversion of the Native Americans to Christianity bring it on faster? Did the presence of the lost tribes in America suggest that America truly was God's new Israel? Such questions divided believers from unbelievers, Jews from Christians, those who prepared for the imminent millennium from postmillennial scoffers who eschewed speculation altogether.

Now two South Sea Islanders had arrived in New York, and Theodore Dwight speculated that they might help resolve these conundrums. Dwight detested Americans like Morton who argued for multiple creations; they contradicted the Bible, were an affront to the

Declaration of Independence and the equality of men before God, and ignored all the evidence of a common origin to be found in the world's languages and cultures. So when he knocked on Morrell's door in the hope of studying Dako's language and culture, he wanted to find similarities with Jewish customs and with Hebrew and Greek languages. He did.

D ako himself would have been equally gripped by the questions of origins as he and Dwight walked together along the lawned paths of the Battery and the harborside. He seems to have enjoyed becoming Dwight's teacher and took his task seriously. He was "frank, simple, and amiable," providing Dwight with information on his people, their culture, and their geography that hindsight now proves to be accurate. Dwight could not have known precisely where Dako was from, as Morrell was keeping this a secret, but he described Dako as "perfectly African" in appearance, with "large, thick lips, curled hair, small nose (a little flattened), with a complexion like that of a dark mulatto" and classified him as belonging to "the Negro race of the Pacific Ocean" that the French explorer Dumont d'Urville had only recently termed Mélanésie. As Dwight noted, there was nothing but conjecture about the nature, habits, and languages of that region, and even that conjecture was founded on works older than those of Captain Cook from the 1760s and 1770s.

Dako spoke English, but he also taught Dwight Uneapa. He made sketches, being "ready at drawing in a rude way," and even built models to describe his houses. He taught Dwight his songs, rhythms, and poetry, apparently singing a little plaintively—though to a Western ear many of the songs would have had a melancholy air—while Dwight noted them all down in his journalist's shorthand. Out of these many long conversations Dwight prepared "enough for a small volume," but he actually published only two short summaries. The manuscripts have not been found.

What is known of Dako and Dwight's conversations derives from the two published summaries, one that appeared in Dwight's book on his American travels in 1834 and the other published a year later in the *American Annals of Education*. In these, Dako describes his upturned bowl of a world, as well as his island of Uneapa (or Ooneeahpah) with its three prominent mountains and its neighbors, Garuby (Garove), Raga (Naraga), Doapa (Munduapa), and Badirry (New Britain). Dwight understood these to be high islands some twenty miles in circumference each, and thirty or forty miles apart, with the exception of Badirry, which was so extensive that Dwight speculated it could be New Guinea or New Ireland. As Dako also spoke of a tremendous explosion and combustion which had destroyed a town and many of the inhabitants on Garuby "a few years since" at the command of the god of the dead, Pango, Dwight rightly deduced that the region was volcanic.

Dako taught about the creative force, "Mariumba," meaning sky or cloud, referred to also as Manaka, or legend. Dwight interpreted this as a single, all-powerful God, "the preserver, and rewarder of the good and punisher of the bad," the "Creator, Preserver and Judge of all." It was exactly the kind of evidence he was searching for to establish ancient links between Dako's South Seas and the biblical world. Dako expanded on the arts of curing diseases, obtaining favorable winds, and producing rain, which were also derived from this deity, but explained that the lesser deity, Pango, presided over "an inferior world," "the abode of the departed spirits of the good, the land of music, where everything is invisible." But the inhabitants of that world were "spoken of as tune púroco—white men," and "Captain Morrell and the crew of his schooner, the Antarctic, were taken to be from it."

Dako also explained the trade between the islands, and how "the articles in demand are found so distributed among them, as to render extensive exchanges convenient, and often necessary to the existence of some of the people." Dwight gathered that there were ostriches (actually cassowaries) on New Britain whose quills and leg bones were traded. Indeed, he was amazed to find out that the islanders used them as a kind of money to purchase spears and wives in a world in which polygamy was restricted to the rich. And he learned a little about the political order and the moral framework within which it worked. These populous islands were governed by "numerous petty princes," who, Dako told him, might quarrel and battle with those of their own island, but never with the inhabitants of others. Wars were unknown between the people of different islands, and "even two deadly enemies who might chance to meet in another [island] would not be permitted to attack each other."

Although Dwight could find no evidence that Dako's people had any social and trading links outside his few known islands, he nevertheless detected several traces of biblical and other ancient cultures in their customs which provided powerful evidence for the unity of humanity. Pango, he thought, bore a strong relationship to the Greek god Pan, in both name and deed. And he saw links with Judaism in the islanders' practice of circumcision.

As their conversations unfolded, Dako found in Dwight someone who would share his sadness and melancholy for the world he had left two years earlier. He even sang to Dwight the soothing nursery song he had sung to his own child, in which he promised to decorate the child's head with the beautiful feathers of the Labi parrot if only he would stop crying—"Eoa, eao, labi labi vivi na potu." Dako spoke to Dwight of his amazement at all that he had seen in America, acknowledging "that there were some good men there," but made it clear that he was impatient to get home—although he promised to return to "Merriky Isle" if possible, and even bring one of his brothers with him.

On Sundays, Dwight took Dako to a Sunday School he oversaw. The islander was suitably fascinated, promising to gather together the children every Sunday when he was home and teach them in like manner. Dwight was impressed. He was particularly pleased that he had been able to speak with Dako before his mind had been adulterated by missionaries or any other educational interference as that meant he had managed to "form an opinion of the mind of a heathen and a barbarian."

Their conversations rolled on into early 1833. Then, in February or March, Monday died. Dwight recorded that the man was "very passionate and disobliging, never accommodating himself to his exile." He was also "never particularly examined by any one, so far as I know, and left nothing behind him, not even a record of his language, that might satisfy our curiosity." Monday had made a further visit to Alderman Meigs in March 1832, apparently to thank him again for his kindness, but whether he actually spoke while he was there goes unrecorded. Apparently Monday's tuberculosis became worse, and eventually Morrell transferred him to a hospital, where he was "attended by careful and skilful physicians, and watched over with paternal anxiety by Captain Morrell." Despite Morrell's effort, though, Monday declined rapidly and died—and with him died half the justification for any investment in Morrell's proposed return voyage, which had suddenly become a much riskier venture. Dako was now Morrell's only return ticket to the Pacific. His value to Morrell increased accordingly, and it seems that perhaps Dako began to realize this.

Even as Dako was providing Theodore Dwight with the evidence for a single human creation, Morrell was probably planning to sell Monday's head to Dwight's antagonists, for whom it would be highly significant. Clearly, Monday had been worth more to Morrell alive, but in death his rare skull was still valuable to craniologists and phrenologists, and it almost certainly found its way into a collection. Such was the fate of the next Oceanian to die in New York, a Fijian chief named Vendovi, who arrived with the federally funded American Exploring Expedition in 1842 and also died of tuberculosis. The Philadelphian doctor, Pickering, who had been so dismissive of Monday's capacity to use a knife had been on this later exploring expedition, and immediately on docking with the ailing Vendovi wrote about him to the skull collector Samuel Morton: "This is to let you know that our Feejee Chief is on his last legs and will probably give up the ghost tomorrow. As you go in for Anthropology, it would be well worth your while to come on immediately, for such a specimen of humanity you have never seen, and the probability is, that you may never have the opportunity again." After Vendovi died, his skull was cleaned and displayed among the trophies of the expedition.

Morton and the craniologists were soon to become celebrated for their new science—and lauded all over Europe, as well, for pioneering a distinctive "American school of ethnology," the most advanced theory of human origins of its time. Nowadays, its "scientific" racism casts such a shadow of embarrassment that anthropologists prefer to forget it entirely and trace their origins to more congenial thinkers much later in the century. And yet we are neglecting this history just as genetic thinkers are once again unstitching human unity, with some even casting New Guineans as rather more Neanderthal (actually, Denisovan) than the rest of humanity. Historians have previously related the way the "American school" guffawed at opponents like Dwight, who held to human unity, and ridiculed them for putting religion and ethics before "rational science." Understandably, perhaps, it is historians who have been more interested in documenting the work of the scientific racists. Yet a little more attention to the likes of Theodore Dwight (and indeed, to African American and Native American scholars of the era who also upheld human unity) would keep us from forever framing this as a contest between the imperfect science of the American school and recalcitrant religious adherents. Those with a conviction in a singular humanity did not simply revert to the Bible; they drew from it the confidence to probe critically the methods and assumptions of their adversaries.

Monday's skull has yet to be found. It was not in Morton's collection, but it was probably acquired for one of the many craniological collections in New York at the time, where it may well rest to this day.

CHAPTER 8

Fame

ঌ৹ও

While Dwight was befriending Dako, Samuel Woodworth had been finishing Benjamin's book, *A narrative of Four Voyages . . . .* Actually, the title went on a bit, as was then the fashion: *. . . to the South Sea, North and South Pacific Ocean, Chinese Sea, Ethiopic and Southern Atlantic Ocean, Indian and Antarctic Ocean. from the Year 1822 to 1831. comprising critical surveys of coasts and islands, with sailing directions. and an account of some new and valuable discoveries, including the Massacre Islands, where thirteen of the author's crew were massacred and eaten by cannibals. to which is prefixed a brief sketch of the author's early life.* The volume had taken Woodworth ten months to write—much longer than the usual hack job—but finally in December 1832 he delivered the manuscript, and the Harper brothers rushed it to publication. Samuel Knapp had finished ghosting Abby's *Narrative of a Voyage* several months previously, but because its force and commercial success depended on Benjamin's work, the Harpers had delayed publication until early 1833. The two books were the lead titles in Harper's list for that winter, and were extensively reviewed in newspapers and magazines across America.

The publishing venture had left Samuel Woodworth frustrated. He had delivered on his contract and absorbed himself in writing a major work, but he would receive neither credit nor royalties beyond the flat fee he had agreed to. To reap a further reward, he began work on a stage play concerning the massacre of the crew of the *Antarctic* and Leonard Shaw's capture and escape. In order to build publicity for both the book and the play, he drew on his contacts in the newspaper and literary world, beginning with John J. Adams, then editor of the weekly *New York Traveller* magazine. In Morrell's *Voyages,* Woodworth had flattered Adams with an eleven-page quotation from a letter he had once penned to Morrell from Panama—and saved himself the bother of writing eleven pages. When Adams promoted the book, he would be puffing himself in the process. It was a shrewd move. Adams wrote a prepublication exclusive, having drawn his information, he said, "from a literary gentleman of some celebrity, who has perused the manuscript, that it is replete with thrilling interest, and abounds with descriptions of startling incidents and hair breadth escapes." Said literary gentleman was none other than Woodworth.

Adams's puff for the book continued: "What is of still greater importance, it comprises more nautical information, sailing directions, and geographical facts than have ever been condensed in the same compass." And while he was at it, he took the opportunity to advertise Abby's forthcoming book: "We shall wait with great impatience the appearance of her narrative which will soon follow that of the Captain. We also understand that this eventful fourth voyage is about being [*sic*] dramatized by the gentleman before alluded to and who we are happy to add, is every way competent to the purpose."

The Harpers' publishing company would not reveal for another 130 years that Woodworth had ghostwritten Morrell's narrative, but Woodworth's close friends in New York clearly knew. One such was George Pope Morris, who had founded the *New York Mirror* with Woodworth a decade earlier. The paper's review of the book clearly relied on inside knowledge:

> This is a highly interesting and instructive work, and of a character that does not often emanate from the American press. The style is just what it ought to be for such a narrative— plain, chaste, correct, and pleasing, without a particle of affectation. The volume abounds with striking incidents and

stirring adventures; but its greatest merit, in our judgment, is the nautical and geographical information it contains, conveyed in language suited to any capacity. The secretary of the navy, we perceive, has signified his wish to have it furnished to every naval officer; and we are convinced, from a careful perusal, that no school or seminary, in which geography is taught, ought to be without it. As the copyright of these pages—there are nearly five hundred of them—must have cost the publishers a good round sum of money, we trust the sale will be equal to their liberality. If Mr. Cooper receives, as we have been told he does, from ten to fifteen thousand dollars for each of his novels! how much ought to be paid to the writer of such a book as "Morrell's Voyages"?

The judicious use of quotation marks around "Morrell's Voyages" and the suggestion that the writer be paid as much as James Fenimore Cooper are evidence that Morris—or perhaps Woodworth himself—wrote this.

The book sold extremely well, running to many reprints and then a new edition in 1841. Some readers went so far as to acclaim it as an important contribution to American literature. The New York jurist Chancellor James Kent, for example, included the work in his well-respected *Course on English Reading,* commending the voyages as "performed with admirable skill, and with enthusiastic spirit and enterprise." But the book's mixture of styles did not please all tastes. The reviewer for the *American Quarterly Review,* for example, suggested: "He writes as a plain sailor might well be supposed to write, but then he inserts so many unnecessary particulars, that he tires his readers while he ought to amuse them."

Although Woodworth had crafted his Morrell as a peculiarly American explorer, a Yankee hero who commanded the respect of his crew, his reading public stretched around the globe. The book was given immediate and detailed review coverage in both France and England. That Woodworth's Knickerbocker friend Washington Irving had been living in London and that James Fenimore Cooper

was then in Paris may have had some influence on the speed of review attention, but the book was also feeding into a genuine appetite
in both countries for stories of new global discovery.

In the Britain, the book rekindled the story of "Massacre Island,"
which again became a news item published widely across British
newspapers. The narrative was also reviewed at length and with much
admiration in the leading literary magazine, the *Monthly Review,* and
copies were ordered by the recently formed Royal Geographical Society. In France, the response was even more enthusiastic. Albert Étienne
de Montémont honored it with an immediate translation, publishing
it as the twentieth volume in his monumental compendium of famous voyages, and thereby placing Morrell among the likes of Magellan, Dampier, Bougainville, Cook, and La Pérouse. The translation
received stunning reviews:

> While searching for new trading products, the hugely adven-
> turous and intrepid Anglo-American, Captain Morrell, found
> charming lands to behold and delicious green islands caressed
> by ocean waves, hidden and protected by coral reefs, and cov-
> ered in fruit, flowers, and the most treacherous race of can-
> nibals that can be imagined. In this sailor's adventures there is
> the material for three or four plays. There are incredible, even
> marvelous, scenes which evoke fear, terror, and pity. There
> are mysterious discoveries—so mysterious that professional
> geographers might easily mock him a little. It is all very spicy
> and above all, not too long.

Within five months of publication even the prestigious *Bulletin* of
the Paris Geographical Society had printed a long abstract of Morrell's fourth voyage and an equally comprehensive analysis of it by no
less than Dumont d'Urville, the leading French explorer of the day.
Having only recently returned from the Pacific, Dumont d'Urville
systematically (and correctly) revealed that all Morrell's "discoveries"
had been described by earlier mariners, and yet he was not harsh in his
criticisms. He accepted that many of the discoveries that had preceded

Morrell were recent and so might not have appeared on his charts. Morrell, he surmised, might genuinely have regarded them as his own. Dumont d'Urville was generous but he was wrong: Morrell had sailed with up-to-date charts. He had simply been somewhat elastic in his interpretations so that he could claim and name these all-important "discoveries." The Frenchman described Morrell as courageous, skilled, and dedicated, and at the end of his analysis offered some advice for Morrell's next voyages: take two watches along to improve accuracy in calculating longitude; make succinct maps or sketches to assist in the identification of islands; and write down vocabulary lists of the various peoples he visited. "It is very annoying," chided Dumont d'Urville, "that he has not let us know the most usual words of the islands of the Bergh and Massacre groups with which he had so many relations. These are most important for those researching the origin and affiliation of the diverse Oceanic peoples." When, two years later, Dumont d'Urville produced his own compilation of "important voyages," he again honored Morrell by reprinting large tracts of his book—even while noting that Morrell's experiences often did not match his own and that the captain's good geographical descriptions were "mixed with extraordinary details that at the least border on exaggeration."

Woodworth was soon ready with the play. When it was staged at the Bowery Theatre—or the American Theatre, Bowery, as it was by now officially renamed—it had a long and successful run. This combined with the book to embed the Morrells' fame still further in popular culture. The patriotic Knickerbocker revolution had been slow in filling New York theaters with American plays, but Woodworth's helped do so. The two main theaters, the Park Theatre on Broadway and the smaller Bowery, had both been designed with the upper classes in mind, and for many years most of their auditoriums had been filled with expensive boxes whose fashionable occupants preferred European comedy, ballet, and opera, along with the expensive international stars who sailed to New York especially to perform them. All this changed, however, in 1830, when a new manager, Thomas Hamblin, took over the Bowery with a new business model. He wanted larger audiences

who might pay less but would fill the house to see popular melodrama that Americans could write, and could be played by less expensive American actors. Soon his Bowery was attracting the masses, just
as cinemas would a century later. It drew an audience, as one of the
ousted elite put it, of journeymen, clerks, porters, apprentices, and
"nameless classes of vicious boys." But this was an audience that Woodworth could please.

The Bowery itself was modeled on the Minerva temple in Athens,
its massive bright white marble and columned portico lit up brilliantly
at night by two grand street lamps sporting a pair of American eagles.
Yet inside its reputation was far less pure: preachers and the preaching
newspapers condemned it, and theater in general, for its sinful influence. They were not altogether wrong. It was not the plays that were
an issue, but the theaters themselves, which were places where many
members of the audience came for illicit sex. Theater owners added
to their meager profits by allowing prostitutes access to the third tier, or
top balcony, and by selling drinks there. Every evening at the Bowery,
Hamblin would arrange for one or other of the city's two hundred
brothels to send its ladies over an hour before the show, so that when
the men arrived they could drink and make arrangements to go out
afterward—or even have sex there and then in the extreme dark. With
eighty prostitutes regularly working the third tier, actors and actresses
were forced to shout their lines. And to reduce disruption as best they
could, theater designers created separate entrances to the third tier
to enable prostitutes and their clients to come and go as quietly as
possible—an architectural feature that has lived on.

The Bowery was more raucous than most. Its third tier was the
definition of depravity, but illicit sex was not restricted to that gallery
alone. Patrons could see "males and females in strange and indecent
positions" in the lobbies, and "sometimes in the boxes." Such was the
union between things theatrical and things sexual that many brothel
managers rented previously fashionable properties near the theaters,
and where possible had the walls between them knocked out. Newcomers to the theater were often more than a little shocked, and respectable women stayed away.

Theaters had not done well in the 1832 season. The cholera that Morrell had encountered in Manila had finally swept into New York, taking so many thousands with its giant scythe that the city's social world all but shut down. Across America many claimed that it was a moral disease—and the loose lifestyles of New Yorkers had brought the affliction so harshly upon them. Certainly, the immoral theaters had been among the first public venues to be shunned—those who could afford to frequent them could also afford to flee town. And they did. The city was eerily quiet and empty. Grass began to grow on Broadway.

But by March 1833 the audience was back. Woodworth had written three theater pieces since the early 1820s, including his Yankee hit *The Forest Rose,* but for eight years he had found it hard to make his plays pay. It was the new fashion of crowd-pleasing American melodrama at the Bowery that tempted his hopes, and with a topical plot at his disposal he quickly turned the story of the massacre of the *Antarctic*'s crew into *The Cannibals; or, Massacre Islands,* a potboiling drama aimed at a popular audience. Stories of captive Americans and their release had long been the stuff of melodrama as the adventurous and destitute had moved west into Native American lands. The success of *The Cannibals* rested on transposing this genre into a nautical adventure. The play went into rehearsal in February 1833 and opened on February 20, "holding possession of the stage" well into May, with revivals throughout the year. To guard their plays against competitors, theater owners rarely printed them, and no copies of the play have survived—no bad thing, perhaps, for Woodworth's posthumous literary reputation.

Captain Morrell (named "Morrington" in the play) was played by the Bowery's lead tragedian, George Jones (who later went on to play Hamlet in London), while Abby's brother, the young logkeeper John Keeler ("Keelson" in the play), was played by another Bowery professional, a Mrs. Conway. Leonard Shaw was presented as a true Yankee tar—and unsurprisingly, as this was Woodworth's play, reviewers found a peculiar and respectful American nationality in his character. They applauded the play itself, and its characters, but were a little disappointed with the less than convincing savages, who could have had "no very correct notions either of spinning or weaving, nor of any other mechanical art, that could supply them with such a reputable wardrobe of coats and round-abouts." By the end of the run, as many as twenty thousand New Yorkers had seen the play—perhaps a tenth of the city's population—and Morrell was still in town. With the book and now the play came real celebrity. His fame soon spread still farther as his heroic exploits filled children's books and magazines. In one article detailing Morrell's descriptions of albatross nesting sites, the writer reminded his young readers, "About a year or more ago he brought two South Sea Indians to this city, who were exhibited in Peale's museum near the Park. They were bloody-minded fellows." Then *Uncle John's True Stories About Natural History* appeared, casting Captain Morrell as a brave seaman. And Peter Parley abstracted several passages of Morrell's book into a new magazine, in which he also printed the only known picture of Dako (see above, Chapter 4).

The picture is a study in deceit. It makes Dako appear to be on his Pacific island, although it was actually a reworking of the sketch which had terrified Dako when he saw it in the empty rooms of Tammany Hall. At home he went without clothes, but here he is draped in white linens from Manila which cover up the only thing he did bring with him: the tattoos on his limbs, chest, and shoulders. The artist was not able to capture the intricately worked headdress with its vibrant plumes of red feathers—it looks more like a proto-Rasta hairdo—but this hardly matters. It is unlikely to have been Dako's. The same is true of the jasper earring weighing down Dako's right ear: jasper was not part of his world. The shell necklaces and spear, too, were all generic Pacific accoutrements.

There are, however, two much darker deceits embedded in the picture. The first is that Dako appears twice: in the larger image we see encoded in Dako's coy smile the promise of a civilizing mission and a contentment with his new lot. But this contrasts with the backdrop of savagery on his island, represented by the bowman watching Dako's "rescue." Dako there is being "saved" from the water and—by implication—from this savagery by the American oarsmen rowing the whaleboat which has been lowered to pick him up.

The second deceit, however, is darker still, and the implications it carried would take America to civil war: it is the deceit represented by his feet. The eminent physician Dr. Pascalis had noted that Dako's leg was inserted "nearly into the middle of the foot." This, he wrote, was characteristic of African feet: a "much protruding heel, a mal-conformation never to be seen in the white races." And that "mal-conformation" was used as part of the creation wars. In this image, the artist calls attention to Dako's feet and their physical difference to emphasize racial difference. So here we have him: Dako dressed up to play into the American debates of the time.

By April 1833, a book-length children's version of Morrell's fourth voyage had appeared under the stolen pseudonym of "Jack Halliard." (This character was pirated from the stock sailor character of children's books of the 1820s, Jack Halyard.) Now American children could read of Dako and Monday's capture, but through the lens of adult deceit: in this work the heroic Morrell did not kill the islanders but played with them, and when they threatened the vessel he "scared them off" by firing cannons over their heads. Children read that the two captives were simply "picked up," became "good" and "well in-formed," and arrived in New York as "friends." Take this passage on the capture of Monday. As the "Ninigo" islanders approached,

> they seemed to think that they had nothing to do but to take possession of the ship, without asking our leave. So they handed us ropes, and bade us tie them fast to the stern of the vessel, and we did so, for we wanted to have a little frolic with them. Then they began to paddle with all their might, dragging the ship towards the shore after them. They were so delighted that they could not help singing and shouting for joy. But their pleasure did not last long. When we were pretty nigh the land Captain Morrell ordered the sails to be hoisted. The wind filled them, and presently we were dragging the canoes away, savages and all, at a great rate. Directly we went so fast that the ropes broke, which saved us the trouble of cutting them. Then the sails were lowered again and the vessel stood still.

The savages then paddled up to us again and began to throw their spears at us. Captain Morrell thought this was carrying the joke too far, and so ordered the cannon to be fired over their heads. The noise and the flames and smoke, and the hissing of the cannon balls amazed them, and they all jumped overboard. There were all at once fifteen hundred curly, black heads in the water all about us. We picked up two of the poor savages and brought them to this country with us. Their names are Sunday and Monday and both of them are now very good well informed men.

As a celebrity explorer, Morrell was being courted as an authoritative voice on all aspects of American seamanship, and he contributed opinions to assorted debates, most notably on the abuse of alcohol by sailors. Before voyaging in the *Antarctic,* Morrell had advertised that there would be no spirits on board his ship and he claimed to have had several hundred applicants for that very reason. In the *Sailor's Magazine* of February 1833 (which published excerpts from his book) he claimed that, even when cramped together for seven months with eighty-five other men, these teetotal seamen were "like brothers towards each other," dutiful, obedient, and healthy. He had no need to impose punishments, he pronounced, and he recommended that shipmasters prohibit spirits in both the cabin and the forecastle. He also hailed the noble savagery of Dako and Monday in contrast to inebriated whites: "Even Sunday and Monday abhor the intoxicated man, and look upon him beneath the brute creation, and say it causes contention, uproar, confusion, and even murder in this country; and these two Pacific Islanders cannot endure the idea of swallowing one drop of this deadly poison."

As Morrell's celebrity grew, his appeal to "commercial men" began to pay off. By early 1833 he had managed to build a coalition of investors into a joint stock company, among whom were "the most respectable merchants of New-York." The consortium was led by Charles Van Wyck, a member of a prominent family whose ancestors had settled in New York when it was still a Dutch colony, an influential member of the Dutch Reformed Church, and the editor of its newspaper, the *New York Christian Intelligencer.* He was also a novice in funding commercial ventures of this type. In the joint stock company, however, he was joined by more experienced traders, among them Charles Oakley, who was, like Morrell, a veteran of the 1812 war and had since built up a business as a tobacco, cigar, and snuff manufacturer. A third investor was Oakley's close business associate Captain Nathaniel Jarvis. Both were directors of the Greenwich Bank and partners in the Greenwich Insurance Company. Jarvis was also a member of the New York Assembly. A fourth investor, Major Paul Babcock, had been a leading figure in Stonington shipping, but had since shifted his interests to the more lucrative trade opportunities in New York. There were other shareholders in the consortium, among them a Mr. Willett and a Mr. Storm, about whom little is known.

This consortium commissioned a new brig to be built in Baltimore, and one evening early in April 1833 its hull was launched from the shipyard of Messrs. E. Tenant and Company. A superb-looking ship, she was a third larger than the *Antarctic,* built for speed, and christened the *Silas E. Burrows* in honor of Morrell's foster brother. Baltimore clippers were reputed to be the fastest vessels on the high seas, and this brig, with its two masts raked back, was designed to the specifications of Baltimore's most respected sea captain, William H. Trott.

Morrell had petitioned Congress to finance a voyage that combined scientific discovery about the South Pole with the alluring profits of trading in Dako's region. The new ship was thus designed to supply both the armament required for the Pacific and the needs of a naval vessel that could cope with the pack ice on her way to the South Pole. Baltimore newspapers proclaimed the city's pride in receiving such a demanding commission. The owners ordered her to be equipped for a voyage that would steer south "as far as practicable." They commissioned William D. Patten and Company to oversee her fitting out, and it subcontracted the more specialist work to carpenters, sailmakers, riggers, and the like. A Mr. Joseph Francis, for example, built the ship's three whaleboats and tenders. Once again, the crew were to be "men of character": alcoholic spirits were forbidden on board, and this time the captain even undertook not to distribute firearms to islanders. Morrell was a moral man. When it suited. No captain enjoyed managing drunken sailors or facing armed islanders. After Oakley advanced money to Trott, the consortium took possession of the vessel, and several crew were hired to help sail her from Baltimore to New York.

In the buildup to the voyage, Morrell had again petitioned Congress several times. In December 1832, he solicited the House of Representatives to cover the costs of looking after Dako and Monday. New York senator Churchill Cambreleng presented Morrell's case, saying that he was soon to take the captives home, and prayed that Congress would refund the expenses he had incurred in bringing them to the United States "and educating them"—now amounting to twelve hundred dollars. With his newfound celebrity, Morrell was asking for three times as much as he had earlier. Then, in February 1833, Morrell petitioned Congress once more, this time for scientific equipment: "praying to be allowed the use of certain nautical instruments belonging to the United States, in an expedition now fitting out from New York intended to penetrate to the South Pole." Both petitions were referred to the Committee on Naval Affairs. They got no farther.

As neither the instruments nor government funds were forthcoming, Morrell and his investors were forced to relinquish the scientific aims of the voyage even before the ship was launched. Morrell was probably mightily relieved, as he would not now have to live up to his fictive South Polar exploits. Theodore Dwight, who was then visiting the Morrells regularly to speak with Dako, picked up on these changes. He wrote in his father's newspaper that, although the discovery element of the expedition had been abandoned, the ship was still being fitted out for a trading voyage and that a number of enterprising young men were to be involved. While he hoped that the voyage would prove "prosperous and lucrative," he enjoined his readers in the larger hope that it would be "a means of conferring great moral benefits upon those poor, ignorant but gentle and docile people."

So although Morrell had arrived in New York in 1831 with a huge debt and a reputation for trading losses that would normally have kept him on shore for life, in just eighteen months he had become an American popular hero and was now the commander of this, the most capable exploring ship his country could build. Perhaps his luck was changing.

It wasn't.

The first problem concerned Silas E. Burrows. The new ship had been named the *Silas E. Burrows* not simply to honor Morrell's foster brother or an investor in the expedition (which Burrows probably was) but to pay deference to his position as an extremely wealthy philanthropist. Burrows had recently donated ten thousand dollars to finance the construction of a massive Masonic marble monument in Fredericksburg, Virginia, over the remains of George Washington's mother, "the Mother of the 'Father of his country.'" He had sponsored prizes for New York's steamboat captains who had not flinched during the cholera crisis. He was a patron of authors, musicians, and artists. In 1833, however, he became embroiled in a scandal that cost him money and honor in equal measure. Morrell's planned voyage was an early casualty of his precipitous fall.

In the early decades of the 1800s, the Burrows family had accumulated a huge fortune by funding a fleet of sealing and whaling vessels. By the 1820s, young Silas had quit the high seas himself and moved to New York, where he invested in shipping that traded down the eastern seaboard to South America. His success lay in his knack for nurturing political support for his commercial activity, most notably with Simón Bolívar, from whom he had gained a monopoly on steamboat lines plying Colombia's main river. But Burrows also needed to cultivate political and financial contacts in Washington, and he found a way in 1828 when he generously paid off the pressing debts of former U.S. president James Monroe. This earned him many introductions, and it was one of these—to Nicholas Biddle, the president of the Bank of the United States—which was to prove calamitous.

Burrows was looking to borrow money to finance further shipping, but in his dealings with Biddle he almost single-handedly generated a corruption scandal that transformed American politics and wrecked its economy.

The Bank of the United States was a highly controversial institution. The federal government had established it in 1816 to improve the government's own access to credit after the War of 1812. Based in Philadelphia, it had been given a monopoly on all federal government deposits, which guaranteed its income and therefore its ability to lend. This gave the bank an extraordinary competitive edge over all the rival state banks, which objected to the unfair advantage. The rivals also accused Biddle and his bank of political corruption, as it seemed all too willing to offer politicians prestigious positions on its board or cheap, preferential credit. This was a fat-cat bank, and the American political world was beginning to turn against it. In Washington the fat cats were the elite of the American Revolution and their children, but the old guard had finally lost its power in the presidential election in 1828 when Andrew Jackson's Democratic Party ushered in the era of the "common man." As the election of 1832 approached, many Jacksonian Democrats wanted to dismantle the bank that supported their opponents, so they lobbied to reject an upcoming renewal of its federal charter and thus force it to close. The battle over the fate of the bank between the old guard and the common man (and rival bankers, of course) soon became an important point of contention in the presidential race.

When Burrows, the financial savior of a former president, walked through Biddle's door looking for credit, the bank president thought he had found a friend. Burrows promised Biddle to use his influence to swing the powerful New York Democrats to the bank's side. What Burrows did not say was that he had intelligence that New York Democrats were going to support Biddle's bank anyway: it was providing credit to most of the city's merchants. Burrows tricked Biddle into thinking that the support would be all his doing. He arranged for Biddle to loan him fifteen thousand dollars, which Burrows then loaned to the most influential New York Democrat, the newspaper editor Mordecai Noah, no less. As far as Biddle was concerned this loan was essentially a bribe to turn Noah to his cause. Burrows kept this from Noah, however, giving him to understand that the money was simply a commercial loan from Burrows's father to help him buy a stake in his paper. Burrows knew that Noah's paper would support the bank, and he took the credit (literally) for something that was going to happen anyway. He took a decent 2½ percent commission on the transaction and, more important, was now in a position to blackmail Biddle: the bank's critics had long complained that the bank subverted the free press, and Burrows knew that if Biddle's secret loan to Noah became known it would be interpreted as a bribe and would destroy the bank. With a veiled threat, Burrows now "asked" Biddle for an unprecedented trading loan of two hundred thousand dollars. Stupefied, Biddle could only stall.

This was all in early 1831. When the *Antarctic* returned to New York later that year and Morrell began looking for investors, Burrows again pressured Biddle, soliciting another loan and threatening to damage the bank. Eventually, in March 1832, Biddle decided to silence Burrows by offering him a loan of thirty thousand if he would clear the bank of the original fifteen thousand loaned to Noah. It seems that this transaction enabled Burrows to inject some money into the joint stock company that Morrell had proposed, and helped forge the coalition of investors in Morrell's venture.

Unfortunately for all concerned, however, President Jackson called a congressional inquiry into the bank's affairs in the run-up to the 1832 election, and all the loans were exposed. The congressional inquiry of May 1832 concluded that Biddle had bribed the newspaper editor, Noah, and his bank stood accused of that of which it had long been suspected: bribery and corruption of the free press. New York Democrats denounced Noah as a traitor, stripped his paper of their support, and encouraged all party loyalists to cancel their subscriptions and cease to advertise in it. As Noah was a Jew, the scandal also fueled anti-Jewish sentiment, most notably in the viciously anti-Semitic journalism of Gordon Bennett. Silas Burrows was disgraced and attacked from all sides. The *Rochester Republican* self-righteously suggested that other sources be explored to finance the monument to Washington's mother: "Better, far better, that the ashes should continue in seclusion than monuments arise through ill gotten lucre and be profaned by dishonored hands."

This "Bank War," as it came to be known, was the key issue on which the 1832 presidential election turned. Each side sought to purchase voters, apparently, at five dollars a head. The city and state banks aligned themselves with President Jackson and purchased Democratic voters, while the disgraced Bank of the United States purchased voters for his opponent, Henry Clay. Jackson was reelected, and after his inauguration he issued an executive order over the objections of Congress to end the deposit of government funds in the Bank of the United States. This precipitated the bank's premature collapse and a credit crunch which soon plummeted America into economic recession.

Silas Burrows was not a popular man. But though the New York papers lampooned him, he weathered the criticism, and Morrell's joint stock company survived. Worse was to come, however. Burrows had now made innumerable enemies on both sides of the political divide: he was a traitor to the Democrats for participating in corruption and the scourge of their opponents for bringing disrepute on their bank and their cause. Then, in early March 1833, just as the *Silas E. Burrows* was due to be launched, he was also accused of the seduction of a young woman, for which he was to stand trial in November.

The ship's name now became synonymous with both corruption and seduction. If ever there were an inauspicious vessel sailing into New York Harbor that June, this was it. Moreover, Monday had died by March, also threatening the profitability of the venture. The combination of events finally put too much pressure on the stockholders, who fell out, leading to "the entire abandonment of the expedition." Morrell's plans for voyaging in the 1833 season were ruined, and with them any hopes Dako may have had for his return home. Crewmen and craftsmen even had to sue the owners to be paid. Each investor suggested that the others were responsible for the debts, and all insisted that the lawsuits among them would have to be resolved before creditors could be paid. By August, the crew and other creditors had taken their case to court, forcing the ship to be seized and sold to pay them.

At the end of July, ill fortune again visited the Morrells when death took their younger son, John Burritt Morrell, "aged 1 year, 10 months and 21 days." Whether Abby had been planning to join Benjamin on the new voyage is unclear, but if so, at the death of her second child her spirit for travel and her willingness to leave her surviving son, William, deserted her.

Benjamin Morrell was in New York when Burrows's seduction case came to New York's Superior Court in November 1833. The downfall of such a prominent figure drew enormous crowds. Burrows was accused of seducing Mary Carew, an orphan who, like Morrell's sisters, had been fostered with his father and then lived with Silas. The prosecution asserted that in October 1832 Burrows had visited her boardinghouse in Vestey Street and left with her to visit Peale's Museum, but that on the way he had taken her to one of New York's many brothels and seduced her. Among the witnesses called in Burrows's defense was Benjamin Morrell's sister Eliza, who suggested that Carew had particularly loose morals and already worked in a brothel. The case became all the more newsworthy as defense lawyers revealed a long-standing feud between the Carew and the Burrows families: Mary Carew's sister, Henrietta, had previously sued Silas Burrows's father for ten thousand dollars' damages when he had reneged on his offer to marry her (he was in his sixties at the time). As the papers reported, "Perhaps on no similar occasion in this country has such an immense number of persons assembled as were gathered together on this occasion. Three thousand people were in court to hear the verdict." There was no verdict. The case went for retrial.

Burrows's disaster had brought down the voyage, but now public and investors' confidence in Morrell was also beginning to crack. Most American readers of Morrell's book marveled at his exploits, but among these were several sailors, sea captains, and investors across the country who had sailed with Morrell, financed him, or sailed to the same locations, and they found serious problems with the events and descriptions in the book. One reviewer acknowledged in June 1833 that he had heard "doubts expressed concerning Mr. Morrell's veracity." Most of his critics, however, could cite specific problems with some of the details, though few were in a position to denounce the majority of it. Only the merchants William Skiddy and Christian Bergh knew just how far the book's inaccuracies cloaked Morrell's serial ineptitude.

Others soon had cause to worry. When members of the main American Missionary Society read Morrell's book and his description of Patagonia, they had been impressed by the "glowing description of the harbours, the forests, the climate, soil, clover meadows, and the numerous and peaceful inhabitants of the western coast of Patagonia." In one passage, Woodworth had taken the liberty of hinting that this coast would be a favorable field for missionary enterprise. The Mission Society took the bait and immediately prepared to dispatch two young men to what they imagined was a lush paradise. They wrote to Morrell for further details, and Morrell replied twice, in January and February 1833, with effusive descriptions of Patagonia's most temperate climate, its fine harbors and rich soils. Its forests, Morrell informed them, teemed with wildlife. One wonders whether it was Morrell who wrote this or the mischievous Samuel Woodworth in one of his more Knickerbocker moments.

When the missionary society sought a reference for Morrell, they chose to write to Silas Burrows. Another mistake. He affirmed Morrell's credentials. It was only when the time came to leave, after the missionaries had been recruited, funds raised, and bags packed in July 1833, that the poor proselytizers realized their fate: the master of the vessel who was to take them—a sealer from Stonington named Captain Clift—let the earnest duo know that they were about to sail to one of the bleakest corners of the earth and had been utterly misled by Morrell's romantic description. Bravely, the missionaries went anyway. But word was getting around.

CHAPTER 9

Return to Dako's Island

ௐ

M ore than half a century after the events narrated in this
history, on a dark, snow-muffled morning in January 1889,
a famous hermit died in Harlem. For over thirty years,
local children had grown up spooked by his massive fortress, which
they knew as the Hermitage, and the tales of what lay within. Editors
at the New York *Times, Herald,* and *Tribune* quickly saw a story and sent
reporters to coax what they could from neighbors and shopkeepers.
The reporters drew a blank, but the building itself and local rumors
about its inhabitant were all they needed to weave something together.

Sitting out of time and place amid the tenement blocks where
124th Street meets Third Avenue, the Hermitage had been modeled
on a frontier fort of the type that helped the U.S. cavalry win Texas
and the West. The thick spiked timbers lashed into its perimeter
stockade towered nine feet high; inside this ran another stockade of
equally massive boards, made even higher in places to foil the prying
of inquisitive neighbors. The man inside was surely rich, and serious
about his seclusion. The Hermit restricted food deliveries to the dark
path that lay between the two stockades and organized their gates so
that the inner one could open only when the outer one was shut. The
building itself was three stories and built like a safe. It was a brick
box, painted white, which stood fifteen feet back in a plot that took
up half the block. Its front door was three planks thick, reinforced

with iron, and studded with rows of round-headed bolts. Neighbors reported to the newsmen that for a third of a century the window shutters had never been opened and that the Hermit could not have let in more than half a dozen callers in all that time. Rumors had circulated for decades about the treasures he kept in the building's vaulted cellar and the beautiful women imprisoned within the house. In the dark of night, some said, the Hermit's voice could also be heard commanding a ship's imaginary crew.

Very rarely, the Hermit had emerged from his seclusion. As New York had expanded to engulf Harlem, he had arranged for tenement blocks to be built on the derelict fields he had inherited long ago. When he left his refuge, he would be dressed in homemade black clothes and shoes, and accompanied by a woman who was dressed similarly. They neither walked together nor exchanged words: he stood five feet five and always strode several paces in front of his taller companion. The census taker was not even sure whether she was his wife, opting instead for "housekeeper." But she had died the previous year, and no one knew their relationship.

The Hermit's relatives were keen to have a taste of his massive legacy, amounting to eight hundred thousand dollars or more, and eventually they arrived in New York to contest the questionable will which had disinherited them. Their successes in court and what the litigation revealed about the Hermit's life soon rekindled a wider interest in him. All the Hermit had asked, reporters now learned, was to be left alone. He had "sworn a boycott against all mankind and was as faithful to his vow as if he considered it sacred." The relatives revealed, however, that the Hermit was an educated man, and unequaled in his travels. As a teenager in 1834, the *New York Times* disclosed, "he went on a three years cruise among the Pacific islands, and on his return wrote a book which was published by Harper and Brothers, recounting fabulous stories of the strange adventures that had befallen him."

The *Sun* probed a little farther into the Hermit's travels. His book, it reported, "was interesting as a specimen of eccentricity," giving new and apparently arbitrary names to islands and archipelagos already discovered and named by Captain Cook. Since that voyage, the Hermit had apparently fought for the Russians during the Crimean War and journeyed from the Black Sea to Finland in the company of the travel writer Bayard Taylor. The Hermit had also penetrated the Amazon River farther than any previous white man and crossed the Rocky Mountains before America's celebrated pathfinder, John C. Frémont. The Hermit had even, claimed the paper, taken the first rocking chair into Oregon.

By 1856, the year the Hermit built his fortress, far across the American continent in the waters of San Francisco Bay another recluse had already been living for five years as the sole inhabitant of tiny Red Rock Island. This recluse's barren six acres still glisten pink in the bay's evening sun, emerging sheer from the sea between Richmond and San Rafael. In 1851 the island's sole inhabitant had turned his back on San Francisco, the city which he had helped to found, and on the state senate, to which he had been elected. Now he lodged alone on the island in a simple log cabin, catching fish from his cottage doorstep and provisioned in all else by a doting and tolerant brother who rowed out to see him once in a while. On this island, said a perplexed biographer at the time, he lived "like a second Robinson Crusoe. He can sit by his fire and shoot the wildfowl he may choose." Like the Harlem Hermit, the recluse of Red Rock stood only five foot five. He had long dark hair, a full sailor's beard and moustache, and a roving right eye that peered somewhat independently toward the heavens. A man who had known him well discerned in him an impish, subversive, almost feminine air: "more than a man in some things and less than a man in others. . . . Of open heart and countenance, and of tender sensibilities, . . . it was these qualities perhaps that gave him that air of boyishness which might easily be taken for effeminacy or a nature trifling."

Divided by a continent and as alone as it was possible to be in their opposite metropoles, these two men had once been inseparable friends as far back as each could remember. As schoolboys aged twelve, in 1827 they had run away together from their prosperous New York City families. Armed with their meager savings and the family rifles, they had simply vanished. Their parents had found good-bye notes saying that they had gone west to seek their fortune, and reasoned—rightly—that the boys would probably track up the Hudson from New York to Albany and then try to follow the newly dug Erie Canal. The boys' parents rushed a letter off to relatives living upriver, who eventually managed to capture the underage duo some hundred miles away as they were passing through the Catskill Mountains.

Five years after this escapade, in 1833, the parents had won their struggle to get the boys through college, but then introduced the two young men to Benjamin Morrell and Dako. Boyhood dreams of going west now changed to fantasies of another kind of journey. The boy who was to become the recluse of Red Rock Island was Selim E. Woodworth, second son of Morrell's ghostwriter, Samuel Woodworth, and his arresting wife, Lydia. Selim Woodworth's boyhood friend, later to become the Hermit of Harlem, began life as Thomas Jefferson Jacobs, though he later changed his surname to Monroe.

Jacobs's father was a prosperous New York tailor who had made his way from Poland in the late 1800s and built up a clothing store on Maiden Lane off Broadway. His fashionable ready-made clothes offered quality and durability "at the very lowest prices." It was not an original boast, but it clearly worked: he managed to educate his children and purchase a farm in the hamlet of Harlem that would eventually turn out to be a superb investment. At school, young Thomas had fallen in with Selim, and the two boys were soon plotting their future together.

Sixteen-year-old Selim Woodworth had been captivated by his father's writing sessions with Morrell at the family home in Duane Street and had surely met Dako at the Morrells' house seven blocks up Broadway. Two years later he determined to abandon his studies and pestered his father for permission to travel. Samuel relented: with ten children to raise, he was not inclined to keep any of them at home longer than he had to. The ghostwriter seems to have induced Benjamin Morrell to take Selim as captain's clerk on the *Silas E. Burrows* and (when that venture failed) on its successor. Morrell gladly accepted, "being by now very fond of the precocious boy."

Both Benjamin Morrell and Samuel Woodworth wanted Selim to undertake the journey for other reasons. Morrell's fame and his improved fortune had depended on Woodworth's melodramatic romanticization of his adventures, and he hoped that a similar book might be written about his next voyage. For Samuel Woodworth, too, the success of Morrell's book and of *The Cannibals* play had provided him with something of a comeback. He had followed up these successes with another play written for the Bowery Theatre, but this had flopped at the box office despite winning a prize for its "best Yankee character," another imaginatively realized "Morrell" figure. Woodworth's and Morrell's was a successful partnership, and both men had a vested interest in making sure it continued. With Samuel's son Selim on board for the next voyage, Morrell could, aided by Selim's writing skill, draft letters to Samuel in New York. Sent via the rather haphazard global postal system of returning whalers and traders, these could be adapted by Woodworth to give them Morrell's literary persona and published in the New York newspapers, eventually to be developed into a second book. Readers in New York (and around America and the rest of the globe) would be able to follow Morrell's adventures more or less as they happened—and later buy the book.

As Selim Woodworth had his father's entrée, he was able to arrange for Morrell to take on his friend Tom Jacobs as a midshipman. Morrell also allowed the two youths the privilege of keeping a journal and making such observations as they liked on condition that, on the ship's return, they not publish anything in relation to the voyage for a specified (now unknown) length of time. Selim Woodworth and Tom Jacobs had both readied themselves for the voyage by studying navigation theory and were surely as disappointed as Morrell at the collapse of his initial plans.

Selim Woodworth and Tom Jacobs, though, were more than just friends. As their lives unfolded it became apparent that these two were men who loved men—in particular, each other, in an attachment that would last until death. The world into which they were born did not define people by their sexuality (the term *homosexual* was not coined until the 1860s), but nevertheless throughout the nineteenth century popular American morality outwardly despised those who practiced male-male love, then referred to as "sodomy" or "buggery." Those drawn to this "other love" had to create plausibly heterosexual sex lives for public consumption, even though in 1830s New York homosexual liaisons were tacitly accepted. Male lovers in the city were able to meet openly at the carnal slum of Five Points or at City Hall "Park," opposite Peale's Museum. Lovers could meet also inside the theaters themselves, amid poets, playwrights, and actors, some of whom were openly effeminate. There was some homophobic press, to be sure, but in the hierarchy of indecency, male love was less of an affront to New Yorkers' sensibilities than heterosexual affairs across "races" or political hypocrisy.

Such issues were aired especially in the city's newly emerging "sporting press": the cheap newspapers and magazines with names such as *The Owl* or *The New York Flagellator and Police Bulletin* that devoted their pages to sexual exploits and connoisseurship. These somewhat fly-by-night publications were usually edited by Jacksonian Democrats whose invective was aimed primarily at exposing the moral hypocrisy of their opponents whenever such men were spotted patronizing brothels or bawdy music halls. Occasionally extreme writers called for male lovers to be executed—as statute permitted—but for many this practice was not taken as a threat to family or wider society in the way that "miscegenation" was, just as an affront to God.

At home, members of Selim's household were among the more tolerant of this "other love," despite their Swedenborgian beliefs. Male love was integral to the literary scene around which the Woodworths' world revolved. Among the many visitors to the household when Selim was a teenager had been the "American Byron," Fitz-Greene Halleck, and his circle.

Selim Woodworth would eventually marry, and Tom Jacobs may have, but neither for love. When they were teenagers New York might have tolerated a male-love subculture, but as the nineteenth century progressed and as their youth ceded to maturity, their bachelorhood would have attracted increasingly unpleasant attention. Woodworth had been the first to wed: his brother Frederick, who had patiently provisioned him on tiny Red Rock Island, eventually convinced him to return to shore and respectability. At the age of forty-one Selim married a sixteen-year-old whom he had not even met. The unfortunate bride, Lisette, had recently arrived from Chile as a governess. Letters in the Woodworth family archives speak of her later having adulterous affairs but also note that Selim was "quite blind to certain rights or feelings of a wife (not intending to be)." One gets a sense of their relationship, lived mostly apart, from a letter Selim penned to Lisette eight years after their wedding: "You have really become a sensible woman at last. I did once despair of your being anything but a frivolous girl, and I never did know how great a prize I had in you, until I was separated from you. You must not 'Flirt' or I will get jealous, and be coming home suddenly to shoot some fellow."

At the time Woodworth left his island seclusion for marriage, Jacobs seems to have been traveling through Russia and the European Arctic in the company of Bayard Taylor, ten years their junior, and the central charm in New York's underworld of male love. (Taylor later wrote America's pioneering gay novel, *Joseph and His Friend: A Story of Pennsylvania,* published in 1870.) One suspects Woodworth may have harbored a certain jealousy toward Jacobs's associates, but it was the year he gave up on Jacobs and married that Jacobs himself gave up on the world and built his fortress.

All this was long in the future. As eighteen-year-olds, Woodworth and Jacobs anticipated that a voyage with Morrell and Dako would be the most romantic of adventures. For Jacobs, "the idea of visiting lonely and fruitful islands heretofore unknown; and of witnessing the habits of Sunday's people and their exultation at his safe return; and above all, the prospect of opening a new and brilliant path to fortune and to fame, combined to adapt this voyage to my somewhat roving and adventurous disposition." For both, as for so many young men of this era, the impulse to go to sea was driven by an urge to flee the strictures of family and society, and by a sense that out in the world beyond their homeland were other ways of life where other ways of thought and love were licensed.

For ordinary seamen, such license extended to the on-deck ban-
ter away from their captains. In these years, American authors who
had gone adventuring in the Pacific found that they were free to include nudity, phallic jokes, innuendoes, and other sexual references
in their accounts. Otherwise forbidden topics, described in ways that
could both entertain readers and sell books, also enabled authors to
hold a mirror to their own world.

After the failure of the *Silas E. Burrows,* Morrell had been charac-
teristically tenacious. As Jacobs was later to write, he "had indulged
too long in exaggerated dreams of wealth and fame that lay within
his reach, to be easily diverted from the attempt to make them real."
Within a year of the collapse of the joint venture, Morrell had again
secured enough financing to mount a voyage. Not all the original
investors had deserted him. Three—Charles Oakley, Nathaniel Jarvis,
and Paul Babcock—together stumped up the capital for a shoestring
expedition. Babcock, in particular, was not going to abandon Burrows. He and Silas's father, Enoch, had been close friends in Stonington, and it had been these two who had welcomed the American
president James Monroe to their hometown in 1817, at which the
president had commended the Burrows family for their part in its defense during the War of 1812. Silas Burrows had since been providing
Babcock's celebrated adventurer son-in-law Nathaniel Palmer with
ships to command. Babcock's reputation was without stain, and it was
enough to keep Oakley and Jarvis in as investors. It is possible that
other Stonington investors injected some money into the venture, too,
including the veteran sealer and merchant Captain Fanning.

Their funds enabled the new company to purchase the hull of a fast
clipper that was already afloat and for sale in Chesapeake Bay. Having
rigged her for speed—her two brigantine masts leaning back to give
her the rakish Baltimore clipper look—they christened her the *Margaret
Oakley,* after Charles Oakley's wife. Only a week before the *Margaret
Oakley* was due to sail, Morrell had managed to have yet another petition presented to the House of Representatives, this time to support
Captain Fanning in his continued lobbying for federal funding of an

exploratory expedition to the South Seas. No one realistically expected such financing to be agreed upon under the incumbent president's administration, but many correctly anticipated a political change after the election in 1836. Morrell, as America's "Captain Cook," might have imagined that the government would invite him to command the expedition on his return.

Morrell probably also invested his own family's money in the *Margaret Oakley*. His aging, lonely, and possibly insane father had died in November 1832, and in the month before sailing, Morrell's younger sisters, Abby and Eliza, had sold the property they had inherited from him in Stonington for $350.

So it was that the brig *Margaret Oakley* sailed from New York for the Pacific on March 9, 1834, on a voyage shrouded in "mystery," though that mystery was cleared up ten years later, in 1844, when a book was published, also by Harper and Brothers, which purported to solve "the mystery which has heretofore surrounded this famous expedition." The real mystery is whether we can believe any of the book's fabulous narrative. Written apparently by Jacobs, it recounts a voyage in which the captain first attempts to reach extreme southern polar latitudes before turning to the Pacific to take "Sunday" triumphantly home and open up trade with his region. In Jacobs's narrative, the *Margaret Oakley* then sails on to explore the islands of the Bismarck Sea and the New Guinea mainland, with captain and crew building friendships in many locations and making occasional forays deep into the New Guinea interior. In all this, the book mixes irrefutable fact and compelling detail with the implausible and the impossible. So, while the geographical accounts of the region and its languages are now known to be very accurate, the crew's encounter with panthers in a land that has never had any, their visit to ornately carved stone ruins entangled with creepers in a region where none has ever been found, and their hunting of cassowaries in grasslands that today are high forest have seemed somewhat less credible.

One copy of Jacobs's rare book sits today on the shelves of the British Museum library, bequeathed by a former owner who was an authority on oceanic curiosities, Harry Beasley. Before offering his volume to other readers, however, Beasley himself felt compelled to warn them in pencil, just inside the pristine front cover, "It would seem from the author's remarks, he has never visited the places he claims to have done." Beasley was heeded, and anthropologists and historians have discounted Jacobs's fabulous narrative ever since. What they have overlooked, however, are the manuscript diaries, sketches, vocabularies, and other jottings that Jacobs's companion Selim Woodworth set down during the voyage which survive in the Woodworth family archive, and which, together with the newspaper reports of the era, enable Jacobs's fact to be discerned from his fiction—and the rest of the story to be told.

While preparing to set sail, the *Margaret Oakley* anchored in the Hudson just off New York's Battery Gardens and took on stores and a cargo of trading trinkets, including tinware, knives, fishhooks, mirrors, iron nails, and reject glass beads for trading among the Pacific Islands. Dako had a hand in choosing the trade goods—ensuring that novel paint colors and religious prints were included. A day or two before sailing, Jacobs and Woodworth were rowed out by a boatman from the Battery Gardens and welcomed by the ship's steward, Antonio Morris, and his son William, the cabin boy. Morris freed a berth for them from the chaos of preparation in one of the tiny officers' cabins, where they slept their first night together. In Jacobs's description: "My friend and myself turned into it, making the most of our room, and sleeping as soundly as if the stirring adventures which filled our imaginations were never to exist save in our dreams."

When Morrell and Dako came on board the next day, Morrell was furious. His financiers had suddenly foisted two commercial agents—or "supercargoes"—on him to control the business side of the voyage. Nathaniel Jarvis and Charles Oakley had together appointed a relative of Jarvis's as their supercargo, the twenty-four-year-old Algernon Sydney Jarvis, while Paul Babcock had appointed as his supercargo his relative Francis H. Babcock. Clearly none of them entirely trusted Morrell, and this enraged him. They even required him to give power of attorney to Francis Babcock. This was the first time Morrell had taken on supercargoes, and according to Jacobs, he regarded them as commercial spies. They posed a constant threat as well: having power of attorney meant they could cancel the voyage at any moment.

This time, Dako traveled in the officers' quarters with the captain, officers, supercargoes, and two young men. He took a top berth above Jacobs and Woodworth in a stack of three. As the success of this voyage depended on Dako, Morrell was taking care to look after him. Dako could doubtless gauge his own indispensability, too, and figure out that the tables had begun to turn—and how they might be turned further. All the bluster of Morrell's American public persona and his heroic command would be meaningless in the tiny wooden cabins of the *Margaret Oakley*. Morrell was the captain, but he was becoming dependent on his captive. Dako was allowed the run of the ship and soon also gained the respect of her crew.

Morrell's first mate was a diminutive, fresh-faced lad of eighteen, John B. Bernadon, Jr., the son of a wealthy Philadelphia shipping merchant who seems to have apprenticed him almost from birth. Second mate was the Englishman William Scott who had sailed as second mate on the *Antarctic* and was devoted to Morrell, not least because the captain had nursed him back to life after a near-fatal illness. With the arrival of two supercargoes, the officers' quarters on the *Margaret Oakley* were extremely cramped. As was usual, the captain had both his own stateroom for sleeping and his after cabin for work. But the others living aft had only their tiny shared cabins, which contained nothing more than two or three berths in a stack, and access to the eating cabin, which barely accommodated the eight of them.

The ship sailed with about forty men on board. Among the crew were at least two African Americans, the cooks George McRae and Philip Luff, a "runaway slave from the pine forests of Virginia" who doubled as the ship's fiddler. Some members of the crew were true veteran sailors, such as Third Mate William Benton, who was attracted by the daring of the expedition, having worked on both slave and pirate ships, and who in his years of sailing had acquired six languages. Others were green hands, embarking on their first voyage.

Even as the ship set sail on March 9, she encountered her first setback. After the crew had walked up the anchor and the sails had caught the wind, her chain stopper failed. Plunging down, its chain lashing at the crew's legs, it brought the ship up to a jolting stop. This episode augured ill for the voyage, as some later reflected.

Families, financiers, and friends came aboard the ship as far as Staten Island, and as they were leaving in the harbor pilot's yacht, Morrell promised his financiers their profits within eighteen months. Neither Abby Morrell nor John Keeler would voyage this time. Abby presumably came aboard to see Benjamin off, then disembarked to join the onlookers watching her husband's ship disappear over the horizon.

The cramped conditions of the officers' cabin soon sparked conflict. In particular, the supercargoes objected to sharing quarters with Woodworth and Jacobs and, for reasons that are unclear, put pressure on the captain to demote Jacobs. Morrell was forced to comply and commanded him to join the crew before the mast. This was a shock for the young man. Not only did he have to give up the comparative luxury of the officers' cabin for the squalor of normal crew quarters— where berths were shared by men on alternate watches—but the duties of an ordinary seaman were far more physically rigorous than he was used to. It also took him away from Woodworth. The only advantage to this new arrangement was that he still had access to Dako.

Jacobs and Woodworth had probably met and chatted with Dako in New York, but it was only once they were all on board the *Margaret Oakley* that their friendship fused. In his memoir, Jacobs writes that he and Woodworth had "been from the first" Dako's "favourites on board; and to us he always communicated his doubts and fears respecting his ultimate return to his native land." Dako, with his tall and immensely strong and proud presence, towered over these two somewhat effete young men, just as he did over the rest of the crew. Morrell had lodged Dako for almost four years, but had made no attempt to learn his language, though he now requested that Jacobs and Woodworth do so. He also asked the two to draw up sketches and maps, some of which survive. Morrell had presumably been keen to rectify Dumont d'Urville's criticism of his earlier *Voyages:* that he had not created vocabulary lists or made maps and drawings. So, in the dim confines below deck or the sun and breeze topside the young men now not only studied Dako's language but also extended their inquiry into his island's historical mythology and everyday life. Dako was a well-practiced and authoritative teacher, having discussed the same matters with Theodore Dwight the previous year. Consequently the young men were able to glean a great deal of trading intelligence from Dako, which would become crucial as the voyage progressed.

The *Margaret Oakley* swept east across the Atlantic to Cape Verde, and then south round the South African Cape. The plan was to sail eastward almost to Australia before tracking north to Indonesia, New Guinea, and Dako's island. But misfortune intervened early. By the time they reached Cape Verde off the west coast of Africa, the ship's decks were leaking and her cargo was so damaged that Morrell had to lay anchor so the crew could waterproof the deck by whacking cotton and hemp fiber soaked in pine tar into the cracks, then covering this with putty and pitch.

Misfortune struck again off South Africa. Jacobs claimed in his account that they were making a detour to the South Polar seas when the ship sprung such a dangerous leak in the massive swell that she was lucky to reach the safety of Mauritius. The trip to these southerly latitudes is pure fiction, though—introduced, perhaps, to suggest Morrell's heroic impulsion to explore the Pole and his desire to fulfill his original promise. The *Margaret Oakley* actually sailed no farther south than Cape Town, although the leak was real enough—in fact, almost catastrophic. By the time it was found, water was several feet deep in the hold, its weight threatening to split the hull in the huge swell of the Roaring Forties. Panicked, Morrell and his crew immediately made ready the three smaller boats stowed aboard so they could push off at any second. The whole crew then spent the two weeks it took to get to Mauritius bailing and pumping out water—a task that was amplified when a sperm whale caught the ship under the stern, and spouted on deck.

Dako, Jacobs, and Woodworth were becoming close companions. At Cape Verde the three wandered over the island of Bonavista and swam together off its beaches. When becalmed on board, they would dive off the ship—Dako fearless even with sharks around. When making good headway, a sport for them and the rest of the crew consisted of harpooning dolphins on the bow wave, at which Dako understandably proved to be the most proficient, although William Scott, the second officer, managed passably well. However much the crew attempted to copy Dako's style of throwing the spear, they could never match his ability, and when they wrestled with him in the rare idle moments it was with equal futility. Dako, however, much preferred the tranquillity of solitude. He soon acquired a reputation as an excellent lookout, settling comfortably on the masthead, where he could discern a sail or land sooner than any other crew member. Later he became principal lookout as the captain navigated the narrow passages through coral reefs. There was little to break the monotony of the voyage except the usual celebration when the brig first crossed the equator and green hands such as Jacobs and Woodworth received the customary initiation: the captain donned the costume of King Neptune with trident and regalia, and lathered each of the novices with tar, shaved their beards with a rusty iron hoop, and plunged them into the sea, recovering them as initiates—or "old tars."

That Dako commanded increasing respect as the voyage unfolded is captured in Jacobs's descriptions:

> Uneducated as he was, he possessed sound practical common sense, and never exhibited anything of a servile or timid temper; his manners, on the contrary, were commanding and impressive, without being proud or ostentatious. He cared little for ornaments, and valued only things of practical utility, which contributed in some way to his comfort and happiness. His notions of comfort and usefulness, of course, differed widely from those of civilized people, as in the delightful climate of his native islands the people wear no clothing. . . . He was always a favourite among our men, was never at enmity with anyone, and had a most inveterate and praiseworthy habit of minding his own business.

Jacobs conveys Dako's "pidgin" English, which was not the "tok pisin" language that developed on his island during the twentieth century.

By Jacobs's recollection, Dako's English was perhaps more reminiscent of the speech of American Indians—or at least its rendition in
American literature: "Cap-in Mo-rel!" "Me tink-e me see land-e!"
"Him look-e too much-e far off!" "plenty high!—me no hab fool-e
you dis time!"

The *Margaret Oakley* arrived off the island of Mauritius on June
12, 1834, in "a leaky state," according to London's *Morning Chronicle*
many months later. The copper-bottomed vessel that the investors
had purchased was flawed, and the supercargoes were obliged to finance
a full overhaul. Slaves in a Mauritian shipyard stripped and repaired the
hull, and reinforced her with a second skin of timber. To settle the account, the supercargoes had to mortgage both the ship herself and her
cargo in what was called a bottomry bond—an undertaking to forfeit
the ship and her cargo if the loan were not repaid with interest.

The refitting was not without its advantages. The reinforced hull
gave the brig increased protection against coral reefs, and in the make-
over Morrell was also able to give her a "warlike appearance," which
"caused the citizens of Port Louis [the capital of Mauritius] to suspect
that we were bound on some piratical or slaving expedition, and this
was soon the general rumor throughout the place." Her sides (the
bulwarks) now extended so high above the main deck that the crew
"standing upon deck, could not be seen by natives in canoes alongside."
Morrell had ten or more cannon ports lit into the bulwarks on either
side which, according to the Mauritian newspapers, only added to
suspicions of her intent. The captain increased the armament, too,
acquiring four new cannons—two twelve-pounders and two eighteen-
pounders. And he shipped several new crew to manage them: "Sailors
who came to ship with us wore very knowing looks, and gave us to
understand that they knew what sort of a craft we were."

Morrell sent his first letter back to Samuel Woodworth from Mauritius, along with a copy of his journal, both presumably composed by
Selim. In New York Selim's father edited them into the public "Morrell's" more literary and poetic style, and published the result in the literary weekly he had founded, the *New York Mirror*. Through the
Woodworths, the magazine's readers began to follow Morrell's jour-

ney from New York to Cape Verde and the Cape of Good Hope, and learned of the leak from which the ship would have undoubtedly sunk had not her pumps worked at the rate of fifty thousand strokes a day. The paper also printed a long extract of Morrell's "new voyages" concerning Mauritius, in which the captain once again came across as the most authoritative and eloquent of American navigators—and once again plagiarized the text word for word from published sources. Fully refitted, the *Margaret Oakley* sailed from Mauritius ten weeks later, on September 2, 1834, cruising via Malaysia and the Celebes and Banda Seas of modern Indonesia, and then southeast along the northern shore of Papua New Guinea, before nearing Dako's tiny archipelago.

The ship was heavily armed with cannon, but now Morrell also issued muskets and cutlasses to her crew. Without much else to break the monotony of life at sea, the officers kept the ordinary seamen busy making sails, cleaning pistols, and practicing their weaponry. Dako learned the use of pistols and muskets like the rest. Morrell also had the crew practice rowing the ship with five long oars to a side, to enable her to avoid dangerous currents in slack winds and to maneuver within small bays.

Once off the north coast of New Guinea, Morrell issued a pair of pistols to each of the crew. He took his time sailing along the coast, trading with the indigenous peoples, whom he found generally friendly. Morrell made Dako responsible for communication, but his languages were of little use, and at times tentative relations built on gesticulation broke down. In what later came to be called Humboldt Bay (now Yos Sudarso Bay), the brig was attacked by "an immense fleet of outrigger canoes" that outpaced her in the light winds. The flotilla generated such a noise from its drums and conches that Morrell again had to direct his men through a speaking trumpet. It was an unequal match. A broadside of eighteen-pound cannon each loaded with 250-piece grape shot created a "scene of fearful devastation" reminiscent of the day of Dako's capture.

As the ship approached Dako's island, Morrell stepped up his commands. No one, least of all the supercargoes, was to know their precise location. He was probably all the more keen to conceal their

The brig *Margaret Oakley* off New Guinea and Yos Sudarso (Humboldt) Bay, from
Thomas Jefferson Jacobs, *Scenes, Incidents, and Adventures in the Pacific Ocean; or, The
Islands of the Australasian Seas, During the Cruise of the Clipper Margaret Oakley, Under
Capt. Benjamin Morrell . . . ,* 1844, frontispiece

whereabouts to forestall anyone on board from realizing that the islands which they assumed he had discovered had actually been on the
charts all long.

The captain confiscated all nautical instruments and forbade anyone to chart the voyage. Even the vessel's speed was no longer reck-
oned in the traditional way—throwing a log in the water and timing
how fast the boat moved away from it—so the logbook contained no
courses, distances, latitudes, or longitudes. Since the battle at Humboldt Bay, Morrell also began to quarrel frequently with the supercargoes over the balance between commerce and exploration, whose
arguments gave him (as he thought) good cause to "crush the owners
and their spies." In this atmosphere of secrecy and suspicion, Selim
Woodworth was concerned enough that the wrong people (including
the captain) might read his journal that he took to encoding in cipher
any private comments or passages critical of people's conduct. He also
encrypted the locations he noted and their trading particulars. Jacobs
was equally careful. He had smuggled his own navigational instruments into steerage, but took the ship's position surreptitiously.

Dako was generally in buoyant spirits at the prospect of returning home, but his anxiety and impatience also became painfully visible. "He could scarcely eat or sleep, and every day he was found sitting in the slings of the fore-topsail yard, leaning with his back against the topmast cross trees." Here he sat for "whole days, gazing at the horizon ahead, apparently absorbed in deep meditation." Eventually, one November evening eight months after the *Margaret Oakley* had left New York, the captain woke Dako to say that his archipelago was in sight. Jacobs relates Dako's disbelief: "What for you too much a pool, Capin Mor-el? You see my island! Suppose me no see my island, me no lik'e you too much!" But when he saw the island "he uttered a shout of heartfelt rapture, which thrilled through every bosom on board."

As they approached the archipelago, Dako instructed Morrell to sail to the smaller island of Naraga, where his mother's relatives lived, rather than to Uneapa, his home, as he needed to know the outcome of the war before he dared land there. That the *Margaret Oakley* arrived at Naraga, and that Woodworth and Jacobs landed cannot be doubted: the engraving in Jacobs's book resembles the island closely: a small volcanic peak emerging from the sea, clad in forest, with houses fringing the beach. Jacobs also described in detail the island's signature feature: the boiling springs on the beach and the culinary opportunity they offered the inhabitants. Islanders congregated by the springs to cook the fish they had landed by simply dunking them in the naturally boiling water.

The *Margaret Oakley* off Naraga, as depicted in Jacobs, *Scenes, Incidents, and Adventures in the Pacific Ocean*, 79

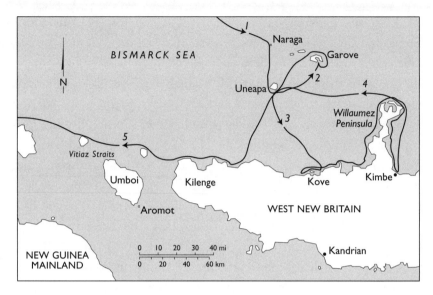

Return of the *Margaret Oakley* to Dako's island, November–December 1834. 1) arrival
at Naraga (Dako's mother's island); 2) arrival at Uneapa (Dako's island) and visit to
Garove; 3) exploring Kove and thence to Kimbe (Dwight's) Bay; 4) return to Uneapa;
5) departure on voyage around the Bismarck Sea (map by Bill Nelson)

As the *Margaret Oakley* neared Naraga, the islanders on shore threatened the vessel with spears and war clubs and loosed off slingshots.
Dako ran out onto the ship's boom, shouting to them that he was
"Telum-by-by Darco" (or perhaps "Terrumbumbyandarko," as "his"
letter published in the New York paper had him). The islanders were
not convinced, shouting back that Pango (whom Jacobs called "Pongo")
had killed and eaten Dako, to which Dako apparently replied, "Pongo
good man." The islanders then argued that Dako was "not white like
you"—associating whiteness with his clothes, perhaps, rather than his
skin color, and the spirit world of which he was a part. So, in a dramatic move, Dako stripped and stood naked before them, revealing his
body and the intricate tattoos that proved his identity and status.

This was enough for the islanders, whose aggression switched to
awe. Next, according to Jacobs, Dako put on a cheap red crown, possibly purchased especially for the occasion, which echoed the feathered
headdresses fashionable on the island. Then he had one of the ship's
boats row him to the reef near shore. Leaving the Americans to with-

draw in fear of attack, Dako then swam alone toward the beach. He was "instantly recognized by his people, who testified their joy and affection by uttering shouts of welcome that might have been heard for miles to seaward," and embraced by all. Jacobs likened his reception on shore to that of Napoleon returning triumphantly to France from his exile in Elba.

The brig had anchored off the island. After an hour or so, Dako returned to the vessel accompanied by a fleet of canoes. He requested permission to spend the night on the island and beckoned Jacobs and Woodworth to join him. The captain remained on board, but the two young men, who after eight months of Dako's tutelage could probably now speak some of the Uneapa language, went with him. On approaching the beach, they were literally carried ashore in the canoe, staying with Dako until the evening. On their arrival:

> Darco [Dako] was encompassed by the oldest men and women upon the island. Some seized him by the hands, others embraced his legs and feet, while several caught him round the neck, and fairly wept upon his bosom. He was much affected by these unequivocal demonstrations of affection, and the big tears rolled down his cheeks.
>
> While this was going on, we were surrounded by a more youthful class, and found it almost impossible to move hand or foot. Some of them wet their fingers and rubbed our hands and arms, to ascertain whether the color of our skin was natural and permanent, or only artificial. . . . Others played with and admired our hair. . . .
>
> Darco was at length enabled to come to our assistance, and caused his people to form a circle around us, that we might sit down and get a little fresh air, and the natives at the same time might have a better view of us. He also told us to keep off our shirts, and thus to show his people that we were willing to conform to their style of dress, and thus to gain their confidence and friendship. . . . The principal chiefs remained inside the circle, and Darco related to them the wonderful adventures

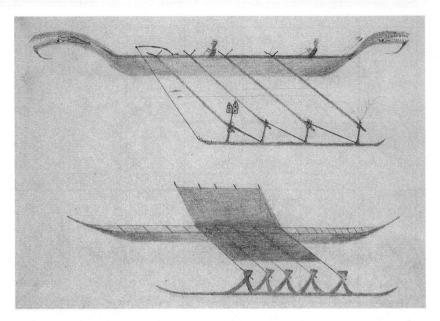

Outrigger canoes from Uneapa and the Bismarck Sea sketched by Selim Woodworth (reproduced by permission of the Huntington Library, San Marino, California)

he had encountered since his strange and mysterious captivity and exile from his beloved country. They listened with the most greedy avidity to his wonderful stories.

According to Jacobs, he and Woodworth then visited "the Palace of Lavoo," a forty-foot-square building with bamboo walls and a palm-leaf thatch, where several elderly leaders had gathered to welcome the returning hero. The youths from New York sat among them, "and they gazed at us in wonder."

The most notable man present, Jacobs writes, was Lavoo himself, "the red warrior." He was a stout, thick-set man, about forty-five years of age, of medium height and with a commanding air. What Jacobs found curious about him, though, were his reddish skin and his long, dark-red hair, while his wife was "the very counterpart of himself in all other respects." Dako told the inquisitive Jacobs that they were brother and sister. What is particularly tantalizing is that Jacobs eventually learned "from various sources" that the island had been settled by a Frenchman named Laveaux, a surgeon from La Pérouse's ill-fated exploring expedition of the 1780s. According to Jacobs, Laveaux had acquired a wife or wives from Dako's island, "and the present red warrior and his wife are the son and daughter of Laveaux, pronounced Lavoo, the name of the present red man." Jacobs also recounts that other islanders frequently called the island of Naraga Red Man's Island.

If this narrative is to be believed, it solves a mystery concerning the fate of the survivors of the most famous of French shipwrecks, in which La Pérouse's two lavishly equipped vessels had gone missing in 1788. Their fate had been the subject of tremendous speculation not just in France but around the world for nearly forty years, until eventually, in 1827, a maverick Irish merchant-captain named Peter Dillon was offered the hilt of La Pérouse's personal sword while trading at the Pacific island of Tikopia. He made a few inquiries and found that this and other articles had come from another island, Vanikoro. He convinced the British government in India to give him command of a survey vessel to check the story out, reaching Vanikoro in September 1827. Here Dillon recovered compelling evidence of La Pérouse's shipwrecks, finally ascertaining the fate of the royal expedition, for which he later received rewards and honors from the French government. After hearing the news of Dillon's discovery, the French naval explorer Dumont d'Urville, who was on an expedition in the Pacific at the time, also made for the site of the wrecks, and was told by islanders there that the French survivors had built a vessel and escaped from the island. The fate of those survivors had remained unknown ever since. Now Jacobs was suggesting that at least one of them had reached the tiny island of Naraga.

Meanwhile, Dako learned on Naraga that his father, Tupi, had died and that his people on Uneapa were still at war with easterners from the mountains who continued to raid their lands. These easterners had even carried off the daughter of Dako's cousin Ragotur. Anticipating a difficult return, Dako encouraged Morrell to take on board two of his friends before sailing. One of them Jacobs names as Wonger, the other Pongaracoopo, Dako's kinsman who had lost an eye and "received a buck-shot near his shoulder-blade" during the battle four years previously in which Dako had been captured. Joining Morrell was a brave act for these two islanders—boarding a ship, possibly of the dead, certainly from an unknown world, perhaps never to return again. As if to enhance their fear, Morrell ordered a cannon to be fired once they were en route, in part to show off to his passengers, but in part, perhaps, to alert Uneapa islanders of his imminent arrival.

With Dako acting as translator for the new passengers, Jacobs was able to relate some insights of their first experiences on board. He describes their amazement at cannonballs and at the report of the cannon, which scared them enormously. Wonger and Pongaracoopo also understood the ship in some way to be a "bottomless pit," the hatch perhaps being akin to a portal to the underworld. They figured, too, that the tin cups, bottles, and tumblers that were part of the crew's everyday equipment were shells that grew on the "coral reefs and sand-spits in the moon." This was not an unreasonable deduction since the islanders believed that the large clay pots they obtained from the New Guinea mainland through their trade networks were also natural shells—a ruse the mainlanders who made these pots maintained well into the twentieth century in order to guard their monopoly of manufacture.

In his book Jacobs develops a narrative excitement around Dako's homecoming. But although his account of the buildup to it can be broadly trusted—the Laveaux enigma, perhaps, aside—Woodworth's journal reveals that the events Jacobs related of the homecoming itself were wishful fiction.

The *Margaret Oakley* carved though the choppy waters for the final twenty-two nautical miles to Uneapa, but as she drew near the familiar bay where the battle with the *Antarctic* had taken place, neither Morrell nor Dako wanted to risk going ashore unannounced. Instead, Morrell had Dako, Wonger, and Pongaracoopo rowed ashore in one of the ship's boats. As they approached the beach, yells rang through the forest and a vast body of islanders descended to the shore fully armed with spears, slings, clubs, and shields. At this Wonger and

The *Margaret Oakley* off Uneapa Island, from Jacobs, *Scenes, Incidents, and Adventures in the Pacific Ocean*, 88

Selim Woodworth's sketch of Dako's island of Uneapa from aboard the *Margaret Oakley* (reproduced by permission of the Huntington Library, San Marino, California)

Pongaracoopo stood up and addressed the astonished crowd "in a loud and energetic strain, accompanied by violent gesticulation." Next the intermediaries took to the water and swam ashore, where they were welcomed, and "soon the joyful cry of 'Telum-by-by Darco! Telum-by-by Darco!' rang through the forest in all directions." After two hours "a splendid war-canoe put out of a cove, manned by fifteen warriors, or chiefs of noble blood, who paddled for the vessel," followed by a fleet of smaller canoes, each laden with gifts of fruit for the ship. The Uneapa chiefs stepped from the wide platform of the war canoe and came aboard the *Margaret Oakley,* where they embraced Dako, hustled him back into the canoe, and hastily paddled to shore. The whole fleet followed, apparently chanting a greeting song, accompanied by drums. "They soon entered the cove, and were lost to our view."

At this point Jacobs's published version of events ventures into pure fiction. In his narrative, later the next day Dako returned to the vessel, having been crowned "King of Nyappa," and explained that he could bring the "mountain people" who were suing for peace to unconditional and bloodless subjection, but in the meantime he would organize the collection of tortoiseshell, pearls, and other valuable commodities. None of this happened. What took place was much simpler. Woodworth's journal entries for the *Margaret Oakley*'s arrival at the islands are lost, but when his journal picks up the story again, it is clear that, once ashore, Dako simply vanished.

For Dako, the homecoming was not all that he had hoped. His desire to return to his wife, Vakale, and his son, Tupi, had sustained him during his protracted exile in New York. Vakale, however, had not waited for him. Those on the islands still remember the event in their oral histories:

> There was a man whose name was Dako whom the white people kidnapped. . . . They thought he would be a good servant and put him to work until they were ready to bring him back. But his wife was grief-stricken over him. . . . Now his wife had sat grieving but finally another man had married her and she ceased. He said, "Why are you grieving? Your husband won't come back. He's dead." So he took this woman and married her. So when the poor fellow came back he had no wife. He too sat down and grieved.

Dako's odyssey had not ended as it was supposed to. Nor was it over.

CHAPTER 10

Missing

 భఙ

Now that Dako had disappeared, it seemed as if Morrell had circumnavigated the world for nothing. He could surely sense the bitter anger of his investors and the rising tensions with their agents on board. It would be futile, and possibly dangerous, to land. Given the carnage that he had inflicted in this very harbor four years earlier, any landing would require overpowering force, yet to use that force would be to undermine peaceful trading relations, the font of all profit.

Morrell waited for another day, his ship anchored off the reef, rocking aimlessly with the waves. Perhaps Dako might appear from a thatched hut or a grove behind the beach just as nonchalantly as he had vanished. Eventually the sun plunged into the tropical sea, and throughout a second humid night the watch chatted on deck and scanned the watery phosphorescence for the splash of a swimmer. The captain ordered a lantern to be lit and hung in the rigging to guide Dako. But nothing happened. After yet another day of increasing despair, the enormity of Morrell's loss began to shatter his self-delusion.

The trapped captain took out his frenetic anger on the crew, insisting that the decks be scrupulously swept and then scrubbed and scrubbed again. The next morning Morrell upped anchor and made for the nearby volcanic island of Garove, whose eruption Dako had

The *Margaret Oakley* entering the Garove harbor of Havana Kapou (Big Mouth), from Jacobs, *Scenes, Incidents, and Adventures in the Pacific Ocean,* 91

once described and where, he had told Theodore Dwight, there was a cave portal leading to the ancestral world.

Garove Island is an exploded caldera. Its residual volcanic rim curves round like a horseshoe to enclose a superb natural harbor some five miles in diameter with a narrow entrance linking the crater to the sea. As the *Margaret Oakley* glided into the harbor, the sea became eerily calm and the wind slackened in her sails. Looking up at the steep, forest-clad crater rim protected from the ocean's fickle winds, Morrell realized the harbor's potential: here was an ideal place for a trading colony. The location offered a perfect opportunity—but without Dako, it would be someone else's paradise, make someone else's fortune. Huts and hearth smoke revealed that parts of the island were inhabited, but the Americans did not attempt to make contact.

In disbelief that Dako could have let him down so badly, and desperate for the introduction he needed to tap into this verdant economy, Morrell ordered the *Margaret Oakley* to return to Uneapa, drop anchor, and wait. Again in vain. The whole mission was in jeopardy, but this time the optimistic captain would not be able to talk his way out of trouble.

Morrell and the supercargoes had very different views on how to respond to this calamitous setback. Having recently come under attack and witnessed the terrible bloodshed during the battle off Humboldt Bay, the supercargoes had no desire for a repeat encounter. They proposed to cut their losses, quit the region, and head for Manila or Canton, where they could acquire the usual trading cargo of silks and teas and still come out with a reasonable profit. For Morrell, however, such an option spelled ruin: he would return to New York to face ridicule. No El Dorado. No story. Overruling the supercargoes—that is, commandeering the vessel from the delegated authority of its owners—was deemed an act of piracy. This did not deter the captain. Jacobs put it later, Morrell "released himself unilaterally from all obligation to prosecute the voyage for the owners' benefit. . . . He changed the objective and sought to lay the foundations for trade in this region at their expense, and at some future time to return, in a vessel of his own, and reap the profits. This meant conducting a thorough exploration of Tropical Australasia; to enter all the most dangerous and unknown places with apparent recklessness."

The young supercargoes were powerless in face of the intransigent captain, whose dictatorial power also carried the crew. Trapped, they could only register their dissent and hope to exert their authority at the next port, a scenario Morrell would now do everything to avoid. In this mood of recklessness and desperation, he initiated a voyage that was so audacious that no one has since believed that it actually happened. Selim Woodworth's journal shows that it did.

In the captain's favor was a loyal crew who had shipped for adventure and fortune, not trade. He also had an extremely maneuverable and well-armed vessel, and two young linguists on board who could get by in the Uneapa language at least. While Dako had been with them, Morrell, Woodworth, and Jacobs had also gleaned a great deal of intelligence about the trading opportunities in the region. Morrell knew that Dako had himself traded with the Kove people on the north coast of New Britain, and had noted down some names and locations. Indeed, he knew of some of the influential figures there, including Dako's trading partner Tantargeely, whom the Americans could safely presume spoke Uneapa. He also had intelligence on other powerful individuals in settlements farther along the New Britain coast. Morrell's emerging Plan B was therefore to attempt to make

contact with the people on the Kove shores and through them forge
wider trading links wherever he could. Having opened communication, he would proffer presents and, if possible, commission communities to collect cargoes of tortoiseshell and pearls in preparation for
his return some months later. With luck he could also prospect inland
for gold and other valuables such as sandalwood.

So without Dako or any other intermediary, Morrell sailed for
the coast of New Britain and attempted to establish contact in the
Kove region. Jacobs gives a sense of how out of the ordinary this new
mission was. "The scenes through which we had already passed, the
mysterious region we had now entered, and the view of the towering
and verdant mountains of Bidera [New Britain], tended to inspire us
with a feeling as if we had taken a final leave of civilized life, and
entered a new and unknown world. With a swift and well-armed vessel under his feet, and a large and chivalrous crew at his command, far
away from the control of law, Captain Morrell in a measure became
'outlawed,' and so did we all."

The crew were more than a little nervous about setting ashore. As
Jacobs explains, "Before we began to penetrate the mystery that hung
over it, every step we took was taken with hesitation and terror."
Woodworth's journal places the ship off Kove on November 25, 1834,
about a week after Dako disappeared. The *Margaret Oakley* was forced
to anchor at some distance from the coast, as Morrell did not dare
venture closer, having discovered that the water was a bay of shoals—
in this case, of reefs as well. Instead, he equipped the ship's three small
boats with masts and sails, a blunderbuss and a winch, and sent them
off to explore. This part of the northern coast of New Britain had
genuinely never been visited by Western vessels before, or if it had their
exploits had never been charted. Large distances remained entirely
blank on Arrowsmith's navigation charts, which even indicated that
New Britain might be two islands.

To the east of the *Margaret Oakley*'s anchorage was a promontory
that the sailors called Sambarlow's Point. Their first attempt at contact was to chase a solitary canoe which had put ashore there to escape them. Having pulled in, too, the Americans managed to hail the

The *Margaret Oakley*'s three boats, the *Invincible,* the *Tempest,* and the *Sylph,* were used to explore shallow bays and rivers. From Jacobs, *Scenes, Incidents, and Adventures in the Pacific Ocean,* 218

frightened canoeists, who, as related in Woodworth's journal, took them to be the same cannibalistic deities that had stolen Dako so many years before.

> Although we could not see them, they being in the Bushes, we invited them to come out and receive some presents but they said that they were afraid that we had come to take them away to Eat, as God had done previously at Nyappa by taking Darco. We told them that we were not God but people like them but they did not believe us. We also told them that we had just brought Darco home and that he had been in our Country; but all of our conversation was of no use; they would not show themselves; and all the time begging of us to go away. We finally told them what we came for and asked them if they had any Tortois Shell, they said they had, and if we would go away that they would put some in an old tree that lay in the watter; we then pulled the boat towards the tree and layed some pieces of old Iron hoop on the tree and pulled away. The natives soon came out and took the Iron and left in its place 4 pieces of Shell which we took and thanked them promising tomorrow to call and see their friends on Jarvis Isle.

That Woodworth and Jacobs could speak Uneapa sufficiently for this conversation to have taken place might astonish us, but the encounter must have been all the more bizarre for the canoeists whom they had cornered. Could their pursuers be the "lonely spirits" of those who had died in the bush without proper funerary rights, living in eternal solitude haunting the living whose company they craved? Could they perhaps be the ghoulish monsters of the forest that at times take human form but who, driven by the desire to eat human flesh, chase those they find alone? Both interpretations were possible, but Woodworth's journal makes it clear that the canoeists assumed immediately that they had been cornered by a "god"—we can presume the spirit Pango—who had taken Dako and who commanded the dimension of the dead whence he led the departed.

Kove men sometimes visited Uneapa for long periods to learn the language and build trading friendships, so Dako's language was well known along the coast. If these randomly encountered canoeists are anything to go by, the inhabitants of this part of New Britain's shoreline also knew all about Dako's capture. The visitation at Uneapa several years before had entered the local sagas, and although in them Pango had then been repulsed by the islanders, it was only at the expense of enormous destruction and the abduction and presumed death of Dako. Terrifyingly, these new visitors shared the same corpselike pallor and strange loose skin of Dako's abductors. They also seemed to emit weird ethereal sounds (the boatswain's whistle, fifes, and perhaps the French horn and drums which the sailors used to coordinate the boats) to communicate not just with each other but undoubtedly also with the spirit world whence they derived their power.

From the first day of the voyage, Morrell had taken against the younger of the supercargoes, Algernon Jarvis. The captain now vented some of his frustration by using the dangers of first contact to make life particularly uncomfortable for him. As trade was his job, Morrell seems to have reasoned, Jarvis should be the one to initiate it. Next day, the captain dropped the unfortunate young man on a sandbank that lay off a beachside village on one of the many inhabited offshore islands. Morrell presumably hoped that the unarmed Jarvis sitting alone on his sandbank would not only allay local fears but also act as a lure. But the behatted and forlorn supercargo attracted no one. Despondently, Morrell instead led a party ashore—at the sight of which the villagers abruptly fled. The Americans did not know what to do, but decided to hang some cutlery and beads on the brightly painted house-of-respect as a sign of trade. On their return the following morning they found that the villagers had roasted a pig for them, but had left the articles hanging just where they had put them. Selim Woodworth again managed to establish some kind of dialogue with the villagers. It turned out that what the Americans construed as gifts and an overture to trade had been interpreted by the islanders as an assertion of possession: "They believed, as I learn't afterwards, that the god had put [the objects] on this House and that they would return to take up residence there."

The islanders reasoned that these apparitions did not appear to be bound by the predictable and well-understood natural and social rules that dictate human behavior. While some of their visible features appeared human, their sulfurous weaponry and its control over life and death suggested powers far beyond the capability of mortals, and the gratuitous carnage they had wrought in Uneapa revealed a wholly different morality. Now the beads and cutlery they had left also revealed powers and creative abilities that set them apart. Not only were metal and glass unknown substances to the islanders, the fact that all the pieces of cutlery were identical meant they could not have been made by the hand of man. They must belong to the spirit world.

Those gathered on the shore cast suspicious, nervous looks at the Americans and their otherworldly objects. Then, to end the standoff, Morrell took down the knives and beads and gave them to their leader, or *mahoni,* a man named Peo Lioo, who was "much pleased with them and expressed his thanks by offering us some cooked Cocoas and Roast Pig."

To build on these signs of friendship, the Americans returned to the island the next day and invited the elderly Peo Lioo into the boat.

He agreed but "had difficulty in getting clear of his people. They thought we were going to eat him. . . . We showed him everything that we thought would amuse him, and we made him a present of a Red cap, a calico shall, an Axe and some beads." An elderly woman with a large sore on her back also courageously ventured up to Morrell to seek a cure, which he promised to attend to. Gaining the islanders' trust was slow work, but at least on this tiny island the Americans were feeling somewhat more secure, so the following day Morrell and Woodworth took one of the small boats several miles up a navigable river on the mainland that lay behind the island. This river, they found, was lined with high rainforest and apparently deserted. As nature's nerve-racking cacophony surrounded them, the unsettled Americans fired muskets in reply.

The *Margaret Oakley* had no doctor on board, but Selim Woodworth was designated the closest thing, and that evening he returned to the island to treat the woman's sore with Harlem Oil—the popular kerosene-based cure-all that most American ships carried. That she solicited medical help so soon after meeting these apparitions suggests something of how the strangers were perceived. People often accredited the power of healing to otherworldly knowledge and intervention.

Establishing contact required patience. Next the Americans tried their luck a few miles farther west, at another tiny islet village marked by seven coconut palms. Its leader, they thought, was Dako's friend Tantargeely. As ever, at the sailors' first appearance the villagers fled the beach. But on this islet there was nowhere to hide, so its inhabitants dealt with the intruders as they would with any other tricky spirit powers invoked during their ceremonies. Approaching cautiously, they began to dance in formation, singing and swaying coconut fronds, as was done at funerals and festivities. Since the islanders' understanding of these beings focused not only on their marvelous powers but on their almost insatiable desire for hogs and roast pork, they carried with them a slain pig, which they placed in the sailboat as a peace offering and gesture of respect. They then ceased singing and approached the landing party as they would do if friendship had been established. Their lore maintained also, however, that these spirits were not invulnerable: if the islanders were clever enough they might out-trick or even annihilate them.

Communicating again in the Uneapa language, Woodworth found out that Tantargeely had died and been replaced by another mahoni. He arranged for the landing party to meet with the new leader the following morning. This time the islanders rapidly overcame their initial fright and began to crowd around the Americans' landing boat while the ship's two other boats patrolled, armed, slightly offshore. In the confusion the beached boat's retractable rudder disappeared. In response, Morrell, through Woodworth, threatened the old men in the village: "If they did not find it instantly . . . he would make thunder and lightning and kill all of the people and knock down all of the huts." Morrell had the swivel gun on one of the offshore boats loaded with bar shot (a spinning anti-personnel missile, resembling a dog's bone) and ordered the crew to stand and raise muskets to shoulder. At this, an elderly man—presumably the mahoni—emerged waving the rudder, and "shouting to us not to sink the island," swam out with it to the launch, which by then had put to sea. Again the power the Kove people attributed to the Americans is palpable: local mythology held that Pango was able not only to sink islands but to cause earthquakes, bring tsunamis, erupt volcanoes, and eject the massive lava bombs that so closely resembled cannonballs. The sulfurous fumes of musket fire and the thunderous report of the cannon—Morrell was careful to carry out practice drills in the vicinity of the villages—left the Kove in little doubt about his powers.

It was not just the islanders who purloined things, however. Over the next week, until December 2, the three small boats visited and revisited several islands. Intrigued by the locals' obsidian, tools, and spearheads, the Americans helped themselves to what they found in the freshly deserted villages, along with hogs, chickens, breadfruit, coconuts, and other items. In each case, they left behind beads and metal knives in what they imagined was reasonable compensation. Every encounter carried an element of suspense. On one island, when Morrell hopped on shore to receive a hog, he forgot to lay down the dramatic-looking harpoon he was carrying. The villagers fled in terror.

There was little actual violence. The only documented instance occurred when a canoe followed one of the Americans' boats and the unnerved crew fired a musket to scare the pursuers away. Whenever they ventured onto a beach, the sailors were under orders to fire a musket if they faced any danger, as this would attract the support of the other boats and their cannon. Equally, a cannon shot from the ship or an ensign raised on its mast was a signal for the landing parties to hurry back aboard.

As respite from the tension of these encounters, Morrell sought out uninhabited islets far offshore where the crew could relax and swim. On one occasion they found a rich bed of sea cucumbers and collected hundreds for the ship's cooks to prepare. The empty pearl oyster shells which littered both the beaches and the burned-out hearths of overnight fishing camps on these islets were also theirs for the taking. These mini-paradises offered a break from the vigilance and anxiety of contact encounters, and a taste of the pleasures of colonization—until the enchantment was shattered by the sight of a fifteen-foot saltwater crocodile.

For two weeks the Americans traded as best they could with whichever locals they managed to meet. On board, the crew spent their mornings mending the sails and rigging as usual, and polishing the knives, cheap cutlery, and mirrors that the islanders found so appealing. Dako, it seems, had helped Morrell choose his trading cargoes well. Yet trading was hard: inhabitants invariably deserted their villages before the Americans arrived. The most successful encounters were on the tiniest islands, where the villagers had nowhere else to go. But tiny islands brought tiny rewards. Morrell needed to find richer lands.

After a week, he left the Kove region, sailing eastward along the New Britain shore, and continued his tentative exploration in the direction of the volcanic Willaumez peninsula, where one of its volcanoes was currently erupting. In one bay he anchored to collect fresh water and fuel, and when prospecting there for sandalwood encountered an armed party decked out with "huge teeth and beads with green leaves in their heads" who spoke a different tongue and promptly fled. Here Morrell not only felled trees for fuel but also planted an experimental garden of maize, pumpkins, beans, and turnips, testing these crops in New Britain for the first time. The landing party were, notes Woodworth, astonished at a massive tree from which projected vast buttresses of roots, snaking out, he claimed, over four acres. This was monumental nature such as they had never seen.

And so they moved from bay to bay, past the erupting volcano, round the Willaumez peninsula, and into the massive Kimbe Bay. Morrell named it Dwight's Bay after Theodore Dwight, whose intelligence on the geography of the region—gleaned from Dako—he seems to have been using. Each stop brought surprises, such as the gift of red-painted hogs "covered with small beads passed round their necks and legs." Morrell even led a nervous single-file trek up into the heavily forested mountains, where he left beads and butter knives every hundred yards on felled trees "to attract these natives." Just why Morrell supposed butter knives would come in handy for the locals is unclear, but they attracted no one. One visit to some boiling springs resulted, Woodworth recalls bluntly, in death. His journal reverts to notes: "Boats started to visit the Boiling Spring that we saw coming in the Bay. The skirmish with the natives, their fine appearance, shields, women fight, we shot a man in a tree, their hospitality &c." Morrell's ambitions to open trade peacefully were failing. His prospecting had as yet come to nothing: no cargo and no enduring relations with any of the villages. Instead, by killing a man, he had again evoked the animosity of one group of villagers, and presumably of their trading friends, too. In desperation, he abandoned his exploration and returned to Uneapa to search for Dako.

Uneapa was barely a hundred miles away and, anchoring the ship off the island, Morrell hoisted an ensign during the daytime and a lamp at night as a signal to Dako to come aboard. But nothing happened. The following day, Woodworth and the boatswain, William Benton, took a boat to search more extensively for the missing man:

We rowed along the shore inside of the reef and continually kept hollowing for Darco, but all was of no use, he came not. We then pulled around in a bight on the north side. Here is a town and we saw a canoe but the natives were so timid that I could not get any news of Darco. One of their men came out on a Rock and told us that we could not find him here but go around to the S. West side that he lived there. I wanted to go near this man but he ran in to the bush. We then pulled along towards the west end untill our boat grounded. We then rowed here through the surf in deep watter and kept along outside of the reef. We saw the ensign hoisted as a signal for us to come aboard and at the same time a man runing and runing down the Surf to-wards us, but [Benson] wood not wait for the man and we started on board, and squared away for Bidera.

Was the figure running so urgently toward them Dako? Others in the boat wanted to stay and find out, but the boatswain refused to wait. As Woodworth put it later, he "would not stop, as he sayed, for any of the damned negroes."

With attempts to trade with the Kove having come to naught, Morrell was proving to be as bungling in his new status as pirate as he had been as captain. He was losing direction. He ordered the *Margaret Oakley* to weigh anchor and sail back to mainland New Britain, but this time to head farther west toward some of the other places Dako had told him about. At the spot where "Mohire" apparently lived, Morrell could find no anchorage and sailed on, to where the "Celingies" (now known as Kilenge) lived near the northwest point of New Britain at Cape Gloucester. By this time it was mid-December, and the northwest monsoons had begun: a season of heavy rain, high winds, and rough seas when even local sailors dared not venture into the open seas. The winds were too strong for the *Margaret Oakley* to anchor safely.

Morrell sailed on, beginning a clockwise circuit of the Bismarck Sea that would eventually lead him back to Dako's island. He made

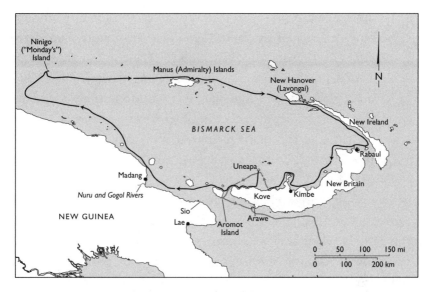

Route of the *Margaret Oakley* around the Bismarck Sea, December 1834–January 1835, and then departing to Australia via Uneapa, Aromot Island, and Arawe, January–February 1835 (map by Bill Nelson)

rapidly up the coast of New Guinea before steering east toward the Ninigo archipelago, the low-lying group of coral atolls and lagoons where Monday had been captured. Here again Morrell could not anchor safely: the weather was too unpredictable and he would have been exposed to attack. And without Monday they would have been unable to conduct trade. Morrell could only reflect on what might have been and sail on, arriving at the Manus (Admiralty) Islands on December 22.

Inhabitants of Manus were accustomed to the visitations of traders. Scrawled notes by Woodworth over the next weeks reveal that in several locations the Americans traded iron bars or hoops for pigs and shell, but that negotiations were fraught. As Woodworth describes, discerning the "going rate" of trading items was not easy:

> If you are in want of Provision the best articles are empty bottles and small beads on short strings, and for one of their bags full of cocoas give them one bottle and for 6 cocoas 1

short string of beads, and in the same ratio for Fish; and for
Hogs, 1 Piece of Bar Iron. If you give them more than above
prices for these articles you spoil the trade in buying shell. It
is well to give each individual after he has sold his shell a
small present of a Fish hook or a few Buttons or beads and tell
them that it is a present, or in other words Cow-wash. Treating them in this manner gives them a good opinion of you
and they well exert themselves to get shell for you.

The senior supercargo, Francis Babcock, went ashore on a number of
occasions, but on one at least, contact turned out to be violent—
resolved only when crew monitoring proceedings remotely by telescope from the *Margaret Oakley* ordered a cannon broadside fired in
warning.

Woodworth's journal entries covering the next three weeks are
missing, but Jacobs provided detailed descriptions of events that do
not appear to be fabricated. According to Jacobs's account, Morrell
lingered at the island of Manus, finding it rich in shell, and then
headed east to New Hanover, then down the southwest coast of New
Ireland, across Saint George's Channel, and back to the north coast
of New Britain, before approaching the familiar waters of Kove from
the east. Jacobs provides extensive accounts of their trading and skirmishes during this time, but all contact remained ephemeral.

By January 20, 1835, the Americans had more or less completed
their circuit and were approaching the volcano on the Willaumez peninsula they had left six weeks previously. Erupting now with enormous
force, its flames arced high into the night sky and lava poured down the
mountainside as a massive plume of smoke formed a "perfect column"
to the upper atmosphere, where it was pushed to one side by the winds.
In the darkness under the volcanic clouds, the Americans anchored in
the cove where they had earlier planted their garden and found that
the pumpkins were doing well but not the maize. Their previous visit
had clearly made an impression on the locals, and the garden and the
power of their iron axes seem have been the cause of some awe: "The
trees that we had felled on our cutting wood here before had aston-

ished them very much. They had hung on the stumps of each, a piece of white bark with figures and hirogliphics carracters painted on them in red paint."

The myths that helped New Britain's people place the intruders spoke of a parallel world of the dead whose inhabitants raised pigs, gardened, and hunted in much the same way as the living. Yet their pigs usually appeared as rats, rocks, or snakes to the living, and their fields and groves were similarly transfigured. Now, however, the locals were faced with an actual garden, which had not only been created with miraculous speed, but out of which had germinated a variety of hitherto unknown plants. This was the kind of hybrid place where the spirit and the physical world merged—and which might provide a portal between them. The glyphs painted on the bark were surely akin to those that are still to be found in the area inscribed on the rocks which mark such portals.

The painters of the glyphs called out to the *Margaret Oakley,* and Morrell and Woodworth rowed ashore to present them with seeds for the crops they had planted. This was all part of Morrell's emerging plan to establish a trading colony in the region. If he was unable to reap sufficient profits from this expedition alone, perhaps he could salvage some financial return from its wreckage by laying the grounds for a future venture.

CHAPTER 11

Tables Turned

ღღ

A s soon as the *Margaret Oakley* doubled the point and came into view of Kove, her crew sensed that something had changed. Canoes that would before have fled now came alongside to trade. When a canoe was hit by a heavy wave and sank, its occupants resurfaced smiling at the brig, jovially retrieved their dugout, bailed it out with shovel-like scoops, "and soon overtook us laughing at the accident as though it had not happened." In some of the other canoes Woodworth recognized familiar faces, including a "man with a sore arm" whom he had treated earlier with his Harlem Oil (treating sores having become his specialty). It was this man who revealed to Woodworth the cause of their newfound welcome: just two days previously, several canoes had arrived from Dako's island with the news that Dako had not been killed all those years ago but had returned in Morrell's ship—a ship that was now being warmly welcomed. This was the news Morrell needed, and his uplifted crew were impatient to hear more.

For several days, though, there was a frustrating silence as gales roughened the sea, grounding the Kove canoes, which had been pulled high up off the beach, and swamping the Americans' boats when they impatiently ventured out to trade. In the meantime, encounters with Kove people were now accompanied by good humor instead of mutual fear. Morrell was not only trading confidently, he was also distributing seeds and explaining through Woodworth what they were and how to plant them.

It was about six weeks since they had left Dako at Uneapa, but finally the Americans received definite news of him. They were anchored in the waters off one of the larger offshore islands and had invited its aged leader, Lewie (called "Nomer" by Jacobs), and his wife, Heydee, aboard ship. From Lewie they found out that Dako "had been here and had given the people the name of Capt. Morrell and when alongside today they wanted to see him. When they saw he was king of the God-Ship they all shouted for joy and kept continually calling for Capt. Morrell. Darco had also told them of the wonders of America which they also kept repeating."

Kove's people now reasoned that Dako had not only traveled to the parallel realm but that he had also returned safely and had even managed to strike up a close relationship with its powerful leader, Morrell. Dako would surely have described New York's brick-built houses towering several stories high, perhaps even the glistening marble of the White House. Maybe he described the horse-drawn carriages and sleighs, the experience of skating on frozen rivers and the silence of the snow, the dead forests that miraculously regrew annually with the new warmth. He must also have related tales of the human crush at the "Cannibal Show" set among the monstrous curiosities, of the circus, of the harbor, of Broadway, and of the sexual slums of the Bowery. He might also have conveyed the allure of the church and the powers it professed. He may even have brought his sketches back to Uneapa. However, there is no evidence that such descriptions disabused his Kove and Uneapa friends of their belief that he had been transported to a miraculous spirit domain. Quite the reverse: each word he uttered would only have reinforced such an interpretation. What is more, representatives of this spirit world were now visible in all their strangeness through the ship portal.

Dako had brought definitive news of the world to which the people of Uneapa would travel when death took them or, more correctly, when the ships of the dead ferried them there. Through his testimony the islanders could now derive a clearer picture of their own future.

These wonders of America did not belong to a faraway, unattainable world, but one to which all would eventually travel. Inhabitants who were drawn from the hills and surrounding villages to see the "god ship" were not simply curious about a novel sight but excited by the rarest of all phenomena—a portal to the land of the dead from which Dako had proven that it was possible to return.

That Dako could have described many of the Americans as having Melanesian-like complexions, and that several of those on board the *Margaret Oakley* (the African Americans among the crew) indeed had such complexions, only enhanced the islanders' certainty that this was a vessel that had sailed across the horizon to a land where their own ancestors were now living. Unsurprisingly, Captain Morrell—or "Cap-in Mor-el" as he was now dubbed—was fast becoming even more celebrated here than he had been in America. As news flashed though the region's extensive gifting networks, word of Cap-in Mor-el traveled far more quickly than he did, and there was no one now who would not be interested in a visit.

Dako's endorsement of them transformed the fortunes of Morrell and his crew. Some brave young islanders now wanted to board the *Margaret Oakley,* including one of Lewie's sons, Garrygarry. In an act of enormous trust Lewie even allowed his precious son to voyage with the Americans, despite panicked protestations from the boy's mother, who, as he was trying to board the brig, "got hold of his legs so tight that he could scarce get from her." Lewie gave Garrygarry a string with five knots tied in the end that indicated the five moons (months) that Morrell now promised they would be gone. He also presented Morrell with a string of beads as a pledge for the safe return of his son at the stipulated time and solicited a gift in return, which the captain was happy to offer along with other presents. Then, according to Woodworth, the old man "gave his son a great deal of advice. Finally the captain told Lewie that he would be a good father to his son, and those on the canoe then left, crying." Garrygarry's brothers paddled alongside to see him off. Even then his father and a fleet of canoes accompanied the ship out to sea, and when they could go no farther "set up such crying and lamentations, that almost brought tears in our eyes." This was clearly no ordinary departure. It was more like a funeral: Garrygarry was now embarking with Cap-in Mor-el on a voyage to the parallel world of the dead. But he was doing so voluntarily. In many eyes it must have seemed that his action was akin to suicide.

After he was aboard, the sailors had Garrygarry washed and shaved, cut his hair, and found some clothes for him. By Woodworth's account he was well contented and ate a "hearty dinner." If this was the way of death, then it could be a lot worse.

The "ship of the dead" soon arrived at Uneapa. Anxiously, the sailors again waited for a canoe to come out to greet them—and again in vain. The captain then ordered a boat ashore with Babcock "to see or hear something if possible of Darco." As he approached, some islanders waded out toward him: a good sign, since in previous attempts the Americans had hardly gotten near enough to speak to anyone. When Babcock's boat reached the beach, more islanders approached and signaled for the occupants to wait. Shortly afterward a man ran swiftly into the water whom Babcock and those watching from the ship immediately recognized as their "old friend Darco." He was naked and much thinner than when they had last seen him. But he was "hailed by three cheers from the boats crew. He soon had the hands of his old shipmates and was so overjoyed that he continued talking in his own tongue for several minutes."

Others on the island were still wary, however, and worried that if Dako were taken on board again he might never return. To allay these fears, Dako arranged for Babcock and one of the other hands to remain on the island as hostages while Dako and some of his family took the boat out to the *Margaret Oakley*. As they came alongside, Dako jumped up over the rail and on to the deck, where he was "soon in the arms of Cpt. Morrell (who stood at the Gangway to receive him) and wept like a child for several minutes and it started the tears in the Capt's eyes also." (Woodworth wrote these words in cipher: the captain's self-image was not of a man who shed tears, it would appear, let alone shed them in the arms of a naked man from a "cannibal island.") For both Morrell and Dako, however, these were tears of relief as much as camaraderie. Dako could now access the treasures he knew would flow to his island from the ship, and Morrell finally had the prospect of a successful trading venture. His decision to overrule the wishes of the supercargoes and remain in the region had been vindicated. No one would now dare accuse him of piracy. Dako's tears also presumably had an element of ritual—on Uneapa public tears and wailing were performed in honor of the living and the dead alike.

Dako was embraced by all the crew, who "wished him a hearty welcome." A further glimpse of Woodworth's own emotion can perhaps be found in his notes on the Uneapa language, in which he provides translations for "'I thought Darco you was dead' (*Gow tat tie Darco ago te matrey*); 'Where is your house?' (*Kener camea Rumacker?*), and 'I love you very much' (*Gow to logo rumebu aga kerer*)."

Dako eventually calmed down sufficiently to tell his erstwhile companions what had happened to him since they had seen him last. As Woodworth recounted in detail, on the day that Dako first returned to his people, he spent time catching up on events until "he know not how long he had been on shore." But when he prepared to return to the ship's boat waiting for him on the beach, "his friends followed after him and would not let him come." Afraid that Dako might be conveyed away from them once more, "they got around him and held on him," until eventually the boat returned to the brig. Dako later tried to return to the ship in a canoe, but again his friends detained him until at last the *Margaret Oakley* could wait no longer and set sail. "He sayed it almost broke his heart to think how disapointed we would feel at his not returning and cryed like an infant but it was to no avail, the Brig was gone and Capt. Morrel perhaps would think him treacherous."

Though Dako's thoughts then were for Morrell, his first thoughts had been for his wife, Vakale, and his young son, Tupi. And herein lay the tragedy that had kept him from the ship. Dako's wife and son are remembered on the island to this day for the grief they both bore following Dako's abduction: the tears they shed and the mourning gaze they cast over the ocean for an interminable time after his departure. When Dako described his family to Dwight in New York it is clear also that the memory of Vakale and perhaps of his other wives was sustaining him in his exile. But in his absence he knew that other suitors would tempt Vakale. It was not customary among his people for a widow to remain unmarried. Vakale had held out. But not for long enough.

Dako's father had died in his son's absence, having lost his son to Pango and his daughter-in-law to another husband, and the wars he had been waging when Dako was abducted had still not been resolved. Hostilities continued, rendering the whole island unsafe. After his initial ecstatic welcome and with the brig gone, Dako had no option but to return to island life and the new authority that was thrust upon him now he had inherited his father's mantle. Yet his treasures and riches had remained on board the ship. Dako had only fantastical memories and stories of a place beyond the horizon of the upturned bowl, as well as a knowledge of languages, manufacturing skills, and religions that lay beyond all imagination. After four years of captivity recalling island life in his dreams and to inquisitive Americans, he could not revert easily to the day-to-day life on Uneapa. He became depressed. The strong and confident man became listless and could hardly eat.

So when Morrell had returned to the island in his fruitless search for Dako six weeks before, on December 13, and Dako had spotted the boat sent looking for him, he had desperately tried to reach it. But once again he had been held back by "a great many of his people," and by the time he had broken free, the boat—under Benton's impatient command—was already departing. Dako had swum out as far as he could, but the surf on the reef was too dangerous and, as Woodworth related furiously, "The ill natured scoundrel that had command of the Boat would not stop." The ship had been almost within his grasp. Dako, abandoned, wept for an hour, and, as he related, "every night he could not help weeping."

Nevertheless, the trading season was approaching, and Dako arranged for five canoes to cross the sea to New Britain, presumably to rekindle links with his family's long-standing Kove gifting partners. When they returned he received the news that the American ship had been there, and that Morrell would return. Heartened, he and a companion had built four large trading canoes—two of which Dako claimed were as large as the *Margaret Oakley*'s long boats—and collected shell to take with them to New Britain. These canoes were now only four days away from being launched, and he had been planning to make the crossing in "half a moon."

The Americans had arrived off Uneapa at 6:00 A.M., but despite the intensity of the reunion, they were gone by midday. They had dared not disembark, let alone stay on the island. Perhaps they knew about the war raging with the easterners and feared for their safety. More likely, though, they recalled that during Morrell's earlier voyage, he had killed many of the youths from the very community in which he was now anchored—a fact that was unlikely to have been forgotten by their bereaved families.

Before they parted, Morrell and Dako agreed that the captain would return within five months, in preparation for which Dako would gather plenty of shell. Morrell also gave Dako the equipment he needed to instill calm and some authority on the island. He took Dako to his cabin and put together "a regular fit out." According to Woodworth the items included "axes of all kinds, adzes, knives, plane irons, Gumbles, Cloth, looking Glasses, Fish hooks, Beads, Pistol and all the necessary appendages as to a beautiful spear that we got in the Isle of France, Cutlasses, Orniments, seeds, Crockeryware, tin horns, and pans and cups & a great many articles too numerous to mention." Jacobs also mentions a musket, a harpoon, hatchets, a draw knife, a cleaver, bar iron and iron hoops, calico, beads, and carpenters' tools. Woodworth added: "The Capt. also put a Grind stone all ready mounted in the boat for him, when he went ashore, to finish his canoe."

This was a cargo the like of which had no precedent on Uneapa. Perhaps it also included items that Dako had acquired on his own account in the United States. His sketchbook? Swedenborgian texts? Every item was extraordinary to the islanders and could only reinforce their view that Pango and these foreign spirits were the font of all invention. All Dako could do now was give Morrell a fine hog and some coconuts and bid him good-bye until five months' time.

Meeting up with Dako had been a huge relief for the whole crew. And now, with Dako's interventions and with Garrygarry on board—the son of an influential local leader and a willing intermediary and interpreter—they were finally able to gain the extraordinary access to the region's vast trading area on which the voyage was premised. Morrell and the *Margaret Oakley* were still "Pango" as far as the people of the region were concerned, but this extraordinary spirit and its cortege, which had been so destructive, venting volcanic fire and wreaking carnage four years ago, had now become a more predictable, reciprocating moral being: of the other world, to be sure, but possibly more human, too. These beings had odd habits and powers, but they could laugh, smile, and relax; above all, Dako had managed to establish an exchange relationship with them and an enduring sense of mutual obligation.

Morrell now tried to visit as many friendly locations as possible to capitalize on this newfound goodwill, and at each he commissioned cargoes of tortoiseshell, pearl shell, and pearls for his return. Garrygarry, who spoke Uneapa, could communicate with Woodworth and Jacobs, and these two young men now applied themselves also to learning a pidgin version of Garrygarry's own Kove language, which served as a trading lingo throughout the region. But more than that, Garrygarry developed into an eager intermediary himself. He had witnessed the unprecedented display of material largess that the Americans had showered on Dako and so could report firsthand tales of their wondrous cargo. Garrygarry's word also carried special weight as he was perceived as speaking on behalf of his father, whose influence extended far. And Morrell wore Lewie's necklace, which may have been taken as a visible sign of the old man's favor.

Garrygarry took Morrell straight to the heart of the regional trading network. This was a tiny coral islet called Aromot, which lay a hundred yards off the much larger island of Umboi, located in the Vitiaz Straits between New Britain and New Guinea. Known to the Americans as Gonoro (Gonoreah), probably through a misunderstanding, Aromot had long operated as a stopover for traders between these two shores, and had become a key node for the trading networks that linked the two land masses.

Nowadays visitors have christened Aromot the "Hong Kong of the South Pacific" for its densely packed houses, but even then it was an extraordinarily bustling place. The architecture revealed the precarious nature of the inhabitants' existence. Huge tides, storm surges, and even occasional tsunamis regularly overcame the island's coral reef protection, so houses were raised on stilts four or five feet from the ground, their floor beams lashed to sturdy log uprights buried deep in the sand. However, the house walls spoke of different dangers. A single skin of vertical bamboo strips is no defense against a well-sharpened spear tipped with obsidian or cassowary bone, but with double the skin and the inner bamboo spread horizontally, as was the norm here, these raised houses became impenetrable citadels.

The *Margaret Oakley* arrived off Aromot on the evening of February 6, 1835. The change in the Americans' fortunes is made clear by the rich, detailed journal entries that Woodworth provides of their visit. As they anchored, some inhabitants welcomed them tentatively with a hog, several baskets of yams, and a few coconuts. As darkness fell, in an attempt to demonstrate their mystique and power, Morrell ordered the crew to fly the huge kite with its dangling lantern that was designed to help errant longboats find the brig at night from even a great distance. Their efforts almost stopped the islanders from approaching the ship. Early the next morning the island's leader, Mahseelow, arrived in a canoe with another hog, but his people had found the kite so alarming that he had evacuated all the women and children from the island, sending them over to the mainland before daylight, perhaps expecting a fight. This hog was an offering of peace.

Using Garrygarry as interpreter, a much-relieved Mahseelow soon invited the Americans ashore, and after breakfast Woodworth, Jacobs, the captain, and some crew bravely took up his invitation. Jacobs describes Garrygarry's importance to the Americans: "We landed, and Garry told them who we were and what we had come for." The leader ushered his visitors onto the elevated wooden stage at the town center that was used for important deliberations. Built of logs and bamboo and raised on stones and log piles, the stage was shaded by a huge tree and surrounded by a grove of coconuts, under which a vast crowd of onlookers had gathered, repeating the chant "Cap-in Mor-el."

The people of the region, despite having lost some of their trepidation, continued to regard the Americans as creatures from the white world of the dead, a misconception that Morrell and his crew did little to dispel. Although there was no merit in terrifying their potential trading partners, there were definite advantages to nurturing their own mystique—as became clear in their introductions. Translating through Woodworth and Garrygarry, Morrell had had words with Aromot's leader, who then introduced the captain to the assembled crowds. According to Jacobs (whose rendition is perhaps not entirely to be trusted), he declaimed:

> Beloved people; you have looked at Oorro (the sun) from day to day, and at Tiecoe (the moon), Maryomber (sky), and Neto-Neto (stars) from night to night, and witnessed their regular revolutions. These are all controlled by Timboca who has now come to visit you in the person of Cap-in Mor-el, who is a mighty and powerful Mahhone (king), and has come to exchange the productions of Tiecoe for those of Gonoro. He never eats his enemies, or fights, except on the defensive, and then he destroys the foe with the *ballum bally* [cannon] of Oorro!

Aromot islanders were used to relating the myth of the cosmic tree that had swayed and fallen in mythical times, its branches distributing the different specialties that each location brought to the region's trading network, thereby establishing the divine economic order. A question that seemingly vexed everyone gathered at Aromot was how the Americans fit into this economy. As Woodworth's diary puts it, after Mahseelow introduced the newcomers, he "began to name the limbs of the tree that overhung us": "he has a different name for each one." Mahseelow was presumably outlining their mythical trading geography in the hope, perhaps, of placing the visitors in the order of things. If so, his aim was lost on Morrell's company.

It was now also becoming clear to the Aromot islanders—just as it had to the people of Uneapa—that it would be possible to establish some kind of trade friendships with these spirits. Dako had probably instructed Morrell on the conventions employed in trade throughout the Vitiaz Straits region; in particular, the importance placed on delayed reciprocity (that is, giving during one encounter and then receiving in equal measure at another, sometime later). Following his introduction, Morrell began to nurture such a friendship with his host by inviting him and a few elders into his world on board the *Margaret Oakley,* where he presented Mahseelow with gifts in order to prompt eventual reciprocation. By boarding, these visitors may not have seen themselves as entering the parallel world, but in local interpretation they came close. In Woodworth's version of the visit: "The old chief accompanied us [on board], we showed him everything that we thought would please him and gave him many presents. He was very much pleased and promised to do all he could to collect shell against our return and went ashore again." Morrell's plan was starting to work; the people of Aromot had begun expanding their welcome.

During the rest of the day the *Margaret Oakley* attracted more and more attention from the myriad trading canoes that passed through Aromot on their journeys between New Guinea and New Britain, thereby spreading the word of Morrell's arrival in both directions. Having met with such a positive welcome, the captain decided to linger. Before breakfast the following day, he took a swim with Woodworth and some of the crew off an exposed reef, where they could also dig up fresh sand to clean the ship's deck. He then had paints made up, and went ashore with some of his men to paint the leader's canoes and the front of his house with their wondrous new colors— and also to daub several of the men, who particularly loved the bright, novel vermilion red.

Morrell had also brought ashore the ship's carpenter to lend a hand in boat building. The larger trading canoes used by the islanders were twin-masted and rigged like schooners. To make such craft oceanworthy, local builders raised the sides of the dugout logs that served as their hulls by lashing three-foot-high timber boards above

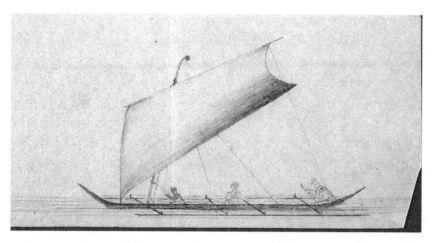

Sailing canoe presumed to be from Aromot Island. Sketch by Selim Woodworth (reproduced by permission of the Huntington Library, San Marino, California)

them, and sealing the joints. To their sterns, they lashed wide covered railed decks, which projected out over the sea on either side. Steered with a large paddle for a rudder and stabilized by outriggers, these were the vessels that enabled Aromot's people to trade across the straits between New Guinea and New Britain. The islanders were astonished at the power of the carpenter's drill as he shaved out the holes necessary to lash the raised side planks to the dugout hulls. It accomplished in seconds something that would have taken a local man hours to carve with shell and stone tools.

Now the captain was again called to the council stage, leaving Woodworth and Jacobs to wander off on their own. They came across the house-of-respect, beautifully built out of round logs and thatched with coconut and palm leaves. They entered to find it "very pretty . . . being carved and painted." In the center lay what they took to be the chief's rough bed, built of small poles. Although the building's walls were quite low, the roof towered up some twenty-five feet, and the two huge pillars that supported the ridgepole were lovingly carved with fish, snakes, lizards, and crocodiles, and painted "in all of the variety of collors possible." The ridgepole itself was also carved and colored to resemble a crocodile.

As the two rummaged in the darkness, behind a screen partition they discovered the embalmed body of a child, wrapped in leaves and lying on a bed of sticks, with a solitary living cockatoo watching over it, attached by a cord. The young Americans had no idea of the body's significance but continued their search for other novelties, including an impressive array of fishing nets and some old baskets hanging from the roof which "appeared to be done up very attentively." But the bird must have spoken of their presence, for just as they were opening one of the baskets, a guard discovered them. "He appeared quite astonished at finding any one in here, as he was left as sentry to prevent intruders, but was not near when we went in. As soon as he saw what we were about he ordered us out of the place, and was quite offended at our taking such liberties with things they hold in such awe. He was soon passified, when he explained to us that they were heads of deaseased Kings. They were embalmed in vessels of wood and sealed up tight and suspended in these baskets to prevent I suppose the rats from devouring them." What the guard would have made of these two young living dead caught in the act of unpacking the embalmed skull of a venerated leader can only be imagined.

This elaborate house-of-respect was decorated with designs that had turned it into a place explicitly devoted to communicating with the ancestral world. Given the sacred and secret musical and ritual instruments it contained, which gave access to the powers of the other world, entry to the house was strictly regulated; any woman found to have entered might have been put to death. But once the bemused guard had overcome his shock, he allowed the two intruders to go on their way. Jacobs and Woodworth had surely stepped into several such empty houses in the previous weeks while exploring villages that had been deserted on their arrival, and so were used to defiling the sacred. Yet in every defiling act, unknown to them, the young men, as revelations of the spirit order, were reshaping local knowledge of it.

Not overly perturbed by being discovered and oblivious to the magnitude of their transgression, the two continued their explorations on the island, eventually being conveyed by dugout over to the mainland to inspect the yam and sweet potato plantings there, and the tobacco gardens which supplied the locals with their rough cigars.

Morrell, meanwhile, had sent the ship's boat and a diver on an unsuccessful errand to prospect the lagoon off the island for pearl shell. As he toured the island, the inhabitants continued to chant his name. In local dialects, "Cap-in Mor-el" was beginning to sound suspiciously like either "Kapi Molo," or "Moro," the names of powerful creators revered locally. Just as in Uneapa, where the captain had become woven into local mythology as Pango, so here perhaps some were conceiving of him as an apparition of Kapimolo, their mythical ancestor—a human who was perceived as a progenitor of the economic and social order. And if Morrell were Kapimolo, then might those close to him—Woodworth and Jacobs—be his children, they wondered. By which local marriage? With which local wife? Just whom might these apparitions be related to?

It was such questions that were surely vexing the islanders as the Americans weighed anchor the next day, having been showered with gifts of a sow, plantains, coconuts, yams, and sugar cane. Theirs had been an unhurried departure—after a good swim and the daubing of another of the island's canoes, Woodworth had had time to present the old leader with some Harlem Oil and a bottle of Dr. Lee's Patented "Billious Pills." Morrell had not acquired much tortoiseshell at Aromot, but he had traded for a couple of good pearls and, most important, the islanders had agreed to build up a cargo of shell and pearl to await his return later in the year.

By now Morrell had left commissions for cargoes at several locations around the Bismarck Sea. Since other Western ships rarely entered these waters, and since he had now set up a number of personal reciprocal arrangements, he had effectively built himself a nice little monopoly. The captain's extraordinary capacity to fall into disaster was thus, as ever, matched by his equally extraordinary capacity to clamber out of it. Moreover, just as the words of Samuel Woodworth back in New York had transformed Morrell's callous deceit into heroic celebrity throughout Europe and America, so now the oral traditions

of the Bismarck Sea were reconstruing his actions of sheer acquisi-
tiveness as heroic generosity.

With his future cargoes assured, and any accusation of piracy cir-
cumvented, Morrell could now put his mind to restocking and refitting the *Margaret Oakley*—long overdue after five months at sea without
touching port. He set his sights on Port Jackson (Sydney Harbour) in
Australia, but he was in no particular hurry. Still with Garrygarry
aboard, he wanted to prospect for further trading opportunities en
route.

His first stop was a group of islands called Arawe, at the extreme
southwest of New Britain, but even with Garrygarry's assistance, making contact with the inhabitants was impossible. At this point Selim
Woodworth's journal for the first time reveals that some of the crew
were falling sick, including Woodworth himself. Until then, the visitors' reactions to the heat, humidity, mosquitoes, and sand flies, and
the ill health associated with all these, had remained remarkably absent from his journal. The ailing Woodworth now confided that he
felt too ill to accompany an interior trek that Morrell undertook, although he nevertheless reported on it. Every village the Americans
passed through was deserted. According to Woodworth, the captain
"saw in one house 8 baked human heads strung on a pole." They understood these to be "trophies of war; the heads are of their enemies."
Over the next days, Morrell led a number of similar expeditions,
stealing five of the heads, which would sell well in New York and
Philadelphia. These were the rare skulls of South Sea islanders that in
the hands of Samuel Morton and others would illuminate God's creative intent and the number of naked and languishing Adams Michelangelo should have daubed in God's act of creation on the ceiling of
the Sistine Chapel, as well as how many Eves God should be nurturing under his arm.

The captain also purloined some of the large wooden shields
painted with the baffling swirls that are characteristic of this region's
artwork, but by now he understood local customs sufficiently to leave
axes, beads, and knives in hopeful exchange for them. Some of these
deserted villages had enormous defenses. One where the Americans

stopped, up on a hill, could only be entered by two small gates built into a stockade wall about ten feet high. Within stood a tower about twenty feet high, and "on the top there [was] a large pile of stones which the natives ha[d] to defend their village." Despite such defenses, the Americans had walked right in, to a deserted silence.

The crew could no longer hope to establish trading contacts, for they had moved out of the Vitiaz trading area where Garrygarry could translate. Even so, they landed at every opportunity and took whatever they could, especially the skulls "to be seen in every house," as well as all the spears, war clubs, and other objects they could manage.

During the voyage south and east along the southern shores of New Britain the *Margaret Oakley* was occasionally attacked by canoes, which the sailors usually repulsed with small arms. But on one notable occasion, the Americans killed two men and wounded six. They picked up three of the injured men and a boy, whom the mate Benton promptly "struck in the head with a cutlass, wounding him severely." Woodworth was clearly angry at such unnecessary violence and reports the incident in cipher. Reverting to plain text he wrote on:

> When we got the natives on board they were unable to speak for terror thinking that we were agoing to kill them. They proved to be enemies of our Garry's people and as soon as he found it out he dispoiled them of their orniments as trophes of war and also wanted to kill them but the Capt. would not permit him. . . . We took them all below and dresed their wounds, the little Boys head was shaved and washed and sowed up, the wound was very deep quite to the skull and about 3½ inches long fore and aft his head. The little fellow was not more than 11 or 12 years old but stood it like a man without uttering a groan or showing the least sign of fear. One of the men had buck shot in the left elbow and bled profusely. We could feel the shot but it was so painful to the man that I bound it up without extracting them; another of them had one ball in his back just below his left shoulder blade. We could not feel it any were near the wound and bound it up.

He had also one in his left arm. He did not appear to feel it; another had been shot in the fore part of his head, the ball had entered the forehead just above the right eye and had come out just in the edge of his hair. The same man had a ball in the top of his head, between the scalp and skull. . . . We had no instruments to extract the balls, so we done them up without. The Capt. then gave each of them a number of presents and put them all in their canoe which we picked up and sent them ashore. Two of them was able to paddle so they made out to get on shore with the determination never to try the like to another vessel.

Compare this journal entry to the sanitized version that made it into print from Jacobs, who clearly knew the mortal implications of leaving shot to fester in a wound:

We probed the wounds, extracted the balls, scarified them with the bistoury, and dressed them in the best manner we knew how, with adhesive plasters, lint, opium, and basilicon. Then we placed the natives in their canoe, presented them handsome colored engravings, iron, beads, and mirrors, and told them that they were free. Heretofore they had remained as unmoved as statues; but, at this exhibition of our kindness and generosity, their feelings overcame them, and with tears they invited us to come on shore, and, promising not to attack us again, they paddled away.

The Americans now left New Britain for Australia, but wherever possible as they voyaged south past Bougainville and the Solomon Islands, they solicited shells, food, and local tools such as spears, paddles, and war clubs from the canoes that approached them, acquiring these over the side of the boat in exchange for cutlery, beads, bottles, and the like. Morrell and the supercargoes permitted all the ship's crew and officers to trade for these items on their own account, each packing his curiosities into his own secure wooden chest in the hope of selling them in Port Jackson or freighting them home from there.

There were further violent incidents. On March 1, for example, the captain led a volley of musketry that shot and killed a visitor who had started for their canoe with an ax. Once out of the Bismarck Sea, the "god ship" had definitely reverted to devilish type, with Garrygarry an apprentice like the rest. The gratuitous violence that boatswain Benson doled out with racist pleasure was surely stirred by his own lowly place in the line of command, but it accorded with the attitudes of southern slaveholders. Woodworth hated Benton—not only because he had ignored Dako when he had swum after them, but also for the way that he lorded it over Jacobs in the forecastle. Woodworth was probably not alone in his hatred—the African American cooks, Verae and Luff, must also have shared his feelings. Yet all were desperate to earn something out of the voyage beyond their meager salaries—and if that meant snatching what they could from the "cannibal islands," then so be it.

CHAPTER 12

Sydney Respite

ක

The *Margaret Oakley* passed the lighthouse on South Sydney Head, reaching Sydney Harbour (Port Jackson) on Monday, April 13, 1835. This British colony in Australia had been born indirectly of the American Revolution, which had ended the transportation to America of British convicts, who had until then been sold to the plantations in Virginia at twenty dollars a head. With America off-limits, British prisons began to fill up. A solution was found after three convict ships made it to Australia—first to Botany Bay and then to Port Jackson, arriving in 1788 to establish the British Penal Colony. The invading colonists also introduced smallpox, which killed more than half the indigenous population, and then they displaced the rest. By the time of Morrell's arrival the colony's settler population had swelled to eighty thousand, and Sydney, its capital, was a city of some fifteen thousand.

As the brig approached the harbor, the coast appeared as an unbroken line of precipitous sandstone cliffs. These took the full force of the huge Pacific waves that the ship had been riding for about seven weeks, and which sent a dense spray up to the cliff tops hundreds of feet above it. Even though the harbor entrance was two miles wide, it was well concealed by nature, though marked by the beckoning lighthouse. To the crew of the *Margaret Oakley* entering the harbor for the first time, its tranquillity would have been palpable, calm as a lake, vast

and secure. The town of Sydney itself lay on a hilly peninsula between two of the bay's innumerable coves and inlets.

The *Margaret Oakley* was the finest vessel that had been seen in
Sydney for some time—well manned, well armed, and remarkably
fast. Customs officials checked her cargo of tortoiseshell, curiosities,
and so on, but the Americans had little to show for their trading: just
238 pounds of tortoiseshell, a cask of whale teeth, and twenty bottles
of the pungent and medicinal cajuput oil (Tiger Balm) that they had
picked up en route to Dako's island in modern-day Indonesia. How
much of the cargo that was unloaded at the portside for customs inspection was actually sold is uncertain, but local newspaper reports of
the time reveal what else the *Margaret Oakley* was still carrying: 130
kegs of gunpowder, 200 pounds of shot, one case of bullet molds, one
keg of lead, two cases of fouling guns, nine cases of muskets, three cases
of tinware, sixteen cases of cutlery, one case of fishhooks, three cases of
mirrors, three crates of crockery, and quantities of nails, iron pots, whaling gear, iron hoops, cauldrons for boiling sea cucumbers, saws, and a
case of prints and glass beads.

One reason Morrell made for Sydney was cockroaches. His ship's
holds and cargo had become infested with the worst variety, which
they had picked up in Mauritius along with the usual rats. After anchoring, he immediately arranged for the cargo to be discharged and
the vessel to be smoked thoroughly with charcoal, sulfur, and mercury. The crew also cleaned the brig from stem to stern and gave her
a coat of fresh paint.

Removed from the rest of the "civilized" world by two very
large oceans, and reliant on passing ships for news from elsewhere,
local newspaper reporters were a little disappointed—and somewhat
astonished—that the *Margaret Oakley* had "seen but one vessel since
she left New York and brings no ship news." However, they still described her as "the admiration of everyone who has had the pleasure
of going on board, both on account of her build, and the exquisite
neatness of her trim." The papers were also alert to the size of her
crew—forty men (many more than was usual for a trader)—and the
caliber of her guns for "protecting the vessel from any attacks from

the natives of the South Sea Islands where she is bound for trading purposes."

Morrell was back in a land where his book had already brought him celebrity. The Australian papers soon found out that he was the Morrell who had "once been attacked, losing many of his crew," and had written the book from which they had published the more melodramatic extracts. An Australian whaling captain named Russell was happy to confirm Morrell's veracity, having himself touched at "Massacre Island" soon after Morrell and seen the remains of his tree fortress. Sydney's papers were also full of praise for Morrell's literary skills, placing him "at once amongst the writers of the modern school of nautical literature." His *Voyages* had, they said, caused "some sensation" in England. The first copy that reached London from New York had been ordered by a Mr. Barrow, secretary of the admiralty, no less. It was an honor indeed for the colonists in this remote outpost of empire to have the celebrated American navigator and writer among them.

Morrell's arrival happened to coincide with the first ever Saint George's Day celebration in Sydney. Australians of Irish origin had long held dinners to celebrate Saint Patrick's Day and the Scots Saint Andrew's Day, but even after forty-seven years there had been hardly enough English unity to organize a Saint George's Day bash. Morrell was invited to represent the United States at the inaugural dinner on the evening of April 24, 1835, along with the governor, the colonial secretary, and about a hundred other dignitaries at the most splendid feast the colony had ever seen. As the guests raised their glasses for toast after toast, one was eventually offered to "Captain Morrell and the American Navy." It was cheered with "three times three." Morrell then returned the compliment with a toast to "England and America, the friends of the brave and patterns of humanity"—which may have left the audience rather flummoxed.

During his month in Sydney, Morrell found himself in the newspapers on many occasions. In one instance he assured a journalist that with a select cargo worth twenty thousand dollars he could realize four hundred thousand in two or three years on his current ventures. This was relished by the town's journalists, who desperately wanted it to be true. They had heard such claims before but were "happy that the same views are entertained by the writer of the narrative, whose competency to judge upon the point is wholly undisputed." In reality, however, having been away for over a year, Morrell had so far managed to acquire only about a thousand dollars' worth of shell. Other much more successful Pacific traders were in port, including the Irish captain Peter Dillon, whose *Narrative and Successful Result of a Voyage* had far eclipsed Morrell's *Voyages* in significance and whose discovery in 1826 of the wreck of the French expedition commanded by the comte de La Pérouse had led to his being fêted by the grateful French government—which also paid him a handsome pension for life. As Morrell learned, the same generous pension was due to anyone who brought news of any survivors of La Pérouse's shipwrecks—an opportunity he would keep in mind.

Architecturally, Sydney at the time was much like New York had been sixty years earlier: a mix of original wooden buildings laid out in rather haphazard streets and more recent prosperous brick and stone constructions organized within a grid of blocks. The Broadway of Sydney was George Street. Lined with shops, it also counted the theater, the jail, the barracks, and the market among its attractions. Wagons laden with wood and provisions made their way into town along the unpaved and rutted roads leading to the center. Rather than the slaves who had built eighteenth-century New York, however, it was convicts, dressed in yellow trousers and blue or red shirts, who laid out Sydney's roads, fired its bricks, quarried its stones, tended its crops, cut its fuel, and built the town. Convicts also refitted the whaling and trading boats for the profit of the owners of the wharfs which lined the next cove. Some convicts were managed by the colony, but others were "apprenticed"—sold almost as slaves—to the free farmers and mechanics who had sailed out to Australia to make a new beginning or who had served out their own time and now become citizens.

For Garrygarry the visit to Australia was extraordinary—as it was supposed to be. Morrell hoped that a brush with modernity would make the lad an even more helpful intermediary. Morrell had no interest in launching Garrygarry in a new "Cannibal Show": there was no market for one. "Melanesians" were nothing new here, having frequently shipped to the city on the whaling vessels that used to hire or kidnap them for work on board. Sydney was also an entrepôt for the dried, tattooed Maori heads and other curiosities that found their way to the world's museums. In any case, for Morrell Garrygarry was not an anonymous savage but his ally and the wellspring of his future success, with whom he could communicate through Jacobs and Woodworth.

It was they, then, who were deputized to look after Garrygarry. The two decided to dress him up in a suit of the captain's old clothes, with stockings and slippers to match and a white beaver hat, and took him ashore to see "the wonders of the moon"—one of the locations of the parallel world, according to Garrgarry's sacred geography. Garrygarry was amazed at the shops, taking a full half hour in one to examine each object, while Jacobs and Woodworth waited patiently for him out in the street. He also inspected closely the novel fish at the fishmonger's, and was particularly taken with a pile of bricks, treasuring in particular one that he began carrying around with him after he realized that four-story houses could be built of such materials. On an excursion out of town he was just as impressed by plows, wheeled carts, and a wheelbarrow. A man on horseback and a pony and trap proved equally stunning to a youth for whom the largest land animals previously encountered had been hogs, dogs, and cassowaries. Jacobs also describes Garrygarry's amazement at the sight of cows, though he thought their milk somewhat inferior to the coconut variety.

On the evening of April 23, the Americans took Garrygarry to see a double bill at the Theatre Royal, taking in August von Kotzebue's pioneering melodrama *The Stranger,* translated from the German, and a comedy classic, *Raising the Wind.* But plays were not all he would have seen at the theater. Much like in the Bowery in New York, sex also featured prominently. Australia was already home to horseracing, cricket, regattas, and theater, but, despite the delights of each, these were also all fronts for the gambling, drinking, and sex work for which Sydney was famous. In this new colony, men hugely outnumbered women. Many male convicts who escaped—or were freed—took up with aboriginal women, and, as in all frontier towns, there was a ready market for paid sex. Sydney was a city of brothels, with the theater at its heart. Respectable people shunned the Theatre Royal. As one gentleman put it: "If there is little reason to consider the theatre as a school of virtue in England, there is no reason whatever for regarding it in that light in New South Wales." Reviews of the performances Garrygarry attended suggest that although audiences were somewhat thin, those who came were kept in a continual roar of laughter by the performance of "Mr Simmons as Jeremy Diddle," whose amorous intentions toward an heiress and her fortune went badly wrong in a mix-up with a maid. Jacobs and Woodworth had some trouble keeping Garrygarry still during the play and occasionally had to restrain him from making loud remarks. By way of contrast, on the following Sunday the two young men took the islander to church. When the parson started to pray, Garrygarry sat bolt upright and "laughed at the audience," whereupon Jacobs was obliged to push him down into a praying attitude. Beyond the occasional onboard prayer session, this was Garrygarry's first brush with Christianity, which must have seemed strangely inconsistent with the debauched revelry of the theater.

It was mid-April, and the Australian winter was approaching. The crew now resorted to woolen clothing and shoes. Shoes, however, "gave us no little pain; we had gone barefooted so long that all our shoes were too small for us." For Garrygarry, too, Australia was not all amusement and pleasure. First he had run out of betel nuts, to which he was surely addicted, and then he fell ill, troubled first by chilblains and then by a bad cold—which "was a thing entirely beyond his understanding; for he had never been affected with such a thing during his whole lifetime."

As for Morrell, his mistreatment of his young assistant supercargo, Algernon Jarvis, had paid off. Jarvis left the ship in Australia, sailing directly to the United States at the first opportunity aboard the wool-trading vessel the *Black Warrior*. Many years later Jarvis looked back on his time on the *Margaret Oakley* almost nostalgically, recounting with pride the story of how Morrell had named "Jarvis Island" after him—despite its being far from their route and already so named by

1821. The departure of the supercargo meant that Jacobs could return to the officers' quarters and share his cabin with Woodworth again. The two studied navigation together and drew up charts under the direction of the captain. Morrell also acquired two new crew who hailed from the more frequented regions of the Pacific: "Jack" Woahoo (Oahoo) from Hawaii and "Tomme" (John Otahitia) from Tahiti. Each man had had the ill luck to be captured, drunk, on his respective island by crews of whalers who had then abandoned their captives in Sydney. If we can take Jacobs's word, these two risked shipping with Morrell in the hope of meeting with vessels bound for their homes.

After three weeks in Australia, having taken on new provisions of salt beef, ship's biscuit, and dried fruit, the *Margaret Oakley* made ready to sail. Morrell also stocked up at private horticultural gardens on seeds and grapevines that he wanted to test in Uneapa and New Britain. The brig weighed anchor and made directly for New Britain. It had taken her crew seven weeks to prospect their way down to Australia, but they managed to return to Aromot Island in just under five, arriving there on about June 3.

The Woodworth family archives hold no journal sections for this next period, and it becomes harder to distinguish events as they actually unfolded from the imaginative interpretation of the voyage that eventually appeared in Jacobs's book. There exists, however, an extraordinary manuscript account documenting "commercial intelligence" written by Selim Woodworth which provides an account of an annual oyster-gathering festival that took place at Aromot—renowned all over New Britain and nearby islands for its large white pearl shells. This festival drew people from the entire region. That the Americans were permitted to join in reveals the warmth with which they were now regarded.

Woodworth describes the scene: the political leaders and their best divers from all along the northern shore of west New Britain sailed in for the festival, arriving from Kove (Tanta-mile-e-lew-eys) at the "east end," from Kilenge (Celingies) to the west, and from the

"Noris-ies," presumably between the two. The pearl divers were all women, as it was believed that men could not find the shell, and "the gift of seeing it is only bestowed on the women." Woodworth was a little skeptical of the explanation, attributing this division of labor rather to the men's laziness, but such diving—free diving to almost a hundred feet—was (and remains) quintessentially a girls' and women's specialty in the region and enwrapped in lore.

Woodworth joined one of the diving canoes which gathered in large flotillas of fifty or more, and set off in the calm of the early morning for the pearl grounds located on an extensive reef some distance off the island. When all the chiefs were ready to send down their divers, the master of ceremonies blew on a large conch, signaling the women to dive in unison. Amid the howling of conches, the beat of drums, and the shouts of children, each diver, armed with a basket in one hand and "sinking stones" in the other, swam down to the reef, transferring her stones to the basket as she went to help with her descent. As soon as the divers had disappeared beneath the surface, the tumult stopped. Dead silence followed as the whole fleet and Woodworth waited in anxious expectation of the divers' success.

Soon the silence was interrupted, perhaps by the return of a short-winded woman who had been unable to remain down long or—better—by one who had filled her bag and released her sinking stones. After the first simultaneous dive, each diver would return to the reef in her own time. If she was lucky and returned to the surface with shells, her team would "set up another shouting and blowing while those that has had no luck remain silent." This continued for two or three hours, until the master of ceremonies struck his outrigger with a paddle to signal the end of the competition. The flotilla of canoes then headed to shore, "voices keeping time with their paddles and the women and children shouting at an unfortunate fisher as they pass his canoe."

Back on shore, the men took charge of the oysters, carrying them to the town's raised stage while the women dispersed to prepare a lavish feast. This was accompanied by dancing and singing, although the elders of the island and the assembled chiefs "never join in these sports." Instead they retired to the council stage to talk over weighty affairs while the young people partied in the chief's large hall. The inhabitants of Aromot tried to entertain their visitors, and Woodworth describes the women as the "Bells of the Evening." The festival continued until near dawn, but even as guests retired to sleep "they [were] often interrupted by the women that [were] continually serving out some refreshments to their visitors."

The movements of the *Margaret Oakley* between her arrival at Aromot on about June 3 and her departure from the region on about July 21 are hard to figure out. The main source is Jacobs's book, which is not to be entirely trusted about either the nature or the chronology of events. According to Jacobs, the Americans stayed at Aromot for only a day before taking Garrygarry back to Kove, where they stayed for a little over a week, then spent three or four nights with Dako on Uneapa. They then sailed to the Manus (Admiralty) Islands, where they traded and explored for almost three weeks. Afterward, they returned for one last short visit to Uneapa and another to Kove before heading away from the region. All in, Jacobs's descriptions account for just over five weeks, and taking into consideration nights and days spent voyaging between these places, his timings more or less work.

The warm welcome the Americans received when they returned to Aromot appears to have been reproduced at every destination, although Jacobs's account of Garrygarry's return to Kove is not completely credible. According to Jacobs, Garrygarry's father had died while he had been away, and his people were attributing his demise to Morrell. They were therefore astonished to see the captain turn up with Garrygarry, whom they had come to accept would not be returning from the dead. According to this account, Garrygarry was installed as leader of his people in an elaborate ceremony which bears several resemblances to Woodworth's account of the Americans' reception at Aromot. If Jacobs's version of events is true, it was unlike anything that has been recorded in the region since.

More credible are Jacobs's accounts of cassowary hunting in the grass fields of the interior. Standing four feet high, but bouncing higher when running at speed, these flightless, emu-like birds were prized by Kove people: their feathers were used as head regalia, their beaks as charms, their quills as an export for Uneapa's marriage currency, and their bones as spear tips. Wild cassowaries can be ferocious, using their horny projecting foreheads to deliver a mighty head-butt and the dagger-like claw on their inner toe in a murderous slash. Jacobs accurately described beaters driving them over interior grasslands, known locally as Kunai, toward a line of men armed with spears (in his case a musket). Although New Britain's vegetation is essentially forest, Jacobs's description of the hunt is supported not only by Woodworth's sketch map, which shows rolling hills, on which he drew a cassowary feather, but also by his journal, which describes "the Ostrich planes so called from its being the principal grounds that the natives hunt these Birds." Grass plains can result from the fire and ash of volcanic eruptions, and similar grass plains can be found today.

It is credible, too, that by now Woodworth and Jacobs had acquired a fairly good knowledge of the local pidgin from Garrygarry. Once ashore, Jacobs continued his study: "I quartered myself with the family of a friendly chief, and endeavoured to learn all of the language that I could, and so did W[oodworth]. . . . We picked up many words, particularly names of things, from the children who came to play with us, and examine our hair and try to wash off the 'white paint' upon our bodies, so as to make us the same color as themselves."

Morrell's "ship of the dead" was by now freely circulating in these seas, and he could count on a welcome at every anchorage. Unfortunately for Morrell, however, the treasures promised him at each stopping point turned out to be meager, nowhere near satisfying the requirements of the remaining supercargo, Babcock. The Vitiaz trading network into which he had inserted himself was simply not as rich in shell, pearl, and the like as he had assumed it would be. Now Morrell would have to look for more lucrative sources of revenue: sandalwood or even gold.

CHAPTER 13

Dako's Dominion

ιΟ

The cargo that Dako received from Morrell before the *Margaret Oakley* upped anchor for Australia transformed his life. His
return from an epic journey with these treasures recalled stories on the island of another man who had entered the world of the
dead through the cave portal in Garove and had also returned with
miraculous provisions. But Dako had arrived with many more otherworldly things than had ever come through that cave—adding to the
islanders' perception of him as strangely gifted. Moreover, the route
through the Garove cave portal had become blocked deep in mythical time, but now Dako had found an alternative, far more rewarding
entrance via Morrell's ship. And that ship would come again. Dako
had managed to do what had only been spoken of before: establish an
enduring gifting relationship with the dead. Humans had entered a
new era.

To this day Dako's descendants recall the bewildering things he
acquired: "When the time came for him to return they filled up a
box for him. It was really full. There were all kinds of things: waist-
cloths, trousers, beads, all kinds of things for decorating the body, all
kinds of paint—red, white, green—they placed inside. They took this
man that they had captured, and when it was time for him to go, they
filled this great box. It was two feet high. They gave him all these
good things—beads, a belt, and other things—and they took him

back. They gave him a shotgun and cartridges and some blades and brought him back." Modern islanders recall in particular the returning hero's musket: the power it gave him and the fear it instilled. He "stood up and began to shoot pigs. When he shot the pigs, everyone fell down for no good reason. They thought they would all die from the gun. They all fell down and lay there." In keeping with tradition— and as told in other stories about those who had returned from the reefs of the dead—Dako set about distributing his newly acquired gifts, in particular snippets of beautiful colored calico. Recipients likened their gifts to flowers: "When Dako came back he showed all the things he got from the white people. Clothes for example. People divided the clothes into little pieces and shared them out. They made them into decorations. Like flowers. They weren't for covering the body. No, they had nice colours. They were beautiful things." Dako had also solicited from Morrell paints in novel colors, especially some prized greens, that he knew would amaze his fellow islanders.

Having learned the potency of gifts and weaponry from his father, and now armed with prodigious quantities of both, Dako turned to transforming the political landscape of his island. He and his people not only possessed the material forces of power—guns, cutlasses, lances, and the like—but also the enduring relationship with the parallel world that supplied them. This added a certain invincibility. When the Americans returned to Uneapa after their Australian respite, they found that the war between eastern and western Uneapa was over. Those who "fell down and lay there" before Dako included not only his own people, cowed by his weaponry and his fury at losing his wife to another man, but also their long-standing enemies from the eastern mountains. As Jacobs notes, it was primarily the muskets that had had such a dramatic effect: "He had terrified the mountaineers into submission by the thunder which he seemed to draw from the clouds with his fire-arms, and had restored his people to peace and happiness."

Those who had lain down before Dako determined to find him a new wife. As it is now recalled, they got up and "began to talk softly: 'What are we going to do about this man here? He is going to kill someone because of this.' So now they were all scared. They were frightened of Dako's pandianga [gun]. They all trembled and later they gave him a young woman." His new bride was named Takari. As his descendants relate: "Takari had children by him and our lineage descends from this family." By the time the Americans had returned, Dako had not one but two new wives and a homestead in the hills near the border between east and west. Perhaps having ancestors from both sides of the political divide made him well placed to create the conditions for lasting peace.

It was not just Dako's relationships on the island that had changed, however. When Morrell had first pulled him out of the sea, Dako had become his captive and slave. In America, as Dako learned English, he became aware that Morrell's future depended on him, just as much as he depended on Morrell, and their relationship had become more balanced. Dako had been able to explore New York City and its factories, churches, and schools as a free man and to count among his visitors and friends some of the most radical scholars of the United States. On the voyage home, Dako's authority and command had increased. He had sailed in the cabin with the officers, rather than before the mast with the crew; he had been given the freedom of the boat and had become Woodworth and Jacobs's teacher, initiating the young men in new ways of looking at the world which had transformed their lives and desires. After he was back in his home waters, however, his relationship with Morrell had changed again. His disappearance had reinforced his awareness of the captain's dependence on him. With Dako missing, Morrell had made some reckless decisions, which threatened to transform him in the public mind from hero to outlaw. Although they were not to know it, by preventing him from returning to the ship Dako's friends had empowered him still further in his relationship with his erstwhile captor. It was only when Dako broke his silence, contacted Morrell, and helped him with his trade that the captain's future had started to look more secure—and the threat of outlaw status was lifted on the back of potential economic success. Now Dako was engaging with Morrell not only on his own terms but in an exchange relationship in which he was firmly in control.

With the *Margaret Oakley* anchored safely within Uneapa's fringing reef, her crew were finally assured of a welcome ashore, and they took full advantage, sporting with the islanders on the beach and visiting their houses. Women and children came to look at the ship, too, clambering on board, astounded at all they saw. They began using her bowsprit rigging as a diving board. Some women, we can presume, also discovered that the newcomers were not quite as dead as they had first supposed. Jacobs insinuates in several passages that island women had sexual relations with the sailors. But sex, or even marriage, with the dead would not have posed an insurmountable conceptual problem for the islanders. Local mythology often describes marriages between humans and vuvumu—and the many new technologies, skills, and ideas that derive from such connections. Societies of the dead, as the islanders understood it, are much like those of the living. In deep time, such liaisons were said to have been far more common and links between the living and the dead more frequent. Only later had the parallel worlds of true humans and spirits become so divided, and after a few generations the spirit blood running in true human veins had been watered down. The new order brought by Morrell and Dako was, in many ways, simply a return to a mythical older one.

Woodworth enjoyed playing up his miraculous powers. On one occasion on the mainland of New Britain he put on quite a performance at his beachside clinic. He first delineated a curing "space" on the dry upper beach by marking a circle in the sand and told the patients and the onlookers pressing in, with mothers holding up their children to get a better view, to stand outside it. He then filled up the sand groove with gunpowder. Next to the medicine chest in the center of the circle, he also prepared a large rocket flare and a "blue light" on a pike. The rockets were usually used as signals from the ship, while the blue light was a naval flare that could be seen for miles and was used to orient lost boats at night. At dusk, when the healing session was done, Jacobs described how Woodworth fired the rocket and lit the blue light and gunpowder circle, which combined to cast "an unearthly glare in the dark green foliage of the forest"—and entertain as well as terrify the crowd.

Soon after they arrived, Dako took Jacobs and Woodworth up to the new house that he had built on the southern slope of Mount Kumbu, with sweeping views of the verdant valley, the breakers on the reef, and the huge sea and horizon. Here he introduced his two young friends to "his two wives," who "had fallen in love with Darco since his return." Dako had decorated his house with American-style fretwork and surrounded it with a suburban garden, laid out with coral sand paths and bamboo fences, where he now carefully planted the grapevines and peach and other trees which Morrell had brought him from Australia. So much did he treasure these new plants that he assigned four people to carry them to his garden. Inside his house Dako had hung up his clothes and gun as if they were museum curiosities that visitors could contemplate as protective armor and sources of power. One islander had apparently asked Dako to show him how the musket worked. Rather than refuse, Dako had overloaded it so that the recoil would inflict a severe blow. This, Jacobs wrote, deterred the rest of them from "aping the thunder of heaven." The gun was soon treated with fear and reverence, as none but Dako could work it.

Woodworth and Jacobs also discussed his future with Dako. They asked him to return to New York, but he declined. He was happier on his island, he said, "where people no want money to get married and support a family." Rather, according to Jacobs, Dako encouraged the young men to remain on the island. Indeed, Jacobs describes Dako's close friend Ragotur insinuating that Jacobs should marry Ragotur's fifteen-year-old daughter Tewatse, whom he knowingly left in Jacobs's company while he was staying at Dako's house one night. In the evening as they discussed the subject around the flickering red light of a flaming candle spiked on a spear, both Ragotur and Dako urged Jacobs to marry and settle on Uneapa: "Darco told me how much happier I could live here than in a cold, dreary country, where the wants are many and but ill supplied, and where the people cut each other's throats to obtain money, or commit suicide for the want of it." Dako also promised to build for Jacobs a "fine house upon the opposite side of the glen," while Tewatse promised she would keep

Thomas Jefferson Jacobs on Uneapa, from Jacobs, *Scenes, Incidents, and Adventures in the Pacific Ocean,* 276

the house and garden, make the mats, and cook the food. Her entreaties were unlikely to win Jacobs's particular heart.

While they were in the hills, Dako told the two young men a curious story that had been passed down the generations and which both Jacobs and Woodworth believed to be founded upon fact, even if it had been distorted with the retelling. It was the account of the island's evacuation following an apparition of Pango. Tantalizingly, it seemed to relate to an earlier European visit to the island. In Dako's rendition, according to Jacobs—who claims to have taken great efforts to transcribe it accurately—Pango visited Uneapa "a long time ago, or, in Darco's broken English, 'too much a moon,' before he was born." There was a mighty tempest, accompanied by an earthquake and a tsunami, which threw fish, shellfish, and coral inland. In its wake, easterners from the highlands observed Pango approaching the island. Apparently Pango had "many heads, each of which [was] furnished with a long black horn, projecting from the forehead and covered with fire. The eyes in each head were large and fiery; the mouths of huge breadth, and armed with teeth of enormous size. He was also furnished with a great number of arms and legs, long as our lower studding-sail booms, which served, like the legs of a centipede, to walk with. Out of each mouth was blown a flame of fire, which killed his enemies from a great distance, and the sound of his voice was like distant thunder."

The easterners presumed this apparition was their enemies' doing, deducing that an exasperated Pango had come to settle their foolish disputes and might, in his anger, sink the whole island. They sent a delegation to the west to sue for peace, and Dako's ancestors, only now themselves perceiving the approaching Pango, accepted. But Pango continued to advance "with his numerous wings and limbs in constant motion, until he came as close to the shore as the surf would permit, and surveyed that part of the island where Dako's village was situated, with great minuteness, for some time. He then turned about and started in the direction of Naraga," nodding his head as if he would say, as Dako expressed it, "Never mind! bom-by me come back and eaty you!"

Inferring from Pango's departure that he had come to sow peace, the islanders were subsequently shocked to find that many fishermen and traders were going missing out at sea. Then Pango reappeared, devoured some fishermen, and burned their canoes. The united islanders counterattacked, luring Pango into a trap with a decoy canoe, so that when he next rose "from the bottom of the sea" and came at them, "spouting streams of fire," the islanders ambushed him with a fleet of heavily armed canoes. But Pango, as Dako put it, "speak thunder and lightning too hot cause him too much mad! him killed too many my people!" Only one islander survived. "Pango kill too many with his tongue!" which was very long, and "break my people all a pieces!" Pango then plundered so many houses and murdered so many islanders that their combined chiefs finally resolved to evacuate the island and settle on the faraway uninhabited island of Mundawpa. Their departure left Uneapa depopulated.

At this time a young western woman named Peepe had fallen for an easterner chief and eloped with him to a mountain retreat. This chief stoked rumors that Pango had eaten her, but when the island was evacuated, he proved to be false-hearted and emigrated without her, leaving his lover pregnant and alone on the island. Peepe had twin boys, who soon began helping their mother to fish, collect fruit and coconuts, and eventually even to spear boar.

Peepe warned her boys against Pango, and as they grew into men they planned revenge and secretly built a war canoe, with which they successfully ambushed and decapitated Pango, exhibiting his bleeding head first to their mother and then to those who had fled to Mundawpa. These twin heroes precipitated a counter-emigration and eventually became great leaders, from whom Dako himself was directly descended; he "still recounts the story of his ancestors, with the fullest faith in its authenticity."

With the islanders' return to Uneapa, the ancient feuds between easterners and westerners were revived. Not long afterward, a column of smoke was seen over the distant island of Naraga, and the Uneapa people sent an expedition to investigate, including the heroic sons of Peepe. They discovered two children, a boy and a girl, of fair complexion who told them that their mother had just died. She was one of Pango's supposed victims, and the delegation buried her, but some had become so enchanted by Naraga that they settled there and adopted the fair orphans as their own. These children and their descendants, unlike the rest of the islanders in appearance, became known as the Red Men of Naraga, which was apparently why the island is sometimes called Naraga, "Red Men's Island," or, as Jacobs wrote, the Island of Lavoo, the Red Chief.

Jacobs noted the sincerity with which Dako related this story and speculated that it must have been founded on incidents connected with the ill-fated expedition of La Pérouse: "Why is it improbable that the vessels of La Pérouse were stranded upon some of the numerous coral shoals which abound in the vicinity of these islands, during the continuance . . . ?" He also speculated that, perhaps as a result of a mutiny, a small boat had arrived off Uneapa which had been mistaken for Pango. "French officers or sailors, with their cocked hats trimmed with gold lace upon their heads, would not look to their terrified imaginations unlike men with horns growing out of their heads, and fiery eyes; and their muskets held in an aiming position, might be likened to very long tongues that 'spit fire plenty, and break my people all a pieces!'" Jacobs was probably unaware that Dumont D'Urville had discovered that some survivors of La Pérouse's shipwrecks had actually built a small escape craft from the debris and departed the shores of Vanikoro, never to be heard of again.

This account suggests that Uneapa islanders had encountered European or Asian vessels deeper back in their history. Jacobs argued that his own deductions were strengthened by "the fact which we ourselves witnessed, that these natives refused to receive their own beloved prince when clad in clothing." As he concluded: "If the tradition of the devil's visit to Nyappa [Uneapa] is not connected with the fate of the lamented La Pérouse, it certainly must be with that of some civilized white men; and a mystery here remains to be solved!" And if the mystery was linked to "Lavoo" and La Pérouse, then its solution would attract plaudits from the French government—and perhaps a pension, too.

The next day, Dako showed Morrell something he thought would interest him: reefs where there were some fine sea cucumbers. For lack of cauldrons and know-how Dako had been unable to cure any for the Chinese market, as Morrell would have preferred, but he knew there was a future in them. Dako also took Morrell on a tour into the interior of the island to prospect for timber. And one evening the crew were treated to some of the lewd dances of the region in which men and women "amused us by dancing round a blazing fire, performing grotesque and curious antics" to the rhythms of castanets and drums. The lyrics of the songs that accompanied the dancing were, Jacobs thought, "part of an historical love-tale connected with Lavoo (the red warrior) and his wife, the precise meaning of which I could not comprehend."

While Morrell had been away in Australia, Dako had completed his new trading canoes and, like the islanders of Aromot and Kove, had built up a cargo of tortoiseshell for the captain. Morrell was now plugged firmly into the vibrant exchange networks of the region and the trade opportunities they offered. To help him further, Dako arranged for Wonger and Pongaracoopo—the two relatives who had accompanied him on the return journey from Naraga to Uneapa—to travel with the *Margaret Oakley* and act as intermediaries on one last circuit of the Bismarck Sea. These two voyaged with Morrell for three weeks, visiting, among others, the Manus Islands, which the Americans had now realized were the best source of tortoiseshell in the region.

Finally it was time for Morrell and his crew to take leave of Dako and the Bismarck Sea. The captain lingered on Uneapa for two or three days, checking on the state of the plants Dako had planted, giving and receiving further presents, and preparing wood, water, and vegetables for the voyage ahead. What was given and what was received goes unrecorded. Suffice it to say that with each exchange Dako and Morrell's relationship was sealed more firmly, more predictably. Jacobs, Woodworth, and others presumably also made their own gifts to Dako and his fellow islanders. If any of the islanders now sought to voyage to America, they were refused: Dako and Monday's time in America had been costly, and Morrell did not want to repeat the experience. Besides, he already had all the links with the region he needed. Surprisingly too, given how close the crew had become to Dako, there was little emotion in their parting. But by this time, Morrell's coming and going had become regular. He would be back, they felt sure.

Morrell then sailed over to Kove to take leave of Garrygarry. Apparently Garrygarry was now married to the beautiful daughter of a prominent man named Karpo. In his book, Jacobs takes care to describe her almost naked form in a more sexually alluring way than he could ever get away with when describing a Western woman, and topped off his portrait with a description of her tortoiseshell earrings and hair ornamented with a carved comb and flowers. Jacobs also portrays his final farewell here as more emotional than that from Uneapa. Kove was a place where the Americans had been able to relax and sleep in the village houses, with no sense of the latent anger that there must have been on Uneapa, where Morrell had once wrought such slaughter. Describing their departure, Jacobs puts tears in the eyes of Garrygarry's people as they entreat him to stay. Perhaps it was true.

But this leave-taking was just the end of the beginning as far as Morrell and his newly acquired friends around the Bismarck Sea were concerned. Despite Dako's help, the cargo that the captain had amassed in the region was insignificant—and Dako would have recognized this, too. In Australia, Morrell had sold 238 pounds of shell, and on this later leg of the voyage he had picked up a mere 143 pounds more. As shell was worth only about $5.50 a pound in China at this time, his entire cargo was worth just $1,900—a full two orders of magnitude short of the $120,000 he had promised to Baltimore's "Commercial Men." He had plenty of trading cargo left, but there was nothing to trade it for. Morrell had not acquired any bird of paradise feathers either, nor any dried sea cucumbers and ambergris, and consequently this voyage, like his last, was heading toward commercial failure. All it had done so far was create potential. Morrell was, as ever, on the threshold of great things and huge profits. He had truly done what no other "whiteskin" had done before or would ever do: he had built an enviable and unique set of trade friendships across a region where other traders dared not venture. In the long run he could build on this to attract consignments of tortoiseshell, sea cucumber, and sandalwood; he had also built a platform for other prospecting that might be far more valuable, and a monopoly that was unlikely ever to be challenged. But all this was still to be developed.

The young linguists and most of the crew also realized the commercial opportunities that were available, but like Morrell they knew that a different business model was needed to make them pay. Together they were hatching plans along with the captain to establish a colony on the near-perfect harbor island of Garove, which they felt they could make their own and turn into both a trading hub for the region and a much-needed secure stopover for Australian merchantmen and whalers. Since neither the current cargo nor the crew were adequate to this task, the best they could do was pin their hopes on attracting investors in a future voyage. Morrell, however, had promised his investors short-term results, not long-term prospects. To have any hope of raising the financing for a return voyage and the colonization project, he first had to turn a profit on the current trip.

The captain and the remaining supercargo, Francis Babcock, had two options. One was to prospect for gold, the second to join in the American trade with China. Until now, Babcock had been either astonishingly patient with Morrell or powerless to prevent him from crisscrossing the Bismarck Sea in search of cargo. But Babcock was now surely eager to earn his commission and turn the current voyage to profit for his employers, and thus himself. First they would search for gold. Then they would head for China and pick up a trading cargo for New York.

From the moment Europeans set sight on the northern coast of the New Guinea mainland in the 1520s, all visitors had envisaged it as a source of immense wealth. The first Spaniard to arrive off its shores, Álvaro de Saavedra Cerón, named it Isla del Oro, "Gold Island," and this helped fill every meager encyclopedia entry on the land with romantic allure until well into the nineteenth century. It was a prophetic assessment which has since turned out to be surprisingly correct: gold mining is now vital to Papua New Guinea's modern economy (and to the prosperity of at least some). But from Cerón's visit to Morrell's more than three hundred years later no known prospecting had been carried out. Morrell now had the platform, the contacts, and the confidence to begin.

He was still not to be hurried, though. According to Jacobs, the ship sailed west at a leisurely pace for six days, covering just a hundred miles along the New Britain coast and anchoring in various locations so her crew could explore coves and rivers, and visit the homes of local political leaders. From Cape Gloucester on the extreme west coast of New Britain, Morrell then made across the Vitiaz Straits to the New Guinea mainland, covering the hundred miles within a day. Here he anchored off the village of Sio, a nodal point on the New Guinea mainland for trade with the people of Aromot. Sio's inhabitants specialized in pot production, and their clay pots often found their way through the region's gifting networks to islands as far away as Uneapa, passing through many hands along the way. Morrell had probably learned of Sio's trading importance from his contacts at

Aromot, but he would certainly have been able to deduce its significance from the profusion of sailed trading canoes drawn up on its beaches.

The people of Sio were presumably primed by their trading partners from Aromot, and welcomed the *Margaret Oakley,* but her otherworldly occupants may not have been the objects of as much amazement as they were elsewhere in the region. Ships like Morrell's passed by fairly frequently—the Vitiaz Straits, which the village overlooked, were on one of the preferred routes between Australia and China, Japan, the Philippines, and Singapore. The villagers would also have heard in detail about the events that had unfolded when the ship had visited Aromot, because Sio was the island's main trading partner. Having now no local interpreters on board, Morrell relied on Woodworth and Jacobs, who could speak the region's trading pidgin well enough. With their help he was able to procure a few pearls, pearl shell, and tortoiseshell, but what he was really after was gold. Knowing the importance of ingratiating himself with the local chiefs, he invited a number of them on board and, according to Jacobs, "entertained them sumptuously." He then gave them "many valuables," after which "they informed us that gold-dust and diamonds abounded in the interior." A deal was struck: the villagers would collect these for the Americans "and have them ready against our return." Whether there is any truth in this account is open to question, but there certainly was gold to be found in the hinterland of Sio, as today's mines there testify.

Rather strangely, the villagers then proceeded to entice the Americans to take their ship's boat into the almost circular cove that lay a short distance from the village's islet. Here they encouraged the crew to rake the sea bottom. The sailors were excited. Maybe they would find pearls. Instead—to their dismay but to the villagers' apparent delight—they pulled up a large earthenware pot. The Americans did not know about the villagers' regional monopoly on the manufacture of clay pots, or that in order to protect that monopoly they were used to tricking potential trading partners into thinking their pots were actually the shells of giant deep-water mussels, available only in this particular cove. Whether their trading partners in New Britain were really so gullible is questionable, but many had interpreted the ship's pots and pans as rare shells in exactly the same way. The Americans were merely baffled.

Weighing anchor, Morrell navigated the *Margaret Oakley* another hundred miles northwest along the New Guinea coast until he reached the mouth of a river that is now called the Gogol. This was over four hundred feet wide, but because it was then the dry season only a narrow channel of water was finding its tortuous way down to the sea through the gravelly riverbed. This was the opportunity Morrell had hoped for. He picked a team from among the crew to explore the interior via the riverbed and, according to Woodworth's journal, announced that they "were now about to penetrate a country that no civilized man had yet dared to explore—a country which the best authorities inform us is peopled by a race of men called *Haraforas*." Morrell's *Universal Geography,* one of the few books that he had on board, noted of New Guinea that the Haraforas were very savage and lived in "hollow trees"—although this was about all it had to say on the subject.

Taking blankets, provisions, and trading articles in bags secured to poles carried between the shoulders of two men, the Americans stoically set out into the unknown, tramping along the riverbed in single file and crossing the stream regularly to shortcut meanders. Impenetrable forests hemmed them in on either side. At dusk on the first night they camped on a secure island at the confluence of the Gogol and Nuru Rivers. The next morning they set off up the latter, spending the whole day searching for signs of diamonds and gold, but to no avail. That night they camped on a rocky bluff, which they fortified as best they could after hearing voices in the forest.

It was early the next morning that they had their first encounter with local people: a hunting party who "stood motionless and speechless," naked and uncircumcised. More used now to making contact, the Americans held up trinkets and made friendly signs, but the men fled to an overhanging bluff before daring to take another look. One shouted at the sailors, who approached and with much difficulty

Prospecting for gold up the Gogol and Nuru Rivers on the New Guinea mainland, from Jacobs, *Scenes, Incidents, and Adventures in the Pacific Ocean,* 297

managed to give them beads and the like. After this the Americans were invited to follow the men up the river, across valleys, and past cultivated fields on a rolling plateau covered with coconut, banana, and bread-fruit groves, as well as other trees they did not recognize. They had entered the lands of the Garia people, and as they approached some thatched houses a crowd gathered to greet them in wonder. They were soon introduced to the chief of the village, Bivartoo, whom they presented with gifts, while he reciprocated with fruits. Having so rapidly won his trust, the Americans were able to use his village as a base, staying there overnight. The next day, having ascended a mountain for three miles, they at last stumbled on one of their prospecting objectives, sandalwood. They cut some samples and returned to the village.

Bivartoo apparently told the Americans, using sign language, that over the mountain there was a great valley (the Ramu Valley) through which coursed a vast river upon whose banks lay the ruins of cities built by a race of men who were now extinct. Enormous animals, with great teeth and moving noses, apparently now roamed the valley. Sign language can lead to curious interpretations.

Garia people nowadays relate a story passed down the generations that long before the region was colonized in the 1870s, white people had come up the Nuru River. These visitors were spirits who spoke the "language of the gods" and brought gifts from their world of the dead. Some of these gifts were, apparently, white and came from ancestors who had died "good deaths" (that is, naturally, or at least in the right place and somewhat under their own control). Other, red gifts were from those who had died badly, the victims of maleficent intentions of one sort or another. Researchers who recorded such stories in the mid-twentieth century were perplexed, not knowing that a trading mission of Morrell's era might have ventured this far into the interior. They assumed these accounts must relate to an expedition of the German colonial forces four or five decades later, and that the people retelling these oral histories had a poor notion of time.

After their partial success, Morrell's interior party backtracked to the coast, where the brig was awaiting them. They sailed a few more miles, then anchored to prospect again. Where they hove to is unclear, but they were well received by a second coastal trading community. These communities had trade links south, along the coast, so it can again be presumed that they had been forewarned of the *Margaret Oakley* and her otherworldly occupants. From this new anchorage, Morrell made a second inland journey, this time in search of gold, in the company of several of the principal chiefs. Woodworth picked up what he had heard before: that there was a great valley in the interior, a massive river and "a singular race of people" there. His intelligence was partially correct, although it would not be until the 1930s that the existence of huge populations in the valleys of the New Guinea highlands would become known to the outside world. Modern traditions from the vicinity where the Americans were based include stories of white men who had landed long ago and slashed their way through the bush to the top of the coastal mountain range using steel knives. Locals had subsequently congregated from all around to observe the blade cuts on the trees and compare them with what their own stone axes could do. Traditions hold that some of these white people had even made themselves understood and, before sailing away, had promised to return.

Now as Morrell sailed up the coast of New Guinea, he was leaving the region where he was known and could communicate with the inhabitants. Indeed, he was approaching the Yos Sudarso (Humboldt) Bay, where he had battled so ferociously on his way down into the region. He had more or less given up on interior expeditions, though he did want to explore the mouth of the Sepik River and sail up the vast Mamberamo. It is probably no coincidence, then, that before heading north, Morrell paused in a quiet cove and ordered that the white waterline running the length of the *Margaret Oakley* be painted black, and her blood-red gun ports be similarly daubed. She was now entirely black. He had perhaps picked up from Dako that in Uneapa lore there were two "ships of the dead" that conveyed people to the parallel world. Therefore, not only would the appearance of the *Margaret Oakley* differ from what it had been, but the inhabitants of Yos Sudarso Bay might respect and fear her all the more and keep away if he needed to anchor her while the small boats explored the rivers. The crew, however, had a different interpretation of why they had to blacken the ship. A black ship was the classic sign of piracy, and rumors abounded about Morrell's intentions. As it happened, these events were occurring on or about July 10, the day on which, across the world in America, the Margaret Oakley after whom the brig had been named, the wife of Morrell's financier Charles Oakley, died.

Morrell's prospecting had come to almost nothing: no gold and no diamonds—only sandalwood, and even then it was in a place far in the interior, and not easily accessible. He had managed to jettison one supercargo in Australia; his other, Babcock, must by now have been completely exasperated. When Morrell blackened the vessel it was perhaps a warning to him, too. But given how unfruitful Morrell's search for his El Dorado had turned out to be, Morrell was left with no choice but to steer reluctantly for China, as Babcock wished, to the huge maritime trading city then known as Canton (Guangzhou). Here Babcock could reasonably hope to secure a safe cargo of silks and teas, both of which could be sold at immense profit in New

York—all the more so if the supercargo could arrange to pick up a cargo in time to reach the city for the lucrative spring trade in 1836. But the enormous profits would go to the merchants who could stump up the capital for the cargo. Morrell and his backers would simply be paid their freight charge. The life of a merchantman was low risk but offered a small reward—the very antithesis of Morrell's preferred business model.

It was mid-October 1835 before the *Margaret Oakley* entered Canton's vast bay, nudging her way carefully through a thick carpet of Chinese fishing craft before heaving to in the outer harbor at Lintin, where she dropped anchor. Immediately, small covered boats drew up offering food, knick-knacks, and laundry services. This was the capital of commerce—and most welcome to the brig's crew after two thousand miles of open sea.

The imperial government of the Qing dynasty was suspicious of foreigners but recognized that China needed their trade. Exterior commerce was restricted to the "Provincial Town" of Canton, and there to just thirteen authorized merchants, known as the Cohong. Each member of the of the Cohong guild had constructed a substantial two- or three-story building set back from the banks of the Pearl River, and these thirteen "factories," as they were known, formed an impressive show of Western architecture unique to China's empire. Only here were Western merchants allowed to live and trade. Moreover, each trading nation was allocated a particular Cohong and factory. The resident American trading agents were confined to the Kwang-yuen hang, or "factory of wide fountains"—not that there were any. In front of it stood a huge flagpole with an equally large Stars and Stripes rippling in the wind, which signaled to all the passing river trade that this was the factory of the "flowery flag country." Behind the building lay bustling Old China Street, and beyond that the labyrinth of narrow lanes that formed the abode of more than a million people, all off limits.

The factory of wide fountains was the only place in China where Babcock could secure a cargo of tea. But first he had to take a ship's boat from Lintin Harbor to the Chinese customhouse near Macao, twenty miles away, then sail on to Canton to see what cargo might be found and whether there was any mail.

The factory of wide fountains was presided over by the American consul, Peter W. Snow, who doubled as commercial agent for most of the American firms. This was not a good posting for him. His factory was divided into three or four houses, each with a warehouse below and an elegant apartment above, but this complex was more or less the limit of his life. Foreigners were only allowed out into the square in front of the factories leading the hundred yards down to the river known as Respondentia Walk, which was fenced off and reserved for them. In the evening, merchants from all the foreign countries emerged from their respective factories to exercise, pacing up and down the square like tigers in a cage. Their wives and children were forbidden to join them: no foreign woman could enter the emperor's dominions. A Western woman had once ventured into her husband's factory, and all trade had been stopped, all servants withdrawn, all provisions cut off until she left. The merchants could not be denied access to the river, though, and they all took up rowing and sailing, organizing regattas that pitted factory against factory, nation against nation. In the oppressive heat of summer, commercial agents were also allowed to row two miles downstream to a set of fenced-off gardens and pagodas that were neatly arranged for their benefit on the banks of the river. But this was the limit of their freedom. For all other entertainment, they would have to travel outside China. Portuguese-owned Macao, known for its balls and masquerades, beckoned.

It was not difficult for the trading agents to procure teas and silks. In the highlands of China where the tea was grown, contractors purchased it from producers and then sold it to a class of wealthy tea merchants, who transported it down the rivers and canals to Canton. Here the merchants placed it in charge of brokers, who conferred with the thirteen Cohong to sell it to the foreigners. The silk industry located in and around Canton also supplied brokers, who sold the silk to the foreigners via the Cohong. In short, everything passed through these thirteen, monopolistic Cohong. As individuals, how-

ever, these Chinese merchants (hong) hardly profited from their monopoly. Rather, it was the aristocrats to whom the Cohong were
themselves answerable who creamed off the profits. These same aristocrats also forbade any hong, under pain of death, to befriend or favor any foreigner under their care. Should a foreigner misbehave, it
was their hong who took responsibility. And once a hong always a
hong; they could never quit their posts. They had all the pain but
little of the reward of the trade.

Babcock had hoped to secure a cargo destined for the United
States. Seven or eight American merchant houses used to trade with
Canton from their bases in Boston, New York, and elsewhere down
the eastern seaboard. More or less annually these merchant houses sent
their orders for teas, silks, and the like to their Canton agent—usually
Snow—whose job it was to arrange for their purchase, storage, and
shipment. For decades (indeed, centuries) European-American merchants had been shipping out silver dollars to pay for their orders: a
risky business and costly in insurance. By the 1830s, however, China
was awash with silver, and the Chinese themselves preferred imports.
Instead of silver, American merchants had begun to pay in credit
notes backed by the most trusted British banks, with which the Chinese merchants could then buy imports.

Snow would not have entrusted a cargo to just any merchant vessel that stopped by. Babcock, though, was employed by one of the most
renowned merchant houses in New York and, unusually, he even held
power of attorney over his captain. Added to that, the captain, Morrell, had a global reputation as a navigator as well as a fast and impres-
sively armed brig. This was a freighter Snow could trust, and he
readily agreed to load her with the most valuable cargo he could find.
Babcock sent word back to Lintin Harbor for Morrell to sail upriver
posthaste to take it on.

Sailing up the Pearl River was not a cheap or easy exercise. First
Morrell had to purchase the permits to trade from the Chinese customhouse. Next he had to pay a ship's pilot sixty dollars to conduct the
Margaret Oakley to anchorage in Canton's Whampoa Harbor, seven
miles below the city. The captain was also obliged to hire a security

merchant (who would make sure he paid the taxes), a linguist (who delivered permits for shifting cargo from the warehouses and for tracking it), and a comprador (who controlled the provisioning of the ship). All in all, this would have cost a staggering twenty-five hundred dollars, except that Morrell, like most traders, took on board from one of the ships in the outer harbor some rice to deliver to Canton, which carried exemptions and brought the transaction costs down to a thousand. The pilot took the *Margaret Oakley* up the river, through the narrows of Bocca Tigris, defended by its eight forts, and into Whampoa Harbor. Here Morrell was to wait for his cargo to be brought from Canton in smaller craft.

Before Morrell entered port, he would also have had to declare that he had no opium aboard. The Chinese authorities were doing all they could to keep opium out, whereas the British East India Company was doing everything it could to bring it in. The more addicts the company could feed, the more silver the company had spent on Chinese goods it could claw back. Four years later the tension between the imperial authorities and the East India Company would lead to the First Opium War, heralding China's "Century of Humiliation." Morrell, however, did have opium aboard—a whole chest full. He had acquired it en route to China at Sulu in the Philippines and probably sold most of it to the Chinese smugglers who visited ships when they anchored in the outer harbor of Lintin. But he may well have retained some for himself. Although not much discussed, opium use was not unheard of among ship's officers at the time. It was, after all, sailors who had introduced opium in the eighteenth century to the seaports of America and Europe, where it was by now commonly consumed. In the 1790s a perceptive commentator observed that among the women of Nantucket, America's whaling capital, "A singular custom prevails. . . . They have adopted these many years the Asiatic custom of taking a dose of opium every morning, and so deeply rooted is it that they would be at a loss how to live without this indulgence; they would rather be deprived of any necessary than forego their favorite luxury." The habit was not confined to ladies' circles either: an eminent physician took "three grains every day after breakfast, without the effects of which . . . he was not able to transact any business." A history of hidden opium use aboard the whaling and trading fleets in the Pacific has yet to be written, but it was certainly going on, as the death notifications of sailors attributed to opium overdoses attest.

Back at the factory of wide fountains Snow ordered pre-purchased cargo to be released from the warehouses, transferred to the *Margaret Oakley,* and loaded aboard. Each chest had already been inspected long before and sealed in lead or wax with both the inspectors' marks and the American owners' initials: CLR, D&L, JPC, RBF, JHM, MT, BB, and BS&Co. This cargo, which had cost $150,000, would fetch some $250,000 if Morrell kept his promise to reach New York within ninety days. A lot of people had a lot at stake that he would get there, and on time.

CHAPTER 14

Shipwreck

ᘐ

Neither Morrell nor the *Margaret Oakley* ever reached New York. Before sailing from Canton the captain had pared the crew down for what was now a simple trading voyage. He also let go of two of his officers: Second Officer William Scott and Third Officer William Benton, both of whom found positions on Bombay-registered ships that plied their trade between India and China. These ships were crewed by Indians, but commanded by European-American captains, who usually owned their own boats and preferred to have European-American officers. On board the *Margaret Oakley,* Selim Woodworth and Tom Jacobs were now promoted to full officers.

The *Margaret Oakley* weighed anchor in Canton on November 14, 1835, but the voyage was blighted from the start. Just two days out, the brig lost her rudder in a severe gale. According to Jacobs, in order to regain some maneuverability and avoid running ashore, Morrell was forced to lighten his load by jettisoning a significant weight of tea chests—a story later greeted with some skepticism by his insurers. Whatever actually transpired, the captain certainly nursed his ship into Singapore harbor for repairs, arriving there on November 28. Mysteriously, however, he then spent a full thirty-five days in port. Not only had he cost his cargo's insurers an enormous sum by throwing the tea overboard, but with this delay he was also losing the valuable time advantage he had to catch the high spring prices in

America—diminishing the profitability for the cargo's owners. To settle the costs of the ship's repair, too, and of her stay in Singapore, the supercargo Babcock was forced to sell a further 370 of the twenty-nine-pound tea boxes. Even this simple trading leg of the voyage was becoming a disaster.

One reading of events is that Morrell had begun to defraud his insurers. No one really knows how much tea was thrown overboard. It is feasible that the captain sold some of this "lost" tea in Singapore. Monitoring the cargo was in part the supercargo's responsibility—but it would have been exceptionally difficult for Babcock to keep track of all the chests as they were being heaved overboard in a panic in the midst of a gale. In any case, Babcock did not query Morrell's actions. He seems either to have trusted Morrell or been complicit in the theft—or powerless to control him.

Another reason for the delay in Singapore, perhaps, is that Morrell was robbed, or at least claimed to have been. One stormy night, between three and four in the morning, so he reported to the Singapore authorities, a thief entered his cabin while he was sleeping (perhaps in an opium-induced stupor). The thief apparently broke open his trunk and carried off his telescope, a Malay cutlass, and, more strangely, some letters and newspapers. When Morrell reported the burglary he also reported his surprise that the more valuable possessions lying around his cabin—his timepieces, pistols, cash, opium, and curiosities—were not taken. Yet the captain knew full well that the real value of this voyage did not lie in any of these, but in the ship's papers and the navigational details and trading potential they would have contained. If the robbery were Morrell's fiction, its value surely lay in the "lost" cargo manifests, which made it impossible for the owners ever to distinguish what had been thrown overboard and what had been sold. The Singapore authorities presumed that something must have scared off the thief. More likely, however, it was an inside job—or never happened at all.

Whether coincidentally or not, Jacobs suddenly left the ship. Tensions must have reemerged in the cabin, as Jacobs and Woodworth would probably not otherwise have separated from each other, but

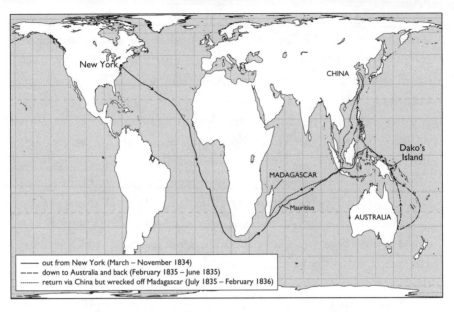

Voyage of the *Margaret Oakley,* March 1834–February 1836 (map by Bill Nelson)

whether it was tensions between the two youths, or between them and the captain, can only be speculation. Somewhere within the cracked mirrors and acrid smoke now beginning to enshroud the fate of the ship and its cargo, it is plausible to see Jacobs himself having stolen back his own confiscated documentation and some of the charts he had been so carefully drawing up before making off. As the profitability of the China leg of the voyage was by now looking doubtful, those bonds built when the ship's crew were unified in their desire to return to colonize Dako's island were likely to be loosening. Jacobs declared publicly in his book that he was "keen on seeing other parts of the world at a more leisurely pace," but this leisure was certainly not offered by the brig onto which he transferred: the *Ann,* under Captain Abell. She left Singapore on December 6 and made directly for Demerera, in British Guyana. True, Jacobs made a small excursion up the Demerera River, but he soon sailed on to Halifax, Canada, and from there to New York, arriving in late July 1836.

The *Margaret Oakley,* on the other hand, set sail more than three weeks after the *Ann,* on New Year's Eve. Despite a considerable number of tea chests having been thrown overboard, there still remained 400 full tea chests aboard the ship, each at eighty pounds, 450 half chests, and 630 boxes at thirteen pounds each. Also in the hold was a full cargo of silks. In Canton, Snow had loaded 315 cases of sewing silk and cases and cases of the higher quality boxed "pieces" (individual shawls or silk handkerchiefs).

With Jacobs gone, Morrell now shared the officers' quarters with only three people: First Officer John B. Bernadon, supercargo Francis Babcock, and Second Officer Selim Woodworth. Their relatives would have been tracking their voyage home from the reports of vessels which they met, or "spoke," along the way—as would the ship's owners and insurers, who were more concerned with profits than people. Lists of these encounters at sea were published in the "Shipping" section of port newspapers and republished around the globe. It was thus reported in New York that after Singapore, the *Margaret Oakley* passed through the Sunda Straits—the gateway from the Pacific to the Indian Ocean between Java and Sumatra—and was then seen passing Java Head on January 9. A month later she was again spoken not far from Mauritius, but after that there was silence. She had been due to drop anchor at Cape Town in South Africa, but another vessel leaving there for America on March 7 reported that she had not arrived. Newspapers around the world now reported the *Margaret Oakley* as missing. Describing her as a "rakish looking brig of 230 tons, built in Maryland in the year 1834," they "alert[ed] the world to her cargo belonging to American houses worth from one to two hundred thousand dollars."

Some American newspapers soon reported that the captain's wife, Abby Morrell, had received a letter from her husband, dated at Mauritius, but this turned out to be idle rumor. Month after month, relatives of the crew scanned the shipping news with decreasing hope. Like many ships at this time, the *Margaret Oakley* was given up for lost. Morrell's financiers, the owners of the cargo and their insurers, became equally despondent. Then, after six months of silence—a period which usually suggested that a vessel had been lost with all hands—a report seeped out that the brig had foundered on the beach at Fort

Dauphin (today Totagnaro) on the southeastern tip of Madagascar. It had taken five months for her marooned crew to send word of their whereabouts to the American consul in Mauritius, but he had immediately dispatched a vessel to their assistance. Initial reports suggested happily that all the crew were saved and about two-thirds of the cargo recovered. This was not exactly the case.

Given that the crew had not got word out for five months, one might infer that Fort Dauphin was an isolated beach village far from any lines of communication. Not so. Global shipping had come to Fort Dauphin three centuries earlier, after the first European castaways arrived in the 1500s. In 1643, when the king of France grandly granted the whole island of Madagascar to a French company, the Société Française de l'Orient, the man charged with establishing the colony had chosen its bay for his capital and called it after the dauphin, the future Sun King, Louis XIV. The French also built a defensive fortress there with massive lime, sand, and cement walls upon a commanding hill which overlooked the harbor. Their nascent colony soon forged links with the local Antanosy people, many of whom were themselves descendants of shipwrecked Portuguese sailors and whose ruler was a Portuguese speaker who had lived previously in Goa on India's western coast. But the French occupation increasingly depended on suppression and violence, which eventually provoked the Antanosy to expel them in the 1670s. Where the French had failed to capitalize on the port's trading opportunities in ebony, cattle, and beeswax, the newly independent Antanosy began to succeed on their own account, developing exports to the growing slave centers on the islands of Mauritius and Réunion, which lay directly en route from Madagascar to India.

Later in the seventeenth century Fort Dauphin acquired a new importance when some of the pirate ships which preyed on European traders to India began provisioning at the harbor and selling their hauls there. The pirates sold their captured ships and cargoes principally to New York–based merchants. One pirate, Abraham Samuel— the son of a Martinique planter and his black slave—even became the town's leader. He had been wrecked off Fort Dauphin, but the local

Antanosy queen declared that his tattoos matched those of her lost son and she made him her heir. This reign of pirates was suppressed in the early 1700s, and the town readapted to the export of cattle and other foods to Mauritius, Réunion, and, increasingly, America. Several independent European traders then managed to settle and make a living purchasing cattle from the interior and driving them to the port, where they slaughtered, salted, and dried them and sold the beef to the French and American navies, whaling fleets, and slave plantations. The enormous beef exports from the pasturelands of Madagascar's interior literally fed the global economy.

The French attempted to recolonize the town, first in 1768, then in 1819, after which they held it for six years, and their occupation "put an end to the vexations which the small party of French, whom commercial affairs retained on the coast, had been subjected to." The new French contingent continued to trade cattle, but also built Fort Dauphin up as a slaving base where larger slave ships could take on captives purchased from around Madagascar and the East African mainland. Predictably, a considerable rum distillation and sex industry also evolved to serve the ships. Visiting captains found it virtually impossible to control their crews while in port. Crews even used to force their captains to sleep on shore while the working women visited the ships. Fort Dauphin was anything but a sleepy beachside village; it boasted a history of globalization to match that of New York.

This was the place where Morrell and his crew had apparently been holed up incommunicado for months. Morrell knew his investors would soon demand an explanation from him—and an accounting for their cargo. Morrell set down his version of the events leading to the wrecking of the *Margaret Oakley* in a legal protest in which he asserted his innocence. On February 10, 1836, he claimed, he had discovered that rats had gnawed through all six of the 160-gallon casks of water in the hold. Having lost his entire water reserve, he put the crew on short rations and made immediately for the most convenient harbor, Fort Dauphin. Given the notoriously unpredictable winds in the bay and the fact that anchors could easily slip in the harbor's shifting sands and violent currents, he knew that stopping there would be difficult, but he had no choice. He reached port on February 14, and laid anchors fore and aft about a quarter of a mile offshore.

On his arrival, Morrell was met by Madagascan government officials and a Frenchman, Albert Dargelas, who had married a local woman. He had embraced the life of the Antanosy and acted as interpreter. Over the next three days, it was Dargelas who helped Morrell organize the woodcutting to make new water barrels and to collect the water itself. But the crew were facing problems getting everything aboard under increasingly heavy seas and a freshening wind. On the afternoon of February 18, disaster struck. Morrell was ashore buying fresh provisions when an anchor chain broke. First Officer Bernadon, in charge of the ship at the time, could not prevent her from being shunted by wind and waves onto the beach, where the onslaught of the waves quickly breached her hull. Within twenty minutes, water was three feet deep in her hold.

To save the cargo, Bernadon immediately launched the ship's three boats, and another boat, belonging to a Frenchman, Pierre Aubanque, came to her assistance from ashore. Woodworth later supplied the absent Jacobs with a vivid description of events. A sudden gale had added to the rough seas, Jacobs wrote in his account, and the vessel "plunged and staggered, and the waves completely buried the bow, sweeping the deck. The anchor dragged, and another was let go, but to no purpose." The ship was driven broadside onto the beach, her timbers split. The crew broke open the hatches, and all hands raced to save the cargo with the boats. Two hundred Malagasy villagers had collected on the beach, all willing to lend a hand, and the captain got them to form a chain reaching from the vessel to the shore, some in boats and canoes, others standing in the water. The Malagasy soon landed the cargo, but "amid a scene of great confusion," with "many a box of costly silks, satins, crapes, and handkerchiefs ornamenting different parts of their persons, while under their arms were boxes of tea, bundles of sewing silk, and other valuables the like of which the natives had never before seen." Morrell "paced the beach to and fro like a maniac, with a brace of pistols in his hands, threatening to blow out the brains of the first man who broke open a box."

The captain could only despair, his visions shattered and his kingdom sunk. His frown and cold command were now directed at those who, antlike, emptied his colossal wreck, now destined for the sandy depths. He could not police the chaos, and he lost a fair amount of cargo to the "helpers." A hundred bottles of medicinal cajuput oil that he had purchased in Singapore were "lost," while the sago he had also acquired was ruined by seawater. Once the cargo was unloaded, and the crew were ashore, Morrell put the chests and crates under armed guard and secured them with tents made from the ship's sails.

In all, Morrell claimed officially to have saved 115 of the 400 full tea chests, 230 of the 450 half tea chests, and 380 of the 630 tea boxes—that is, about 40 percent of the tea cargo. He also recuperated 360 cases or boxes of silks, which was by his estimation about half the total. Three cases of chinaware, a case of ink, and eight cases of pearl shirt buttons were also among the items recovered.

It was the boxes of curiosities gathered from around the Bismarck Sea, however, which were to cause the most trouble. Some of these chests had drifted ashore at the foot of the bay, and when an inquisitive Malagasy opened one, he was more than shocked to find it stuffed with dried skulls. As Jacobs writes, the Malagasy were horrified and "held a convention over them, and concluded that the crew of the *Margaret Oakley* were a set of piratical cannibals, who had been cruising along the shores of Madagascar, eating the people and preserving their skulls. This came near causing a bloody outbreak of savage fury upon our party, and it was only by consummate tact on the part of the captain that the enmity of the natives was allayed."

"Consummate tact," in this instance, probably meant payment. Morrell rewarded with part of the cargo the governor, port officials, and Dargelas, all of whom had helped him protect it from being "plundered by the natives." As time went on, Morrell also had to pay the townspeople in kind—which he was forced to do on diminishing terms because of the tremendous quantity of "China goods" which had been "stolen from the wreck by the natives and which had been floating in the market."

Morrell quickly purchased a few storehouses from Dargelas and others in which to stow the cargo and spent the next two months building new storehouses and putting the cargo in order (which presumably required him to break some of the merchants' seals). But if Morrell is to be believed, disaster struck again when, toward the end of March, a fire in one of the storehouses destroyed several more cases of silk, the ship's sails and rigging, and nearly all the crew's clothes and bedding.

Fort Dauphin had been a heavily frequented port, and in the past the Americans could have counted on being able to send for help from Mauritius rapidly. But ships were now putting in only rarely. In the late eighteenth and early nineteenth centuries the people of the Imerina kingdom in northern Madagascar had grown rich on slavery, and in 1825, while allied with Britain, had captured Fort Dauphin and began to colonize the Antanosy people. Their Imerina king had installed his cousin as governor; the governor in turn used the town as a base during his military campaigns against surrounding peoples. After the king died in 1828, his successor, Queen Ranavalona, continued this policy, but she attempted to eradicate Christianity, too. Some missionaries had been disrespectful to the local healers who had miraculously pulled her through a dose of smallpox (although only after it had ravaged her beauty). Furious, she dismantled treaties with Britain and France, expelled all the missionaries, and in 1835—the year before Morrell's shipwreck—outlawed Christian worship. She needed little help from European powers to support her army. A Frenchman named Jean Laborde who had washed up on the island's shores in 1831 had helped her develop the iron furnaces and industrial complex to produce heavy cannon and other weaponry. Unluckily for Morrell, the *Margaret Oakley* had been shipwrecked at the very time when the queen's well-equipped forces were attacking recalcitrant peoples in the south of the island, using Fort Dauphin as a base from which to launch their ruthless campaigns. Regular traders knew to steer clear.

It took Morrell almost two months to secure the cargo fully, but the crew were becoming impatient. The captain's next move was to send the supercargo, Babcock, to a port farther north with local guides in the hope of finding a vessel to send news of the wreck to Mauritius. While Babcock was away, a vessel did arrive at Fort Dauphin, although her officers seem not to have been interested in helping the Americans. This was a French ship from France's colony at Réunion which brought the disturbing news that "a war between France and America was daily expected." As Morrell was living as a guest of the French, this was unsettling. American and French newspapers were reporting in mid-1835 that diplomatic relations had been suspended between the two countries and that "the blight and curse, the desolation and demoralization of war seem about to fall on us." For forty years, American merchants had been lobbying the French government to repay damages incurred by American citizens during the French Revolution, and in 1831 the two countries had finally negotiated a treaty settlement of five million dollars. The treaty had been ratified by both governments, but the French Chamber of Deputies would not stump up the money. The United States was now threatening war.

Far from being saved, then, it seemed that Morrell was more likely to be dispossessed by the very French who had assisted him. He judged it best, "all circumstances considered," to destroy all the letters and papers pertaining to his voyage, and burn them "with his own hands." He claimed that this was to keep the ship's documentation and secrets away from the French. For the captain, destroying the papers also had the benefit of keeping the ship's log and the cargo manifests, invoices, and accounts of the voyage out of the hands of the owners and insurers. Moreover, he destroyed not only his own documents but also those of the absent supercargo, Babcock: that is, all the records of the cargo transactions in China and Singapore. This conveniently covered his tracks. In his deposition, Morrell wrote that he "had assumed that duplicates of all letters and papers had been forwarded to America by the supercargo." But if Babcock had not done this—as Morrell seems to have discerned—Morrell had now destroyed all evidence Babcock might have had concerning both the tea he had discarded off Singapore and, more important, the cargo that had been saved in Madagascar.

This French ship that brought news of impending war was probably the *Estelle,* which was on a trading voyage out to the west coast
of Madagascar and Mozambique. Six weeks later, in mid-June, en route
home to Réunion, the *Estelle* arrived with news that the impending
war had been averted. Her commander, Captain Voil, was a great deal
more helpful this time. While in port, he accompanied Morrell and
many of the *Margaret Oakley*'s crew, along with all the French expatri-
ates, to the governor's residence up at the fort to witness Morrell's legal protest, the official document in which the captain attempted to
absolve himself of responsibility for the wreck and its losses. After
Captain Voil returned to Réunion, he sent news of the wreck to the
American consul in Mauritius.

The American consul, a trader named Paul Froberville, immediately dispatched a relief vessel to Fort Dauphin while sending news to
New York that the *Margaret Oakley*'s crew and about two-thirds of her
cargo had been saved. Babcock, the supercargo, he reported as missing,
presumed dead, as no word had been heard of him since he departed
on foot to find another port about three months previously.

The relief vessel, when it appeared, took only eleven of the *Margaret Oakley*'s crew members to Mauritius, leaving the others to guard
the cargo. Selim Woodworth oversaw this first contingent to travel, and
when he arrived in Mauritius, he published a letter in the local paper
thanking the American consul "for his kind and affectionate treatment." He also thanked the captain of the relief vessel for saving them
and providing protection "from the insults and abuse of the natives."
The five months at Fort Dauphin had clearly not been easy for many
of the shipwrecked sailors. There were tensions between the Americans and the French, and between Queen Ranavalona's forces and the
city's inhabitants, but more worryingly, given the queen's propensity
for putting Christians to death, there were also tensions between the
Americans and her representatives in town.

About a third of the crew had accompanied Woodworth on the
first relief vessel, including the African American cook Phillip Luff,
the Tahitian "Tomme" Otahitia, and the ship's boy Robert Mills. Not
all the crew, however, had had such a difficult time in Fort Dauphin.

Two—probably the other cook, George Verae, and the Hawaiian, "Jack" Oahoo—apparently became "great favorites" in the town. They married and settled there, developing a business salting beef and curing hides.

Notably absent from the first relief ship was the captain himself and most of the cargo. Either the relief vessel could not accommodate the bulk of the cargo, taking only about two hundred cases of silks and some tea, or the Malagasy authorities would not permit its release. Or perhaps Morrell did not want the cargo to be sent to Mauritius at all.

In Mauritius, the American consul ensured that the crew were looked after but nevertheless took the usual precaution of distancing himself publicly from any debts that the sailors might incur in port. Finally the supercargo, Babcock, returned from the dead, having eventually found his own passage back to Mauritius. He now set to work with the consul to recover the remainder of the cargo—authorizing the sale of part of it to raise the money needed to look after the sailors. He also had to pay off the debt that the *Margaret Oakley* had taken on in Mauritius on the voyage out, when she had had her hull rebuilt.

Babcock and the consul soon commissioned a second relief vessel, the larger brig *Deux Frères,* to sail to Madagascar to fetch more cargo. Babcock went with it and managed to gather up a valuable shipment, but again it represented only a small proportion of the full cargo. And once again, Morrell remained steadfastly at Fort Dauphin with the rest of the goods. Babcock and the consul sold the cargo that they had retrieved early in October, and then the supercargo returned on a third relief expedition to Madagascar, once more on the French schooner *Estelle,* hoping to recover both more cargo and Morrell. But when he returned to Mauritius in November, it was still with only a meager amount of cargo. And Morrell remained at Fort Dauphin.

The "indefatigable" Babcock was certainly earning the respect of the underwriters in trying to track down the missing cargo. Morrell, however, was not. For some reason he was not cooperating. For the owners of the cargo and its insurers in New York, a loss on this scale was almost unprecedented. On receiving news that most of the cargo had been saved, they immediately dispatched a fast schooner, with agents aboard, as a relief vessel. This was the *Catharine Wilcox,* under a Captain Osgood, which arrived in Mauritius on about June 1, 1837. But she managed to secure only $25,000 net worth of cargo. In all, about $40,000 had been raised from the sale of the cargo that had reached Mauritius, but some $15,000 of this had been reclaimed, partly by those who had loaned Morrell money for the repairs during the voyage out in 1834, partly by those who were out of pocket for having rescued the crew from Mauritius, and partly by the owners of the relief ship *Catharine Wilcox* herself. The insurers remained highly suspicious that the only cargo recuperated so far was the plain black-and-white silks, the cheap teas, and other bulk articles. None of the "fancy silks" or other more valuable articles had yet been found. According to the insurers, cargo worth about $110,000 at purchase prices was unaccounted for. Their suspicions were raised still further when they discovered that when Morrell had initially sent Babcock away from Fort Dauphin, he had gained a free hand over the cargo and burned all Babcock's papers along with his own.

Worse, when the *Catharine Wilcox* had arrived in Mauritius, the insurers' agents found that Morrell and the rest of the cargo had not yet arrived from Madagascar. So they sailed to Fort Dauphin, where they were baffled to discover that the captain whom they had come to relieve had vanished along with the rest of their valuable cargo, seemingly with no forwarding address.

Morrell and some (if not all) of the remaining cargo were not in Madagascar because they were at that very time plowing the high seas on board a British-registered ship, the *Rio Packet,* heading for London. By absconding, Morrell had damned himself with both the owners and the insurers. If he had wanted to, he could have worked for them on the beach after the wreck. But he had despised the owners from the start, and his clever legal protest—which would absolve him of all responsibility for the wreck and its loss—simply mocked his insurers. He respected none of them. It would be rash to attribute Morrell's flight simply to fear that the latent stain of piracy hanging over him that might now be used against him, or that the mysteries over the disappearing cargo would suggest criminal intent. Although he must have nurtured these fears, there was something more positive to his moves—they left him in control.

The *Margaret Oakley* had always been Morrell's empire, but in his mind he had extended his dominions over the islands of the Bismarck Sea as well. There he was revered not only by his adoring crew but, as "Pango," by the inhabitants of an entire world over which he held extraordinary powers. The captain of the "god ship" had tasted reverence and seems to have found it addictive. In the Bismarck Sea he was king of kings. Everything belonged to him: the ship, her crew, the islands. The future colonization he was plotting would merely be an extension of his existing delusion. Years later Jacobs would say that Captain Morrell was not so abandoned a man as many supposed, and that "after the wreck of the vessel he became partially insane." But perhaps the wreck had less precipitated his madness than rendered a more profound insanity visible. Sailing with the residual cargo to Mauritius would have been abdication. By heading for London to sell it Morrell retained his majesty—and a cargo worth more than enough to fund his colony.

Unknown to Morrell, though, his movements had been picked up by the American consul at Cape Town, Isaac Chase, who had been informed by the magistrate of Saldanah Bay, some sixty miles north of Cape Town on the Atlantic coast, that Morrell had been on board a British ship that had provisioned there. In March, Chase wrote to the *New York Journal* (and presumably to the American consul in London) that Morrell "of the famed 'Antarctic'" was now traveling with the British brig *Rio Packet,* commanded by Captain Dench, which had arrived in Saldanah Bay from Madagascar. The captain had apparently told the magistrate that he had lost his ship at Fort Dauphin, and that "the greatest part of the cargo of his vessel was saved and on board of the Rio Packet now bound to London." Having heard reports that Morrell had been seen in Lima on the west coast of South America, Chase was suspicious. He may have had his facts wrong, but he was right to be suspicious.

CHAPTER 15

Morrell Adrift

༺ᘓᘓ༻

T he *Rio Packet* arrived at Gravesend, a customs post in the
Thames estuary, on April 28, 1837. All London's outward-
bound vessels were inspected here closely prior to departure,
causing a bottleneck on the river. Morrell disembarked and paid his
shilling for the "long ferry" which took him the twenty miles west
into London. Each meander in the river revealed yet more of the interminable shipping, moorings, and warehouses that humbled visitors
with the extraordinary power of the British Empire.

Morrell left his steam ferry at London Bridge and walked up to
the salerooms of the opulent East India House in Leadenhall Street,
in the City, through which China tea and silks were sold. On the portico, propped up on half a dozen massive Ionic columns, was a huge
allegorical sculpture of George III protecting the commerce of the
company. Atop stood a statue of Britannia, ruling over the figure of
Asia, which was seated on a dromedary.

Morrell wanted to convert the cargo into cash—but the cargo was
not his to convert, and he made no effort to contact the owner's agents
in the City. His conduct was definitely criminal. Unfortunately for him,
however, news of his impending arrival had already reached the American consul, Thomas Aspinwall, who probably had been alerted by his
South African counterpart, Chase. So although Morrell managed to sell
some of his teas and silks at the daily auction in the East India Company

salerooms, "the prompt and judicious measures of Col. Aspinwall, the American Consul at London" ensured that the whole proceeds of these sales, together with goods unsold, were secured for the benefit of the owners and underwriters. In all, however, the consul managed to recover only about ten thousand dollars' worth of goods and notes.

Morrell's conduct appeared all the more suspicious to Aspinwall and the insurers because the cargo chests, which had been sealed in Canton, had been opened and resealed after the wreck, hiding their provenance. As the goods could not be attributed to their original shippers, the insurers were now not even able to recover the part of the cargo that remained in London, for they could not prove exactly whom it belonged to.

It was now more than a year since the wreck, and Morrell passed on the legal protest, authenticated by the Malagasy governor of Fort Dauphin and other representatives of "Her Majesty the Queen of Madagascar" to the consul, who in turn passed it on to the insurers. The American insurers repudiated the whole document, dismissing the Malagasy signatures as "unreadable and unimpeachable names." But while they did not believe a word of his protest, there was nothing they could do to Morrell while he remained outside U.S. jurisdiction. The majority of the cargo—worth something between one hundred and two hundred thousand dollars at 1836 prices—was still missing. The insurers would have to pay up, and hope to collect from Morrell if they could track him down.

Morrell was temporarily broke and in a bind. If he had stashed more of the missing cargo, how was he to recover it? Having been caught trying to sell cargo clandestinely, Morrell had no intention of returning to America to face the insurers, but his high-minded and lofty self-importance never deserted him: he now imagined that his celebrity and contacts would extricate him from this difficulty, and even earn him the command of a British trading ship that would take him back to the Pacific. Morrell's new reputation, however, was beginning to eclipse his old one; moreover, just as the skulls from New Britain had come to haunt him in Madagascar, so now his ghostwritten self came to haunt him in London.

Samuel Woodworth had portrayed Morrell not only as a modern merchant-adventurer with a penchant for poetry but also as a fervent American republican: a brash Yankee, critical of European imperial ambitions—especially British and French ambitions. Morrell now found himself at the heart of imperial Britain, and though there had been appreciation there for the adventurous and scientific elements of his *Voyages,* there had been considerably less enthusiasm for the book's more nationalistic and flamboyant passages. Morrell, it might be recalled, had been incarcerated in Dartmoor prison during the War of 1812, at a time when his ghostwriter-to-be had been editing the anti-British newspaper *The War.* Unsurprisingly, Morrell's ghostwritten narrative overflowed with Knickerbocker republican spirit, casting British and French explorers as "vassals of some petty despot."

Neither Woodworth nor Morrell could have foreseen when they published the *Voyages* that Morrell would end up destitute in London and wanted for fraud in the United States. When he tried to solicit command of a ship from one of those same English vassals, the foremost sealer and merchant-explorer of the Antarctic Charles Enderby, the said vassal had "heard so much of him that he did not think fit to enter into any engagement with him."

Having failed to persuade any British merchants to offer him command of a ship, Morrell convinced himself that perhaps his reputation in France might be strong enough to secure a command there. His *Voyages* had been translated in the country's most prestigious publication and had received glowing reviews in Paris and a full commentary by France's foremost geographer and navigator, Jules-Sébastien-César Dumont d'Urville. In France, Morrell was *the* American explorer.

To be sure, Dumont d'Urville had been somewhat critical of the captain's tendency toward hyperbole, but he nevertheless considered his book important enough to publish extensive extracts in his own compendium of voyages. Others in France had also marveled at Morrell's trading activities and maritime knowledge in the Pacific, including Gabriel Lafond de Lurcy, who had met Morrell in Manila in 1830 and eventually published a book that presented him in a strongly sympathetic light. Morrell's fame had even reached the French king, Louis-Philippe, who, according to Dumont d'Urville, was very familiar with the *Voyages*. The king, however, was rather irritated by the thought of France's being outdone by America in Antarctic exploration. (He was probably also less than happy at being cast in such a popular book as a "petty despot.") So the year previously, when Dumont d'Urville himself had been struggling to persuade the French navy to finance another Pacific exploring expedition, King Louis-Philippe had unexpectedly offered him full backing—on condition that Dumont d'Urville also explore the extreme southern polar latitudes to locate the land mass of Antarctica, which the numerous icebergs and accounts by many whalers indicated must surely be there. Dumont d'Urville—who was not a polar navigator at all—had been perplexed, even horrified by this royal request: "I had read the travels from which the king must have drawn his plans; these could only have been from the journals of Weddell or of Morrell. Now of these two navigators, both simple seal hunters, the latter was already known to me as an inventor of stories, and the veracity of the other still had to be proven." Resigned to fulfilling the royal desire, however, Dumont d'Urville was finding in the spring of 1837 that Morrell (or at least his book) had become a rival. To prepare for his southern polar voyage Dumont d'Urville decided to visit London on a ten-day fact-finding mission, arriving on April 26, 1837.

So, as fate would have it, Morrell had arrived in London just two days after Dumont d'Urville. Each must surely have heard the news of the other's presence, although if there was a meeting it goes unrecorded. Dumont d'Urville had come expressly to visit the eminent Antarctic explorers of the Royal Geographical Society, the most famous of whom was Charles Enderby, the man who had rejected Morrell's request so bluntly.

Two months later, when Dumont d'Urville was back in Paris preparing his ships, he must have been shocked to discover that Morrell had written to the Paris Geographical Society offering his services to the French government in the hope of commanding one of Dumont d'Urville's own vessels for his expedition:

London June 20th

To the Geographical Society, Paris,

Gentlemen, having been informed that an Expedition is now fitting out for a Voyage of discovery & Survey, towards the South Pole, and having made myself already [familiar] with the Antarctic seas, Indian Ocean & South Seas &c &c, I beg leave to offer my services to the French People and will engage to place the Proud Banner of France ten degrees nearer the South Pole than any other Banner has ever been planted, providing I can obtain the command of a Small schooner of from 120 to 150 tons Burthen, properly manned and equipped. If the Society will have the goodness to communicate the foregoing to the government to[o] & they will be pleased to pay my expenses to & from Paris, I will appear before them on the receipt of this and give them my ideas and plans on the subject of an Antarctic expedition.

I have also to inform that body that during my last voyage of discoveries in the Pacific Ocean (which voyage has but just terminated) I discovered many Islands, Harbours, Reefs and Shoales hitherto unknown to the civilized World; and on one of those Islands which I visited; Mr La Voo (the Surgeon of La Pérouse's Ships) died in 1834. I also saw two of his children &c———

Your answer to this will be looked for with anxiety as I am about to sail for [the] United States of America. I have no other means of recommending myself to you than by referring you to the Published account of my Voyages which Narrative was [set?] before the world in 1832. Published in New York.

I am Gentleman

Yours &c.

[signature] Benj M

Mr. B. Morrell Jun

17 Lucas Street, Commercial Road, London

The French monarch's desire to send Dumont d'Urville on a voyage to the South Pole seems to have been piqued by France's rivalry with America. In May 1836, the United States Congress had finally agreed to finance a major "Exploring Expedition" of the sort that Fanning, Reynolds, and Morrell had been lobbying for. Louis-Philippe did not want France to be outdone again (he was not to know that it would take two years of extensive public debate and political procrastination before an American exploring expedition would eventually sail). Thus the idea of a French expedition being captained by an American—especially Morrell—was almost unthinkable. Yet Morrell's letter attempted to entice a broader French interest by suggesting that he had news of the surgeon of La Pérouse's famous expedition, whose children Woodworth and Jacobs had apparently met on Naraga. According to Jacobs's later account, Morrell himself did not go ashore at Naraga and was thus entirely reliant on Woodworth and Jacobs for his information. And Woodworth and Jacobs, if they met Lavoo's children at all, did so just once, very briefly.

The French Geographical Society passed Morrell's letter on to the Ministry of Marine Affairs, where a M. Thupinier referred it to the minister himself. Thupinier advised that the proposal to offer Morrell command of a vessel was unacceptable, but he nevertheless thought that Morrell should communicate his ideas concerning the forthcoming expedition. A member of the Paris Geographical Society had discussed this with Thupinier, who had thought that the most important issue was the news of Lavoo's children. Thupinier suggested that the Society reply that it could not cover the costs of Morrell's trip to Paris but would be very grateful if he could nevertheless communicate to the expedition members his ideas relating to the Antarctic Pole and more precise information on the children of M. Laveaux. In particular, could Morrell identify the location of the island where he had met the children, so that the French navy could instruct a vessel to visit it and see whether Laveaux's children had retained any of their father's papers? Realizing that Morrell was "influenced by money," the Society was to remind him about the Constitutional Decree, which granted a pension to whoever could provide news of La Pérouse or bring back a member of his expedition. Thupinier thought that perhaps Morrell would be eligible for one if he could prove that the children of one of the surgeons were alive. He reasoned that if their father had died as recently as 1834, he would have taught his children French and given them valuable information on the fate of the expedition.

On August 4, 1837, the minister formally thanked the Paris Geographical Society for passing on Morrell's letter and requested precise details on where he had found Laveaux's children. The president of the Society in turn relayed the minister's request to Morrell. There is no further correspondence. Dumont d'Urville was in a rush to get the expedition under way, and it may be that, in part, he wanted to avoid having to deal with Morrell. He departed for the Antarctic on September 7.

The information concerning Laveaux remains enigmatic to this day. Given that Morrell now had such good trading relations with Uneapa, Naraga, and other islands and coastal settlements around the Bismarck Sea, and given how jealously he guarded his potential monopoly—now his only lifeline to an elusive fortune—it is understandable that he would not have wanted to reveal the whereabouts of Lavoo's children to the French. Yet by indicating that he had this information and then withholding it, he did nothing to impress the French authorities. Indeed, quite the reverse. From being perceived as an American hero in France, Morrell suddenly became an American fraud. His deployment of the children to obtain command of a vessel, whether genuine or a bluff, had ignominiously backfired.

Morrell's attempt to sell the cargo and his apparent hesitancy to return to America also angered the owners of the *Margaret Oakley* and the insurers of her cargo. In early January 1838, the captain's creditors and insurers published their scathing version of his frauds in the *Boston Daily Advertiser*, and this account was republished in newspapers across America as a warning to anyone who might consider having dealings with him. Their aim was to destroy his reputation, and they succeeded. The *Rhode Island Republican* republished the insurers' story under the headline "Captain Benjamin Morrell," beginning it: "Many of our readers will remember this person as the reputed author of a book purporting to be a narrative of his adventures on four sealing voyages, which was published a year or two since and made a good deal of noise, in consequence of the extraordinary discoveries he pretended to have made—albeit many presumed to doubt their truth."

The insurers' account went on to note that Morrell had succeeded in persuading some highly respectable merchants to finance his fifth trading voyage to the islands he claimed to have discovered, which were "the key to unbounded riches unknown to any other mortal." They then gave an overview of the voyage to Mauritius and the refitting and rearmament there, for which Morrell had taken out a mortgage on his ship but which had "excited the suspicions of the authorities." The insurers were unable to say what he had done in the Pacific, as where he went next was "involved in mystery." All they knew was that he had arrived in Canton in October 1835 with only about two thousand dollars' worth of tortoiseshell and most of the original articles he should have traded with islanders in "'*terra incognita*,' the '*Eldorado*' which *he only* knew of." When Morrell had offered to get a freight to the United States in ninety days, he had been successful in securing one only because his supercargo, Babcock, was "a young gentleman of respectable connections and standing," who "was supposed to control, in a great measure, the proceedings of Morrell."

The aggrieved insurers and owners then provided a detailed account of the *Margaret Oakley*'s final voyage from China and its unending list of irregularities, including their bemusement and anger at Morrell's throwing overboard part of his valuable cargo after his rudder broke and his failure to inform them about this; the length of his stay in Singapore to mend the rudder; the cost of the repairs; and how much of the cargo had been sold to finance them. They were equally unimpressed by Morrell's account of the wreck and his explanation of why the news had taken so long to reach them; by how little of the cargo had been recuperated; by his saving only the least valuable items; by his disappearance from Madagascar; and by his decision to open and destroy the supercargo's papers. "The reader will readily comprehend why he opened the papers," they wrote, suggesting as well that Morrell had quickly managed to "get rid of his supercargo." They were also shocked by Morrell's departure for London, by his removal of the owner's marks on some of the cargo, and, not least, by his attempt to sell cargo that was clearly not his.

As far as the insurers were concerned, Morrell had been working neither for his ship's owners during his voyage from New York to the Pacific nor for his cargo's owners during the voyage from Canton. He had defrauded them all. The last the insurers had heard of Morrell was that he was in France "persuading the Government that he knew the place where La Perouse was lost, and could point out the descendants of the unfortunate navigator, now existing on some island known only to him." The accusation went on: "We shall probably next hear of him on board some exploring vessel bound to the Pacific, and it is to be hoped that he will enlighten the public and especially the owners of the Margaret Oakley's cargo, in many points thereunto relating which (like the island) are only known to him: and finally, it is to be hoped that his new work will differ from his old one, in as much as we now want facts only, which in this case will be much more saleable than his former fictions."

Since his leaving China, Morrell's vertiginous fall could perhaps be attributed to a cascade of innocent disasters and misjudgments. And yet the same cruel genius that had impelled Morrell to accomplish the impossible when forging links with the people of the Bismarck Sea appeared to have become more calculatingly criminal when faced with each unfortunate event. Morrell had now lost the trust of everyone who could have helped him, bar those who had sailed with him on the *Margaret Oakley*. He was, however, still a free man. What was he to do?

CHAPTER 16

Father and Son

ﾛﾟ

I n late 1834 Samuel Woodworth had received the first installment of Morrell's new narrative from the journal his son Selim had sent from Mauritius on the *Margaret Oakley*'s outbound journey. This was also the last installment. Samuel edited it and published it in the *New York Mirror* in January 1835—with most of its text plagiarized directly from Charles Grant de Vaux's 1801 *History of Mauritius*. From then until the ship was reported missing in the New York papers in July 1836, news of the *Margaret Oakley* was scant. Algernon Jarvis, the assistant supercargo whom Morrell had treated so badly, eventually made it back from Australia in September 1835, rejoining Charles Oakley's tobacco business. Jarvis might have been the source of rumors about Morrell's untrustworthiness that were beginning to circulate in New York, although at the time Jarvis quit, Morrell's decision to remain in the Bismarck Sea seemed to have been vindicated. After the *Margaret Oakley* went missing, however, and as news of the fate of both the ship and her cargo began to filter back to New York, the rumors about Morrell's dubious integrity gained strength.

When Tom Jacobs eventually landed in New York in July 1836 after leaving the *Margaret Oakley* in Singapore, he was anticipating a warm reunion with Selim Woodworth. Instead he was told that his beloved companion was missing, believed dead. Jacobs was also greeted with the stories circulating among merchants and insurers that

Morrell had either turned pirate or absconded with the cargo and formed a settlement on a remote Pacific island. Whether Jacobs credited such hearsay for the hope it offered that Woodworth was alive or had more confidence in his inside knowledge and reasoning cannot be known, but certainly Woodworth's absence upended his life. Jacobs himself had had a good voyage home. From Singapore he had sailed to Saint Helena, and thence to Demerera in Guyana, where he had been offered the job navigating a brig, the *Atlantic,* to Halifax. From Halifax it had been a short hop to New York. Now, incapable of waiting for Woodworth, Jacobs found solace in travel. Initially he worked on a trading vessel to the West Indies, then undertook an overland trek to the American Far West in an era before wagons would attempt it. This was the dream for which he and Selim Woodworth had eloped when they were twelve.

According to Woodworth family legend, Selim's parents had abandoned all hope of seeing their son again after the *Margaret Oakley* had been reported missing for several months. But both Algernon Jarvis and Jacobs had surely brought letters and news of the voyage from the Pacific. Samuel Woodworth had received copies of the sections of Selim's journals which lie in the family archive to this day. One account seems to have been sent from Australia, presumably having returned with Jarvis, and another from Canton, presumably having returned with Jacobs. So the family was stunned but encouraged when newspaper reports appeared charting the wreck of the *Margaret Oakley* off Madagascar, the rescue of her survivors, and the curious movements of her captain, cargo, and supercargo.

Three months after the voyage had begun in March 1834, Samuel Woodworth had taken up a second ghostwriting challenge for Harper and Brothers on the back of his success with Morrell's *Voyages.* His luck as a playwright had run out, and his paltry income as a poet had left him in "the most poetical circumstances"—destitute. Crowds of other writers in New York were now standing on his shoulders, and it hurt. So he happily accepted the offer of employment as private secretary to Commodore John Downes at the Charlestown Navy Yard in Boston and to ghost a sympathetic account of the commodore's excesses during a "punitive" pulverizing of Sumatran ports. This was a curious job for a poet, but it made sense given Woodworth's track record with Harper and Brothers, whom Downes had lined up to publish the quasi-official *Voyage of the United States Frigate Potomac under Commodore Downes*—nominally written by Jeremiah N. Reynolds, who had sailed on the ship's final leg.

Woodworth moved with his family to Boston and worked for the commodore and Reynolds for almost two years, first arranging puffs of pre-publicity about Reynolds's capacity as a writer and then whipping up interest in the tale. When this employment came to an end, Woodworth ensured that his resignation letter and Downes's laudatory acceptance of it were published in the *New York Mirror,* informing all literary America whom he had been working for—and, by inference, what he had been doing. "Reynolds's" book was a hit (despite its massive, unnoticed plagiarism) and, as its writer, Woodworth wanted some recognition.

Woodworth had given as his reason for resigning his poor eyesight. He was certainly ailing. Three months after he returned to New York, in February 1837, he suffered a disabling stroke. Never a wealthy man, he suffered still further when the debts were called in of an unnamed friend for whom he had rashly offered his house as surety. Reports suggested that Woodworth was "too conscientious to retain anything for himself when he might have done so." One might even speculate that the friend for whom he had offered his house as surety was none other than Morrell.

By June 1837 reports of Morrell's attempt to sell part of his cargo in London had filtered through to New York. From being lauded as a daring navigator and children's hero, Morrell was fast becoming better known as a fraud, a pirate, and a criminal. That Samuel Woodworth had ghosted his *Voyages* had also become common knowledge. When the New York *Sun* reported on Morrell's letters to the French Geographical Society in June 1837, it added that his voyages had been "prepared by Woodworth."

By this time Samuel Woodworth was surely realizing that his Knickerbocker nationalism had created something of a monster in

Morrell, and that he himself was also possibly implicated in the captain's criminal deceit. Moreover, Samuel, as a father, may also have felt that he was complicit not only in deceiving his fellow Americans but also his own son Selim. He had entrusted his beloved boy, baptized with his own penname of Selim, to a hollow hero—and one whom he had himself partially fabricated. In sailing with Morrell, Selim had become victim to the romanticism and sentimentality that his father had spun. For many months Samuel Woodworth must have believed that his son was lost because of it.

But one morning in the summer of 1837, while Samuel was recovering from his stroke, Selim simply reappeared at the family home on Pearl Street. According to family tradition, there are two versions of this story. In one, "He had told none of his family of his return, but climbed up the drain pipe and got into his own bed where he was discovered the next morning by his grandmother." In the other, "He came into the yard in a way that alarmed his young brother, Frederick, who met him, pistol in hand, thinking he was a robber. But the rough looking sailor laughed and said, 'Don't shoot. I am Selim.'" Since Woodworth family lore also has it that Selim was the sole survivor of the wreck, one might be somewhat skeptical of both these accounts. In any event it would have been quite a homecoming. Selim soon paid a visit to Tom Jacobs, now back from his trek and living on the family farm in Harlem. They had shed tears when Jacobs had departed the *Margaret Oakley* in Singapore; now, when Woodworth surprised Jacobs at his home, it "was some moments before we spoke, but we grasped hands and eyed each other."

Selim had returned to find his father destitute and unable to work following his stroke. But Samuel Woodworth had a gift for infectious friendship. He had always attracted like-minded spirits, and they now rallied round him in his illness and poverty. By August 1837 his friends had begun to organize benefit events for him at New York's main theaters, the National and the American (Bowery). Among those friends were some very influential people. The committee organizing the benefits was chaired by none other than the mayor of New York, Aaron Clark, and run by George Pope Morris, editor of the

New York Mirror, which he and Samuel had co-founded in 1823. Making an eloquent address to the first meeting of the committee was Jeremiah N. Reynolds, whose by-now best-selling work Woodworth had so recently ghosted. Others involved were Colonel Knapp (Abby Morrell's ghostwriter), and the ever-loyal Mordecai Noah.

New Yorkers rallied to help their ailing but much-loved author, and even those who could not make it to the benefit pledged money, while the stars of American theater agreed to perform for free. (One donor was the newly elected president of the United States, Martin Van Buren, who sent twenty dollars.) Few other writers would have been honored in this way. Woodworth's supporters were not necessarily fans of his poetry, and even those who were, were not seeking to endorse it. What they appreciated was Woodworth's support for others who had tried to live by the pen, his perseverance, and his exemplary "life of great, but unprofitable, literary labor." The performances in November 1837 yielded Woodworth more than three thousand dollars (seventy-five thousand in today's money), a sum that, according to *The Courier,* would "place the beneficiary beyond the reach of want for the residue of his life."

Talk of exploration was permeating political and popular circles across America. Congress had finally authorized the United States Exploring Expedition in 1836, endowing it with a vast budget of $346,000, but its departure had been delayed time and again. Disputes arose over who was to command it, which ships were to be deployed, and who was to be appointed to the prestigious scientific posts. By the time the expedition finally sailed, in August 1838, Reynolds, its prime mover, had been completely set aside. Many senators expressed the popular view that the whole thing was a waste of public funds. It had its origins in John Symmes and Reynolds's dubious "holes at the Poles" theory, and even though Reynolds had by now dropped the idea, this history left a legacy of cynicism—as did the great expense of the enterprise, which suggested more pomp than practicality.

But the American reading public still could not get enough of books that offered either first-person accounts of voyages or descriptions of them. Among those who seized on the genre was a little-known writer named Edgar Allan Poe. He had just completed some tales, which Harper and Brothers had refused to publish, and was making a precarious living as an editor for the literary magazine the *Southern Literary Messenger*—hampered by both his drinking and by his incisive criticism, which offended many of America's aspiring writers. Poe was desperate to get published himself, and for once he listened to the advice of friends and publishers who suggested he write a nautical novel, as it was guaranteed to sell. Poe toyed with the genre, publishing in the *Messenger* in January 1837 what were to become the first installments of *The Narrative of Arthur Gordon Pym of Nantucket*. Then, between February and April, he began to recognize the full potential for a tale of an American man breaking the bonds that held him—and if he could do this as a nautical hoax as well, so much the better.

Poe's plot for his new book combined the visionary holes at the Poles ideas of Symmes and Reynolds with the (presumed) verisimilitude of Morrell's *Voyages*. When Poe began writing in late 1836, Reynolds's and Morrell's reputations were both riding high, but by mid-1837, when Harper and Brothers announced his book, Reynolds was being cut out from the Exploring Expedition, Morrell's reputation had begun its free fall, and Woodworth had been publicly identified as Morrell's ghostwriter. By early 1838, when Poe was completing the book, Reynolds had turned into a bitter man writing angry public letters to the secretary of the navy, and Morrell was on the run. The works of Morrell and Reynolds thus not only provided Poe with the plot and authenticity he needed, but, as they were also both actually spun by the Swedenborgian wordsmith Woodworth, implied much more about perception and reality. That the novel ends with the main character, Pym, entering the white world of the dead so feared by the Pacific islanders even suggests a meeting with Dako, or at least a reading of Theodore Dwight.

By the time Poe's novel was published in July 1838, almost half of it was drawn either directly or in paraphrase from Morrell's *Voyages*. Poe was fully aware of who had written both Morrell's and Reynolds's narratives. As Woodworth's youngest daughter recalled later in life, Poe was among the many writers who corresponded with her father and regularly visited the family home. Poe enjoyed such "diddling," as he called it, characterizing his borrowings as a combination of "ingenuity, audacity, nonchalance, originality, impertinence, and grin." Ever since Washington Irving had kicked off the Knicker-bocker revolution in 1809 with his playful history of New York, the diddle had sustained New York humor and satire. An exemplary "grin" had only recently been pulled off by the editor of the *Sun,* Benjamin Day, who in August 1835 had managed to convince New Yorkers of the discovery of sophisticated life on the moon. Even the normally cautious had been drawn in—which had the desired effect of expanding enormously the newspaper's circulation. That Poe drew on Woodworth's two ghostwritten books can be read as a tribute to Woodworth: respect from one diddler to another. But Poe's published novel was less a work of parody or plagiarism than of visionary genius—and perhaps a dig at his publishers, who had declined to publish his original treasured stories, but whose preferred maritime tales all turned out to be diddles themselves.

To Samuel Woodworth's dismay, his recently returned son Selim soon began plotting with Tom Jacobs to return to Dako's world and establish a trading colony on Garove. The two were probably also corresponding with the fugitive Morrell. Dako was awaiting their return, as were others around the Bismarck Sea who had been building up cargoes for them. That return was already a year behind schedule.

While aboard the *Margaret Oakley,* Selim had taken careful notes of all the materials and financing that would be needed for such a trip, and had jotted down the commercial potential of the various locations they had visited. He now scouted for a suitable vessel, finding one in the brig *Active,* which was then anchored in New York Harbor. The veteran explorer and sealer Captain Fanning, who had long been lobbying for the United States Exploring Expedition, had proclaimed that the *Active* would be the perfect exploring vessel and had recommended her for the expedition. She was small—her deck just seventy-nine feet long and twenty feet across at the beam—but she was quick and much more maneuverable than the lumbering vessels that naval commanders usually preferred (and which they eventually chose for the expedition). Now she was for sale at a knock-down price. But Selim's dream was to go unfulfilled.

Samuel Woodworth was very concerned by his son's plans, and to avert them he managed to "procure a commission in the Navy for him" so that Selim could join the official U.S. Exploring Expedition instead. As a result of his ghosting activities, Samuel was now well connected with the navy, and given Selim's command of Pacific languages, Samuel did not find it difficult to have his son engaged as a midshipman. Selim was commissioned on June 16, 1838. The next month he was ordered to duty with the Exploring Expedition, which was finally on the verge of sailing.

Selim, though, quite literally missed the boat. According to naval accounts his orders to join the expedition were not forwarded to him soon enough. By the time he responded to a duplicate order, the expedition had already set sail. In its place, on November 20, 1838, Selim was ordered to join the USS *Ohio,* which was sailing for duty in the Mediterranean.

An underlying aim of Samuel Woodworth's strategy may well have been to separate Selim not only from Morrell but also from Jacobs, and parted they were. For two years they remained apart, as Selim began the slow climb up the navy ranks while Jacobs worked the faster route to becoming a sea captain on trading ships, taking time out to explore the Texas interior. The lives of these two had been intertwined from childhood, and their time on the *Margaret Oakley* had surely sealed their bond of intense friendship in a way that nothing else could. What united them still was their combined dream of revisiting the Pacific. It was their point of unity; their joint project; their correspondence; their way of being together. Together they had walked the islands of Mauritius, Aromot, and New Britain; set up clinics on assorted beaches; and learned and laughed in the languages of Dako and Garrygarry. Together, too, they had mistaken fools' gold for the real thing, and captained the small boats that had explored the islands of the Bay of Shoals. The south Pacific was their paradise, away from the stifling constraints of family life in bourgeois New York: a place where they were free to be themselves. And their dream was to return to it. Now Selim's father had separated them.

On the long days aboard the *Margaret Oakley,* Selim had begun also to draft a novel. But if this act of composition was impelled by the shadow of his father, the content revealed a son's agony with that father. Indeed, not just agony but fury. Only fragments of Selim's draft novel remain, and perhaps only fragments were written, but these traces dwell exclusively on a son's revolt against his father and suggest a much darker side to Selim than is apparent in his journals.

Selim's untitled novel is set among the quaysides of Toulon and Marseille in the French Mediterranean, where he was now serving, and tells the story of Eugene. Eugene's father, a naval captain, resolves that his son is now old enough to accompany him on board ship, but Eugene, unable to envisage living as "a boy under the severity of his father," becomes "frantic with disappointment and vexation." He retires to his room, throws himself on his bed, and weeps. There he also spins schemes to avoid the inevitable, although he "well knew the character of his father who when once determined nothing could alter." After relapsing into melancholy, he plots and executes his eventual flight. In all this, Eugene's anguish is enhanced by an intense jealousy of his older brother, Piere (*sic*), who has inexplicably avoided Eugene's fate: "I am doomed to be the victim of a tyrannical parent but you [Piere] are left to act the pleasure of yourself and be the dutiful son of an affectionate father." Eugene's jealousy is extreme: "We are both flesh and blood yet I am to be treated like an infant and you a man." Selim's draft is fiction—yet the hollowness it portrays of a son's duty and affection toward his father suggests that it is also autobiographical. If Selim's private anger at his father was similarly divorced from his apparent devotion—a familiar slippage—it becomes one of some consequence, as his journal (on which I have relied heavily for the story so far) was not a private one but addressed to that father.

So who was the real Selim? The wholesome, keen-to-please young man who religiously wrote his journal at sea so that his father could use it as source material for another best seller? Or the novelist depicting a tortured, bitter relationship with his father? Or was there another Selim still waiting to get out, more cynical and more worldly than either?

CHAPTER 17

The Lost Colony

ᠭᠥᠯ

Morrell was a wanted man in America and had run out of options in Europe. As long as he stayed in England, however, he was beyond extradition and clear of justice. In London he was nearly destitute, lodging in a boardinghouse on Lucas Street, off Commercial Road in one of the East End's poorer quarters. If he had made off with the unaccounted-for cargo, he must have salted it away: he clearly had no access to the fortune it was worth.

Morrell's insurers had powerful circumstantial evidence that he had stolen more of the cargo than he had attempted to sell in London, and they were trying to track it down. Perhaps he had stashed some away in Madagascar, or even in Mozambique? The *Rio Packet,* on which both Morrell and the cargo had been conveyed to London, had been trading in both places; she also sailed in the company of another American brig, the *Richmond,* to which Morrell could easily have transferred the cargo. The *Richmond,* sailing from Salem, Massachusetts, frequented Mozambique's slave port of Quillimane on the Zambezi estuary, and it is possible that the cargo was sent there. There are other possibilities, too. Morrell might have offloaded the cargo at Cádiz, as the *Rio Packet* had touched there en route for London, and Morrell, who spoke Spanish, knew the port well.

From his unlikely base in the East End, Morrell was planning either to return to Dako's region, where once again the promise of trade might bring him salvation, or to recoup the cargo (or perhaps both). Having failed to gain command of a British or a French ship, he eventually paid his passage to the Caribbean, probably via Cádiz, apparently arriving at Havana, the hub of the slaving empire there, in the autumn of 1837. He had strong links with Spanish traders in Havana through his merchant friends in Baltimore, and could perhaps talk his way into a command, even if it was of a slaver.

The exact movements of Benjamin Morrell from this time on are unclear. By several accounts, he managed to gain command of a clipper astonishingly quickly. Who would have backed him remains a mystery, but that someone apparently did so suggests that it was probably a close friend. Morrell sailed in the summer of 1838, the first shipping season after he arrived. While no one knows who financed the voyage, there is less mystery surrounding its purpose: according to Jacobs, Morrell was heading back to Dako's island and the Pacific. But those who testify to this voyage agree that Morrell did not make it. All concur that he sailed only as far as Mozambique, where, according to Jacobs again, he died: "It happened to be a very sickly season in this proverbially sickly place . . . [and] by the last account received, he took the prevailing fever and suddenly died."

Reports of Morrell's abrupt death in Mozambique first emerged in Boston in December 1839, and the date of his demise was put at March of that year. American obituaries were not complimentary. The account in the *Boston Daily Advertiser* identified Morrell as the former commander of the *Margaret Oakley,* which "was run ashore at Madagascar, and but a small portion of the property was recovered." Not concerned about speaking ill of the dead, the writer continued: "His history was an eventful one, and would fully sustain the old saying, that if rogues were to exercise half the ingenuity in any honest calling, which they do to make themselves the pests of society, they might obtain competency, if not wealth, and die respected."

French sources also date Morrell's death to 1839, but put it two months earlier, in January. Mozambique was a dangerous place at the time, and it was not just fever that could kill. In December 1838 the lower-ranking soldiers of the Portuguese army garrison at Quillimane led an insurrection, and after pillaging the town they attempted to hijack a ship and sail it to freedom in North America. The uprising failed, and its ringleaders were captured and executed. Could Morrell have been killed in the unrest?

French sources are also more specific about Morrell's last actions. After confirming that his initial attempts to obtain the command of a French ship were unsuccessful, the *Biographie universelle* continues: "He eventually turned to the merchants of Havana, who listened. He sailed on the ship *Christine,* which sailed for the east coast of Africa in September 1838. This enterprise was very unfortunate. The vessel was wrecked near Mozambique, and the captain died of fever in this city in late January 1839."

While the French and American accounts appear to confirm each other in the main, closer inspection reveals a telling inconsistency. As was reported widely around the world at the time, the *Christine* was indeed wrecked off Mozambique, destroyed in a hurricane, but this happened in January 1840—a whole year after Morrell's supposed death. The *Christine* was a Cuban slaving ship visiting the popular Mozambique shores under the command of one "Gaspard" (a classic Spanish sailor's pseudonym).

Whatever their individual veracity, all these reports cumulatively suggest that Morrell was for a time involved in slaving between Havana and Mozambique. Newspapers around the world carried the story of the hurricane that wrecked the *Christine,* but it was the fate of her companion ship, the *Amélie,* that became notorious. During the first phase of the hurricane the hatches had been battened down and three hundred of the nine hundred slaves aboard died of suffocation and want of food. When the gale recommenced, the hatches were closed for a second time, and a further four hundred perished before she made Mozambique Harbor, "whither she repaired for the purpose of getting a farther supply."

The French reports of Morrell's death in Mozambique after the wreck of the *Christine* thus associate the captain with slavery and hypocrisy. Morrell's published *Voyages* provided vivid, scathing accounts of slavery and slavers—Woodworth had added these passages to secure

Morrell the readership and respect of missionaries and abolitionists. Now here he was, apparently, working with the most callous of Cuban slavers. Yet if Morrell was aboard the *Christine* the year she was wrecked, then it was a year after he had supposedly died.

News of Morrell's death in Mozambique unleashed rather than curtailed further criticism. Many of those who had earlier credited his narratives or financed his trade and had subsequently felt deceived, tricked, or humiliated were keen to express their feelings. For the French, no more proof had been needed of Morrell's dishonor after he withheld information about the location of the Lavoo children: either his humanity was wanting or his truthfulness. Dumont d'Urville, who had initially recognized Morrell as a respected rival, could respect him no more. When Dumont d'Urville returned from his polar and Pacific exploring voyage, it was to huge acclaim. He had hoisted the French Tricoleur in a new region of Antarctica on January 21, 1840, naming his landing place and a slice of the continent after his wife, Adélie. He also added further Pacific "discoveries" to his earlier clutch. Dumont d'Urville had become France's explorer hero, its leading Pacific analyst, and president of the preeminent Paris Geographical Society. But rather than ignore Morrell, Dumont d'Urville damned him in two successive books about his own voyages.

In one volume, Dumont d'Urville relays the opinions of American consuls he met in two Chilean ports, both of whom suggested that Morrell was a liar. They also apparently told Dumont d'Urville that any attempt he might make to find the Lavoo children would be foolish. The consul in the port of Valparaiso was a Mr. Hobson, who doubled as an agent for New York merchants. Dumont d'Urville asked him for news of Morrell because he "still held in his heart" Morrell's discovery of the two children. Hobson was apparently quick to state that he had no actual news but that this navigator was not considered reputable. Morrell's book was a tissue of lies, he said, and the history of the children of the surgeon of La Pérouse was a fable dreamed up by Morrell to entice the French government into giving him a ship.

Farther up the coast of Chile, at the port of Talcahuano, Dumont d'Urville met a second American consul, a former sea captain now acting as a trading agent, named Paul Delano. Delano informed Dumont d'Urville that he had known Benjamin Morrell since 1823, when Morrell had commanded the *Wasp*. Delano stated bluntly that Morrell's account of that voyage "was not true." This, Delano thought, "did not add credence to the alleged encounter with the children of the Surgeon of La Pérouse."

Dumont d'Urville had what he needed to absolve himself of any responsibility for not following up on Morrell's supposed intelligence concerning the children of the lost Lavoo. These consuls, however, like the rest of America, were unaware of all that had transpired on Morrell's most recent voyage aboard the *Margaret Oakley*. In particular, neither Dumont d'Urville nor the consuls knew anything about the elaborate commercial groundwork that Morrell and his crew had prepared at Dako's islands. Morrell could not let the French know where he had encountered the children of Lavoo as it would have jeopardized his trading monopoly in the region.

In the other volume, Dumont d'Urville again attacked Morrell, but on a different issue. The Frenchman had tried to visit the location of one of the American's most important discoveries, the ruins of the early Spanish settlement of Philippeville overlooking the Magellan Straits in a place now known as Puerto Hambre, or "Port Famine." Samuel Woodworth had written into Morrell's voyages several hoaxes and exaggerations about this region, not foreseeing that his playful Knickerbocker diddling might later impel missionaries and explorers alike to linger in the desolate place. Dumont d'Urville did not see the funny side:

> Those who have had the courage to read the pretended voyages of the American Benjamin Morrell could recall that he claims to have visited the ruins of Ancient Philippeville in June 1827, founded by Sarmiento, that he had recognized its ramparts, its forts, its church, its prison etc. He ends even by

declaring that it would not take much work to rebuild them. From their appearance, Morrell's accounts seemed to me to be exaggerated. Yet as they also carry some truth, I had not yet become certain that M. Morrell could assert entirely false accounts with such assurance. I communicated the extract of the American concerning the ruins in question to my officers on both ships, and asked them to inform me of the discoveries that they could make of this sort. Nothing was discovered which resembled these ruins in the radius that they took in every direction all around the anchorage, and it was impossible that anything escaped their multiple investigations.

In this report, however, Dumont d'Urville is no more reliable than Morrell. Not only does he exaggerate Morrell's descriptions, but he is factually incorrect: the fort and ruins were there—and we have that on the authority of no less than Charles Darwin, who visited the same "Port Famine" on December 26, 1833, ten years after Morrell but six years before Dumont d'Urville. Darwin's description of the fort and the ruins of the town matches Morrell's: "The buildings were begun in very good style and remain a proof of the strong hand of old Spain." Dumont d'Urville was simply trying to discredit Morrell.

Whether Morrell ever left Cuba and, if he did, whether he arrived in Mozambique and, if he did, whether he died there remain intriguingly open questions. Abby Jane Morrell was still only twenty-nine in 1837, and she had not seen her husband for three and a half years. She had presumably been corresponding with Benjamin in London, and she probably transferred funds to help him sail for the Caribbean. Moreover, she certainly sailed to the Caribbean herself at the same time as Benjamin, presumably to be with him. Yet she did not go to Cuba. Records show that in February 1838 she returned to America from the island of Saint Thomas, then part of the Danish Virgin Islands, hundreds of miles southeast of Cuba. It seems possible that she met up with her husband there, or perhaps in Venezuela. Ships bound for New York from Venezuela usually called at Saint Thomas.

In the 1830s Benjamin Morrell's brother, the sea captain Jeremiah, had gone to work for Silas Burrows in the Venezuelan maritime town of Puerto Cabello, and his son (also named Jeremiah) still lived there. Given also that news of Morrell's death derived from Boston, where Abby had been living, was it possible that those reports were not all that they seemed?

If Morrell did sail from the Caribbean, it was certainly without Tom Jacobs and Selim Woodworth, who were now both settled into their respective seagoing careers. As reports of Morrell's death reached them, the two realized that the trading monopoly in the Bismarck Sea had passed to them. They began working again on plans to return to Dako's region.

By mid-1841, Woodworth and Jacobs had finished polishing their plans to establish a colony in the horseshoe harbor of Garove Island. Indeed, this had become their obsession. Even while Jacobs had been longing for Woodworth's return from the wreck, he admitted that "the settlement and lucrative trade of the lovely and benighted Morrell's Group was ever uppermost in my mind, and occupied my sleeping and waking thoughts."

Similar colonization schemes had been proposed for other Pacific islands. In particular, a British missionary, the Reverend John Williams, had suggested a less commercially driven plan. In his 1837 *Narrative of Missionary Enterprises in the South Sea Islands,* Williams had proposed that a settlement on one of the South Sea islands could be established where passing ships might refresh and refit without being exposed to danger—something travelers to and from the new Australian settlement were then seeking. Williams proposed that the colony be established in the "Navigators Group" (now Samoa), and extolled the virtue of its harbors, land, soil, and timber. Whether Woodworth and Jacobs took direct inspiration from Williams or whether they simply shared his views is not clear, but they certainly read his suggestions, which fueled their dreams and lent them legitimacy. Williams himself did not live to see his dream become a reality. He was eaten on Erromango in 1839.

Selim Woodworth's navy job was flexible enough to allow him periods of extended leave. Having detached himself from the *Ohio* on August 3, 1841, he took three months' leave allegedly "for the purpose of visiting Milan, in Italy." U.S. immigration records reveal, however, that he traveled to Havana, arriving in New York from there in December 1841. While Woodworth was on board the *Ohio,* he could not do much to further his dream, but a letter from him to Jacobs reveals how far their colonization plans had advanced.

An incomplete copy of this letter, now in the Woodworth family archive, attests not only to the ambition of its author but also, shockingly, to the cynicism in Woodworth's plans to exploit everyone else involved: investors, collaborators, colonists, islanders. In one paragraph he writes:

> Another thing I would propose: that is to have everyone engaged in the Expedition to sign articles, similar to the Shipping Articles of a Whale Ship's papers. Remember, on shares everybody [that is, everyone would be paid in future shares of the profit], no wages, and impress it on the minds of all our employees, the wealth of "The Company." It will act as "Terrorum" to keep them in subjection, and the name of "the company," the "President." "The Board," Governor &c. will be something they cannot comprehend, and will necessarily awe them into respect, and they will be more ready to obey their Officers. We must establish a Store, and as no one will embark without some money, the necessity of which we must impress upon all, informing that they will want it at the different ports we may stop at, to procure refreshments, it will all come to our coffers ultimately. In fact I want to establish a special currency, and American coin if it can be done, and as soon as the natives understand the nature of money, and begin to love it and appreciate it, we can then introduce a spurious article.

This is not the Selim Woodworth with whom we have, until now, been familiar. Only here in his letters to Jacobs does he reveal this other self. Selim was a teenager when he quit New York to be apprenticed to Morrell. In his journal of the voyage of the *Margaret Oakley,* upon which we have been so reliant for our account of the ship's adventures, he comes across as a good man. But his journals are not the outpourings of the intimate thoughts of a modern teenage diarist; they were composed with a readership in mind—his father certainly, the readers of his father's new book, posterity perhaps, and even his better self. And the attitudes shown within the journals are indeed those that a compassionate father might hope for of a dutiful son: he is a friend to Dako, considerate to those he meets, and a companion to us, his readers, as he leads us genially through this unfamiliar world. Somewhere along the line, however, Woodworth the man and Woodworth the journal writer parted company.

Woodworth the man had ever so quietly become an entirely different person. It is only now, as he began to spin his own colonization plans privately with Jacobs, that this sinister new Woodworth appears in written form. This Woodworth was forged in apprenticeship to a man who soon would be "wanted" the world over, and who was prepared to extract everything he could from all those he encountered within it. The journal remains as truthful a record of events as we have, but it could not be more misleading about the temperament of its author.

When Selim's youngest sister, Mary Josephine, recalled their father later in the century, she described him as almost childlike in nature and so loving and forgiving that he could "see wrong in no one and had faith in all." Samuel was universally cheerful, always hopeful and bright. If he had a failing it was that he was too generous for his own good and self-denying "to the last degree." As a husband and father he was both loving and devoted, yet firm and positive in guiding his children, who all looked up to him with adoration. Hers was a magical memory, but it is confirmed by virtually everyone who knew Samuel. A more perfect, successful parent could not be imagined. And yet Selim ran away from him at age twelve.

Selim worshiped his father, but as the few draft pages of his novel suggest, there was a latent anger in his feelings as well. His father may have been loving, but he had surely also been somewhat distant, and not only in a way a father inevitably would be when he had ten children. Samuel was forever escaping to the intertextual world of poetic composition or into the creative and social world of the Knickerbockers. He seems to have loved his second son, but what is love without attention? Samuel's writing life was in part an evasion from his growing children and a denial of the poverty into which his world of authorship had forced them. Perhaps in every shared look between father and son there was a pleading to ignore this distance; but the pleading would prove the lie. A harsh truth for Selim was that Samuel was infatuated more by his words and his wife than by his children. So when years later Selim's sister recalled their mother unbinding her golden hair, letting it fall in stunning curls that never silvered with age down to her knees, she was recalling the enduring subject of Samuel's muse, not her mother's own embrace of parental warmth. "He and our mother were in every respect a perfect unity."

It was Morrell, not father Samuel, who had been by Selim's side during his late teenage years. Morrell had become Selim's surrogate father—doubly so as his actual father had been complicit in binding the two together. Samuel had been writing Morrell's *Voyages* when Selim was an impressionable teenager, which had captivated the boy. Then he had entrusted Selim to Morrell on the voyage which was to be his initiation into the wider world. With three long years in the liminal space of the *Margaret Oakley,* betwixt and between New York and New Guinea, with all familial bonds broken and Morrell as his tutor, Selim's outlook on life was bound to change. If Selim had ever been molded in his father's image, he emerged after three years of learning at the knee of a man who knew no restraint and no fear reforged in Morrell's likeness. He, like Morrell, had learned to mock those on whom he depended.

Men who had known Morrell in New York, such as Jeremiah Reynolds, describe him as "[seeing] through a glass dimly"—a man of instinct, perhaps, and attentive to it, but hardly reflective. Yet those, like Selim Woodworth, who shared his life at close quarters were captivated by his genius. Not only Woodworth and Jacobs but also Scott and Bernadon, Morrell's first and second mates on the *Margaret Oakley,* had became devoted to this man with immense plans who was always on the threshold of great things: a man who had enlarged their minds and expanded their horizons. Morrell opened their eyes to a way of seeing and being that would have shocked his ailing ghost-writer to the core.

Selim's private letter to Tom Jacobs, which shows such a different side of his character, outlines in detail the plans for the colonization voyage. The first sections deal with obtaining a vessel: the recipient—who is not named but whom we can properly assume to be Jacobs—should exert himself to obtain the capital needed for the expedition. Woodworth calculated that ten thousand dollars would be sufficient, but that if they could double the amount their plan would become a certainty. Jacobs was to look into several options for securing the vessel and trading capital. The first and best would be to find a shipowner with an idle craft who would be willing to invest her as capital. "Give the owner to understand that the craft alone is not much, but the great expense of the expedition is the outfit, say $15,000. He will not know the difference."

Woodworth's second suggestion was to purchase a smaller craft more cheaply, but on credit, paying only the interest to the ship-owner. The New York papers that he had received while aboard the naval ship on which he wrote this letter were reporting 160 vessels lying at anchor in the harbor, unoccupied or unemployed, whose owners, he thought, "might like to sell on these terms." In particular, Woodworth knew of a certain Peter Harmony, a New York merchant who had profited hugely from the illegal export of Cuban slaves to America, and who was, notoriously, the trader whose captives had seized the ship, the *Amistad,* that was transporting them into slavery in 1839. Woodworth encouraged Jacobs to make an offer to buy a schooner from Harmony, or even his brig *Malek Adhel,* which had been impounded in New York pending an accusation of piracy. "If we can obtain a craft on those conditions, we had better do so. The interest installments we can readily pay ourselves and can fit out for the voyage if we cannot obtain others to join us."

A third, more devious way of obtaining a vessel would be to encourage some of New York's "pilot boys" to voyage with the expedition in their own craft. At this time the New York Harbor pilots were facing new legal restrictions which were rendering them destitute. Perhaps the more adventurous among them might be enticed to join the voyage as partners? And once at the islands, they could be made, noted Woodworth cynically, "tired of the business" and forced to sell their craft "at our own price."

A colony would take several ships to establish, and Woodworth anticipated commissioning whaling ships to deliver other colonists and their material needs, including the bricks and planks required to build the first houses, all at a cost of a thousand dollars. They would also need to ship good timber boards to manufacture the flat-bottomed boats they would use to harvest sea cucumbers from the reefs.

Woodworth next requested Jacobs to call on the Missionary Society and try to attract a missionary and his family to embark as well—a scheme that gives some sense of how useful missionaries could be to traders:

> Offer him every facility for converting the heathen. Say that we will build him a house and do everything in our power to make him comfortable. It will give a respectable caste to the Expedition, and it will prove to be the best protection against the natives that we could employ. And in one year after he becomes established, we can do as we desire with all the natives. He can be employed in teaching them English and make us a complete set of "Interpreters." We will find the material from each Island that we may want to trade with; it would occupy too much of our valuable time to instruct them, and [the Missionary] could be thus employed, while we are engaged in more important occupations.

But though Woodworth needed missionaries he could not abide sailing with them. "Offer the missionaries passage in the vessel," he suggests, "but at the same time, observe that our craft is small and uncomfortable, but advise him to take passage in the Whale Ship that is soon to sail for the Islands, and a passage can be obtained very moderately." Woodworth also anticipated recruiting a young surgeon whom he had befriended on the ship where he was currently serving. Apart from providing medical assistance, he wrote Jacobs, the man was a gifted botanist and chemist who would be "eminently useful in discovering, among the thousand medicinal plants peculiar to those Islands, something valuable as an article of export,—herbs, barks, dye woods, &c." This scheme also derived from the Reverend John Williams, whose *Narrative* had extolled the skills of an Italian botanist, M. Bertero, on Tahiti. Bertero had astonished missionaries and islanders alike "by the cures he effected with medicinal herbs. When a patient came to him for relief, M. Bertero without going twenty yards from the spot, would often point out some herb which, used according to his directions, produced in numberless instances the most beneficial effects." Bertero had found two thousand new specimens, but he and his precious cargo had perished at sea—which provided Woodworth, Jacobs, the surgeon, and whoever else was involved in their voyage added commercial opportunity.

Woodworth's letter also contained an outline of the profit-sharing. Colonists joining this proposed expedition were not to be paid. They were to be offered shares in the eventual profits, which would be divided along the model of a whaling expedition, and accordingly everyone engaged would have to sign shipping articles akin to a whale ship's papers. Those who invested capital would receive a percentage of the profits, and employees would also get a "lay," or profit share. The "governors," such as Woodworth and Jacobs, would receive perhaps a fiftieth each of the profits, the mechanics a ninetieth, the sea cucumber curers a hundredth—each according to the value of his services. As payment would be based on shares, Woodworth would not need the liquidity for wages, and could use the needs of the company as his "Terrorum."

Most startling, however, Woodworth aimed to exploit not just the investors, missionaries, and colonists but above all the islanders with whom they were to trade. Woodworth imagined that he could

introduce U.S. coins—silver half-dollars, quarters, and dimes and copper pennies—as trading currency around the Bismarck Sea, and then,
once the currency had taken hold, substitute counterfeit coins and si-
phon off the region's wealth. Had Dako and his people ever meant
more to Woodworth than profit, those feelings were long in the past.

Fortunately for everyone except the two planning the expedition,
no one could be found to back it. Raising money was harder than
Woodworth and Jacobs had imagined, made all the more difficult by
the fact that the two of them had been associated with Morrell and
were proposing a venture that seemed to be building on Morrell's
widely reported criminal delusions. After the voyage of the *Margaret
Oakley,* as Jacobs remarked, rumors had been "injurious to the reputation of those most closely connected with the enterprise." No one
except those who had been aboard the ship realized the true trading
potential that Morrell's expedition had established in the region.

But though Woodworth and Jacobs had no credibility with the
merchants of New York, they did not give up. They collaborated for
the next two years on writing a book-length account of their voyage
on the *Margaret Oakley* whose aim was to set the record straight, restore their own reputations, and thus help raise capital. This was the
book published in 1844 under Jacobs's name that I have been using in
conjunction with Woodworth's journal to relate the events of the
voyage in earlier chapters. The story of the book, however, now becomes part of the bigger story, just as the story of the books written
by Benjamin and Abby Morrell have been. The two young men
needed to publish a narrative which would advertise the trading opportunities of the region by revealing how close Morrell had come to
commercial success—while also concealing the precise location of
Dako's island in order to guard their monopoly. Harper and Brothers,
of course, added to this agenda that the book had to sell, so once
again the adventure elements would need enhancement. There would
have to be some diddling.

To help in this endeavor, Woodworth managed to ensure that his
naval duties were confined to New York or nearby Philadelphia between December 1842 and early 1844, when the book was published.

This was made easier at the death of his ailing father, in December 1842. Samuel's first stroke in 1837 had left him paralyzed down his left side, but he had recovered enough to walk with a stick and to write. His second stroke, probably early in 1842, confined him to bed. The third one killed him. His demise was signaled by the press as the passing of a national treasure, and the navy granted Selim three months' compassionate leave and then agreed to his requests for a position in New York so he could be near his family and study at naval school in Philadelphia (from which he graduated as a midshipman in May 1844), and for a further six months' leave to support his brother, who was suffering from a "serious illness."

The extra time enabled Selim and Tom to finish their book. It is unclear when they began it, but internal evidence suggests that Samuel Woodworth had been part of the original writing team. Despite his poor eyesight and the strokes, he could still write, and did so almost up to his death. The new book's curious authorship is more or less signaled to the knowing. Many of its geographical "discoveries" are named after Knickerbocker writers and associates of Samuel Woodworth. There is a "Cooper Bay," an "Irving Bay," a "Reynolds Bay," and an "Audubon Island." There is even a "Woodworth Bay," named for Samuel Woodworth himself. Moreover, the book is stacked with poetical quotations, whether explicit or embedded in the text, drawn from poems that appeared in print in 1840 and 1841, prior to Samuel's death.

The published narrative had a typically effusive title: *Scenes, incidents and adventures in the Pacific Ocean, or The islands of the Australasian seas, during the cruise of the clipper Margaret Oakley, under Capt. Benjamin Morrell. Clearing up the mystery which has heretofore surrounded this famous expedition, and containing a full account of the exploration of Bidera, Papua, Banda, Mindoro, Sooloo, and China seas, the manners and customs of the inhabitants of the islands, and a description of vast regions never before visited by civilized man.* The volume was published solely under Jacobs's name, but Selim Woodworth had been a major collaborator. Many of the passages rely too closely on his manuscript journal to have been written independent of it, and Selim also sent expanded passages to Jacobs which he (perhaps with his father's help) had developed on the basis of his journal. At least one such passage is to be found among Woodworth's papers. Many of the engravings in the book were also taken from Selim's own sketches, the originals of which remain still in his family archive.

As with Benjamin Morrell's ghostwritten *Voyages,* the authors introduced passages to enhance their adventures or burnish their characters. They attribute the leaky state of the boat early in the voyage to Morrell's heroic attempts to reach the South Polar latitudes, rather than the ship's poor construction, and recount a wholly fictitious and rapturous welcome and coronation for Dako on his return to Uneapa rather than admit his embarrassing disappearance. Indeed, according to this account, both Dako and Garrygarry were crowned kings of their lands. Inland journeys are enhanced in length, and discoveries of fortified villages become discoveries of ancient ruined towns (though there may indeed be some ruins that have not since been discovered). Jacobs also describes how the Americans met the children of La Pérouse's surgeon Lavoo on Naraga, implicitly refuting Dumont d'Urville's published dismissal of Morrell's claim two years previously. Since the manuscript of Woodworth's journal does not cover the Americans' visit to Naraga, however, whether the passage in the narrative describing the meeting with Lavoo is accurate or fiction remains open to question to this day.

The book takes an unashamedly "republican" view of the exploration. It reviews earlier expeditions to "tropical Australasia" based on extensive research, but only to expose the violence and ignorance of those earlier explorers, who "knew little or nothing about the country, except the general trend of land in particular places as seen in the distance. . . . They were afraid to land, on account of the warlike cannibals which were supposed to inhabit the islands." This contrasts with the warm relations that the American expedition struck up in the region.

The book also doubled as a prospectus for a future voyage. Just as Morrell had kept the location of Dako's Uneapa and Monday's Ninigo islands secret in his *Voyages,* so Woodworth and Jacobs intentionally disguised all the commercially significant locations in their book. They omitted Dako's island and its archipelago from the published maps and camouflaged their location in the text by introducing false long sea journeys to mislead the reader into thinking that these islands were probably somewhere east (not west) of New Ireland. An appendix reproduced Reverend Williams's plans for the establishment of a colony on Samoa, a further inducement to investment.

Jacobs and Woodworth could not revive Morrell's reputation—to attempt to do so would be to undermine their own. Rather, the narrative presented Morrell's various maneuvers in context, hoping that readers would at least understand them. Morrell intended, Jacobs claimed, "to do right when he started, and if others had dealt with him as he expected them to do, the voyage might have prospered. But many things occurred which the world cannot appreciate, and which in a measure justified (as he thought) his conduct. I am inclined to the belief that Captain Morrell was not so abandoned a man as many suppose."

In every passage of Jacobs's work, authenticity is overruled by the need to attract financial backers. It highlights successful prospecting in every commodity the Pacific can offer, conceals commercial risks, and avoids moral censure that could undermine investor confidence. As Garove Island was to be the main colony, it suits Jacobs to describe it as uninhabited—although Woodworth's manuscript maps reveal otherwise. Above all, the book conceals how dependent Morrell had been on Dako; how Dako's disappearance had jeopardized the entire voyage; and how even the most carefully laid plans of potential investors in the region could easily unravel. Episodes of cold-blooded killing that apparently made even Woodworth ashamed (he encrypted them into his journal) are reforged into moments of compassion, as the young Selim expertly extracts musket balls from the wounded and patches them up. Their looting of skulls and other "curiosities" are recast as "fair exchange" when trinkets are left in their wake. The constraints of commerce and colonization can even be discerned in a passage that was drafted but excluded from the published version. These few leaves of manuscript still languishing in the Woodworth family archive recount a hike that Morrell and his men made inland on the volcanic Willaumez peninsula during which the writer infers the presence of severed limbs roasting over cooking fires from a simple observation of wood smoke. Such an account would have no place in a book that was presenting the region as safe for trade and colonization. The published book dismisses most "cannibal talk" as reflecting outsiders' fear of the unknown or local fears of American outsiders. In the one place it acknowledges cannibalism, it is not as "savagery" but as a retribution for the savagery of European intruders: "an act of vengeance to appease the manes of their ancestors, who may have been cruelly treated, or murdered in cold blood, by some ancient bigoted and ignorant European visitors."

The backstory for all the literature, plays, and exhibitions that these unfolding odysseys offered up to the American public reveals that they all bear the imprint of commercial imperative. Like Jacobs and Woodworth, Benjamin Morrell was tempted by the ripe fruits of profit hanging low on Dako's island, waiting to be harvested by the first European or American who arrived, but while Morrell was displaying Dako and Monday to the public, his massive debts were playing their part in ordering his every move. The literary and theatrical productions could alter fortunes—but they had to say the right thing and have the right effects. Samuel Woodworth created a Benjamin Morrell as the heroic Yankee explorer to support Morrell's private and federal fundraising. Samuel Knapp presented Abby not only as a good wife but as a patriotic activist for American sailors that gave her a moral shine attractive to ethical (and federal) investors. Indeed, with the possibility of federal funding for exploration, the patriotic arguments for expanding American influence overseas found in all these works dovetailed with private commercial advantage. Private interests were kicking out a literature that helped forge a national identity—accentuated by the small circle of patriotic Knickerbocker writers drafted to help.

Jacobs and Selim Woodworth's book appeared solely under Jacobs's name, presumably to guard Woodworth's growing naval reputation, and was greeted with mixed reviews. Several magazines, including the *New York Mirror* (still edited by Samuel Woodworth's former colleague George Pope Morris), praised the book and printed extracts from it. Most were more critical. Some questioned its truthfulness, while others were concerned by Morrell's callous treatment of investors and islanders alike: "We must condemn the course often avowedly pursued towards the natives and the unnecessary effusion of human blood." The book sold most of its print run, making it "a success," but Harper and Brothers did not reprint it and copies are now rare.

Jacobs and Woodworth were probably less interested in the reviews and sales of the book than in its power to attract investors. By the time it was published, they had been away from Dako's island for nine years, but the idea of returning fueled their desires as strongly as ever. Investors, however, were not forthcoming, and Selim Woodworth returned to his naval duties, first carrying dispatches overland to the Pacific Squadron in 1846, and then leading a relief expedition in 1847 to extricate the infamous Donner Party. Those who encountered Woodworth during these ventures ridiculed his pomposity, ineptitude, dishonesty, and frequent inebriation. Yet he earned respect where it mattered, and settled as a leading citizen of Yerba Buena, or as it was soon to become known, San Francisco.

Sometime in 1849—thirteen years after they had left the Pacific— Jacobs again captained a vessel round Cape Horn to visit Woodworth in San Francisco. The main purpose of his voyage was to bring a group of "Forty-niners" through the Golden Gate to join the gold rush, but it was also in part to resurrect the pair's colonization plans, for which he had finally got some backers. Jacobs's bark seems to have been partially financed by investors who called themselves the California and Pacific Ocean Exploring, Trading and Colonisation Company. These investors may well have included Silas Burrows, who was now in the process of moving to San Francisco himself, as well as Jacobs and Woodworth. The joint stock company wrote to Woodworth formally at a date sometime between 1849 and 1851 inviting him to command an expedition from San Francisco to islands in the

Pacific. Woodworth's naval and administrative skills would have made him attractive to the investors, but in addition he was familiar with the islands and knew "the language of the Natives." The expedition's destination again was Dako's island.

The investors' plans were carefully laid out, but they also authorized Woodworth to make any adaptation that was likely to enhance the expedition's success and profit—and since he was being paid on a percentage basis, it was very much in his interest to do so. The plans were modeled on the earlier colonization scheme, but had expanded to include locating the huge guano deposits that had accumulated over millennia on several Pacific islands and islets and for which there was now an insatiable global demand. Indeed, these deposits had become strategically important for the United States, and the company was hoping that "national advantages would accrue from their work." Through their "California and Oregon Delegation" the investors sought endorsement from the U.S. government, also hoping that Woodworth could retain his naval rank and position, since this would give the enterprise respectability and national protection.

This expedition was to consist of three ships. The first, a bark of 300 tons, would carry emigrants and stores for the whole expedition. In the procurement lists, the company envisaged taking a range of artisans and professionals: a watchmaker, a surgeon, an apothecary, a chemist, a metallurgist, a botanist, a surveyor, and a minister. Scientists were needed to prospect for botanical and mineral resources. The first ship would take twelve artisans and three scientists with their families, along with the usual complement of captain, three mates, ten seamen, two cooks, two stewards, four servants, a boatswain, a gunner, a carpenter, an armorer, and a sailmaker. A second ship—a schooner of 150 tons—would carry the trading cargo and would also transport some experienced California miners and their families. A third, smaller steam tug would support the flotilla: as it did not rely on sail power, it would enable the expedition to continue to trade under difficult winds. This vessel would also convey a couple of engineers and four foremen. All ships were to be well armed and equipped "to resist any attack from any hostile natives that the expedition may encounter."

All in all, these plans were budgeted at $40,000 inclusive of armaments, trading cargo, provisions, and sundries—surprisingly little given the scale of the endeavor. Budgets were calculated down to the last item, revealing the practicalities of private colonization. A shopping list for the colony came in at $6,440. Its armaments included 100 revolvers, 250 rifles and muskets, 20 cannon (32- and 24-pounders), powder, shot, shell, shrapnel, and grape. Among the tools needed were those for the blacksmith, carpenters, masons, stonecutters, shoemakers, tailors, and tinmen. The engineering equipment included a steam engine, saw mill, grist mill, and forge, as well as the iron, steel, tin plate, sheet lead, copper, brass, zinc, and solder wires to work with. For the first houses, the expedition would transport sashes, doors, carpets, furniture, crockery, tinware, glassware, hardware, stoves, nails, clocks, mirrors, and cooking utensils. For farming and trade, seeds were to be purchased as well as agricultural and mining equipment, including harnesses, wagons, and carts—and large pots for curing sea cucumbers. For clothing and drapery, the list was enormous, including blue drill, muslin, cotton thread, needles, thimbles, scissors, knives, ribbons, flannel, linen, hats, boots, shoes, stockings, shirts, drawers, buttons, tape, and handkerchiefs. Food to be taken included rice, cornmeal, wheat pipes, barley, beef, flour, sugar, molasses, coffee, beans, oil, vinegar, preserved meats, vegetables, preserved fruits, pepper, mustard, dried fruit, pickles, onions, butter, tea, lard, and olive oil. And alcohol was now acceptable: whisky, wine, ale, and porter were on the list, along with the yeast powders needed to ferment more.

But all these elaborate preparations came to nothing. What happened to unstitch such a carefully planned operation is not clear. Perhaps the investors realized that they could accrue easier profits through the California gold rush. Perhaps there was a more personal falling out. Whatever the reason, Woodworth and Jacobs were again frustrated in their effort to live their dream together. And Dako's islands were once again spared American colonization.

On the *Margaret Oakley,* Woodworth had sailed with Morrell and the officers, whereas Jacobs had been relegated to the crew before the mast. And in everything he attempted, Woodworth was Morrell's protégé: with his own grandiose plans, he was always on the threshold of the next success—but somehow always failing. Even Jacobs, Woodworth's companion and observer, was never entirely Woodworth's man. For reasons we can now only speculate about, Jacobs left Woodworth and San Francisco.

Woodworth now became increasingly impulsive, erratic, prone to outbursts of anger, and, by several accounts, a drunk. Between 1849 and 1851 he helped establish the vigilante committee that tracked down and annihilated a band of desperadoes known as the "Sydney Cove" gang. But rumor had it that while honing in on the gang Woodworth had been keener on the embezzlement of public funds and alcohol than vigilance. And yet Woodworth was elected the first senator for Monterey in the California State Senate of 1849.

Despite such apparent success, it seems that Woodworth's life had lost all purpose. The Pacific dream was over. Jacobs had gone. And everyone else had simply revealed their imbecility by not backing him. If he could have exterminated the world he perhaps would have; instead, he turned his back on it—a hermit's impulse being the flip side of the sociopath's. As the powers of darkness now claimed him for his own, he secluded himself on tiny Red Rock Island. Just one letter exists from him to Jacobs from his sanctuary. It is not dated, but it was clearly written some years after the two parted, and in it he expresses the somewhat forlorn hope that Tom might join him on a sailing cruise in the Mediterranean. Perhaps it was never sent.

> Dear Tom
>
> I have defered writing to you until this late day, not because I had forgoten you but I have had so many letters to write and so little to fill them, that I dispared attempting to fill a sheet. I have heard occasionaly from my brother Fred. I understand that you have made another Tour to the western country &c.
>
> You recolect that some time ago (about the time we were fitting out the expedition for the Paciffic Ocean Trading Com-

Selim Woodworth, ca. 1850–1855, from *The Annals of San Francisco: Containing a Summary of the History of the First Discovery, Settlement, Progress and Present Condition of California,* ed. Frank Soulé, John Gihon, and Jim Nisbet (1855), 794

pany) we talked of starting an expedition for pleasure,—a cruise in the Mediteranean.

There is now an Expedition about fitting out, that I think will prove a splendid affair. There is every prospect of its proving successfull as it will start under better auspices than our projected one. . . .

We propose purchasing a Clipper Brig of about 250 tons burthen, a fast sailing craft, on the M[argaret] O[akley]'s model and size will be just the thing.

But Woodworth's Mediterranean cruise with Jacobs was not to be. He continued his life as a hermit until 1856, when his brother Frederick eventually managed to draw him back into society and persuaded him to marry. Between 1858 and 1860 Selim developed a copper mine on Elide Island, farther down the Californian coast, and then rejoined the navy during the Civil War. Outwardly he also reverted to his father's more compassionate nature. Under the guidance of his brother Frederick and wife, Lisette, and as their wealth accrued almost effortlessly from their city land, their extended household became a liberal stronghold. They even took in and protected the radical African American entrepreneur and civil rights activist Mary Ellen ("Mamma") Pleasant and her husband, John. Mary Ellen had become famous before the Civil War for disposing of her hard-earned capital by donating thirty thousand dollars to bankroll her abolitionist friend John Brown's (failed) insurrection.

Woodworth's life has left enough traces for us to discern something of this later character, but the paper trail for Jacobs is far less easy to follow. Jacobs was not even called Jacobs for much longer. In January 1846, less than two years after putting his name to the book published by Harper and Brothers, he petitioned the New York State legislature to change it. Many petitions for name changes would be accepted later in the century, most famously for the Astors and the Steinways, but in the 1840s they were rare. Name changes might be requested to perpetuate a family name, show gratitude for benefits received, or to escape ridicule, association with undesirables, or confusion. Jacobs's first application in 1846 was rejected. But he persisted, and in 1851 he became Thomas Jefferson Monroe, with the stated reason that "James J. Monroe of St. Louis, offers to pay him $500 and give him other pecuniary advantages if he will assume legally the name of Thomas J. Monroe." James J. Monroe seems to have been a well-known silversmith, and perhaps Jacobs met him as he passed through Saint Louis on one of his tramps west. It seems more likely that Monroe was a friend of the family, as Tom's brother, William, also took the name Monroe, though never formally.

The newly christened Tom Monroe left only secondhand accounts of his subsequent life and enigmatic travels, and while there is no known reason to question their credibility, corroborating evidence remains elusive. That he made another overland trip to California was noted by Woodworth in the extant letter to him, and sources published after his death place the trek during 1853. Sometime between October 1853 and February 1856, Monroe apparently captained a vessel to the Crimea during the Anglo-Russian (Crimean) War, where he fought in several engagements, presumably, like many Americans, for the Russians against the British. He also claims to have traveled with the writer Bayard Taylor "all through Russia from the Black Sea to Finland" between late 1856 and 1857. Monroe does not feature in any of Taylor's known works and letters, but absence of evidence is, as ever, not evidence of absence—especially if the two were lovers. What is certain, however, is that Monroe had begun to construct his Harlem fortress in September 1856; if he did travel with Taylor, it would have been completed in his absence. It would therefore have been on his return that he began to isolate himself and swear his "boycott against all mankind." It is tempting to link Tom's turn to seclusion with Selim's marriage in 1856, but again there is no evidence.

Many years later, in January 1871, a telegram must have arrived at the Hermitage in Harlem bearing news from San Francisco that Selim Woodworth was dangerously ill. Tom instantly arranged for a new passport, packed his bags, and sailed to San Francisco, taking the fastest route, via Panama. But he was too late. Selim Woodworth had died on January 29, at the age of fifty-five. By the time the Harlem hermit himself died, on January 15, 1889, after another eighteen years of seclusion, Dako's island had finally fallen under colonial control—not to the United States but to the German Second Reich.

Epilogue: "The Cannibal" and the Captain

ഗ്രൂ

Before dawn on the morning of December 15, 1943, units of the 112th U.S. Cavalry embarked on their landing craft and cranked up their outboards, heading for the Arawe shores of New Britain to establish yet another beachhead in the battle for the Pacific. Escorting the mission was the naval destroyer USS *Woodworth,* which had been operating off the coast of New Britain for two weeks. She had been named for Selim E. Woodworth, identified in naval literature as a celebrated naval captain from the American Civil War who had commanded armored attack vessels on the Mississippi, eventually earning the personal commendation of President Abraham Lincoln. By some accident of history a vessel bearing Selim's name had finally returned to the islands that had so shaped his life.

It was a full century since Woodworth had helped his friend Tom Jacobs complete their book. Neither the two friends nor any other Americans had made it to the islands to trade and pick up the cargoes which Dako's people on Uneapa, Garrygarry's at Kove, and the Aromot islanders and Sio villagers had promised to prepare for them in 1835. No one ever delivered the wonderful treasures which were promised in exchange. The islands remained "uncontacted" for another generation.

European traders began to visit in the 1870s. Then in 1884 Germany asserted control over what it named the Bismarck Sea. There were profits to be gained from coconut copra, and the coconut palms of Uneapa and Garove attracted traders who "purchased" large tracts of the islands for plantations. Soon after the start of World War I an Australian expeditionary force overcame German resistance in the islands, and after the armistice Australia acquired the mandate to administer them. But in 1942, Japan seized and occupied New Britain, establishing it as a forward base in the country's South Pacific campaign. American and allied forces wrested back control in 1944, and after peace was restored in 1945, Australia once again administered the islands as part of the combined territories of Papua and New Guinea. The territories acquired independence together as Papua New Guinea in 1975.

The traders who visited Dako's islands in the 1870s imagined that they were making "first contact." Any traces of Dako's long stay in New York or of the American sailors' sojourn in the region were overlooked. There are no more written records about Dako, and no record at all indicating whether he lived into the colonial period. By the time of Uneapa's colonization in the 1880s he would have been in his late seventies or older. It was his daughter who welcomed the colonizers. Neither colonizers nor subsequent scholars visiting the islands ever realized that an islander had long ago starred in his own show on Broadway or considered what his legacy on Uneapa and the region might have been.

After the *Margaret Oakley* left, the islanders appear to have patiently awaited the Americans' return. A British vessel commanded by a mutineer named John Francis King inadvertently arrived off Dako's mother's island of Naraga in 1842. Thinking that he had made a new discovery, King named it Gipps Island after the Australian governor whose justice he knew he would eventually have to face. King was most surprised to find that the islanders were keen on trade and not hostile at all. This was in stark contrast to the aggressive way in which the same islanders had greeted Morrell upon his return there before they realized that Dako had come back with him. King knew nothing of those events, which had occurred seven years previously. He traded across the bulwarks of his ship and sailed on. But the

islanders' spirit of welcoming visitors faded fast. "Blackbirders"—
navigators who captured people to work as laborers in the Pacific
plantations—visited the islands in the 1870s, with the result that by
the 1880s the first colonial visitor to the islands, Otto Finsch, reported
that the people were extremely wary of foreign vessels.

Nevertheless, the islanders initially got on well with the white
colonizers, who they imagined just wanted to plant tomatoes, and
recognized in them a chance to reforge links with their ancestors in
the parallel world. Dako's daughter even helped demarcate a garden
for a German colonizer. But the Uneapa people were soon to experience a form of colonization that was as exploitative as what Woodworth and Jacobs had once plotted. Within a few years the best land
on Dako's island had been acquired by Europeans, who made a fortune exporting copra. The Germans also levied a head tax, which
forced men to find paid work and enter into a new economic order as
laborers and migrants. In 1897, a smallpox epidemic nearly wiped out
the populations of Garove and spread through the other Vitu Islands.
Bodies were left unburied, and the islanders who survived were in no
state to resist the Germans.

The island on which Dako's mother lived, Naraga, suffered a different fate. People began dying of a variety of mysterious causes for
which their descendants still blame sorcery and the powerful vuvumu, Laupu, who had become weary of their cooking food in the
island's hot spring. Curiously, Tom Jacobs had written a letter to the
New York *Sun* in 1845 noting that many islanders had succumbed after eating fish that were ailing because of volcanic activity. Volcanoes
have long been a source of mercury, which builds up concentrations
in fish and thus contaminates the entire food chain. Eating fish caught
locally and cooked in the naturally boiling springs of Naraga would
eventually have brought on fatigue, tremors, seizures, numbness, de-
pression, muscle weakness, memory loss, and irregularities in movement, speech, and sight. Eventually, in the 1920s, the last survivors
quit the island—including perhaps the descendants of those who survived the French expedition of La Pérouse—leaving it completely
deserted. And so it remains.

In 1871, in a prelude to European colonization of the region, a maverick young Russian named Nikolai Mikloucho-Maclay settled on the coast of New Guinea fifteen miles south of the meandering river up which Morrell and his crew had trekked prospecting for diamonds and gold. Maclay thought he was the first white man to become familiar with the region. As with Morrell, the people whose land he settled on took him for a celestial being "from the moon" because of the ship he arrived on, the goods he brought, the clothes he wore, and the fear he seemed to lack. Yet when eventually he learned the local language and made friends, he found that some of the people among whom he had settled could speak to him about a land with iron axes, Western clothing, and houses that were several stories high: a land which they associated with their creator god, Anut.

Many miles to the south, the first German missionaries to settle on the Siassi island of Tami also encountered a curious story: the first white man to land there was the mythical god Panku (Pango), who could change himself into different beings. He also apparently stole a woman from Umboi Island by whom he fathered two boys, Ngamet and Kapi-molo. The family traveled on to the Willaumez and Uneapa region, then returned to the little island of Aromot. Here Panku changed himself into a snake with a human head. And that was the last they saw of him until some more white people came to settle. Unaware of Morrell's existence, the missionary dated these events to about 1840, and thought that the stories related to the captain of a whaling ship, with Kapi-molo resembling "Captain Molo" . . . or something similar . . .

Historians of the region tend to make the rather obvious point that we all learn from events. Inhabitants of Dako's island and neighboring shores understood the arrival of Morrell, his crew, and his cannons according to their own way of looking at the world—through the lens of what outsiders like to call mythology. But as the story unfolded, events transformed that very mythology. The ship's cannons sent a new reality and new evidence into previous thoughts. Without access to events prior to contact, historians have often found it easier to consider much indigenous mythology as if it were timeless and invariant. By pushing back the documented history of this region by a generation or two, as we have been able to do here, we can discern how the mythology documented in the twentieth century was shaped—sometimes unexpectedly—by earlier events in the nineteenth, offering an inkling of a new intellectual history.

Myths are no longer told on Uneapa about the spirit Pango. He dominated its cosmology in the 1830s, but today's stories are of other beings. This is not, however, because Pango has been superseded or suppressed, but because the parallel white world of the dead over which Pango presided has become ever more manifest as Uneapa has been drawn into the postcolonial globalized world. Today, *pango* is simply the local word for white people.

In the stories related on Uneapa today specifically about Dako, he is described as having been kidnapped by Germans rather than Americans. It was not until World War II that islanders re-encountered Americans, when the United States captured New Britain from the Japanese. For much of the twentieth century, islanders have been uncertain about where the various white people come from. Even now some still equate distant places such America, Rome, Australia, Japan, Israel, and the moon with the lands of the dead. Among these have been practitioners of a religion adherents call the Kalt Misin (Cult Mission), some members of which once sought to write to the spirits of the dead living in America. Indeed, mischievous critics of this cult on the island played a trick on the leader by forging a reply from his dead brother in America.

The legacy of Dako on Uneapa belongs to the islanders. Oral accounts concerning his capture nowadays relate that the whites had captured him primarily for instruction: "The whites had not caught him to injure or kill him. No they just wanted to give him knowledge by teaching him. So they took him to the ship and looked after him and helped him and dressed him in clothes. Then he stayed with them. They kept teaching him and he was partly able to communicate."

Samuel Woodworth inserted into Morrell's book the idea that Dako and Monday might either become missionaries to their home peoples or "prepare the minds of their countrymen to receive and

protect missionaries." This was surely a self-serving script. Nevertheless, the idea that Dako learned American religious practices was also
recalled by the ethnologist Theodore Dwight, who accompanied
Dako to Sunday schools, where "he took a deep interest in some simple religious instruction which the children received in his presence."
Like all Uneapa islanders, Dako had been schooled in a variety of
theories of creation, and was surely interested in the theology of his
captors and their knowledge of the powers behind creation and catastrophe, if only because these might explain his captors' extraordinary
power. We recall Dwight's observation that Dako "promised on his
arrival at his island to collect the children every Sabbath, and teach
them in like manner." Modern accounts from the island suggest that
the inhabitants were aware of the Christian church long before it arrived: a community leader in north Uneapa "claimed that his mother
had received a prophecy from the powerful spirit Mataluangi foretell-
ing the coming of the Catholic Church. This spirit also told her that
when the missionaries arrived he, the spirit, would leave, returning
only at the end of the world."

The teaching to which Dako had been most exposed during his
stay in New York, via the Woodworths, was Swedenborgianism. It
also seems likely that Dako and Selim would have discussed religious
matters during the long voyage to the island. The *Margaret Oakley*'s
library had few books, but among them was the Swedenborgian *New
Jerusalem Magazine* (the others were a Bible, Cook's *Voyages,* two geography books, a history of Rome, a classical dictionary, a pictorial
geography, a French dictionary, two books on chemistry, and one on
astronomy). The modern Kalt Misin religion on the island dovetails
with the teachings of Swedenborg on the nature of the spirit world.
Both assert that the spirits that associate with humans and shape their
lives can derive from other worlds. Just as Samuel Woodworth gave
George Washington the voice of a Native American in his novels, so
devotees of Kalt Misin on the island believe that it is not only the
spirits of their own ancestors whom they attract and who determine
their being but also the spirits of Americans who shape their lives and
thoughts. With such a cosmopolitan society of spirits able to drive

thoughts and emotions, it becomes sublimely hard to discern what it is to be "us" and what "them."

Meanwhile, back in America, the memory of Dako was kept alive for many years by the radical anthropologist who had interviewed him. Theodore Dwight had become one of the founding members of the American Ethnological Society, which first met in New York in 1842. At one of the early meetings Dwight read a paper based on his interviews with Dako. The paper was never published and is now lost, but according to the proceedings of the society it was titled "Notice of the Uniapa Islands, a small group near New Guinea, and of the habits, language, &c. of that portion of the black race by which they are inhabited, from materials derived from a native." Over the next few years, Dwight spoke regularly about the material he had collected during his interviews with Dako, and commented on what he thought were peculiarities in the Uneapa language. The anthropologist also described Dako's mathematics and his geometrical terms, noting that the language had names for seven different triangles, which may have been significant in Uneapa as both decoration and a navigational aid. As much as thirty years later, in the 1860s, Dwight was still corresponding about Dako with linguists at the Smithsonian Institution.

Gradually, however, as the reputation of Benjamin Morrell descended into infamy, the story of the captives fell out of history and into fiction. Those who have recently encountered traces of "Sunday" and "Monday" in the American historical record have dismissed them as Morrell's "faux cannibals."

But just as Dako's experience of America may have persisted unnoticed on his island and in the regional mythology, so the American experience of Dako has lived on in American popular culture—albeit well disguised within its fiction. In particular, Dako infiltrated one of the most famous novels of the time, *Moby-Dick*. In Herman Melville's masterpiece of the duel between humanity and the mythos of a white whale, he reconjures Dako as Ishmael's compelling companion Queequeg the harpooner. It is after he has shared a bed at the inn with the Pacific Islander that Ishmael extols: "Better to sleep with a sober cannibal than a drunken Christian."

There are several known sources for Queequeg, but one scholar argues that Melville drew many aspects of his character from Jacobs's rendition of Dako. Melville had purchased Jacobs's *Scenes, Incidents, and Adventures . . .* together with Morrell's *Voyages* from Gowan's Bookstore on Liberty Street, off Broadway, in April 1847. Queequeg resembles Jacobs's Dako in a number of ways: the dexterity of his spear throwing; his being the son and heir of a king; his "inveterate and praiseworthy habit of minding his own business"; and his manner of speaking—which Jacobs and Melville render in a similar way. There is something of Queequeg in Garrygarry too. He and the harpooner shared a common interest in wheelbarrows, both fell ill with a chill which developed into a fever, and both sported a beaver hat.

There is, however, more to Melville's assimilation of Dako than detail drawn from Jacobs's book. As we have seen, Melville at the impressionable age of twelve would have seen Dako when the "Cannibal Show" came to the Albany Museum in October 1831. In particular he would have noted the novel tattoos covering Dako's (and later Queequeg's) legs, chest, and arms. These are not mentioned by Jacobs, but they were described by journalists covering the show, as was Dako's feathered headdress and shell necklaces. The young Melville would have appreciated Dako's size and strength as well: "his muscular form of remarkable perfection and portly aspect."

Melville may well have introduced a character based on Dako in his first book, *Typee,* which gives an account of his journey into the "Terrible valley of Typees" on the Marquesas island of Nuku Hiva (though it proved to be not so terrible after all). To sustain his narrative, Melville fleshed out his own experience on this island, where he had absconded from a whaling vessel, by drawing on other works. Whether Melville ever met a real leader of the Typee, by the time his readers encountered the leader Melville called Mehevi, the man had taken on the body and character of Dako: a superb-looking warrior, with a headdress of towering plumes of tropical tail feathers mixed with those of the cock, and with necklaces, earrings, a beautifully crafted spear, and elaborate tattoos displayed "on every noble limb." Those who had seen Dako in America would have no difficulty picturing Mehevi, and that may have been Melville's strategy. Dr. Pascalis, the eminent New York physician who had examined Dako, wrote of him that he had a muscular form, of remarkable perfection, and his commanding rank and authority were denoted as much by his numerous tattoos on the limbs, chest, and shoulders as by his various ornaments. As Melville wrote: "The warrior, from the excellence of his physical proportions, might certainly have been regarded as one of Nature's noblemen, and the lines drawn upon his face may possibly have denoted his exalted rank." Dako has lived on quietly in American mythology just as he has in Uneapa.

Following Morrell's sudden death, his life began to attract a great deal of controversy. For many, he was "the biggest liar" or "the Munchhausen" of the Pacific, largely because of the false claims embodied in Samuel Woodworth's ghostwritten work. For others, swayed by both Jacobs's description of the way Morrell had overruled his supercargo and Morrell's attempts to steal the Chinese cargo, he was a pirate. Yet others have been more respectful, believing in his fictitious account of the voyage to the southern latitudes and attributing him with the discovery of huge deposits of guano. Those skeptical of his claims in life, however, have not questioned claims concerning his death—though anyone who has looked for hard evidence to corroborate it have looked in vain. One nautical historian, Henry Stommel, attempted unsuccessfully in the 1970s to find Morrell's grave in Mozambique. His efforts to locate a grave or gravestone in Maputo were fruitless, as were his searches of the port master's archives, the national archives, and the civil registry. Nothing at all could be found that was connected to Morrell's arrival or his death.

The reason for this is that Morrell did not die in Mozambique. Four years after his reported death, the captain gave proof of life, to those who knew him, in the form of a letter dated August 11, 1843, to Theodore Dwight's *New York Commercial Advertiser*. This letter was simply questioning the claims of a sea captain concerning his discovery of a new Pacific island. The captain in question was one George Netcher (or Nitcher), who had published an article in the American papers early in August 1843 explaining that while whaling on his bark *Isabella,* he had discovered an island that he wanted to name Eadie's Island. The letter of retort, signed simply "Morrell," revealed that the captain was not only alive but seemingly also in New York.

That the letter was signed "Morrell" is far from unequivocal proof that it was written by Captain Benjamin Morrell—his was a common name for a sea captain at that time. Yet the information contained within it could only have been written by someone who had been aboard the *Margaret Oakley.* "Morrell" describes the disputed island's location and provides further descriptions of the island during La Pérouse's first voyage and accounts of it during Dumont d'Urville's subsequent visit. He then goes on to explain that he saw the island again in February 1835 on the way to Australia when voyaging "down the Solomon Archipelago, touching at, and trading with the natives of all the inhabited islands of the group." The timing matches exactly Woodworth's journal for the voyage of the *Margaret Oakley* from the Bismarck Sea to Australia. The letter writer also gives a great deal of nautical information concerning the details of his voyage. On his own arrival off this island, he writes, he also believed that he had made a new discovery, but when he began trading with the islanders who approached hesitantly in canoes, he saw that they already had several European articles. Moreover, although the islands were not on his older charts, when this "Morrell" arrived in Sydney, he had purchased a copy of Dumont d'Urville's newly compiled chart of 1834 which located the island and named it Nitendi. The writer concludes: "I have by examining my charts and private journal, become satisfied beyond doubt, that 'Eadie's Island' and 'Nitendi' are one and the same thing."

This letter was unlikely to have been a hoax: its significance in revealing that Morrell was alive would be clear only to people who knew the details of the voyage of the *Margaret Oakley* (which is not mentioned by name in the letter). And in 1843, the voyage of the *Margaret Oakley* was a complete mystery to all except those who had been aboard her. It is conceivable that Thomas Jacobs, Selim Woodworth, John B. Bernadon, Algernon Jarvis, or Francis Babcock wrote it, yet it seems unlikely. Jacobs and Woodworth were working on their book at this time in order to rehabilitate their reputations and had no incentive to rekindle debates about Morrell, let alone suggest that he had faked his own death. Jarvis and Babcock had been super-cargoes, not sailors, and did not have the navigational knowledge contained within the letter. Bernadon was on a voyage to Cuba when the letter was published.

The letter did not evoke any further discussion concerning the fate of Benjamin Morrell at the time, and its significance has gone unnoticed until now. Why Morrell might have taken this opportu-nity to leave a calling card remains a matter for speculation. Perhaps it was a veiled threat to Jacobs and Woodworth, who were about to publish their own version of events on the *Margaret Oakley,* and who would have been able to figure out its meaning. Perhaps, like many criminals, he could not resist flaunting himself.

Several of Morrell's family had relocated from Stonington to Puerto Cabello on the Caribbean coast of Venezuela, where Benja-min's nephew Jeremiah continued to live. In 1847 Jeremiah sold the last of the Morrell properties in Stonington. Abby Jane Morrell her-self can be placed in the Caribbean several times after her husband's supposed death, returning from there to New York in 1839, quite pos-sibly en route back from Venezuela. She can also be placed in New York in 1841, when newspapers relate that she was robbed of a watch worth fifty dollars, but otherwise she has vanished from documented history. She remains well known in literary circles for her contribu-tion to women's nautical writing and for her advocacy of sailors' rights—but only by those who overlook Colonel Knapp's authorship. Abby, a most elusive celebrity, features only once more in the writ-ten record: in June 1850 she arrived in New York, again from Puerto Cabello.

So it seems most probable that Morrell staged his death at the end of 1838 in Mozambique to evade the insurers who had been pursuing him and the cargo. Mozambique was an excellent place in which to "die": there was no American consul there to ask questions. More-over, Madagascar and Fort Dauphin were just across the sea. Morrell might even have retrieved the remainder of the missing cargo if he had salted it away there and then hitched a ride to Venezuela on one of the innumerable Cuban slavers bound with their mortal cargo for Brazil, Cuba, and the Spanish Main. Although it has been impossible to track the fugitive Morrell down definitively (he covered his tracks well), it seems likely that he spent his final days in Venezuela, probably in the vicinity of Puerto Cabello, living under a false identity a long way from American justice—but still connected within the trading worlds which were his life. If so, he would not have been the last American outlaw to seek refuge in South America.

Puerto Cabello boasted one of the finest harbors in the world, where large vessels could be secured "by a single hair." Long before Bolívar, the Liberator, had won the country's independence from the Spanish crown, the neck of land where the town had grown up had had been cleaved from the mainland to leave a false island now dominated by a massive fort. Its streets had been laid out on a grid and paved, and the stone quay sides all beautifully crafted by prisoners. Overshadowed by huge trees by day and lit by oil lamps at dusk, it was the perfect place for a fugitive sundowner. If traces of Benjamin Morrell are to be found, they are more likely to be in a Venezuelan graveyard than in Mozambique. Morrell really could return from the dead.

༢

Notes

This work casts new light on many people whose lives have not previously attracted much attention from historians. I am sure that among readers there will be those who know something more of these events, and others who hold private documents relating to them and the complex cast of characters. I would be enormously grateful to receive any such information. A work of history is always provisional. One of the reasons for writing a work of this nature is the hope that it may bring to light further evidence and surprises.

Bibliographical Note

As this book relates not only to the odysseys of Dako and Morrell, but also tells the story of the people who narrated them, and how these narrations themselves influenced unfolding events, the text itself serves as an explanatory note for several of its key sources. The narratives of the Morrells and of Jacobs are particularly unreliable, but with the reappearance of the manuscript journals of Selim Woodworth and several key articles about Dako written by Theodore Dwight, as well as myriad details from elsewhere, it has been possible to read these narratives both for what they say of past events and for their place in the unfolding story.

A second significant key to the telling of these events has been missing entirely from the work and will not be found, either, in the bibliography. This is the Internet and the electronic access and search facilities it offers for books of the era. This work could simply not have been written ten years ago. The nineteenth-century American newspapers that are central to this work no longer need be thumbed through for years at the risk of ingesting period dust and disease but can be searched in seconds from a quiet office overlooked by Sussex's beautiful South Downs. I thank the technology, and the minds and the laborers behind it. From my same office, I can access for free the corpus of early newspapers from Australia and Singapore; pay a little for the astonishing historical databases that genealogical organizations now can provide us with; and pinpoint and order like pizzas specific archival copies from libraries across America, Europe, and Australia. Such access is transforming the granularity with which histories of this period can be written, who writes them (attracting anthropologists more used to "being there"), how they are written, and why.

Prologue

On the celebrations, see *New York Evening Post* and *New York Commercial Advertiser,* February 22, 1833. On museum, see, e.g., *New York Evening Post,* January 6, 1831. Quotes "perfectly natural . . ." and "most remarkable . . . ," E. Williams 1833: 173; "splendid and . . . ," *New York Evening Post,* February 19, 1833: 3. On play, "Dramatizing a dream," and quotes "wild, uncultivated . . . ," "dark mulatto . . . ," and "the two specimens . . . ," see *New York Mirror,* March 16, 1833: 295. On Dako's performing, see *New York Evening Post,* February 22, 1833: 3. Quotes "faux cannibal" and "domesticated Pacific Islander . . . ," Gibson 2008: 6. On "reverse anthropology," see Wagner 1981: 31–34. On discerning captives' perspectives, see, e.g., McLean 2012: 610–612. On the narrative history debate, see, e.g., H. White 2009, C. Jones 2013. On "snatching guilty pleasures," see McLean 2012. On transnational American studies, see, e.g., Rowe 2011, Fishkin 2005. On "Black Atlantic," see Gilroy 1993. On the Pacific, see Matsuda 2006, 2012. On the strategy of "following" things, see Marcus 1995.

Chapter 1: The Island

On the battle and its aftermath, see Bergh 1888, Keeler n.d., "Log," November 13–15, 1830, A. Morrell 1833, Halliard 1833. Quotes "literally covered . . . ," "several young . . . ," Bergh 1888; "we fired . . . ," Keeler n.d., "Log," November 14, 1830. On the speed of the *Antarctic,* see Bergh 1888. On events at "Massacre Island," see B. Morrell 1832a, Keeler n.d., "Log," October 15–November 4, 1830, and 1831, B. Pearson 1984. On Morrell's *Universal Geography,* see B. Morrell 1832a: 190. Quote "doomed to . . . ," Malte-Brun 1827: 307. On Uneapa dress and weaponry, see Bodrogi 1970, Keeler n.d., "Log," November 14, 1831. On cacophony method and speaking trumpet, see, e.g., Selim Woodworth n.d., "Journal": "Commercial Intelligence"; Jacobs 1844: 72. On Dako's ("Sunday's") age and physique, see Jacobs 1844: 24, A. Morrell 1833, Th. Dwight 1834: 185. Quotes "African," "were very . . . ," "Savages etc." 1831: 365; "remarkably strong . . ." and "No one . . . ," A. Morrell 1833: 205. On tattooing, see "Savages etc." 1831. On "family" tattoo designs for Siassi islanders in the region, see, e.g., Pomponio 1994, though the prevalence and meaning of Dako's tattoos remains mysterious. On dangling ear lobe and quote "dark copper," see *Massachusetts Spy,* September 14, 1831: 4. Information on earlobe practices from Blythe pers. comm. On Dako's first impressions, see Th. Dwight 1834. On first contact interpretation and quote "The face . . . ," see Connolly and Anderson 1987: 110. On Uneapa cosmology (upturned bowl, vuvumu, pigs, Mataluangi, Pango, etc.), see Blythe 1992, 1995. On seismic Pango, see Th. Dwight 1834, 1835. On black (cannon) ball, see Jacobs 1844: 86. Cannon balls were found off the shore of Naraga Island in 2009 (Jean Guillou, pers. comm.). On Pango's depredations, see Jacobs 1844: 95–103. On battle events and quote "Expect some . . . ,"

see Keeler n.d., "Log," November 14, 1830. On decorated canoes, see Selim Woodworth, "Papers"; information also from Blythe pers. comm. On Uneapa reefs, see Hair
and Magea 1995. Information on Dako's residence from Blythe pers. comm. Quotes
"remarkably well formed" and "warrior and . . . ," Keeler 1831: 2; "smile pleasantly . . ."
and "like a bear . . . ," Jacobs 1844: 24. On Dako's "obliging air," see Th. Dwight 1834,
1835. On Dako's treatment aboard, see "From the New York Standard" 1831. On white
"invisible" parallel world, Uneapa "myths," and ships of the dead, see Th. Dwight 1834,
1835, Blythe 1992, 1995, pers. comm., Fairhead and Blythe unpublished, Lattas
2001, 2005. Quotes "white, nearest to . . ." and "good go . . . ," Th. Dwight 1834: 187.
On the link of flying "ships of dead" to horizon mirages, see, e.g., Powell 1883: 200.
On Pongaracoopo, see Jacobs 1844: 85. On Dako's status, see, e.g., Jacobs 1844 and A.
Morrell 1833. Dako's father's name and the island political structure are from Blythe
1978 (also pers. comm.) and Byrne 2005. On the ship's departure, see Keeler n.d.,
"Log," November 15, 1830. Vakale's reaction was narrated by Rave and Tatau on Un-
eapa in 1980 to Jennifer Blythe, who was then unaware of Dako's story; she forwarded
the information to me. Quote "jumped overboard . . . ," "From the New York Standard" 1831. The island is now also called Unea (or Bali), the language being Uneapa.
Th. Dwight (1834, 1835) spells the island name "Uniapa," and Jacobs (1844) "Nyappa."
Jacobs called Dako's father "Mogagee," but island oral accounts identify him as "Tupi"
(Jennifer Blythe pers. comm.). Uneapa people often have two names. That Dako was
the firstborn (oldest son without older sister) is discerned from the respect paid to him,
and his being in line to inherit his father's position (A. Morrell 1833: 205, Jacobs 1844).
Tumbucu status was inherited in Uneapa (Blythe pers. comm.), contrasting with Kove
society; see, e.g., Chowning 1987b. On island agriculture and livelihood, see, e.g.,
Blythe 1978. On internal and external political relations and fighting between east and
west Uneapa, see Th. Dwight 1834, 1835, Jacobs 1844, Byrne 2005, Blythe 1978, pers.
comm., Rhoads and Specht 1980, Riebe 1967. On population, see "From the New York
Standard" 1831. On island kinship practices, see Blythe 1978, 1992, 1995. An oral account of the intra-island conflict by Bito Saropo (Tumbuku of Vorai) and others was
given to Blythe in 1980 (pers. comm.). On the stone figures, see Riebe 1967, Byrne
2005. On island polygyny, see Th. Dwight 1834. On Dako's three wives, see A. Morrell
1833: 205. Vakale is the only wife mentioned in the tale of the kidnapping narrated by
Rave and Tatau on Uneapa in 1980 (Blythe pers. comm.).

Chapter 2: The Captain

On Benjamin Morrell's earlier life, see especially B. Morrell 1832a. On Abby
Morrell's description and quote "remained silent," see A. Morrell 1833: 50. On Mor-
rell's popularity, see, e.g., testimony of William Scott in Petrie 1844: iii; Jacobs 1844.
Families who entrusted educated youth with Morrell include parents of Oscar
Sturtevant, Samuel Geery, Thomas Jacobs, and Selim Woodworth; see B. Morrell 1832a,
Jacobs 1844. On China trade, see, e.g., Dudden 1997. On sealing history, see Busch 1985.
Tasman passed Uneapa in April 1643 (Tasman 1895) and Bruni d'Entrecasteaux in early
July 1793 (Bruni d'Entrecasteaux 2001). Other visits had been made to the Bismarck Sea

but not Uneapa: see, e.g., Schouten 1619 (for Schouten and Le Maire in 1616); Dampier
1729 (for Dampier in 1699–1700); Carteret 1965 (for Carteret in 1767); Bougainville
1772 (for Bougainville in 1768); J. Hunter 1793 (for Hunter in 1791); Dumont d'Urville
1832b (for Dumont d'Urville in 1827). Malay and perhaps Chinese ships may have
passed too, as may unknown whalers. On La Pérouse, see, e.g., Dunmore 2006. On
Morrell's using Arrowsmith, see B. Morrell, 1832a. Maps from Bruni d'Entrecasteaux's
expedition were published by Beautemps-Beaupré in 1807 and incorporated into Arrowsmith's charts; Morrell's version marked Uneapa as Merité Island (Keeler n.d.,
"Log," November 13, 1830). On navigators avoiding Melanesia, see Chappell 1998: 17,
Gray 1999, Howe 1984: 281–287. On Western racism, see, e.g., Dumont d'Urville
1832b, Ballard 2008: 124. Dumont d'Urville quotations cited from Douglas 2008: 9–10.
On "cannibal" talk, see, e.g., Obeyesekere 2005, Biber 2005. On problems of translation, see Chappell 1998. On the investors' perspective, see B. Morrell 1832a, Skiddy n.d.
On sealers and the Antarctic islands, see Busch 1985, Mitterling 1959. On Stonington
and the Pequod, see, e.g., Timothy Dwight 1823: 19–26, with quotes "The former . . . ,"
"doze away . . . ," "the life . . . ," and "a moving vegetable . . . ," on 19–20. On Morrell
family history, see B. Morrell, 1832a. On the drownings, see "Equinoctial Gale" 1815,
B. Morrell, 1832a. On adoptions, see Burrows 1976: 1172–1181. On Morrell's first marriage, see "Married" 1820. On Morrell's later Antarctic claims, see B. Morrell 1832a, in
contrast with quotations "without making . . ." and "at a cost . . ." from "Voyage of
Discovery" 1824. On father's advice and quote "a speedy . . . ," see B. Morrell 1832a:
142. Quote "very pretty . . . ," Lafond de Lurcy 1844: 351. On Abby's family, see A.
Morrell 1833. On Keeler's studies at navigation school, see Keeler n.d., "Log," end
page, and Stommel 1984. On Skiddy and Morrell, see B. Morrell 1832a and Skiddy n.d.
On Antarctic investors and design, see Bergh 1888, B. Morrell 1832a. On Antarctic's
maiden voyage, see "Shipbuilder Bergh" 1883. On seal collapse, see Busch 1985: 36.
The Antarctic returned with only 6,270 fur sealskins; see New York Evening Post, July 23,
1829: 2. Quote "Mr. Bergh . . . ," Skiddy n.d. On Abby Morrell's refusal and quote
"earnest and unceasing . . . ," see B. Morrell 1832a: 342. On women's voyaging, see
Druett 1991, Whipple 1954. On investors' refusal, quote "considering it . . . ," and
Abby in ship's locker, see Skiddy n.d. On temperance ship, see "Sailing Without Grog"
1829. On Antarctic crew, see B. Morrell 1832a and "Heathen Massacre" 1831. On sailors
as writers, see Blum 2008, and, e.g., for Ames, Lang and Lease 1975, R. Richards 2007.
On crew, officers, and illness, see B. Morrell 1832a. On Manila as trading hub, see
Coulter 1847. For a description of Manila, see Bennett 1832, Stewart 1831. On Morrell
and Hubbell, see Lafond de Lurcy 1844: 338, B. Morrell 1832a, A. Morrell 1833. On fear
of the Antarctic, see Lafond de Lurcy 1844: 338–339. On Hubbell, see Hubbell 1881. On
Abby, see Lafond de Lurcy 1844: 351, A. Morrell 1833: 50–54. Quotes "All was as . . ."
and "My youth . . . ," A. Morrell 1833: 51. On Abby's hiding, see Stommel 1984.
Whether Abby hid when departing the United States, when leaving Manila, or both
remains ambiguous. On departure, see Keeler n.d., "Log," April 12, 1830, B. Morrell
1832a, A. Morrell 1833, Stommel 1984: 27. On voyage to Carteret, see B. Morrell 1832a.
The Carteret Islands (containing Morrell's "Massacre Island") are the Kilinailau Islands. On portent and quote " 'A little bird, as black as ink,' . . . ," see Ward 1967: 243. On

events at Kilinailau, see B. Morrell 1832a, Halliard 1833, A. Morrell 1833, Keeler n.d., "Log," May 28, 1830, Keeler 1831, and newspapers cited in Chapter 4, below. Important inconsistencies in narration of events at Kilinailau are discussed in B. Pearson 1984. On Morrell's twelve-thousand-dollar loan, see Skiddy n.d. On adaptation of the *Antarctic,* see Skiddy n.d., B. Morrell 1832a. On attempted recruitment of Lafond de Lurcy see Lafond de Lurcy 1844: 352, B. Morrell 1832a, A. Morrell 1833. Quotes "We could . . . ," Lafond de Lurcy 1844: 352; "made a declaration . . . ," Tooker 1888. On peace "nego-tiation," see Morrell 1832a: 440. Quote "in cutlery . . . ," B. Morrell, 1832a: 440. On visit of Australian whaler (Bourn Russell) and initials in tree, see N. Jones 2008: 21. Andrew Cheyne found the ruins of Morrell's castle in 1844; see Cheyne 1852: 73–74. For kidnapping precedents, see Chappell 1998. For a dubious eyewitness account of events on Kilinailau (Carteret Islands), see Becke 1908. On Morrell's intention to re-turn, see B. Morrell 1832a.

Chapter 3: At Sea

On death of Kilinailau captive and quotation "hove his . . . ," see Keeler n.d., "Log," November 12, 1830. On location of "Monday's" island, see Jacobs 1844, Stom-mel 1984. On capture of "Monday," see A. Morrell 1833 at, e.g., 81 and 204, Halliard 1833. Quotes "near two thousand . . . ," Keeler 1831: 19; "The report . . ." and "picked up . . . ," A. Morrell 1833: 82, 204. On appearance of Monday, see A. Morrell 1833. Quote "nature ha[d] . . . ," Keeler 1831: 1–2. On Monday's comportment aboard ship, see "South Pacific Islander" 1831. On inference of Monday as criminal or slave, see "From the New York Standard" 1831. Quotes "Every kindness . . ." and "He wandered . . . ," A. Morrell 1833: 205. On terrorizing captives and quote "They are extremely . . . ," see "From the New York Standard" 1831. On islanders considering Americans as cannibals, see Selim Woodworth n.d., "Journal," November 24, 1834. On Dako's account of cannibal monsters, see Jacobs 1844: 95–103. The practice of eating bodies killed in battle is from Blythe pers. comm. On Dako eating shark and quote "great satisfaction," see "From the New York Standard" 1831. On ship life, see B. Mor-rell 1832a. On social world, cuisine, routine, etc., on board, see, e.g., Dana 1840, Whip-ple 1954, Druett 1991. On going barefoot, see Jacobs 1844: 246. On Vancouver's volumes, see Skiddy n.d. On Abby's pregnancy, see A. Morrell 1833. On vinegar see B. Morrell 1833: 487–488. On temperance ship, see "Sailing Voyage Without Grog" 1829. On ship music, see B. Morrell 1832a: 409. On Uneapa music, see Th. Dwight 1835. On Malaz tree myth and quote "and—oh boy . . . ," see Pomponio 1992: 44–46. That Tan-targeely was well known to Dako can be deduced from Selim Woodworth n.d., "Jour-nal," and events in 1834–1835. On Kove society and trade, see Chowning 1972, 1978a, 1978b, 1987a, 1987b, 1990, Chowning and Swadling 1981, Harding 1967, McPherson 2007. On trade, see, e.g., Pomponio 1992: 54–58, Blythe 1978. On gifting friendships, see McPherson 2007. On uses of the cassowary, see Th. Dwight 1834, 1835, Powell 1883 (also from Blythe, pers. comm.). On seasonal cycles, see, e.g., Pomponio 1992: 54–58, Blythe 1978. Quote "They may never . . . ," McPherson 2007: 143. Information on firstborn celebrations, houses-of-respect (or "men's houses"), women's economy, and dress and makeup from Blythe pers. comm. On Manila visit, see B. Morrell 1832a, A. Morrell 1833. Quote "citizens of . . . ," B. Morrell 1832a: 468. On Cavite and Manila society and politics, see Bennett 1832. On Burrows and Bolívar, see "How Silas Burrows . . ." 1897 and Anderson 1962: 44. On relations with Hubbell, see B. Morrell 1832a, A. Morrell 1833. Quotes "The importance . . ." and "Had it not . . . ," B. Morrell 1832a: 469; "On our arrival . . . ," A. Morrell 1833: 87; "perfidious machinations," B. Morrell 1832a: 469. On departure, see B. Morrell 1832a. On hiding the islands' location see Stommel 1984. Benjamin Morrell (1832a) is overt about the commercial reasons for withholding information on these locations. On Hubbell's death, see Hubbell 1881. On passing Cádiz for Bordeaux, see B. Morrell 1832a, A. Morrell 1833. On fight at Bordeaux and quotes "preserve themselves . . . ," "at the sacrifice . . . ," and "unequivocal indications . . . ," see "Letter from Bordeaux" 1831. On loan, see Skiddy n.d.

Chapter 4: The "Cannibal Show"

On New York at the time, see, e.g., E. Williams 1834a, 1834b, Hardie 1827, Th. Dwight 1834, Goodman 2009. On Corlears Hook, see Gilfoyle 1992. On the *Antarctic's* arrival, greeting, birth of son, and family news, see A. Morrell 1833, B. Morrell 1832a. Quote "as one . . . ," A. Morrell 1833: 229. On news coverage of arrival, see "Massacre in the South Pacific" 1831. On debt see Skiddy n.d. Quotes "objects of much . . . ," "Remarkable" 1831; "to their homes," "Cruise of the Schooner Antarctic" 1831. On church service, see Ward 1967: 252. On Chase and quotes "a new era," and "a relation . . . ," see "New York Seamen" 1854. On newspaper rivalry, see Goodman 2009. Quotes "circumstances attending . . ." and "Capt Morrell . . . ," *Courier and Enquirer,* August 30, 1831. Republications of the article appeared in, e.g., *Boston Weekly Messenger* and *Columbia Centinel* on August 31, 1831, the *American Traveller* and the *New Bedford Mercury* on September 2, 1831, and the *New York Observer* on September 3, 1831. On Noah, see Sarna 1981, B. Morrell 1832a: xv, xvi, 462. On Canal Street address, see B. Morrell 1833. On Noah and Tammany Hall, see, e.g., Myers 1901. On Tammany show "Two Cannibals . . . ," see "Exhibition. Cannibals" 1831. The pamphlet is in Keeler 1831. On debates on humanity, see Chapter 7, below. Quotes "The South Sea Islanders . . . ," Keeler 1831: 1; "have no idea . . . , " "Adventures of a Sailor" 1831; "and large shawls," "South Sea Cannibals" 1831a, 1831b; "in a style," "South Sea Indians" 1831; "the clear large . . ." and "a supreme contempt," "Adventures of a Sailor" 1831; "noble," "much better shaped . . . ," "not so . . . ," and "though there . . . ," *National Aegis,* September 14, 1831: 2; "Of these antipodean . . . ," Pascalis 1831. Image and quotes "wonderfully affected" and "gave signs . . ." in "Captain Morrell" 1833. On Dako as an artist, see Th. Dwight 1834, 1835. Material on the Uneapa palate, art, and its ontology from Heerman 2001, Blythe pers. comm. On Pacific art as an inspiration to European art, see Peltier 2001. On the Peales' museums, see Sellers 1980a, 1980b, E. Williams 1834b: 188–189. On Barnum museum, see Barnum 1855. On Hiram Powers, the Cincinnati Museum, the cannibal waxworks, and the tension between "self improvement" and populism, see Dunlop 1984. Quotes "actual embalmed . . . ," Dunlop 1984: 537; "an arrangement . . ." and "one of the . . . ," *New York Evening Post,* September 8, 1831: 2; "evinced signs . . . ,"

"Savages etc." 1831. On transfer of show to Peale's Museum, see "Cannibals" 1831b and "Public" 1831. Quote "a determination . . ." and on circumstances of the escape, see "Savages etc." 1831. On escape, dress, aims, collaboration, and quote "sulky and sad," see "South Sea Cannibals" 1831a; see also "Natives of the Pacific Ocean" 1831 and "South Sea Cannibals" 1831b. On nightlife, Canal Street, and Five Points, see Gilfoyle 1992. Quotes "ready to tumble," Foster 1849: 23; "where black and . . . ," Gilfoyle 1992: 38; "worse, by far . . . ," Cohen, Gilfoyle, and Horowitz 2008: 69. On morning in Manhattan, see Th. Dwight 1834. On missing Monday and quote "it is to be . . . ," "Fugitive" 1831. For the rumor that Monday might be sent to Georgia, see "Card: Captain Morrell" 1831. Quote "an act of . . . ," *Philadelphia Inquirer,* September 12, 1831: 2 (quoting *Courier and Enquirer*). On recapture see "Card: Captain Morrell" 1831, "South Pacific Islander" 1831, and "South Seaman" 1831. On capture by Meigs, see "Captain Morrell, in announcing . . ." 1831. Quotes "I hailed him . . . ," H. Meigs n.d., "Diaries," September 9–12, 1831; "made him various . . ." and "He still appears . . . ," "Card: Captain Morrell" 1831; "He seems to think," *Middlesex Gazette,* September 21, 1831: 2; "We are glad . . . ," *Albany Evening Argus,* September 13, 1831. On Dako's solo show in absence of Monday, *The American* (New York), September 14, 1831: 3. On the continuation of the show, see, e.g., *The American* (New York), September 23, 1831: 3. Quote "Any gentlemen . . . ," "Public" 1831. On criticism of show and quotes "If it is intended . . ." and "the case of . . . ," see "We cordially concur . . ." 1831. On the "Esquimaux," see Wright 1987. Quotes "part wolf . . . ," "Esquimaux Indians" 1821; "They are losing . . . ," H. Meigs n.d., "Diaries," September 25, 1831.

Chapter 5: The Tour

On Albany museum and show, see Fergusson 1831–1832: 592. On "protégés" and quote "make good . . . ," see *Albany Argus,* October 11, 1831: 3. On Melville's youth in Albany, see Parker 1996. On Queequeg, see the Epilogue, below. On Morrell's gifts to the Albany museum, see B. Morrell 1832a. On travel to Philadelphia and the description of the city, see, e.g., Kemble 1835: 17. On pre-publicity and venue, see "South Sea Islanders" 1831a. On the ourangoutang, see "Philadelphia is at Present . . ." 1831. Quote "with human . . . ," *National Gazette* (Philadelphia), September 24, 1831: 2. On Masonic Hall, see "Two Savages" 1831. On Pickering, see C. Pickering 1848: quotes "belonged to . . ." and "I think I can recall . . ." are on p. 168 and "Malay race" and "openness and . . ." on p. 115. On Baltimore rakish captains and quote "something between . . . ," see Kemble 1835: 100. On Matthew Kelly, see, e.g., Footner 1998: 140, B. Morrell 1832b. On Baltimore Museum show, see "Two Savages from the South Pacific" 1831, "Cannibals" 1831b, and "South Sea Islanders" 1831a. Quote "such fearful . . . ," Jacobs 1844: 23; "The cannibals will . . . ," *Baltimore Patriot and Mercantile Advertiser,* November 29, 1831. On Baltimore circus and quote "equestrian marvel . . . ," see Varle 1833: 36. On Mr. Frimble, see "Living Statue" 1831. On circus schedule, see "Theatre and Circus" 1831a, 1831b. Information on benefit for Dako and Monday and quote "the first American . . . ," "Theatre and Circus" 1831b. On the National Museum, see "V." 1832: 247, "National Museum" 1831, "Two Savages from the South Pacific Islands" 1831.

Quote "somewhat enlightened . . . ," *Philadelphia Inquirer,* November 10, 1831: 3. On
the history of human zoos, see, e.g., Poignant 2004, Blanchard, Boetsch, and Snoep
2011, Qureshi 2011. On frustrations with theorization and representation of "human
zoos," see Liauzu 2005, McLean 2012. On the electric eel, see "Gymnotus Electricus,"
New York Evening Post, August 25, 1831: 2. Quotes "induce a . . . ," "two natives . . . ,"
and "be reimbursed . . . ," "Petition of Benjamin Morrell" 1831. On lobbying for a
voyage of exploration, see, e.g., Joyce 2001, Stanton 1975, Sachs 2007. On Morrell's
polar ambitions, newspaper support, and "Memorial," see "Expedition to the South
Pole" 1832; see also *Baltimore Gazette,* January 16, 1832: 2, *Boston Courier,* January 19,
1832: 1, *New Bedford Mercury,* January 27, 1832: 1, and "South Polar Seas" 1832. Quotes
"register his name . . ." and "We have seen . . . ," "Expedition to the South Pole" 1832;
"one of the finest . . . ," "South Polar Seas" 1832; "confine the objects . . . ," *Sailors
Magazine and Naval Journal* 3–4 (1832): 193; "total failure," B. Morrell 1832a: 341. On
Skiddy and quote "famous for . . . ," see Skiddy n.d. On sale of *Antarctic,* see, e.g., *New
York Evening Post,* March 3, 1832: 3, *New York Morning Courier,* September 27, 1834: 1.
Quotes "wonderful dexterity," "Peale's Museum," *American* (New York), January 24,
1832: 3; "Capt. Benjamin . . . ," B. Morrell 1832b. On Dako and Monday's return to
Peale's Museum and their speaking English, see "Peale's Museum," *American* (New York),
January 24, 1832: 3. On Monday's experience and quote "No kindness . . . ," see Jacobs
1844: 14. On Dako's speaking English, see also "South Sea Islanders" 1831b. On letter
purportedly by Dako and quotes "I write from . . . ," "Whence did . . . ," "annihilated
with . . . ," "resolved not . . . ," "to keep . . . ," "The son of . . . ," and "I sometimes . . . ,"
see Terrumbumbyandarko 1832. On Pomingo, see "Letter from John Sevier" 1788.

Chapter 6: The Books

On Bolívar's last words, see Murphy 2012. On "festivals, games . . . ," see Smith
and Woodworth 1831. On James Cook's needing writing help, see Currie 2005. On
Burrows and Samuel Woodworth, see Woodworth and Bochsa 1832. On Ploughboy,
virtue, and the Yankee character, see Conforti 2001. For an analysis of Woodworth's
racism, see J. Richards 2000; on the play see also Dorson 1940, Coad 1919. On the Morrells' relations with the Harpers, Woodworth, and Knapp, see Exman 1965. On Abby
as "first American woman . . . ," see "Theatre and Circus" 1831b. For Knapp's works,
see Knapp 1831, 1832, 1834. On the contracts and quote "make a valuable . . . ," see
Exman 1965: 30. On contemporary views of American literature, see S. Goodrich 1857.
History of New York is Irving 1809. Quote "Distressing . . . . ," "Distressing" 1809. On
Knickerbockers' significance, see Springer 1988, Taft 1947: 88, Adkins 1932. On social
life of Knickerbockers and origins of *New York Mirror,* see, e.g., Wilson 1886: 378; see
also Adkins 1932, Crawford 1912, Taft 1947. On Wiley and literary den, see Derby
1884. On Woodworth's life and work, see Taft 1936, Coad 1919. On Woodworth's
looks, habits, music, and friendship with Halleck, see letters of his daughter Mary Josephine Wethered (née Woodworth) in Selim Woodworth n.d., "Papers." Quote "as
some think . . . ," letter of Samuel Woodworth to Benjamin F. Thompson, January 4,
1838, Papers of Samuel Woodworth, 1829–1945 n.d. On Woodworth's interest in

Swedenborg, see Taft 1936. Woodworth edited the Swedenborgian *Halcyon Luminary,*
1812–1813. On Swedenborgian ideas in the United States, see Hobart 1831. On Appleseed, see Hatcher 1947. On Knickerbockers and Swedenborgians, see, e.g., *Knickerbocker
Magazine,* May 1848, 470. On American newspapers, see Goodman 2009. On editors
and political patronage, see Pasley 2007. On Noah, see Sarna 1981. On Woodworth as
the American poet, see "Biographical Sketches" 1838: 664. On Woodworth's depiction
of Morrell, see B. Morrell 1832a. On arguments concerning Liberian colonization, see,
e.g., Fairhead et al. 2003. On Weddell's voyage, see Weddell 1827. Quotes "The anguish . . . ," B. Morrell 1832a: 68; "If there be . . . ," ibid., 466. On Knapp writing Abby
Morrell's book, see Exman 1965, Dunlap 1930: 649–650. A review of Knapp's *Advice in the
Pursuits of Literature,* with quotes "ready sketcher . . . ," "a sprightly conversationist . . . ,"
and "often soars beyond . . . ," is in "Critical Notices," *North American Magazine* 1, no. 12
(October 1833): 392. On Knapp and Freemasonry, see Knapp 1828. For Knapp's "Masonic
feminism," see Knapp 1828, 1834. Quote "the roar," B. Morrell 1832a: 438. On Woodworth and Knapp's friendship, see, e.g., Knapp 1834: title page. On Morrell's knowledge of
Dako, see A. Morrell 1833. Quotes "king of . . . ," A. Morrell 1833: 205; "make them all do
right," ibid., 206; "rather sullen . . . ," "ferocious savages . . . ," "civilized, intelligent . . . ,"
and "would result . . . ," B. Morrell 1832a: 466.

Chapter 7: Dako, God, and Humanity

Biographical sketches of Theodore Dwight, Jr., and his father can be found in B.
Dwight 1874: 231–233. On Dwight's writing on Italy and links with Mazzini, see Th.
Dwight 1824, 1841–1842, 1851, 1859. On Dwight and the American Lyceum, see
American Lyceum 1831. On Mechanics Society and quote "against the bonds . . . ," see
Barnhart 2005: 19. Members of the Lyceum movement who founded the American
Ethnological Society include Henry Schoolcraft and Edwin James. On the American
Ethnological Society as liberal, see Barnhart 2005: 289. On Dwight's support of South
American republicans (Juan Roderíquez, Lorenzo de Zavala, and Joachím Mosquera),
see *American Annals of Education* 4 (1834): 281. For Dwight on Kibby, see, e.g, Austin
1984. On Payne and Indian Removal, see Foreman 1932, Payne 2002. Quote "quiveringly
sensitive . . . ," "American Ethnological Society" 1867. For Dwight's interviews with
Dako, see Th. Dwight 1834, 1835, n.d., and "Geometrical Nomenclature . . ." n.d. Most of
Dwight's manuscripts were lost. Quotes "to feel such . . ." and "one's attachment . . . ,"
Th. Dwight 1834: 188; "if deception . . . ," Th. Dwight 1835: 397; "with the inquisitive
eye . . ." and "never satisfied . . . ," B. Morrell 1832a: 466. On creation debates, see
Haller 1970, Gould 1996, Fabian 2003, 2010, Ballard 2008, Barnhart 2005, Douglas
2008. On "Peter Parley" (including quotations "My young . . . ," "We know . . . . ," and
"God formed . . .") see Parley 1832: 55–56 (paraphrasing W. Lawrence 1822). On Ham and
slavery, and on attitudes to Native Americans, see, e.g., Haynes 2007, Horsman 1981.
On the significance of the short biblical chronology in popular and professional ethnology, see, e.g., Trautmann 1992, Barnhart 2005. On tensions over abolition in New
York City, see Goodman 2009. On phrenology and significance of skulls, see Combe
1830, Gall, Vimont, and Broussais 1838, Davies 1955. Quotes "the foreheads . . . ,"

Spurzheim 1815: 268; "lamentable deficiency . . . ," Combe 1830: 608. On Morton, see
Bieder 1986, Gould 1996, Fabian 2010. Quote "different forms . . . ," Bieder 1986: 58.
On Morton's advertisement for skulls, see "Skulls" 1831. On skull trade in Australia
and the Pacific, see "Traffic in Human Heads," Select Committee on Aboriginal Tribes
1837. On head market, see Bieder 1986, 1990, Fabian 2003, 2010. On global sources of
skulls, see J. Meigs 1857. Quote "Americans who . . . ," Bieder 1986: 65–66. On Lang
against Morton, see J. Lang 1834b, Morton 1839. Quote "Any from . . . ," Cox 1832–
1834: 290, cited in Gall, Vimont, and Broussais 1838: 155. On debates concerning Jewish origins in the Americas, see Boudinot 1816, Smith and Woodworth 1831 (drawing
on Boudinot), Noah 1837. On apocalyptic speculation and concerns with the lost tribes,
see Joyce 2001: 16, Deuteronomy 28:64. Quotes "frank, simple . . . ," Th. Dwight 1834:
188; "perfectly African," "large, thick lips . . . ," and "the Negro . . . ," ibid., 185; "ready
at . . ." and "enough for . . . ," Th. Dwight, letter to Gibbs April 11, 1866, in Th.
Dwight n.d. On Dako's world and geography see Th. Dwight 1834, 1835. Quotes "a
few . . ." and "Mariumba," Th. Dwight 1835: 397–398; "the preserver . . . ," Th. Dwight
1834: 186; "Creator, Preserver . . . ," "an inferior world," and "the abode of . . . ," Th.
Dwight 1835: 398; "spoken of . . ." and "Captain Morrell . . . ," Th. Dwight 1834: 187;
"the articles . . . ," Th. Dwight 1835: 397; "numerous petty . . ." and "even two . . . ,"
ibid., 398; "Eoa, eao . . . ," "that there . . . ," and "Merriky Isle," Th. Dwight 1834: 188;
"form an opinion . . . ," ibid., 186. On the death of Monday, see Th. Dwight 1835.
Quotes "very passionate . . ." and "never particularly . . . ," Th. Dwight 1834: 185. On
Monday's visit to Meigs, see H. Meigs n.d., "Diaries," March 25, 1832. Quote "attended by . . . ," Jacobs 1844: 14. On Vendovi's demise and the sale of his skull, and the
"American school," see Joyce 2001, Fabian 2010, and quote "This is to . . . ," Fabian
2010: 121. On current genetic theory about New Guineans, see Marshall 2011. On the
guffaw of the American school, see, e.g., Barnhart 2005.

Chapter 8: Fame

On publication of the memoirs, see Exman 1965. On Adams's letter, see B. Morrell, 1832a: 231–242. Quotes "from a literary . . . ," "What is . . . ," and "We shall . . . ,"
"From the New York Traveller" 1833; "This is a highly . . . ," *New York Mirror,* December 29, 1832: 203; "performed with admirable . . . ," Kent 1840: 53; "He writes as . . . ,"
"Narrative of Four Voyages" 1833a. On the spread of the "Massacre Island" story in the
United Kingdom, see, e.g., *Bristol Mercury,* December 29, 1832, and the *Caledonian Mercury,* January 14, 1833. On the French translation, see B. Morrell 1834. On rapturous
review and quote "While searching . . . ," see Larenaudière 1834 (my translation). On
reviews by Dumont d'Urville, see his 1833a and 1833b (including quote "It is very
annoying . . . ," 1833b: 276–277, my translation). On Dumont d'Urville's extracts of
Morrell, see Dumont d'Urville 1835: 163–168, 470–477 (quote "mixed with . . . ," p.
163, my translation). Dumont d'Urville published Morrell's account alongside those of
Magellan, Tasman, Dampier, Cook, La Pérouse, Bruni d'Etrecasteaux, and others. On
long run of play, see Odell 1928. On theater history, see Wilmeth and Bigsby 1998,
Bank 1997. Quote "nameless classes . . . ," Everts 1866: 15. On Bowery and sex, see

Gilfoyle 1992, C. Johnson 1975. Quote "males and . . ." and "sometimes in . . . ," Gilfoyle 1992: 110–111. On cholera, see Bailey 2011: 41. On the opening day of *The Cannibals* see *The American,* February 20, 1833: 3. Quote "holding possession of . . . ," *New York Mirror,* March 16, 1833: 295. There were at least twenty-four revivals that year; see Coad 1919: 172. On the performers and play, see "Dramatizing a Dream" 1833 (including quote "no very correct . . ."). On Dako at the Bowery, see *New York Evening Post,* February 22, 1833: 3. Quote "About a year . . . ," "Penguin" 1833: 17; "nearly into . . . ," "Savages etc." 1831: 264. The children's book is Halliard 1833 (quotes "scared them off," "picked up," "good," "well informed," "friends," and "they seemed . . ." are on pp. 139–142). On temperance and quotes "like brothers . . ." and "Even Sunday . . . ," see B. Morrell 1833: 267. On Morrell's success in financing, see *Newburyport Herald,* February 8, 1833: 1. Quote "the most respectable . . . ," Jacobs 1844: 13. On the consortium and its legal struggles, see "Southern District of New York" 1833. On those involved in Greenwich Insurance, see *Laws of the State of New York 57th session,* Albany 1834: 513. On launch of brig and her quality, see *Philadelphia Inquirer,* May 4, 1833: 2, and *Richmond Enquirer,* May 10, 1833: 4. Quote "as far as practicable," *Torch Light* (Hagers-Town, Md.), April 11, 1833: 1. On petitions, see "Petition of Benjamin Morrell" 1833, "Memorial of Benjamin Morrell" 1833. On running a temperance ship and not trading firearms, and quote "men of character," see "Expedition to the Pacific" 1833. Quotes "and educating them," "Petition of Benjamin Morrell" 1833; "praying to be . . . ," "Memorial of Benjamin Morrell" 1833. On dropping the scientific aims and quotes "prosperous and . . ." and "a means of . . . ," "Expedition to the Pacific" 1833. On Burrows's good deeds, see Hetzel 1903. Quote "the Mother of . . . ," *Philadelphia Inquirer,* May 4, 1833: 2. On Burrows and Bolívar, see Gilmore and Harrison 1948. On Burrows's payments to Monroe, see, e.g., letter of Burrows to Monroe, July 15, 1828, Nicholas Biddle Papers, 1681–1933, Library of Congress. On Biddle, Burrows, Noah, Webb, and the Bank War, see, e.g., Govan 1959, Hammond 1947, Gatell 1966, Sarna 1981, letters in Nicholas Biddle Papers, 1681–1933, Library of Congress. Quotes "Better, far better . . . ," "Mother of Washington" 1833; "the entire abandonment . . . ," Jacobs 1844: 14. On the breakdown of the consortium and legal suits, see "Southern District of New York" 1833. On death of John Burnett [*sic*] Morrell and quote "aged 1 year . . . ," see *New York Commercial Advertiser,* July 31, 1833: 2. On first seduction trial and quote "Perhaps on . . . ," see Van Haun and Burrows 1833?: 20. Quote "doubts expressed . . . ," "Narrative of Four Voyages" 1833a: 336. On Patagonia, see Coan 1880, with quote "glowing description . . . ," p. 12.

Chapter 9: Return to Dako's Island

On Hermit and quotes "sworn a boycott . . ." and "he went on . . . , " see "Hermit of Harlem" 1890. On description of Hermitage, see "Hermitage Soon to Be Sold" 1894. On treasure, women prisoners, gigantic bath, and quote "was interesting . . . ," see *The Sun* (Baltimore), August 8, 1894. On second hermit and Red Rock Island and quotes "like a second . . ." and "more than a . . . ," see Bancroft 1887: 247–248. On flight as boys see letter of January 4, 1892, to Mr. J. B. Harrison in Selim Woodworth n.d., "Papers." On Jacobs's name change, see Scott 1984: 43. On Jacobs's father's business (J. T. Jacobs), see *National Advocate,* October 5, 1822, and quote, "at the very . . . ," *New York Statesman,* December 10, 1824: 4. On Hermit's father and farm, and description of Hermitage, see *New York Tribune,* January 7, 1894. On Harlem property, see *New-York Daily Advertiser,* December 4, 1834: 4, and *New York Commercial Advertiser,* November 27, 1828: 1. Quote "being by . . . ," letter of Mrs. Woodworth to Mr. J. B. Harrison, January 4, 1892, in Selim Woodworth n.d., "Papers." Samuel Woodworth's play *The Foundling of the Sea* won a $400 prize funded by the comic actor George Handel "Yankee" Hill, and judged by Washington Irving and Gulian Verplanck, among others. It flopped: see Northall 1850: 20. On Morrell's taking the boys on board, see Jacobs 1844: 15. On homosexuality of the era, see, e.g., Hallock 2000, Benemann 2006, Gilfoyle 1992, Cohen, Gilfoyle, and Horowitz 2008. On Selim's femininity, see Bancroft 1887: 248. On Woodworth's marriage to Mary Lisette [Lizzette] Flohr, see their letters in Selim Woodworth n.d., "Papers." Quotes "quite blind . . . ," "History of Lisette Woodworth," and "You have really . . . ," letter of S. E. Woodworth to Lisette, May 2, 1863, both ibid. On Jacobs's claim to have traveled with Taylor, see "Hermitage Soon to Be Sold" 1894. On Taylor, see Wermuth 1973. On construction of the fortress in 1856 (the year Woodworth married), see *New York Herald,* September 4, 1856: 5. Quote "the idea . . . ," Jacobs 1844: 15. For (homo)sexuality, Pacific voyages, and narratives about them, see Crain 1994, Martin 1979. Quote "had indulged . . . ," Jacobs 1844: 14. On Babcock and Burrows welcoming President Monroe, see Waldo 1818: 111. On the fitting out and departure of the *Margaret Oakley,* see Jacobs 1844. On the petition, see "Memorial of Captain Benjamin Morrell" 1834. On Morrell family property, see history of "8 High St., and 24 Northwest St. Stonington," manuscript, Stonington Historical Society and Museum (with thanks!). Quote "the mystery . . . ," Jacobs 1844: title. On those who have treated the enigmas of Jacobs's book more seriously, see Chappell 1998, Ballard 2009, Stommel 1984. On preparations for departure and quote "My friend . . . ," see Jacobs 1844: 16. On supercargoes, Dako's quarters, officers, and cooks, see Selim Woodworth n.d., "Journal," and Jacobs 1844. Quote "a runaway . . . ," Jacobs 1844: 141. The sailing date appears in *New York Commercial Advertiser,* March 10, 1834: 2. On disputes and friendship with Dako, see Selim Woodworth n.d., "Journal," and Jacobs 1844. Quotes "been from the first " and "favourites on board . . . ," Jacobs 1844: 82. On voyage to Mauritius, see Selim Woodworth n.d., "Journal," and Jacobs 1844. Quotes "Uneducated as he was . . . ," Jacobs 1844: 23; "Cap-in . . . time!," ibid., 24. On the arrival in Mauritius, see Selim Woodworth n.d., "Journal." Quote "leaky state," "Shipping Intelligence," *Morning Chronicle* (London), September 30, 1834. For the bottomry bond and changes to the ship see Jacobs 1844 (quotes "warlike appearance . . . the place," p. 49; "standing upon . . . ," p. 75; and "Sailors who . . . ," p. 47). For the letter from Mauritius, see B. Morrell 1835. On voyage to Uneapa and events there, see Jacobs 1844 and Selim Woodworth n.d., "Journal." Quotes "an immense . . ." and "scene of fearful . . . , " Jacobs 1844: 71–72. On the logbook and quote "crush the . . . ," see ibid., 66. For Woodworth's regular encryption and decrypting system, see Selim Woodworth n.d., "Journal" and "Papers." On Jacobs's navigational equipment, Dako's preparations, and preliminary visit to Naraga, see Jacobs 1844. Quotes "He could . . . ," "whole days," "What for . . . ," and "he uttered . . . ," ibid., 77–78; "Telum-by-by Darco," "Pongo good man," "not white . . . ," "instantly recognized . . . ," and "Darco [Dako] was encompassed . . . ," ibid., 79–81. On Lavoo, see ibid., 83–86, 103 (quotes "the Palace . . . ," "and they gazed . . . ," "the red warrior," "the very counterpart . . . ," "from various sources," and "and the present . . . ," 83–86). On Dillon, La Pérouse, Lavoo, and Dumont d'Urville see Dunmore 2006, Association Salomon 2008, Guillou 2008, 2011, Obeyesekere 2005. Quotes "received a . . . ," Jacobs 1844: 85; "bottomless pit" and "coral reefs . . . ," ibid., 87. On clay pots being regarded as shells, see Harding 1967: 139–140. Quotes "in a loud and energetic . . . ," "soon the joyful . . . ," "a splendid . . . ," and "They soon . . . ," Jacobs 1844: 89. On Jacobs's fictive narrative of events and quotes "King of Nyappa" and "mountain people," see ibid., 89–90. On Dako's vanishing and subsequent events, see Selim Woodworth n.d., "Journal." Quote "There was a man . . ." is from an oral account by Rave and Tatau on Uneapa Island in 1980 (Blythe pers. comm.).

Chapter 10: Missing

On waiting for Dako, I infer from the passage in Jacobs 1844: 90–94 that the trip to neighboring Garove occurred after Dako's disappearance. See map of Garove in Selim Woodworth n.d., "Papers." On Morrell's overruling supercargoes, and quotes "released himself unilaterally . . ." and "The scenes . . . ," see ibid., 116. Quote "Before we . . . ," Jacobs 1844: 112. For the encounter with the canoeists, "Sambarlow's Point," and quote "Although we could not . . . ," see Selim Woodworth n.d., "Journal," November 25, 1834. On Americans' noises, see Jacobs 1844: 130–131. On Jarvis, and quote "They believed . . . ," see Selim Woodworth n.d., "Journal," November 26, 1834. Note: it appears from this and other quotations that either Woodworth was at times writing his journal some time after the events or, when making these fair copies to send home, he adapted them in hindsight. On the islanders' inferences concerning mass production, see Thurston 1994. Quotes "Peo Lioo" and "much pleased . . . ," Selim Woodworth n.d., "Journal," November 26, 1834. Quotes "had difficulty . . ." and story of elderly woman, ibid., November 27, 1834. On Tantargeely island events, and quotes "If they did not find . . ." and "shouting to us . . . ," ibid., November 28, 1834. For events over the week, ibid., December 3–9, 1834. Quotes "huge teeth and . . . ," ibid., December 3, 1834; "covered with small . . ." and "to attract these natives," ibid., December 9, 1834; "Boats started to visit . . . ," ibid., December 10, 1834. For return to Uneapa and quotes "We rowed along . . . ," ibid., December 13, 1834; "would not stop," ibid., February 3, 1835; "Mohire" and "Celingies," ibid., December 14, 1834; "If you are in want . . . ," ibid.: "Commercial Intelligence." The Jacobs material on Manus, New Hanover, and New Ireland is in 1844: 164–189. Quotes "perfect column" and "The trees that . . . ," Selim Woodworth n.d., "Journal," January 21 and 23, 1835.

Chapter 11: Tables Turned

Events on return to Kove including interest in Morrell and "God ship" are from Selim Woodworth n.d., "Journal," January 26–February 2, 1835; events at Uneapa are ibid., February 3, 1835. Quotes "and soon . . ." and "man with . . . ," ibid., January 29, 1835; "had been here . . . ," "got hold of his . . . ," "gave his son, . . ." "set up . . . ," and "hearty dinner," ibid., February 1, 1835; "to see or hear . . . ," "old friend Darco," "hailed by three . . . ," "soon in the . . . ," ibid., February 3, 1835. Information on tears and mourning practices is from Blythe pers. comm. Quotes "wished him a . . . ," Selim Woodworth, n.d., "Journal," February 3, 1835; "I thought Darco you . . . ," Selim Woodworth n.d., "Papers": "Vocabulary of Uneapa"; "he know not how . . . ," "his friends followed . . . ," "they got around . . . ," and "He sayed it . . . ," Selim Woodworth n.d., "Journal," February 3, 1835. Information on Vakale is from the oral account given by Rave and Tatau on Uneapa in 1980 (Blythe pers. comm.). On Dako's father's death, see Jacobs 1844: 81. On the Uneapa wars, see ibid., 81, 89–90, 94–95 (not everything here can be trusted), and Selim Woodworth n.d., "Journal," February 3, 1835. Quotes "a great many . . . ," "The ill natured . . . ," "every night . . . ," "half a moon," "a regular fit out," and "axes of all . . . ," Selim Woodworth n.d., "Journal," February 3, 1835. For Jacobs's list of Dako's cargo, see Jacobs 1844: 90. Quote "The Capt. also . . . ," Selim Woodworth n.d., "Journal," February 3, 1835. On Kove as lingua franca rooted on Siassi trading relations, see Ross 2014. On Aromot's centrality to Vitiaz trade, see Harding 1967. Note: Aromot must remain a provisional location for the island the Americans (perhaps mistakenly) identified as "Gonoro." Today, Aromot elders suggest that the Americans misunderstood their word *kondoora,* meaning "these people whom we do not want to mention," which is often used in contact situations with Europeans (Robert Bugenhagen pers. comm.). On Aromot/Siassi island construction, see Pomponio 1992. Events at Aromot are from Selim Woodworth n.d., "Journal," February 5–10, 1835, unless otherwise identified. (But note that the name Mahseelow was given by Jacobs and is probably incorrect: Jacobs draws many "names" from the Kove language wordlist in Selim Woodworth n.d., "Papers": "Vocabulary of Kove," including Pelacar, Mahseelow, Tiano, Narcolamo, Nomer, Heydee, Rogerrogee, Rugurar, Imburado, Molarpo, Katore, Pio lio, Erugu-Kutar, Loeloe. My thanks to Jennifer Blythe for this observation.) Quotes "We landed . . . ," "Cap-in Mor-el," and "Beloved people . . . ," Jacobs 1844: 199. On divine economic order and culture of trade at Aromot, Siassi, and their region, see, e.g., Harding 1967, McPherson 2007, Freedman 1970, Pomponio 1992, 1994, and analysis in Fairhead and Blythe unpublished. Quotes "began to name . . . ," "he has . . . ," and "The old chief accompanied us . . . ," Selim Woodworth n.d, "Journal," February 7, 1835; "very pretty . . . ," "in all of . . . ," "appeared to be . . . ," and "He appeared . . . ," ibid., February 8, 1835. Woodworth called the house-of-respect the "King's palace." On "Kapi Molo," see, e.g., Thurston 1994, Bamler 1911: 547, Pomponio 1992: 45–46. On Billious pills and Harlem Oil, see Selim Woodworth n.d., "Journal," February 9, 1835. These pills had featured in ships' medicine boxes since the 1790s: see, e.g., *Columbian Centinel* (Boston), April 4, 1798: 4, Jacobs 1844. Quotes "saw in one house . . ." and "trophies of war," Selim Woodworth n.d., "Journal," February 12, 1835; "on the top there . . . ," ibid., February 14, 1835; "to be seen in . . . ," ibid., February 19, 1835; "struck in the . . ." and "When we got . . . ," ibid., February 23, 1835. The cipher read, "m12 9705e7 38 h72 h21d 1c57119h 18d h3m 92v20216," and can be decoded from encryption notes in Selim Woodworth n.d.,

"Papers." Quote "We probed the . . . ," Jacobs 1844: 220. For events en route to Australia after Arawe, see Selim Woodworth n.d., "Journal," February 16–March 30, 1835.

Chapter 12: Sydney Respite

On Sydney (Port Jackson) in that era, see, e.g., J. Lang 1834a. On arrival and cargo, see *Sydney Herald,* April 20, 1835: 3. On fumigation and painting, see Jacobs 1844: 238–239. Quotes "seen but one vessel . . ." *Sydney Herald,* April 13, 1835: 3; "the admiration of everyone . . ." and "protecting the vessel from . . . ," *Launceston Advertiser,* May 7, 1835: 3; "once been attacked . . . ," "at once amongst . . . ," and "some sensation," *Sydney Herald,* April 27, 1835: 2. On Saint George's Day dinner and quotes "Captain Morrell . . . ," "three times three," and "England and . . . ," see *Sydney Monitor,* April 25, 1835 : 2. Quote "happy that the same views . . . ," *Sydney Herald,* April 27, 1835: 2. On Dillon, see Jacobs 1844: 241 and Dillon 1829. On urban layout and convict work, see J. Lang 1834a. On Garrygarry in Australia and quote "the wonders of the moon," see Jacobs 1844: 247–250. On "Melanesians" aboard trading vessels, see Chappell 1998. On heads in museums, see "Select Committee on Aboriginal Tribes." On Theatre Royal show, see Jacobs 1844: 248 and *Sydney Gazette and New South Wales Advertiser,* April 25, 1835: 2. Quotes "If there is . . . ," J. Lang 1834a: 285; "Mr Simmons . . . ," *Sydney Gazette and New South Wales Advertiser,* April 25, 1835: 2; "laughed at the audience," Jacobs 1844: 248; "gave us no . . . ," ibid., 246; "was a thing . . . ," ibid., 248–249. On Jarvis's departure, see *Sydney Herald,* May 18, 1835: 2. On Jarvis's recollections, see *New York Herald,* July 1, 1895. On Jacobs moving to officers' quarters and new Pacific recruits, see Jacobs 1844: 249. The given names Oahoo and Otahitia are from Selim Woodworth n.d., "Journal," "Ship-Wreck crew of the M. O." On departure, see *Sydney Monitor,* May 6, 1835: 2. The manuscript "Commercial Intelligence" is in Selim Woodworth n.d., "Journal." Quotes "east end," "Noris-ies," and "the gift of . . . ," ibid.: "Commercial Intelligence." For women as divers in Siassi and region, see Pomponio 1992, Chowning and Swadling 1981. Quotes "sinking stones," "set up another . . . ," "voices keeping . . . ," "never join in . . . ," "Bells of the evening," and "they [were] often . . . ," Selim Woodworth n.d., "Journal": "Commercial Intelligence." After Aromot, all references are to Jacobs 1844: 256–271. The extensive ethnographic and oral historical research in this region conducted by, among others, Chowning, McPherson, Dorothy and David Counts, Lattas, and Thurston (all cited in bibliography) appears at odds with political structures in the region and ceremonies surrounding the coronation of Garrygarry as described in Jacobs 1844: 255–265. On the multiple uses of Cassowary parts, see Powell 1880, 1883, Chowning 1978a; material also came from Blythe pers. comm. Quotes "the Ostrich planes . . . ," Selim Woodworth n.d., "Journal": "Commercial Intelligence"; "I quartered myself . . . ," Jacobs 1844: 123.

Chapter 13: Dako's Dominion

Information on cargo including quotes "When the time . . . ," "stood up . . . ," and "When Dako . . . ," is from the oral account given by Rave and Tatau on Uneapa in 1980 (Blythe pers. comm.). Note: Blythe was unaware of Dako's story at this time.

Quote "He had terrified . . . ," Jacobs 1844: 94. Jacobs writes of Dako's subjection of the island twice—initially, and implausibly on pp. 94–95 and later (more accurately?) on p. 271. Quotes "began to talk softly . . ." and "Takari had children . . . ," from Rave and Tatau, oral account, Uneapa island 1980 (Blythe pers. comm.). Events in the Bismarck Sea after Australia, in the absence of Woodworth's journal text, rely on Jacobs 1844: 271–277. On women aboard the *Margaret Oakley,* ibid., 94, 271–272. On sex with vuvumu, see Blythe 1992, 1995, pers. comm. For fireworks and quotes "blue light" and "an unearthly glare . . . ," see Jacobs 1844: 126. Quotes "his two wives" and "had fallen in love . . . ," ibid., 272. On vines, ibid., 250, 273. Quote "aping the thunder . . . ," ibid., 95. On gun, ibid., 94. Jacobs's account of divine skill in gun use resembles local mythology; see Thurston 1994. Quotes "where people no . . ." and "Darco told me . . . ," Jacobs 1844: 273; "fine house . . . ," ibid.: 272. On Dako's oral history (which has clearly been inserted into Jacobs's text out of order, and perhaps pieced together from discussions during the voyage out) and quotes "a long time . . . ," "many heads . . . ," "with his numerous . . . ," "Never mind! . . . ," "from the bottom . . . ," "spouting streams . . . ," "speak thunder . . . ," "Pango kill . . . ," "break my people . . . ," "still recounts . . . ," "Why is it . . . ," "French officers . . . ," "the fact . . . ," and "If the tradition . . . ," ibid., 95–104. Quotes "amused us . . ." and "part of an . . . ," ibid., 273–274. On Admiralty (Manus) Islands and departure, ibid., 277–288. For Jacobs on Garrygarry, ibid., 289–291. On Morrell's shell cargo, see *Sydney Herald,* April 20, 1835: 3, and Selim Woodworth n.d., "Journal," October 19, 1835. On plans to colonize, see Chapter 17, below. On history and representations of New Guinea, see, e.g., Moore 2003, Ballard 2009. On Sio (which Jacobs names "Jacobs's Island") see Harding and Clark 1994. Quotes "entertained them sumptuously," "many valuables," "they informed . . . ," and "and have them . . . ," Jacobs 1844: 290–294. On pot mythology, see also Harding 1967: 139–140. Note that the startling conformity of Jacobs and Harding on this point is clear evidence for the veracity of Jacobs's information, however "strange" it may seem. On interior journey and quotes "were now . . . ," "hollow trees," and "stood motionless . . . ," see Jacobs 1844: 294–300. On the language of the gods and oral traditions that surely relate to Morrell's visit, see P. Lawrence 1964: 67–68, 1984: 21. On subsequent interior journeys, and quote "a singular race of people," see Jacobs 1844: 299–303. On painting the ship black, ibid., 302. Note that dates of this part of the voyage can be anchored by a manuscript sketch dated "30th July" in Selim Woodworth n.d., "Papers," that was the source for the image published in Jacobs 1844: 300. On the death of Margaret Oakley, see *Richmond Whig,* July 21, 1835. On going to Canton, see Selim Woodworth n.d., "Journal," September 18–October 24, 1835, and Jacobs 1844: 344–352. On Canton trading, see Bridgman 1833, Ljungstedt 1836, Gützlaff 1838, and "First American Voyage to Canton" 1837. On opium aboard, see Jacobs 1844: 341. On smugglers in Lintin, ibid., 344. On opium on Nantucket and quotes "A singular . . ." and "three grains . . . ," see Crèvecoeur 1904: 210. On owner's initials, see B. Morrell 1836. On cargo's value, see *New York Commercial Advertiser,* July 2, 1836: 2.

Chapter 14: Shipwreck

On reducing crew, see Jacobs 1844: 348. On losing rudder, ibid., 353. On arrival in Singapore, see *Singapore Chronicle and Commercial Register*, November 28, 1835. On robbery of Morrell, see *Sydney Herald*, May 12, 1836: 4. On Jacobs's leaving and quote "keen on seeing . . . ," see Jacobs 1844: 358–359. On the brig *Ann*, see *Singapore Chronicle and Commercial Register*, November 28, 1835. On cargo of tea and silks, see *Singapore Free Press and Mercantile Advertiser*, December 3, 1835: 3. On Jacobs's way home, see Jacobs 1844: 359–360, and *New York Commercial Advertiser*, March 28, 1836: 1. On departure of *Margaret Oakley*, see *Singapore Free Press and Mercantile Advertiser*, December 31, 1835: 4. On the voyage of the *Margaret Oakley*, see *New York Commercial Advertiser*, April 18, 1836: 1 and 2. On *Margaret Oakley* being reported missing, and quote "rakish looking brig . . ." and "alert[ed] the world . . . ," ibid., July 2, 1836: 2. On rumor of letter to Abby, see *New York Evening Post*, October 24, 1836: 2. On Fort Dauphin news, see *Salem Gazette*, November 22, 1836: 3. On Fort Dauphin history, see, e.g., Bialuschewski 2005, Jolly 2004, Brown 1995, Flacourt 1661, M. Pearson 1997, Bennett and Brooks 1965. Quote "put an end . . . ," "Biographical Notice of Fortune Albrand" 1827: 415. On problems facing captains, see Bennett and Brooks 1965: 186–187. Morrell's protest is B. Morrell 1836; see also Jacobs 1844: 363–366. On Dargelas, see Legueval de Lacombe 1840: 352–355. On the shipwreck, see Jacobs 1844: 363–365 and B. Morrell 1836. Quotes "plunged and staggered . . . ," "amid a scene . . . ," "many a box . . . ," and "paced the beach . . . ," Jacobs 1844: 364. Morrell's official list of goods recovered is in B. Morrell 1836. Quote "held a convention . . . ," Jacobs 1844: 365; "plundered by . . . ," "China goods," and "stolen from . . . ," B. Morrell 1836. On the fire see B. Morrell 1836. On Imerina politics, see, e.g., Brown 1995, esp. 127–129. Quotes "a war between . . . ," B. Morrell 1836; "the blight . . . ," "Important News from France" 1835; "all circumstances considered," "with his own hands," and "had assumed . . . ," B. Morrell 1836. On the help from the *Estelle*, ibid. On the consul reporting the wreck and Babcock being presumed dead, see *Public Ledger* (Philadelphia), November 24, 1836: 2. Quotes "for his kind . . ." and "from the insults . . ." and on crew who came with Woodworth, see "Letters of Selim E. Woodworth," *Mauritius Gazette*, August 27 and September 3, 1836. On crew remaining and quote "great favorites," see Jacobs 1844: 365. On consul and debts, see *Mauritius Gazette*, September 10, 1836. For sales of goods, ibid., September 17, October 1, and November 12, 1836. On Babcock and relief vessel, see *Alexandria Gazette*, March 11, 1837: 3. Quote "indefatigable," *Daily National Intelligencer* (Washington, D.C.), March 10, 1837: 3, and July 31, 1837: 3. On *Catharine Wilcox* and suspicions of underwriters, see *Boston Daily Courier*, September 18, 1837: 4, and "Brig Margaret Oakley" 1838. On Morrell and *Rio Packet*, see *National Gazette* (Philadelphia), May 13, 1837: 2. Quotes "after the wreck . . . ," Jacobs 1844: 366; "of the famed . . ." and "the greatest . . . ," *National Gazette* (Philadelphia), May 13, 1837: 2.

Chapter 15: Morrell Adrift

On *Rio Packet* in London, see *The Times*, May 1, 1837: 7, and *The Morning Post* (London), April 29, 1837: 7. On Aspinwall's recovering cargo and quote "the prompt

and . . . ," see *Daily National Intelligencer* (Washington, D.C.), July 31, 1837: 3. On breaking the cargo's seals and insurers' concerns, with quotes "Her Majesty . . ." and "unreadable and . . . ," see "Brig Margaret Oakley" 1838. Quote "vassals of . . . ," B.
Morrell 1832a: 68. On Enderby, and quote "heard so much . . . ," Hamilton 1870: 154.
On French reception, see Chapter 8, above, and Lafond de Lurcy 1844. On French
king's response to Morrell and quote "I had read . . . ," see Dumont d'Urville 1841:
lxviii (my translation). On Dumont d'Urville's visit to London, ibid., lxxii. The letter
Morrell sent to the Paris Geographical Society, June 20, [1837], is in the Archives,
Ministère de la Marine (copy made available to me by Samuel Houssou. Thank you!)
On American Exploring Expedition, see, e.g., Stanton 1975. On Morrell and Naraga,
see Jacobs 1844: 83–86. On Thupinier and quote "influenced by money," see "Com-
mentaire du Ministère de la Marine sur la lettre reçue du capitaine Morrell—Lettre à
Entête du Ministère de la Marine et des Colonies, July 24, 1837," Archives of the Société
de Géographie de Paris (text made available to me by Jean Guillou. Thank you!). On Morrell's dealings with the French Geographical Society and French government, see also
Bulletin de la Société de Géographie de Paris (1837): 65, 128. On insurers and quotes: "Many
of . . . ," "the key . . . ," "excited the . . . ," "involved in mystery," " '*terra incognita*' . . . ," "a
young gentleman . . . ," "was supposed . . . ," "The reader . . . ," "get rid . . . ," "persuading the . . . ," and "We shall . . . ," see "Brig Margaret Oakley" 1838.

Chapter 16: Father and Son

On "Morrell's" letter from Mauritius, see Morrell 1835, which was plagiarized
from Grant 1801. On *Margaret Oakley* being thought lost, see Harrison 1892. On Jarvis,
see *New York Herald,* July 1, 1895. On Jacobs's doings after his return, see Jacobs 1844:
363. Quote "the most poetical circumstances," *New York Commercial Advertiser,* July 27,
1837: 2. On Woodworth's employment by Downes and later resignation, see "Mr. Woodworth" 1836. On Woodworth's stroke, see *New York Commercial Advertiser,* July 27, 1837,
and *Boston Courier,* July 27, 1837: 1. On surety and quote "too conscientious . . . ,"
see Harrison 1892. On Woodworth's authorship of Morrell's book and quote "prepared
by Woodworth," see "Authors and Editors" 1837 and "La Perouse" 1837. On Woodworth family legend and quote "He had told . . . ," see letter to Captain Randall Jacobs,
October 8, 1940, and transcript of radio broadcast at launch of USS *Woodworth,* both in
Selim Woodworth n.d., "Papers." Quote "He came into . . . ," Harrison 1892. On Selim's being the sole survivor, see news clippings in Selim Woodworth n.d., "Papers."
On reunion with Jacobs and quote "was some . . . ," see Jacobs 1844: 363. On benefit
concerts, see *New York Spectator,* October 2, 1837, and "Samuel Woodworth" 1837.
Quote "life of great . . . ," "Samuel Woodworth" 1837. Quote "place the . . . ," *Albany
Argus,* November 7, 1837: 2 (quoting *The Courier*). On Exploring Expedition, see Stanton 1975. For Symmes and Reynolds's "holes at the Poles" theory, see Chapter 5, above.
On Poe, see, e.g., Quinn 1941: 250. On Poe's use of Morrell's and Reynolds's narratives
(but not realizing Woodworth's hand in Reynolds's), see Pollin 1976. On Poe's friendship with Woodworth, see letters of Mary Josephine Wethered (née Woodworth), Selim Woodworth n.d., "Papers." On "diddling," and quote "ingenuity, audacity . . . ,"

see Poe 1845. On the moon hoax, see Goodman 2009. On Woodworth's commercial notes and *Active,* see Selim Woodworth n.d., "Papers." On Fanning's recommendation of the schooner *Active,* see Fanning 1838: 193, 270, 295. On Selim's commission in U.S. Navy and quote "procure a commission . . . ," see Harrison 1892 and "Selim E. Woodworth U.S.N." n.d. On the *Ohio,* see Selim Woodworth n.d., "Log." On Jacobs as a sea captain, see "Destruction of Fish on the Coast" 1845. On Woodworth's novel and quotes "a boy under . . . ," "frantic with . . . ," "well knew . . . ," "I am doomed . . . ," and "We are both . . . ," see Selim Woodworth n.d., "Papers."

Chapter 17: The Lost Colony

On Morrell's Lucas Street address, see letter of Morrell to Paris Geographical Society, March 25, [1837], in Archives, Ministère de la Marine (copy made available to me by Samuel Houssou. Thank you!). On *Rio Packet* sailing with *Richmond,* see *Salem Gazette,* March 18, 1836. On *Rio Packet* in Cádiz, see *The London Standard,* May 29, 1837. On Morrell in Havana, see "Morrell (Benjamin)" 1843. On Havana in that era, see esp. Turnbull 1840. On Morrell's voyage, "death," and quote "It happened to be . . . ," see Jacobs 1844: 365. Quotes "was run ashore . . ." and "His history . . . ," "Death of Capt. Benjamin Morrell" 1839 (quoting the *Boston Daily Advertiser*). See also "Morrell (Benjamin)" 1843 and Stommel 1984. On the insurrection in Mozambique, see "Private Correspondence" 1839. For French sources and "He eventually . . . ," see "Morrell (Benjamin)" 1843 (my translation). On the wreck of the *Christine,* see "Miscellaneous Notices" 1840. On the death of the slaves, and "whither she repaired," see *The Friend* 13 (1840): 327. On Dumont d'Urville's critique of Morrell, see Dumont d'Urville 1842 (quotes "still held . . . ," p. 106; "was not true" and "did not add . . . ," p. 32, my translation). On Philippeville, see Dumont d'Urville 1841: 104–105 and 242 (quote "Those who . . . ," p. 104, my translation). On Darwin's visit and quote "The buildings were . . . ," see Darwin 1988: 209. On Abby Morrell's journeys to the Caribbean, see records of "New York Arrivals" on Ancestry.com (Mrs. Morrell arrived from Saint Thomas, Virgin Islands, on March 5, 1838, age 28; Abigail Morrell arrived February 4, 1839, age 33, from Saint Croix aboard *Eliza;* "Abby Jane Morrell" arrived on *Maria* from Puerto Cabello [Venezuela] on June 5, 1850). On Jeremiah Morrell in Venezuela, see Burrows 1975: 1180. Quote "the settlement and . . . ," Jacobs 1844: 363. On Williams see J. Williams 1837 and Flexner 2012 (which contains an account of his death). On Woodworth's leave and quote "for the purpose . . . ," see "Selim E. Woodworth U.S.N." n.d. The "New York Arrivals" passenger lists on Ancestry.com show that Woodworth arrived in New York from Havana on December 11, 1841, aboard the *Rapid.* Letter (presumed) from Woodworth to (presumed) Jacobs, and quotations throughout, in Selim Woodworth n.d., "Papers." Quotes "see wrong . . . ," "to the last degree," and "He and our mother . . . ," letter of Mary Josephine Wethered (née Woodworth) in Selim Woodworth n.d., "Papers"; "[seeing] through a glass dimly," Mitterling 1959: 66. On pilot boys, see Pennington 1840. On Harmony and the *Amistad,* see, e.g., *New London Gazette,* August 26, 1839. Quotes "by the cures . . . ," J. Williams 1837 (cited in Jacobs 1844: 372); "injurious to . . . ," Jacobs 1844: iii. On Woodworth's navy leave and quote

"serious illness," see "Selim E. Woodworth, U.S.N." n.d. On Woodworth's continu-
ing to write, see, e.g., his letters of November 25, 1837, and January 4, 1838, to Benjamin
F. Thompson, Papers of Samuel Woodworth, 1829–1945 n.d. On bays, see Jacobs 1844
(Cooper, p. 221; Irving, p. 225; Reynolds, p. 74; Audubon Island, p. 305, Woodworth,
p. 186). The passage in the Woodworth papers concerns a trek into the Willaumez
peninsula: Selim Woodworth n.d., "Papers." Quotes "knew little . . . ," Jacobs 1844:
112; "to do right . . . ," ibid., 366. On Garove's population, see sketch map of Garove in
Selim Woodworth n.d., "Papers." The passage on the trek into the Willaumez peninsula is in Selim Woodworth n.d., "Papers." Quote "an act of vengeance . . . ," Jacobs
1844: 64. On representations of cannibalism and its association with colonialism, see
Obeyesekere 2005, Biber 2005, E. Williams 1834b. On American sea literature and
nationalism, see, e.g., Lenz 1991. Quote "We must condemn . . . ," *Southern Literary
Messenger,* October 1844: 640. On Woodworth's crossing to California, see K. Johnson
2008, Morgan 1963: 98–99. On Woodworth and the Donner party, see, e.g., K. Johnson 1996, 2006. The infamous Donner party was a group of emigrants trapped by snow
in the Sierra Nevada en route to San Francisco; some were forced to eat their dead. On
Jacobs's sailing to San Francisco see "Hermitage Soon to Be Sold" 1894. On the California and Pacific Ocean Exploring, Trading and Colonisation Company and quotes
"the language of . . . ," "national advantages . . . ," and "to resist any attack from any
hostile . . ." and the plans, see the copy of a letter to S. E. Woodworth from Directors
of this company [n.d.], Selim Woodworth n.d., "Papers." The list of provisions is in
Selim Woodworth, n.d., "Papers": "Condensed Plan of the California and Pacific Exploring Trading & Colonizing Co." On Woodworth's part in tracking down the Sydney Cove gang and election to California State Senate, see, e.g., "Selim E. Woodworth"
1855 and Bancroft 1887. Woodworth's letter to Jacobs is in Selim Woodworth n.d.,
"Papers." (Note: it is uncertain how reclusive Woodworth was and at what periods. He
was serving in the State Senate until 1851, and his seclusion appears to have followed
this. He was married and building his business starting in 1856.) On the copper mine,
Woodworth's rejoining the navy, and his navy record, see Selim Woodworth n.d.,
"Papers." On Mary Ellen Pleasant and the Woodworths, see, e.g., Eliassen 2006, Bibbs
2012, Hudson 2003. On Jacobs's name change see *Albany Argus,* January 16, 1846: 3 and
Scott 1984: 43 (with quote "James J. Monroe . . ."). Monroe is tentatively identified as a
silversmith in Mack 2005: 120. On Jacobs's brother taking the name Monroe, see, e.g.,
"Harlem Hermit's Estate" 1889. On Jacobs's travels, and quote "all through Rus-
sia . . . ," see "Hermitage Soon to Be Sold" 1894; see also "Hermit of Harlem" 1890. On
Hermitage construction, see *New York Herald,* September 4, 1856: 5. Quote "boycott
against all mankind," *Macon Telegraph,* April 29, 1890: 3. On Jacobs's 1871 visit to San
Francisco, see passport application of January 13, 1871, "U.S. Passport Applications," on
Ancestry.com, and report of his arrival home in *New York Herald Tribune,* May 15, 1871.

Epilogue

On the battle of Arawe, see the article in Wikipedia, http://en.wikipedia.org/wiki
/Battle_of_Arawe (accessed January 31, 2013). On operations of USS *Woodworth* in

escort and in action around New Britain, see http://destroyerhistory.org/benson-glea vesclass/usswoodworth/ (accessed January 31, 2013), and assorted loose news clippings and correspondence concerning the activities of USS *Woodworth* in Selim Woodworth n.d., "Papers." On colonization of Uneapa, see Moore 2003. Information on Dako's daughter, welcome given to colonizers, and demarcation of garden came from Blythe pers. comm. On King's visit, see King 1844. On Finsch, see Finsch 1888. On smallpox, see Blythe 1978; J. P. White 1999. On depopulation of Naraga, see "Destruction of Fish" 1845 and Guillou 2011: 121. On Maclay and quote "from the moon," see Webster 1984: 97–100. For oral account of Anut, see P. Lawrence 1964: 64–65. On Panku, Ngamet, and Kapi-molo, see Bamler 1911: 547. On discerning history shaping "my-thology," see, e.g., Sahlins 1987, 1995. On Uneapa mythology today, see Fairhead and Blythe unpublished. On the Kalt Misin, see Lattas 2001, 2005. Information on writing to spirits in America comes from Jennifer Blythe (pers. comm.). Dako's being captured to be instructed and quote "The whites had not . . ." are from the oral account of Rave and Tatau on Uneapa Island, 1980 (Blythe pers. comm.). Quotes "prepare the minds . . . ," B. Morrell 1832a: 466; "he took a deep . . ." and "promised on his . . . ," Th. Dwight 1834: 188; "claimed that . . . ," Blythe pers. comm. On library of *Margaret Oakley,* see single-page list of books among papers relating to the *Margaret Oakley* in Selim Wood-worth n.d., "Papers." On Kalt Misin theology, see Lattas 2001, 2005. On Dwight's pa-per to the American Ethnological Society, see *Transactions of the American Ethnological Society* 1 (1845): xii. No known copies of the paper exist. On analysis of Dako's mathe-matics, see "Geometrical nomenclature . . ." and *Historical Magazine,* March 7, 1863: 92. On Dwight's later correspondence, see his letter to George Gibbs of April 11, 1866, in Th. Dwight n.d. Quote "Better to sleep . . . ," Melville 1851: 27. On sources for Quee-queg, see Sanborn 2005, 1998: 234–235. Quote "inveterate and praiseworthy . . . ," Ja-cobs 1844: 24. On Dako's tattoos and quote "his muscular form of . . . ," see "Savages etc." 1831: 365. On tattoos, see also *Massachusetts Spy,* September 14, 1831: 4. On Typee, see Melville 1847 ("on every . . . ," p. 84; "The warrior . . . ," p. 85). On Morrell as the "biggest liar" see Mills 2003: 433–435, and as "Munchhausen," see Wray 1848: 219, and Enderby quoted in Hamilton 1870: 154. For criticisms of Morrell see Guppy 1887: "Better Morrell's deeds have been buried in the oblivion which is fitting for such deeds of heartless cruelty" (228). On Morrell's "death," see Stommel 1984. On Morrell's proof of life and quotes "down the Solomon Archipelago . . ." and "I have by . . . ," letter by "Morrell" of August 11, 1843, to the editors of the *New York Commercial Adver-tiser* republished in *New York Spectator,* August 16, 1843: 4. Bernadon was captaining the *Emily* in Cuba on July 26, 1843, according to the Boston *Daily Atlas,* August 18, 1843: 3. On Jeremiah Morrell and Abby Morrell, see Chapter 18, above. On the theft of Abby's watch, see *New York Commercial Advertiser,* February 26, 1841: 2. On Knapp's author-ship, see Dunlap 1930: 649–650. Quote "by a single hair," C. Goodrich 1852: 657.

ʖ◌◌ʖ

Bibliography

Aderman, Ralf M., and Wayne Kime. 2003. *Advocate for America: The Life of James Kirke Paulding.* Selinsgrove: Susquehanna University Press.

Adkins, Nelson. 1932. "James Fenimore Cooper and the Bread and Cheese Club." *Modern Language Notes* 47, no. 2: 71–79.

"Adventures of a Sailor." 1831. *Philadelphia Inquirer,* September 15: 1.

Ambrose, Wallace R., and Robert W. Johnson. 1986. "Unea: An Obsidian Non-Source in Papua New Guinea." *Journal of the Polynesian Society* 95, no. 4: 491–497.

"American Ethnological Society." 1867. *Historical Magazine* 11: 53–55.

American Lyceum. 1831. *American Lyceum, with the Proceedings of the Convention Held in New York, May 4, 1831, to Organize the National Department of the Institution.* Boston: Hiram Tubber.

Anderson, Virginia. 1962. *Maritime Mystic.* Mystic, Conn.: Maritime Historical Association.

Association Salomon. 2008. *Le mystère Lapérouse.* Paris: Conti.

Austin, Allan D. 1984. *African Muslims in Antebellum America: A Sourcebook.* London: Routledge.

"Authors and Editors." 1837. *New York Spectator,* June 15: 3.

Bagley, Will. 2010. *So Rugged and So Mountainous: Blazing the Trails to Oregon and California, 1812–1848.* Norman: University of Oklahoma Press.

Bailey, Dianne. 2011. *Cholera.* New York: Rosen Group.

Balch, Edwin. S. 1909. "Stonington Antarctic Explorers." *Bulletin of the American Geographical Society* 41, no. 8: 473–492.

Ballard, Chris. 2008. "'Oceanic Negroes': British Anthropology of Papuans, 1820–1869." In *Foreign Bodies: Oceania and the Science of Race, 1750–1940.*

Ed. Bronwen Douglas and Chris Ballard, 157–201. Canberra: ANU E-Press. Available at http://epress.anu.edu.au/foreign_bodies_citation.html.

Ballard, Chris. 2009. "The Art of Encounter: Verisimilitude in the Imaginary Exploration of Interior New Guinea, 1725–1876." In *Oceanic Encounters: Exchange, Desire, Violence.* Ed. Margaret Jolly, Serge Tcherkézoff, and Darell Tryon, 221–257. Canberra: ANU E-Press. Available at http://epress.anu.edu.au/oceanic_encounters/mobile_devices/ch08 .html.

Bamler, Georg. 1911. "Tami." In *Deutsch Neu-Guinea.* Vol. 3. Ed. Richard Neuhauss, 487–566. Berlin: Dietrich Reimer Verlag.

Bancroft, Hubert H. 1887. *The Works of Hubert Howe Bancroft.* Vol. 36. San Francisco: History Company.

Bank, Rosemary. 1997. *Theatre Culture in America, 1825–1860.* New York: Cambridge University Press.

Barnes, George. n.d. "Career of Woodworth, with Matters Incidental Thereto." *Saturday Evening [illeg.],* September 28, 1895, 13. In newspaper clippings, Papers of Selim Edwin Woodworth, 1834–1947. Huntington Library. San Marino, Calif.

Barnhart, Terry. 2005. *Ephraim George Squier and the Development of American Anthropology.* Lincoln: University of Nebraska Press.

Barnum, Phineas T. 1855. *The Life of P. T. Barnum by Himself.* London: Sampson Low and Son.

Beautemps-Beaupré, Charles F. 1807. *Atlas du voyage de Bruny-Dentrecasteaux, contre-amiral de France, commandant les frégates la Recherche et l'Espérance, fait par ordre du gouvernement en 1791, 1792 et 1793.* Paris: Dépôt général des cartes et plans de la marine et des colonies.

Becke, Louis. 1908. *The Call of the South.* London: John Milne.

Ben, Carl. 2003. *The War of 1812.* Oxford: Osprey.

Benemann, William E. 2006. *Male-Male Intimacy in Early America: Beyond Romantic Friendships.* Binghamton, N.Y.: Haworth.

Bennett, G. 1832. "Notes on Manilla, Island of Luçonia." *Asiatic Journal and Monthly Register* 7: 21–30.

Bennett, Norman R., and George E. Brooks, Jr. 1965. *New England Merchants in Africa: A History Through Documents, 1802–1865.* Brookline, Mass.: Boston University Press.

Bercovitch, Sacvan, ed. 1994. *The Cambridge History of American Literature.* Vol. 1: *1590–1820.* Cambridge: Cambridge University Press.

Bergh, Henry. 1888. "Biographical Sketch of Christian Bergh." *New York Times,* March 18: 11.

Bertrand, Kenneth J. 1994. *American in Antarctica.* New York: American Geographical Society Special Publication 39.

Bialuschewski, Arne. 2005. "Pirates, Slavers, and the Indigenous Population in Madagascar, c. 1690–1715." *International Journal of African Historical Studies* 38, no. 3: 401–425.

Bibbs, Susheel. 2012. *Heritage of Power: Marie Laveaux to Mary Ellen Pleasant.* San Francisco: M E P Publications.

Biber, Katherine. 2005. "Cannibals and Colonialism." *Sydney Law Review* 27: 623–637.

Bieder, Robert E. 1986. *Science Encounters the Indian, 1820–1880: The Early Years of American Ethnology.* Norman: University of Oklahoma Press.

Bieder, Robert E. 1990. *A Brief Historical Survey of the Expropriation of American Indian Remains.* Boulder: Native American Rights Fund.

"Biographical Notice of Fortune Albrand." 1827. *Oriental Herald* 15: 413–423.

"Biographical Sketches of Living American Poets and Novelists, no. 5: George Pope Morris, Esq." 1838. *Southern Literary Messenger* 4: 663–671.

Blanchard, Pascal, Gilles Boetsch, and Nanette Jacomijn Snoep, eds. 2011. *Human Zoos: The Invention of the Savage.* Paris: Branly.

Blum, Hester. 2008. *The View from the Masthead: Maritime Imagination and Antebellum American Sea Narratives.* Chapel Hill: University of North Carolina Press.

Blythe, Jennifer. 1978. "Following Both Sides: Processes of Group Formation in Vitu." Ph.D. diss. McMaster University, Hamilton, Ontario.

Blythe, Jennifer. 1984. "An Obsidian Source in the Vitu Islands, West New Britain." *Journal of the Polynesian Society* 93: 199–203.

Blythe, Jennifer. 1992. "Climbing a Mountain Without a Ladder: Chronologies and Stories." *Time and Society* 1, no. 1: 13–27.

Blythe, Jennifer. 1995. "Vanishing and Returning Heroes: Ambiguity and Persistent Hope in an Unea Island Legend." *Anthropologica* 37, no. 2: 207–228.

Blythe, Jennifer. pers. comm. Oral history narrated on Uneapa in 1980, recorded and translated, and made available to me in e-mails and conversations.

Boden, Robert. 2005. "Andrew Jackson: The Bank Wars." In *White House Under Fire.* Ed. Bill Rhatican, 17–30. Bloomington: Author House.

Bodrogi, Tibor. 1970. "Zur Ethnographie der Vitu (French) Inseln. Baessler-Archiv." *Neue Folge* 19: 47.

Bogdan, Robert. 1988. *Freak Show: Presenting Human Oddities for Amusement and Profit.* Chicago: University of Chicago Press.

Borneman, Walter R. 1988. *1812: The War That Forged a Nation.* New York: Harper Collins.

Boudinot, Elias. 1816. *A Star in the West; or, A Humble Attempt to Discover the Long Lost Ten Tribes of Israel.* Trenton: Fenton, Hutchinson and Dunham.

Bougainville, Louis de. 1772. *A Voyage Around The World.* Trans. John Forster. London: Nourse and Davies.

Bridgman, Elijah C. 1833."Description of the City of Canton." *Chinese Repository* 2: 145–160, 193–211, 241–264, 289–308.

"Brig Margaret Oakley." 1838. *Rhode Island Republican* (Newport), January 31: 1.

Brown, Merwyn. 1995. *A History of Madagascar*. London: Damien Tunnacliffe.

Bruni d'Entrecasteaux, Antoine-Raymond-Joseph de. 2001. *Voyage to Australia and the Pacific, 1791–1793*. Ed. and Trans. Edward Duyker and Maryse Duyker. Carlton: Melbourne University Press.

Burrows, Raymond Earl. 1975. *Robert Burrows and Descendants, 1630–1974*. Vol. 2. Cleveland: Burrows.

Busch, Briton Cooper. 1985. *The War Against the Seals: A History of the North American Seal Fishery*. Kingston, Ont.: McGill-Queens University Press.

Byrne, Sarah. 2005. "Recent Survey and Excavation of the Monumental Complexes on Uneapa Island, West New Britain, Papua New Guinea." *Papers from the Institute of Archaeology* 16: 95–102.

Byrne, Sarah. 2008. "Practice-Centred Approach to Uneapa Island's Archaeology in a Long Term Context." Ph.D. diss. University College London.

"Cannibals." 1831a. *Baltimore Patriot*, November 25: 3.

"Cannibals." 1831b. *New York Commercial Advertiser*, September 5: 3.

"Captain Benjamin Morrell." 1838. *Rhode Island Republican*, January 31.

"Captain Morrell." 1833. *Parley's Magazine* 1: 23–25.

"Captain Morrell, in announcing . . . ." 1831. *New York Commercial Advertiser*, September 12: 2.

"Card: Captain Morrell." 1831. *New York Evening Post*, September 12: 2.

Carteret, Philip. 1965. *Carteret's Voyage Round the World, 1776–1769*. Cambridge: Hakluyt Society.

Chappell, David A. 1998. *Double Ghosts: Oceanian Voyagers on Euroamerican Ships*. New York: Sharp.

Cheyne, Andrew. 1852. *A Description of Islands in the Western Pacific Ocean*. London: Potter and Paultry.

Chowning, Ann. 1972. "Ceremonies, Shell Money and Cultural Change Among the Kove." *Expedition* 15: 2–8.

Chowning, Ann. 1978a. "Changes in West New Britain Trading Systems in the Twentieth Century." *Mankind* 11, no. 3: 296–307.

Chowning, Ann. 1978b. "First-Child Ceremonies and Male Prestige: Changing Kove Society." In *The Changing Pacific: Essays in Honour of H. E. Maud*. Ed. Niel Gunson, 203–213. Melbourne: Oxford University Press.

Chowning, Ann. 1987a. "Sorcery and the Social Order in Kove." In *Sorcerer and Witch in Melanesia*. Ed. Michele Stephen, 149–182. Melbourne: Melbourne University Press,.

Chowning, Ann. 1987b. "'Women Are Our business': Women, Exchange and Prestige in Kove." In *Dealing with Inequality: Analysing Gender Rela-*

tions in Melanesia and Beyond. Ed. Marilyn Strathern, 130–149. Cambridge: Cambridge University Press.

Chowning, Ann. 1990. "God and Ghosts in Kove." In *Christianity in the Pacific.* Ed. John Barker, 33–59. Lanham, Md.: University Press of America/ Association for Social Anthropology in Oceania.

Chowning, Ann, and Pamela Swadling. 1981. "Shellfish Gathering at Nuka-kau Island, West New Britain Province, Papua New Guinea." *Journal de la Société des Oceanistes* 37: 159–167.

Coad, Oral Sumner. 1919. "The Plays of Samuel Woodworth." *Sewanee Review* 27: 163–175.

Coan, Titus. 1880. *Adventures in Patagonia; A Missionary's Exploring Trip (1880).* New York: Dodd, Mead.

Cohen, Patricia, Timothy Gilfoyle, and Helen Horowitz. 2008. *The Flash Press.* Chicago: University of Chicago Press.

Combe, George. 1830. *A System of Phrenology.* Edinburgh: J. Anderson.

Combe, George. 1841. *Notes on the United States of North America During a Phrenological Visit in 1838–1840.* Philadelphia: Carey and Hart.

Conforti, Joseph. 2001. *Imagining New England.* Chapel Hill: University of North Carolina Press.

Connolly, Bob, and R. Anderson. 1987. *First Contact.* New York: Viking Penguin.

Coulter, John. 1847. *Adventures on the Western Coast of South America, and the Interior of California.* London: Longman, Brown, Green and Longmans.

Counts, D., and D. Counts. 1974. "The Kaliai Lupunga: Disputing in the Public Forum." In *Contention and Dispute: Aspects of Law and Social Control in Melanesia.* Ed. Arnold L. Epstein, 113–151. Canberra: ANU Press.

Counts, David, and Dorothy Counts. 1970. "The Vula of Kaliai: A Primitive Currency with Commercial Use." *Oceania* 41: 90–105.

Counts, David R., and Dorothy A. Counts. 1992. "Exaggeration and Reversal: Clowning Among the Lusi-Kaliai." In *Clowning as Critical Practice: Performance Humor in the South Pacific.* Ed. William Mitchell, 88–103. Pittsburgh: University of Pittsburgh Press.

Counts, Dorothy A. 1971. "Cargo or Council: Two Approaches to Development in Northwest New Britain." *Oceania* 41: 288–297.

Counts, Dorothy A. 1980. "Akro and Gagandewa: A Melanesian Myth." *Journal of the Polynesian Society* 89, no. 1: 33–65.

Counts, Dorothy A. 1994. "Snakes, Adulterers, and the Loss of Paradise in Kaliai." *Pacific Studies* 17: 109–151.

Counts, Dorothy A., and David R. Counts. 1983. "Father's Water Equals Mother's Milk: The Conception of Parentage in Kaliai, West New Britain." *Mankind* 14: 46–56.

Counts, Dorothy A., and David R. Counts. 1991. "'People Who Act Like Dogs': Adultery and Deviance in a Melanesian Community." *Anthropologica* 33, nos. 1–2: 99–110.

Counts, Dorothy A., and David R. Counts. 2004. "The Good, the Bad, and the Unresolved Death in Kaliai." *Social Science and Medicine* 58: 887–897.

Cox, Robert. 1832–1834. "On the Character and Cerebral Development of the Esquimaux." *Phrenological Journal* 8, no. 37: 289–308.

Crain, Caleb. 1994. "Lovers of Human Flesh: Homosexuality and Cannibalism in Melville's Novels." *American Literature* 66, no. 1: 25–53.

Crane, J. W. 1836. "An Address on the Treatment of the Diseases Connected with the Teeth." *United States Medical and Surgical Journal* 21: 330–337.

Crawford, Mary Caroline. 1912. *Romantic Days in the Early Republic.* New York: Grosset and Dunlap.

Crèvecoeur, J. Hector St. John de. 1904. *Letters from an American Farmer.* Vol. 6. New York: Fox, Duffield.

"Cruise of the Schooner Antarctic." 1831. *New York Commercial Advertiser,* August 30: 2.

Currie, Noel Elizabeth. 2005. *Constructing Colonial Discourse: Captain Cook at Nootka Sound.* Montreal: McGill-Queens University Press.

Dampier, William. 1729. *A Voyage to New Holland etc.* London: James and John Knapton.

Dana, Richard Henry. 1840. *Two Years Before the Mast.* New York: Harper and Brothers.

Dark, Philip. 1969. "The Changing World of the Kilenge, a New Guinea People." *Lore* 19, no. 3: 74–84.

Dark, Philip. 1974. *Kilenge Art and Life: A Look at a New Guinea People.* London: Academy Editions.

Dark, Philip. 1999. "Of Old Models and New in Pacific Art: Real or Spurious?" In *Art and Performance in Oceania.* Ed. Barry Craig, Bernie Kernot, and Christopher Anderson, 266–288. Bathurst, N.S.W: Crawford House.

Darwin, Charles. 1988. *Charles Darwin's Beagle Diary.* Ed. Richard Darwin Kenes. Cambridge: Cambridge University Press.

Davies, John. 1955. *Phrenology, Fad and Science: A Nineteenth-Century American Crusade.* New Haven: Yale University Press, 1955.

"Death of Capt. Benjamin Morrell." 1839. *Army and Navy Chronicle* 9, no. 23: 381.

"Death of Ourang Outang." 1832. *Salem Gazette,* August 10: 3.

"Découvertes du capitaine américain Morrell." 1833. *Bulletin de la Société de géographie* 121: 249–270.

Delaney, Martin. 1879. *Principles of Ethnology: Origins of Races and Color, with an Archaeological Compendium of Ethiopian and Egyptian Civilization* Philadelphia: Harper and Brothers.

Delano, Amasa. 1817. *A Narrative of Voyages and Travels in the Northern and Southern Hemispheres: Comprising Three Voyages Round the World; Together with a Voyage of Survey and Discovery, in the Pacific Ocean and Oriental Islands.* Boston: Delano.

Denizet, Alain. 2005. "Simon Lavo, Germignonville chirurgien-major sur l'Astrolabe." *Bulletin de la Société archéologique d'Eure et Loir* 84: 33–50.

Derby, James C. 1884. *Fifty Years Among Authors, Books and Publishers.* New York: G. W. Carleton.

"Destruction of Fish on the Coast." 1845. *The Friend* 18: 149.

Dillon, Peter. 1829. *Narrative and Successful Result of a Voyage in the South Seas, Performed by Order of the Government of British India, to Ascertain the Actual Fate of La Pérouse's Expedition, Interspersed with Accounts of the Religion, Manners, Customs, and Cannibal Practices of the South Sea Islanders.* London: Hurst, Chance.

"Distressing." 1809. *Republican Watch-Tower,* October 31: 2.

Dorson, Richard M. 1940. "The Yankee on the Stage—A Folk Hero of American Drama." *New England Quarterly* 13, no. 3: 467–493.

Douglas, Bronwen. 2008. "Climate to Crania: Science and the Racialization of Human Difference." In *Foreign Bodies: Oceania and the Science of Race, 1750–1940.* Ed. Bronwen Douglas and Chris Ballard, 33–98. Canberra: ANU Press. http://press.anu.edu.au/foreign_bodies/mobile_devices/ch01.html.

Douglass, Frederick. 1854. *The Claims of the Negro, Ethnologically Considered. An Address, Before the Literary Societies.* Rochester, N.Y.: Lee, Mann.

"Dramatizing a Dream." 1833. *New York Mirror,* March 16: 295.

Druett, Joan. 1991. *Petticoat Whalers: Whaling Wives at Sea.* Auckland: Collins.

Dudden, Arthur P. 1997. "The American Pacific: Where the West Was Also Won." In *Studies in the Economic History of the Pacific Rim.* Ed. Dennis Flynn, Sally Miller, and John Latham, 93–103. London: Routledge.

Dumont d'Urville, Jules-Sébastien-César. 1832a. "Sur les isles du Grand Ocean." *Bulletin de la Société de géographie* 17: 1–21.

Dumont d'Urville, Jules-Sébastien-César. 1832b. *Voyage de la corvette l'Astrolabe: exécuté par ordre du Roi pendant les années 1826–1827–1828–1829. Histoire du voyage.* Vol. 4. Paris: Tastu.

Dumont d'Urville, Jules-Sébastien-César. 1833a. "Découvertes du capitaine américain Morrell." *Bulletin de la Société de Géographie* 121: 249–270.

Dumont d'Urville, Jules-Sébastien-César. 1833b. "Observations sur les découvertes du capitaine américain J. Morrell, par M. J. d'Urville." *Bulletin de la Société de Géographie* 121: 270–277.

Dumont d'Urville, Jules-Sébastien-César. 1835. *Voyage pittoresque autour du monde.* Paris: Dupuy.

Dumont d'Urville, Jules-Sébastien-César. 1841. *Voyage au pole sud et dans l'Océanie sur les corvettes l'Astrolabe.* Vol. 1. Paris: Gide.

Dumont d'Urville, Jules-Sébastien-César. 1842. *Voyage au pole sud et dans l'Océanie sur les corvettes l'Astrolabe.* Vol. 2. Paris: Gide.

Dunlap, William. 1930. *Diary of William Dunlap.* Vol. 3. New York: New-York Historical Society.

Dunlop, M. H. 1984. "Curiosities Too Numerous to Mention: Early Regionalism and Cincinnati's Western Museum." *American Quarterly* 36, no. 4: 524–548.

Dunmore, John. 2006. *Where Fate Beckons: The Life of Jean-François de La Pérouse.* Auckland: Exisle.

Dwight, Benjamin W. 1874. *The History of the Descendants of John Dwight, of Dedham.* 1874. New York: J. F. Trow and Son.

Dwight, Theodore. 1824. *A Journal of a Tour in Italy in the Year 1821.* New York: Abraham Paul.

Dwight, Theodore. 1834. *Things As They Are; or, Notes of a Traveller Through Some of the Middle and Northern States.* New York: Harper and Brothers.

Dwight, Theodore. 1835. "Vocabulary of the Language of the Uniapa Islands." *American Annals of Education* 5 (September): 396–401.

Dwight, Theodore. 1841–1842. "Living Sketches of Italy." *American Penny Magazine* 1: 271, 445–446, 454–455, 484–485.

Dwight, Theodore. 1851. *The Roman Republic of 1849: With Accounts of the Inquisition and the Siege of Rome.* New York: Van Dien.

Dwight, Theodore. 1859. *The Life of General Giuseppe Garibaldi, Written by Himself: With His Sketches of His Companions in Arms. Translated by His Friend and Admirer Theodore Dwight.* New York: Sampson Low and Sons.

Dwight, Theodore. n.d. Letters of Dwight to Gibbs. Vocabulary and Notes. National Anthropological Archives, Smithsonian Institution. MS 1078, 1866 [currently mis-archived under Theodore F. Dwight]. Washington, D.C.

Dwight, Timothy. 1823. *Travels in New England and New York.* Vol. 3. London: William Baynes and Son.

Eaton, Joseph. 2012. *The Anglo-American Paper War.* New York: Palgrave Macmillan.

Eliassen, Meredith. 2006. "A 'Colored' Mosaic: The Vibrant African American Community in Antebellum San Francisco." *California State Library Foundation Bulletin* 84: 11–16.

"Equinoctial Gale." 1815. *Connecticut Mirror,* October 2: 3.

"Esquimaux Indians." 1821. *Connecticut Gazette,* February 28: 1.

Everts, William Wallace. 1866. *The Theatre.* Chicago: Church and Goodman.

"Exhibition. Cannibals of Islands in the South Pacific." 1831. *American,* September 2: 3.

Exman, Eugene. 1965. *The Brothers Harper: A Unique Publishing Partnership and Its Impact upon the Cultural Life of America from 1817 to 1853*. New York: Harper and Row.

"Expedition to the Pacific." 1833. *Alexandria Gazette,* March 30.

"Expedition to the South Pole." 1832. *Boston Courier,* January 19: 1.

Fabian, Ann. 2003. "The Curious Cabinet of Dr. Morton." In *Acts of Possession: Collecting in America*. Ed. Leah Dilworth, 112–137. New Brunswick, N.J.: Rutgers University Press.

Fabian, Ann. 2010. *The Skull Collectors: Race Science and America's Unburied Dead*. Chicago: University of Chicago Press.

Fairhead, James, and Jennifer Blythe. Unpublished. "The Spirit and the Gifts." Manuscript in authors' possession.

Fairhead, James, Tim Geysbeek, Svend Holsoe, and Melissa Leach. 2003. *African-American Exploration of West Africa: Four Nineteenth-Century Diaries*. African American Studies Series. Bloomington: Indiana University Press.

Fanning, Edmund. 1838. *Voyages to the South Seas, Indian and Pacific Oceans, China Sea, North-West . . . .* 4th ed. New York: William Vermilye.

Farris, Johnathan. 2004. *Dwelling on the Edge of Empires: Foreigners and Architecture in Guangzhou (Canton) China*. Ithaca, N.Y.: Cornell University Press.

Fergusson, Mr. 1831–1832. "Notes Made During a Visit to the United States and Canada in 1831." *Quarterly Journal of Agriculture* 3: 571–620.

Finsch, Otto. 1888. *Samoafahrten. Reise in Kaiser Wilhelmsland und Englisch Neu-Guinea in den Jahren 1884 und 1885 an bord Deutschen Dampfer "Samoa."* Leipzig: Hirt und Sohn.

"First American Voyage to Canton." 1837. *Army and Navy Chronicle* 4–5: 258–260.

Fishkin, Shelley. 2005. "Crossroads of Culture: The Transnational Turn in American Studies." *American Quarterly* 57, no. 1 : 17–57.

Flacourt, Etienne de. 1661. *Histoire de la grande île de Madagascar*. Troyes: Nicolas Oudot.

Flexner, James. 2012. "Erromango: Cannibals and Missionaries on the Martyr Isle." *Current World Archaeology* 5, no. 8: 33–39.

Footner, Geoffrey. 1998. *Tidewater Triumph: The Development and Worldwide Success of the Chesapeake Bay Pilot Schooner*. Mystic, Conn.: Mystic Seaport Museum.

Foreman, Grant. 1932. "John Howard Payne and the Cherokee Indians." *American Historical Review* 37, no. 4: 723–730.

Foster, George. 1849. *New York in Slices, by an Experienced Carver*. New York: W. F. Burgess.

Freedman, Michael. 1970. "Social Organization of a Siassi Island Community." In *Cultures of the Pacific: Selected Readings*. Ed. Thomas G. Harding and Ben. J. Wallace, 159–180. New York: Free Press.

"From the New York Standard." 1831. *Nantucket Inquirer,* September 24: 1.

"From the New York Traveller." 1833. *New York Broome Republican,* January 3: 1.

"Fugitive." 1831. *New York Commercial Advertiser,* September 9: 2.

Gall, Franz Joseph, Joseph Vimont, and Victor Broussais. 1838. *On the Functions of the Cerebellum, by Drs. Gall, Vimont and Broussais, Translated from the French by George Combe: Also Answers to the Objections Used Against Phrenology by Drs Roget, Rudolphi, Prichard, and Tiedemann; by George Combe and Dr A. Combe.* Edinburgh: Maclachlan and Stewart.

Gatell, Frank. 1966. "Sober Second Thoughts on Van Buren, the Albany Regency, and the Wall Street Conspiracy." *Journal of American History* 53, no. 1: 19–40.

Gellman, David Nathaniel. 2006. *Emancipating New York: The Politics of Slavery and Freedom, 1777–1827.* Baton Rouge: Louisiana State University Press.

"Geometrical Nomenclature of the Uniapa Islands." n.d. Loose leaf in "Records of the American Ethnological Society, Early Records 1840's–1880." National Anthropological Archives, Smithsonian Institution. Washington, D.C.

Gibson, Gregory. 2008. *Hubert's Freaks.* Orlando, Fla.: Harcourt.

Gilfoyle, Timothy. 1992. *City of Eros: New York City, Prostitution and the Commercialization of Sex, 1790–1920.* New York: Norton.

Gilmore, Robert L., and John P. Harrison. 1948. "Jaun Bernardo Elbers and the Introduction of Steam Navigation on the Magdalena River." *Hispanic American Historical Review* 28, no. 3: 335–358.

Gilroy, Paul. 1993. *The Black Atlantic: Modernity and Double Consciousness* Cambridge: Harvard University Press.

Goldberg, David M. 2003. *The Curse of Ham: Race and Slavery in Early Judaism, Christianity and Islam.* Princeton: Princeton University Press.

Goodale, Jane C. 1985. "Pigs' Teeth and Skull Cycles: Both Sides of the Face of Humanity." *American Ethnologist* 12, no. 2: 228–244.

Goodale, Jane C. 1995. *To Sing with Pigs Is Human.* Seattle: University of Washington Press.

Goodman, Matthew. 2009. *The Sun and the Moon.* New York: Basic.

Goodrich, Charles Augustus. 1852. *Travels and Sketches in North and South America: Embracing an Account of Their Situation, Origin, Plan, Extent, Their Inhabitants, Manners, Customs, and Amusements, and Public Works, Institutions, Edifices, &c. Together with Sketches of Historical Events.* Hartford: Case, Tiffany.

Goodrich, Samuel Griswold. 1857. *Recollections of a Lifetime.* New York: Miller Orton.

Gould, Stephen J. 1996. *The Mismeasure of Man.* New York: Norton.

Govan, Thomas. 1959. *Nicholas Biddle, Nationalist and Public Banker, 1786–1844.* Chicago: University of Chicago Press.

Grant, Charles, Viscount de Vaux. 1801. *The History of Mauritius; or, The Isle of France, and the Neighbouring Islands, from their First Discovery to the Present Time; Composed Principally from the Papers and Memoirs of Baron Grant, Who Resided Twenty Years in the Island.* London: Bulmer.

Grant, Jill, and Martin Zelenietz. 1983. "Naming Practices in Kilenge." *Names* 31: 179–190.

Gray, Alastair. 1999. "Trading Contacts in the Bismarck Archipelago During the Whaling Era, 1799–1884." *Journal of Pacific History* 34, no. 1: 23–43.

Guillou, Jean. 2008. *Échos du grand océan.* Paris: L'Étrave.

Guillou, Jean. 2011. *La Pérouse . . . et après.* Paris: L'Harmattan.

Guppy, Henry. 1887. *The Solomon Islands and Their Natives.* London: Swan Sonnenenschein, Lowrey.

Gützlaff, Karl. 1838. *China Opened; or, A Display of the Topography, History . . . etc. of the Chinese Empire.* London: Smith, Elder.

Hair, Cathy, and Vincent Magea. 1995. "Development of a Small Gillnet Fishery for Roundscads in Papua New Guinea." *SPC Fisheries Newsletter* 75: 39–44.

Hale, C. R. 1932–1933. "Headstone Inscriptions, Town of Stonington, New London County, Connecticut." Mss. Stonington Historical Society, Stonington, Conn.

Haller, John S. 1970. "The Species Problem: Nineteenth-Century Concepts of Racial Inferiority in the Origin of Man Controversy." *American Anthropologist* 72: 1319–1329.

Halliard, Jack (Pseud). 1833. *Voyages and Adventures of Jack Halliard, with Captain Morrell.* Boston: Russell Odiorne; Cincinnati: H. L. and H. S. Barnum.

Hallock, John. 2000. *The American Byron: Homosexuality and the Fall of Fitz-Greene Halleck.* Madison: University of Wisconsin Press.

Hamilton, Capt. R. V. 1870. "On Morrell's Antarctic Voyage in the Year 1823, with Remarks on the Advantages Steam Will Confer on Future Antarctic Explorers." *Proceedings of the Royal Geographical Society* 14, no. 2: 145–156.

Hammond, Bray. 1947. "Jackson, Biddle, and the Bank of the United States." *Journal of Economic History* 8: 1–23.

Hardie, James. 1827. *The Description of the City of New York.* New York: Samuel Marks.

Harding, Thomas G. 1967. *Voyagers of the Vitiaz Strait: A Study of a New Guinea Trade System.* Seattle: University of Washington Press.

Harding, Thomas G. 1970. "Trading in Northeast New Guinea." In *Cultures of the Pacific: Selected Readings.* Ed. Thomas G. Harding and Ben J. Wallace, 94–111. New York: Free Press.

Harding, Thomas G., and Stephen A. Clark. 1994. "The Sio Story of Male." *Pacific Studies* 17, no. 4: 29–51.

"The Harlem Hermit's Estate." 1889. *Daily Inter Ocean,* April 9: 7.

Harrison, J. B. 1892. "Scituate's Celebrity." *Boston Evening* [source unclear]. Saturday [date unclear] June 1892. In newspaper clippings, Papers of Selim Edwin Woodworth, 1834–1947. Huntington Library. San Marino, Calif.

Hatcher, Harlen. 1947. *Johnny Appleseed: A Voice in the Wilderness.* West Chester, Pa.: Swedenborg Foundation.

Haynes, Stephen R. 2007. *Noah's Curse: The Biblical Justification of American Slavery.* Oxford: Oxford University Press.

Headley, Joel. 1873. *The Great Riots of New York, 1712 to 1873.* New York: E. B. Treat.

"Heathen Massacre." 1831. *Boston Recorder,* September 14: 148.

Heermann, Ingrid. 2001. *Form, Colour, Inspiration: Oceanic Art from New Britain.* Stuttgart: Arnoldshe.

Heidler, David S., and Jeanne T. Heidler. 2002. *The War of 1812.* Westport, Conn.: Greenwood.

"Hermitage Soon to Be Sold." 1894. *New York Herald,* February 11.

"Hermit of Harlem." 1890. *New York Times,* April 26.

Hetzel, Susan R. 1903. *The Building of a Monument: A History of the Mary Washington Associations and Their Work.* Lancaster, Pa.: Wickbksham.

Hobart, Nathaniel. 1831. *Life of Emanuel Swedenborg: With Some Account of His Writings.* Boston: Allen and Goddard.

Horsman, Reginald. 1981. *Race and Manifest Destiny: The Origins of American Racial Anglo-Saxonism.* Cambridge: Harvard University Press.

House of Commons. 1840. "Class B: Further Series—Correspondence with Foreign Powers Relating to the Slave Trade." In *Accounts and Papers.* Vol. 19: *Slavery Class B, C & D.* Session 16 January–11 August 1840. Vol. 47. London: House of Commons, 1840.

Howard, Warren. S. 1963. *American Slavers and the Federal Law, 1837–1862.* Berkeley: University of California Press.

Howe, Kerry R. 1984. *Where the Waves Fall: A New South Sea Islands History from First Settlement to Colonial Rule.* Sydney: George Allen and Unwin.

"How Silas Burrows Made a Wager." 1897. *San Francisco Call,* September 5: 20.

Hubbell, Walter. 1881. *History of the Hubbell Family Containing a Genealogical Record.* New York: J. H. Hubbell.

Hudson, Lynn. 2003. *The Making of "Mammy Pleasant": A Black Entrepreneur in Nineteenth-Century San Francisco.* Urbana: University of Illinois Press.

Hunter, John. 1793. *An Historical Journal of the Transactions at Port Jackson, and Norfolk Island, Including the Journals of Governors Phillip and King, Since the Publication of Phillips Voyage, with an Abridged Account of the New Discoveries in the South Seas, to Which Is Prefixed a Life of the Author.* London: Stockdale.

Hunter, William. 1882. *The Fan Kwae at Canton Before Treaty Days, 1825–1844.* London: Kegan Paul, Trench.

Hylan, Ken. 1990. "Cargo and Christianity in Kaliai." *Catalyst* 20, no. 2: 167–188.

"Important News from France." 1835. *American Railroad Journal and Advocate of Internal Improvements* 4, no. 7 (February 21): 109.

Irving, Washington (Diedrich Knickerbocker). 1809. *A History of New York* . . . . Philadelphia: Inskeep and Bradford.

Jacobs, Thomas Jefferson. 1844. *Scenes, Incidents, and Adventures in the Pacific Ocean; or, The Islands of the Australasian Seas, During the Cruise of the Clipper Margaret Oakley, Under Capt. Benjamin Morrell. Clearing up the Mystery Which Has Heretofore Surrounded This Famous Expedition, and Containing a Full Account of the Exploration of Bidera, Papua, Banda, Mindoro, Sooloo, and China Seas, the Manners and Customs of the Inhabitants of the Islands, and a Description of Vast Regions Never Before Visited by Civilized Man.* New York: Harper and Brothers.

Johnson, Claudia. 1975. "That Guilty Third Tier: Prostitution in Nineteenth Century American Theatres." *American Quarterly* 27, no. 5: 575–584.

Johnson, Kristin, ed. 1996. *Unfortunate Emigrants: Narratives of the Donner Party.* Logan: Utah State University Press.

Johnson, Kristin. 2006. "Selim E Woodworth." In *New Light on the Donner Party: Rescuers and Others.* At http://www.utahcrossroads.org/Donner Party/Rescuers.htm#Woodworth (accessed January 31, 2013).

Johnson, Kristin. 2008. "Sailor on Horseback: Selim Woodworth Crosses the Plains, 1846." *Overland Journal* 26, no. 1: 5–15.

Jolly, Alison. 2004. *Lords and Lemurs.* New York: Houghton Mifflin.

Jones, Christopher. 2013. "Narrative History and the Collapsing of Historical Distance." Yale University Press London blog, January 10, 2013, http://yalebooks.wordpress.com/2013/01/10/narrative-history-and-the-collapsing-of-historical-distance-by-christopher-jones/ (accessed July 1, 2013).

Jones, Noreen. 2008. *North to Matsumae: Australian Whalers to Japan.* Crawley: University of Western Australia Press.

Joyce, Barry Alan. 2001. *The Shaping of American Ethnography.* Lincoln: University of Nebraska Press.

Keeler, John. 1831. *The South Sea Islanders with a Short Sketch of Captain Morrell's Voyage to the North and South Pacific Ocean in the Schooner Antarctic Belonging to Messrs Bergh, Westerfield, Carnley, Skiddy, Livingston, and Ivers of New York. To Which Is Added a Brief Sketch Of The Sufferings of Leonard Shaw While in Captivity.* New York: Snowden.

Keeler, John. n.d. "Log of Keeler, 1828–31: John Keeler, Journal of a Voyage to the South Seas." Log 339, G. W. Blunt White Library, Mystic Connecticut.

Kemble, Fanny. 1835. *Journal by Frances Anne Butler.* Vol. 2. London: John Murray.

Kent, James. 1840. *Course of Reading Drawn up by Hon. James Kent (Late Chancellor of the State of New-York) for the Use of the Members of the Mercantile Library Association.*

King, Francis John. 1844. "Navigation Through St. George Channel, to the Westward Towards the Coast of New Guinea." *The Nautical Magazine and Naval Chronicle* 13: 12–15.

Knapp, Samuel Lorenzo. 1828. *The Genius of Masonry; or A Defence of the Order.* Providence: Granston and Marshall.

Knapp, Samuel Lorenzo. 1831. *A Memoir of the life of Daniel Webster.* New York: J. S. Redfield.

Knapp, Samuel Lorenzo. 1832. *Advice in the Pursuits of Literature.* New York: J. K. Porter.

Knapp, Samuel Lorenzo. 1834. *Female Biography: Containing Notices of Distinguished Women, in Different Nations and Ages.* New York: J. Carpenter.

Lafond de Lurcy, Capitaine G[abriel]. 1844. *Voyages autour du monde et neufrages Célèbres. Mers du Sud de la Chine et Archipels de l'Inde.* Paris: Administration de Libraririe.

Lamb, Jonathan, Vanessa Smith, and Nicholas Thomas. 2000. *Exploration and Exchange: A South Seas Anthology, 1680–1900.* Chicago: University of Chicago Press.

Lang, Hans-Joachim, and Benjamin Lease. 1975. "The Authorship of Symzonia: The Case for Nathaniel Ames." *New England Quarterly* 48, no. 2: 241–252.

Lang, John Dunmore. 1834a. *An Historical and Statistical Account of New South Wales.* Vol. 1. London: Cochrane and M'Crone.

Lang, John Dunmore. 1834b. *View of the Origin and Migrations of the Polynesian Nation.* London: James Cochrane.

"La Perouse." 1837. *The Sun,* November 6: 2.

Larenaudière [La Renaudière, Philippe François de]. 1834. "Bulletin. Analyse Critique." *Nouvelles annals des voyages* 61: 203–227.

Lattas, Andrew. 2001. "The Underground Life of Capitalism: Space, Persons, and Money in Bali (West New Britain)." In *Emplaced Myth, Space, Narrative and Knowledge in Aboriginal Australia and Papua New Guinea.* Ed. Alan Rumsey and James Weiner, 161–270. Honolulu: University of Hawai'i Press.

Lattas, Andrew. 2005. "Capitalizing on Complicity: Cargo Cults and the Spirit of Modernity on Bali Island (West New Britain)." *Ethnohistory* 52, no. 1: 47–80.

Lawrence, Peter. 1964. *Road Belong Cargo: A Study of the Cargo Movement in the Southern Madang District, New Guinea.* Melbourne: Melbourne University Press.

Lawrence, Peter. 1984. *The Garia: An Ethnography of a Traditional Cosmic System in Papua New Guinea.* Manchester, U.K.: Manchester University Press.

Lawrence, William. 1822. *Lectures on Physiology, Zoology and the Natural History of Man.* London: Printed for the booksellers.

Legueval de Lacombe, B. F. 1840. *Voyages à Madagascar et aux îles Comores, 1823 à 1830.* Vol. 2. Paris: Louis Desessart.

Lenz, William. 1991. "Narratives of Exploration, Sea Fiction, Mariners' Chronicles, and the Rise of American Nationalism: 'To Cast Anchor on That Point Where All Meridians Terminate.'" *American Studies* 32, no. 2: 41–61.

Letter, Joseph J. 2008. "Reincarnating Samuel Woodworth: Native American Prophets, the Nation and the War of 1812." *Early American Literature* 43, no. 3: 687–713.

"Letter from Bordeaux." 1831. *Alexandria Gazette,* August 22: 2.

"Letter from John Sevier to Piomingo [*sic*], December 15, 1788." 1788. *Colonial and State Records of North Carolina* 22: 704–705.

Leyda, Jay. 1969. *The Melville Log: A Documentary Life of Herman Melville, 1819–1891.* New York: Gordian.

Liauzu, Claude. 2005. "Les historiens saisis par les guerres de mémoires colonials." *Revue d'histoire moderne et contemporaine* 52, no. 4: 99–109.

"Literary Notices." 1832. *New York Mirror,* December 29, 1832, 203.

"Living Statue." 1831. *Connecticut Mirror,* November 12: 3.

Ljungstedt, Anders. 1836. *An Historical Sketch of the Portuguese Settlements in China.* Boston: James Monroe.

Mack, Norman. 2005. *Missouri's Silver Age: Silversmiths of the 1800s.* Carbondale: Southern Illinois University Press.

Maclay, Mikloucho. 1975. *New Guinea Diaries (1871–1883).* Trans. C. L. Sentinella. Madang, Papua New Guinea: Kristen Press.

Madden, Richard Robert. 1839. *A Letter to W. E. Channing on the Subject of the Abuse of the Flag of the United States in the Island of Cuba and the Advantage Taken of Its Protection in the Promotion of the Slave Trade.* Boston: William Ticknor.

Mahon, John K. 1972. *The War of 1812.* Gainesville: University Press of Florida.

Malte-Brun, Conrad. 1827. *Universal Geography; or, A Description of All the Parts of the World on a New Plan.* Vol. 2. Philadelphia: Anthony Finley.

Marcus, George. 1995. "Ethnography in/of the World System: The Emergence of Multisited Ethnography." *Annual Review of Anthropology* 24: 95–117.

"Married." 1820. *The American* (New York), April 11: 3.

Marshall, M. 2011. "Breeding with Neanderthals Helped Humans Go Global." *New Scientist,* June 16.

Martin, Robert. 1979. *The Homosexual Tradition in American Poetry.* Austin: University of Texas Press.

"Massacre in the South Pacific on Newly Discovered Island." 1831. *New York Gazette,* August 28.

Matsuda, Matt. 2006. "The Pacific." *American Historical Review* 111, no. 3: 758–780.

Matsuda, Matt. 2012. *Pacific Worlds: A History of Sea, Peoples and Cultures.* Cambridge: Cambridge University Press.

McKeithan, Daniel Morley. 1933. "Two Sources of Poe's Narrative of Arthur Gordon Pym." *University of Texas Studies in English* 13: 116–137.

McLean, Ian. 2012. "Reinventing the Savage." *Third Text* 26, no. 5: 599–613.

McPherson, Naomi. 1994. "The Legacy of Moro the Snake-Man in Bariai." *Pacific Studies* 17, no. 4: 153–182.

McPherson, Naomi. 2001. "'Wanted. Young Man, Must Like Adventure': Ian McCallum Mack, Patrol Officer." In *In Colonial New Guinea: Anthropological Perspectives.* Ed. Naomi McPherson, 82–111. Pittsburgh: University of Pittsburgh Press.

McPherson, Naomi. 2007. "Myth, Primogeniture and Long Distance Trade-Friends in Northwest New Britain, Papua New Guinea." *Oceania* 77, no. 2: 129–157.

Meigs, Henry. n.d. "Henry Meigs Diaries, 1827–1834." 2 vols. Archives of American Art, Smithsonian Institution. 20560 reel 1365. Washington, D.C.

Meigs, J. Aitken. 1857. *Catalogue of Human Crania, in the Collection of the Academy of Natural Sciences of Philadelphia: Based upon the Third Edition of Dr. Morton's "Catalogue of skulls."* Philadelphia: Lippincott.

Melville, Herman. 1847. *Typee; or, A Narrative of a Four Months' Residence Among the Natives of the Marquesas Islands.* London: John Murray.

Melville, Herman. 1851. *Moby-Dick; or, The Whale.* New York: Harper and Brothers.

"Memorial of Benjamin Morrell by Mr. Cambreleng." 1832. *Journal of the House of Representatives of the United States, 1832–1833,* December 11.

"Memorial of Benjamin Morrell by Mr. Cambreleng." 1833. *Journal of the House of Representatives of the United States, 1832–1833,* February 11.

"Memorial of Captain Benjamin Morrell by Mr. Barber." 1834. *Journal of the House of Representatives of the United States, 1833–1834,* March 17.

"Message from the President of the United States to the Two Houses of Congress, 26th Congress, Dec. 9 1840." 1840. Washington, D.C.: Blair and Rives.

Metcalfe, Samuel. 1833. *A New Theory of Terrestrial Magnetism.* New York: C, G & H Carvill.

Mills, William James. 2003. *Exploring Polar Frontiers.* Santa Barbara, Calif.: ABC-CLIO.

"Miscellaneous Notices." 1840. *The Asiatic Journal and Monthly Register* 33: 83.

Mitterling, Philip. 1959. *America in the Antarctic to 1840.* Urbana: University of Illinois Press.

Moore, Clive. 2003. *New Guinea: Crossing Boundaries and History.* Honolulu: University of Hawai'i Press.

Morgan, Dale. 1963. *Overland in 1846: Diaries and Letters of the California-Oregon Trail.* Vol. 1. Georgetown, Calif.: Talisman.

Morrell, Abby Jane. 1833. *Narrative of a Voyage to the Ethiopic and South Atlantic Ocean, Indian Ocean, Chinese Sea, North and South Pacific Ocean, in the Years 1829, 1830, 1831.* New York: J. and J. Harper, 1833.

Morrell, Benjamin. 1832a. *A Narrative of Four Voyages, to the South Sea, North and South Pacific Ocean, Chinese Sea, Ethiopic and Southern Atlantic Ocean, Indian and Antarctic Ocean. From the Year 1822 to 1831. Comprising Critical Surveys of Coasts and Islands, with Sailing Directions. And an Account of some New and Valuable Discoveries, including the Massacre Islands, where Thirteen of the Author's Crew were Massacred and Eaten by Cannibals. To which is Prefixed a Brief Sketch of the Author's Early Life.* New York: J. and J. Harper, 1832. 2d ed.: New York: Harper and Brothers, 1841.

Morrell, Benjamin. 1832b. "To Commercial Men: An Important Enterprise!" Baltimore: N.p.

Morrell, Benjamin. 1833. "Captain Morrell's Views of Temperance." *Sailor's Magazine, and Naval Journal* 5: 266–267.

Morrell, Benjamin. 1834. "Introduction" and "Voyages autour du monde." In M. Albert-Montémont [*sic*], *Bibliothèque universelle des voyages* . . . . Vol. 20. Paris: Armand-Aubrée.

Morrell, Benjamin. 1835. "Mauritius, or Isle of France." *New York Mirror,* January 10: 221–222.

Morrell, Benjamin. 1836. Protest of Benjamin Morrell, Fort Dauphin, Madagascar. 23 June 1836. Papers of Richard P. Waters, 1807–1887. Peabody Essex Museum. MH-14, Box 1, Folder 5. Salem, Mass.

"Morrell (Benjamin)." 1843. *Biographie universelle, ancienne et modern.* (Supplement). Vol. 74. Paris: L.-G. Michaud, 421–427.

Morton, Samuel. 1839. *Crania Americana; or, A Comparative View of the Skulls of Various Aboriginal Nations of North and South America, to Which Is Prefaced an Essay on the Varieties of the Human Species.* Philadelphia: J. Dobson.

"Mother of Washington." 1833. *Rochester Republican,* May 22: 2.

"Mr. Woodworth." 1836. *New York Mirror,* October 22: 135.

Murphy, Jake. 2012. "Any Last Words? A Collection of Funny or Mildly Ironic Final Quotes." At http://www.smashwords.com/extreader/read /212298/5/any-last-words-or-a-collection-of-funny-or-mildly-ironic -final-quotes (accessed January 31, 2013).

Myers, Gustavus. 1901. *The History of Tammany Hall*. New York: Boni and Liveright.

"Narrative of Four Voyages." 1833a. *American Quarterly Review* 26 (June): 314–336.

"Narrative of Four Voyages." 1833b. *Monthly Review* 3 (Sept.–Dec.): 193–221.

"National Museum." 1831. *Daily National Intelligencer,* January 6: 4.

"Natives of the Pacific Ocean." 1831. *Philadelphia Inquirer,* September 12: 2.

Naval History and Heritage Command. n.d. "Woodworth." *Dictionary of American Naval Fighting Ships, Department of the Navy.* At http://www.history .navy.mil/danfs/w11/woodworth.htm (accessed January 31, 2013).

"New York Seamen." 1854. *New York Times,* April 10.

Noah, Mordecai. 1837. *The Evidences of the American Indians Being the Descendants of the Lost Tribes of Israel.* New York: James van Norden.

Northall, William. 1850. *Life and Recollections of Yankee Hill.* New York: W. F. Burgess.

"Numeral Systems of Different Nations." 1863. *Historical Magazine* 7: 92–93.

Obeyesekere, Ganneth. 2005. *Cannibal Talk: The Man-Eating Myth and Human Sacrifice in the South Seas.* Berkeley: University of California Press.

Odell, George C. D. 1928. *Annals of the New York Stage.* Vol. 3: *1821–1834.* New York: Columbia University Press.

Papers of Samuel Woodworth, 1829–1945. n.d. Samuel Woodworth Collection, 1829–1945. Clifton Waller Barrett Library. University of Virginia. Charlottesville, Va.

Parker, Hershel. 1996. *Herman Melville: A Biography.* Vol. 1. Baltimore: John Hopkins University Press.

Parley, Peter (Pseud.). 1832. *Peter Parley's Annual: A Christmas and New Year's Present for Young People.* London: Darton.

Pascalis, Felix. 1831. "Two Savages of the Mass[a]cre Island." *Baltimore Gazette and Daily Advertiser,* September 10: 1.

Pasley, Jeffrey. 2007. "Minnows, Spies and Aristocrats: The Social Crisis of Congress in the Age of Martin van Buren." *Journal of the Early Republic* 27, no. 4: 599–653.

Payne, John Howard. 2002. *Indian Justice: A Cherokee Murder Trial at Tahlequah in 1840.* Norman: University of Oklahoma Press.

Pearson, Bill. 1984. *Rifled Sanctuaries: Some Views of the Pacific Islands in Western Literature.* Auckland: Auckland University Press.

Pearson, Mike P. 1997. "Close Encounters of the Worst Kind: Malagasy Resistance and Colonial Disasters in Southern Madagascar." *World Archaeology* 28, no. 3: 393–417.

Pech, Rufus. 1991. *Manub and Kilibob: Melanesian Models for Brotherhood Shaped by Myth, Dream and Drama.* Goroka, Papua New Guinea: Melanesian Institute.

Peltier, Philippe. 2001. "The Poetry of Oceanic Art." In *Form, Colour, Inspiration: Oceanic Art from New Britain.* Ed. Ingrid Heermann, 8–11. Stuttgart: Arnoldshe.

"Penguin." 1833. *New York Evening Tales; or, Uncle John's True Stories About Natural History* 2: 17–23. New York: Mahlon Day.

Pennington, William. 1840. *A Statement of the Facts and Circumstances Relative to the Operation of the Pilot Laws of the U.S.* New York: M. S. Harrison.

"Petition of Benjamin Morrell by Mr. Verplanck." 1831. *Journal of the House of Representatives of the United States, 1831–1832,* December 27.

"Petition of Benjamin Morrell by Mr. Wright." 1833. *Journal of the Senate of the United States of America, 1789–1873,* February 15.

Petrie, Lt. [Peter]. 1844. *Morrell's Narrative of a Voyage to the South and West Coast of Africa.* London: Whittaker.

"Philadelphia is at Present . . . ." 1831. *Daily National Journal,* November 7: 3.

Pickering, Charles. 1848. *The Races of Man and Their Geographical Distribution.* United States Exploring Expedition, vol. 9. Philadelphia: C. Sherman.

Pickering, John. 1818. "On the Adoption of a Uniform Orthography for the Indian Languages of North America." *Memoirs of the American Academy of Arts and Sciences* 4, no. 1: 319–360.

Pickering, John. 1820. *An Essay on a Uniform Orthography for the Indian Languages of North America.* Cambridge: Cambridge University Press.

Poe, Edgar Allan. 1838. *The Narrative of Arthur Gordon Pym of Nantucket.* Harmondsworth, U.K.: Penguin, 1975.

Poe, Edgar Allan. 1845. "Diddling Considered As One of the Exact Sciences." *Broadway Journal,* September 13: 145–148.

Poignant, Roslyn. 2004. *Professional Savages: Captive Lives and Western Spectacle.* Sydney: UNSW Press.

Pollin, Burton. R. 1976. "The *Narrative* of Benjamin Morrell: Out of 'The Bucket' and into Poe's *Pym.*" *Studies in American Fiction* 4, no. 2: 157–172.

Pomponio, Alice. 1992. *Seagulls Don't Fly into the Bush: Cultural Identity and Development in Melanesia.* Belmont, Calif.: Wadsworth.

Pomponio, Alice. 1994. "Namor's Odyssey: Mythical Metaphors and History in Siassi." *Pacific Studies* 17, no. 4: 53–91.

Powell, Wilfred. 1880. "Field Notes on the Morroop (*Casuarius bennetti*) of New Britain." *Proceedings of the Zoological Society of London,* June 15.

Powell, Wilfred. 1883. *Wanderings in a Wild Country; or, Three Years Amongst the Cannibals of New Britain.* London: Sampson Low, Marston, Searle and Rivington.

"Private Correspondence." 1839. *The Times,* June 3: 5.

"Public." 1831. *New York Commercial Advertiser,* September 6: 2.

Quinn, Arthur. 1941. *Edgar Allan Poe: A Critical Biography.* New York: Appleton-Century-Crofts.

Qureshi, Sadiah. 2011. *Peoples on Parade: Exhibitions, Empire, and Anthropology in Nineteenth-Century Britain.* Chicago: University of Chicago Press.

"Remarkable." 1831. *New York Evening Post,* August 30: 2.

Remini, Robert V. 2001. *Andrew Jackson and His Indian Wars.* New York: Viking.

Reynolds, J[ames] N. 1836. Address on the Subject of a Surveying and Exploring Expedition. New York: Harper and Brothers.

Reynolds, J[ames]. N. 1839. "Mocha Dick; or, The White Whale of the Pacific: A Leaf from a Manuscript Journal." *Knickerbocker* 13, no. 5: 337–392.

Rhoads, Jim, and Jim Specht. 1980. "Aspects of the Oral History of the Bali-Witu Islands, West New Britain Province." *Oral History* 8, no. 8: 10–22.

Richards, Jeffrey. 2000. "Race and the Yankee: Woodworth's *The Forest Rose.*" *Comparative Drama* 34: 33–51.

Richards, Rhys. 2007. "Nathaniel Ames: A Bostonian in the Antarctic in 1821." *International Journal of Maritime History* 19, no. 1: 271–285.

Riebe, Inge. 1967. "Anthropomorphic Stone Carvings on Unea Island." *Journal of the Polynesian Society* 76, no. 3: 374–378.

Ross, Malcolm. 2014. "Reconstructing the History of Languages in Northwest New Britain: Inheritance and Contact." *Journal of Historical Linguistics* 4:84–132.

Rowe, John Carlos. 2011. "Transnationalism and American Studies." Featured articles. Encyclopedia of American Studies Online, 2011, http://www.theasa.net/project_eas_online/page/project_eas_online_eas_fea tured_article/.

Sachs, Aaron. 2007. *The Humboldt Current.* Oxford: Oxford University Press.

Sahlins, Marshall. 1985. *Islands of History.* Chicago: University of Chicago Press.

Sahlins, Marshall. 1987. *Historical Metaphor and Mythical Realities: Structure in the Early History of the Sandwich Islands Kingdom.* Ann Arbor: University of Michigan Press.

Sahlins, Marshall. 1995. *How "Natives" Think: About Captain Cook, for Example.* Chicago: University of Chicago Press.

"Sailing Voyage Without Grog." 1829. *Schenectady New York Cabinet,* November 25: 3.

"Sailing Without Grog." 1829. *Daily National Intelligencer,* November 9: 2.

"Samuel Woodworth." 1837. *Ladies Companion and Literary Expositor* 7: 205.

Sanborn, Geoffrey. 1998. *The Sign of the Cannibal: Melville and the Making of a Postcolonial Reader.* Durham, N.C.: Duke University Press.

Sanborn, Geoffrey. 2005. "Whence Came You, Queequeg?" *American Literature* 77, no. 2: 227–257.

Sarna, Jonathan D. 1981. *Jacksonian Jew: The Two Worlds of Mordecai Noah.* New York: Holmes and Meier.

"Savages etc." 1831. *New England Magazine* 1 (October): 364–365.

Scaletta (McPherson), Naomi. 1985. "Death by Sorcery: The Social Dynamics of Dying in Bariai, West New Britain." In *Aging and Its Transformations.* Ed. Dorothy A. Counts and David R. Counts, 223–248. Pittsburgh: University of Pittsburgh Press.

Schouten, William. 1619. *The Relation of a Wonderfull Voiage Made by Willem Cornelison Schouten of Horne. Shewing How South from the Straights of Magelan in Terra Delfuego: He Found and Discovered a Newe Passage Through the Great South Seaes, and That Way Sayled Round About the World.* Trans. William Philip. London: T.D. for Nathanaell Newbery.

Scott, Kenneth. 1984. *Petitions for Name Changes in the City of New York, 1848–1899.* Washington, D.C.: National Genealogical Society.

Select Committee on Aboriginal Tribes. 1837. *Report of the Parliamentary Select Committee on Aboriginal tribes (British Settlements), Printed with Comments by the "Aborigines Protection Society."* London: House of Commons.

"Selim E. Woodworth." 1855. In *The Annals of San Francisco: Containing a Summary of the History of the First Discovery, Settlement, Progress and Present Condition of California.* Ed. Frank Soulé, John Gihon, and Jim Nisbet, 794–798. New York: Appleton.

"Selim E. Woodworth, U.S.N." n.d. Typescript. Papers of Selim Edwin Woodworth, 1834–1947. Huntington Library. San Marino, Calif.

Sellers, Charles. 1980a. *Mr. Peale's Museum.* New York: Norton, 1980.

Sellers, Charles. 1980b. "Peale's Museum and 'The New Museum Idea.'" *Proceedings of the American Philosophical Society* 124, no. 1 (1980): 25–34.

"Shipbuilder Bergh." 1883. *Evening Telegram* (New York), December 28: 2.

Simpson-Housley, Paul. 1992. *Antarctica: Exploration, Perception, and Metaphor.* London: Routledge.

Skiddy, William. n.d. "The Ups and Downs of Sea Life, 1805–1839." William T. Skiddy Collection (Coll 304). G. W. Blunt Library. Mystic Seaport Museum of America and the Sea. Misc. mss. v. 157, 158. Mystic, Conn.

"Skulls." 1831. *American Journal of Science and Arts* 21, no. 1: 197.

Smith, Horace, and Samuel Woodworth. 1831. *Festivals, Games and Amusements, with Additions by Samuel Woodworth.* New York: Harper and Brothers.

"Southern District of New York." 1833. *New York Commercial Advertiser,* August 14, 17, and 19, and September 10, 21, and 26.

"South Pacific Islander." 1831. *Watch-Tower,* September 19: 1–2.

"South Polar Seas." 1832. *Daily National Intelligencer,* January 27: 2.

"South Sea Cannibals." 1831a. *Albany Argus,* October 11: 3.

"South Sea Cannibals." 1831b. *Watch-Tower,* October 17: 1.

"South Sea Indians." 1831. *National Aegis* (reprinted from the *New York Courier*), September 14: 2.

"South Sea Islanders." 1831a. *Baltimore Gazette and Daily Advertiser,* November 24: 2.

"South Sea Islanders." 1831b. *Baltimore Patriot,* December 1: 2.

"South Sea Islanders." 1831c. *Philadelphia Inquirer,* November 3: 2.

"South Seaman." 1831. *Albany Evening Argus,* September 11.

Springer, Haskell. 1988. "Washington Irving and the Knickerbocker Group." In *Columbia Literary History of the United States.* Ed. Emory Elliott, 229–239. New York: Columbia University Press.

Springer, Haskell. 2001. "Abby Jane Wood Morrell" and "Benjamin Morrell." In *Encyclopedia of American Literature of the Sea and Great Lakes.* Ed. Jill Gidmark, 300–301. Westport, Conn.: Greenwood.

Spurzheim, Johan Gaspar. 1815. *The Physiognomical Systems of Drs. Gall and Spurzheim . . . .* London: Baldwin, Carnbock and Joy.

Spurzheim, Johan Gaspar. 1832. *Phrenology; or, The Doctrine of Mental Phenomena.* Boston: Marsh Capen and Lyon.

Srebnick, Amy. 1997. *The Mysterious Death of Mary Rogers.* Oxford: Oxford University Press.

Stanton, William. 1960. *The Leopard's Spots: Scientific Attitudes Towards Race in America, 1815–59.* Chicago: University of Chicago Press.

Stanton, William. 1975. *The Great United States Exploring Expedition of 1838–1842.* Berkeley: University of California Press.

Steers, B. MacDonald. 1971. *Silas Enoch Burrows, 1794–1870: His Life and Letters; A Compilation of Material, Gathered from Many Sources, Concerning a Rather Unusual Man.* Chester, Conn.: Pequot Press.

Steers, B. MacDonald. 1977. *Silas Enoch Burrows: A Collection of His Letters, 1818–1848.* Chester, Conn.: Pequot Press.

Stewart, Charles. 1831. *A Visit to the South Seas, in the U.S. Ship Vincennes: During the Years 1829 and 1830; with Scenes in Brazil, Peru, Manila, the Cape of Good Hope and St. Helena.* New York: John Haven.

Stommel, Henry M. 1984. *Lost Islands.* Vancouver: University of British Columbia Press.

Strathern, Marilyn. 1992. "The Decomposition of an Event." *Cultural Anthropology* 7, no. 2: 244–254.

Swadling, Pamela, and Ann Chowning. 1981. "Shellfish Gathering at Nukakau Island, West New Britain Province, Papua New Guinea." *Journal de la Société des Océanistes* 72–73: 159–167.

Taft, Kendal B. 1936. "Samuel Woodworth." Ph.D. diss. University of Chicago.

Taft, Kendal B. 1947. *Minor Knickerbockers.* New York: Litton Educational Publishers.

Tasman, A. 1895. *Abel Janszoon Tasman's Journal of His Discovery of Van Diemen's Land and New Zealand in 1642 with Documents Relating to His Exploration of Australia in 1644. Being Photo-Lithographic Facsimiles of the Original Manuscripts in the Colonial Archives at the Hague with an English Translation and Facsimiles of Original Maps to Which Are Added the Life and Labours of Abel Janszoon Tasman.* Ed. J. E. Heeres and C. H. Coote. Amsterdam: F. Muller.

Terrumbumbyandarko. 1832. "From One of the South Sea Islanders." *Baltimore Gazette and Daily Advertiser,* March 27.

"Theatre and Circus." 1831a. *Baltimore Patriot,* November 30: 3.

"Theatre and Circus." 1831b. *Baltimore Patriot,* December 3: 3.

Thomas, Nicholas. 1989. "The Force of Ethnology: Origins and Significance of the Melanesia/Polynesia Division." *Current Anthropology* 30: 27–41.

Throop, Craig. 1998. "'Pigs Are Our Hearts': A Functional Study of the Pig in Melanesia." In *Nucleation in Papua New Guinea Cultures.* Ed. Marvin K. Mayers and Daniel D. Rath, 13–21. Dallas: Summer Institute of Linguistics.

Thurston, William. 1994. "The Legend of Titikolo: An Anem Genesis." *Pacific Studies* 17, no. 4: 183–204.

Tooker, J. 1888. "Biographical Sketch of Christian Bergh." *New York Times,* March 18: 11.

"Traffic in Human Heads." 1831. *The Farmers' Cabinet,* October 22: 3.

Trautmann, Thomas T. 1992. "The Revolution in Ethnological Time." *Man,* n.s. 27, no. 2: 379–397.

Turnbull, David. 1840. *Travels in the West: Cuba, with Notices of Porto Rico, and the Slave Trade.* London: Longman.

"Two Savages." 1831. *Philadelphia Inquirer,* September 5: 3.

"Two Savages from the South Pacific." 1831. *Baltimore Gazette and Daily Advertiser,* November 22: 2.

"Two Savages from the South Pacific Islands." 1831. *Globe* (Washington, D.C.), December 17: 2.

"V." 1832. "Letter from Washington." *New York Mirror* 9: 244–245.

Van den Berg, René, and Peter Bachet. 2006. "Vitu Grammar Sketch." *Data Papers on New Guinea Languages* 51.

Van Haun, Nancy, and Silas Enoch Burrows. 1833?. *Important Trial for Seduction, in the Superior Court of N. York, Before Judge Oakley, Nancy Van Haun vs. Silas E. Burrows, on Wednesday 27th and Thursday 28th November, 1833.* [N.p., 1833?]. Available at http://pds.lib.harvard.edu/pds/view/5810347 (accessed January 31, 2013).

Van Haun, Nancy, and Silas Enoch Burrows. 1834. *Report of the Second Trial of Silas E. Burrows.* New York: Chittenden and Wheeler.

Varle, Charles. 1833. *Complete View of Baltimore.* Baltimore: Samuel Young.

Voto, Bernard Augustine de. 1943. *The Year of Indecision.* Boston: Little, Brown.

"Voyage of Discovery." 1824. *Newburyport Herald,* May 25: 3.

Wagner, Roy. 1981. *The Invention of Culture.* Chicago: University of Chicago Press.

Waldo, Samuel Putnam. 1818. *The Tour of James Monroe, President of the United States in the Year 1817.* Hartford: Bolles.

Ward, R. Gerard. 1967. *American Activities in the Central Pacific, 1790–1870.* Vol. 7. Ridgewood, N.J.: Gregg.

Webster, Elsie M. 1984. *The Moon Man: A Biography of Nikolai Miklouho-Maclay.* Berkeley: University of California Press.

"We cordially concur . . . ." 1831. *New York Commercial Advertiser,* September 13: 2.

Weddell, James. 1827. *A Voyage Towards the South Pole Performed in the Years 1822–24.* London: Brown and Green.

Wermuth, Paul. 1973. *Bayard Taylor.* New York: Twayne.

Whalen, Terence. 1999. *Edgar Allan Poe and the Masses.* Princeton: Princeton University Press.

Whipple, Addison B. C. 1954. *Yankee Whalers in the South Seas.* New York: Doubleday.

White, Hayden. 2009. *The Content of the Form: Narrative Discourse and Historical Representation.* Baltimore: Johns Hopkins University Press.

White, J. Peter, ed. 1999. *Translation of R. Parkinson's Dreissig Jahre in der Sudsee [Thirty Years in the South Seas] (1907).* Bathurst, Australia: Oceania Publications/University of Sydney.

Whittaker, June, ed. 1985. *Documents and Readings in New Guinea History.* Milton: Queensland Press.

Williams, Edwin. 1833. *New York as It Is in 1833.* New York: Disturnell.

Williams, Edwin. 1834a. *The New York Annual Register: 1834.* New York: James Van Norden.

Williams, Edwin. 1834b. *New York as It Is in 1834.* Vol. 2. New York: Disturnell.

Williams, John. 1837. *A Narrative of Missionary Enterprises in the South Sea Islands: With Remarks upon the Natural History of the Islands, Origin, Languages, Traditions, and Usages of the Inhabitants.* London: J. Snow.

Wilmeth, Don, and Christopher Bigsby. 1998. *The Cambridge History of American Theatre: Beginnings to 1870.* New York: Cambridge University Press.

Wilson, James Grant. 1886. *Bryant and His Friends.* New York: Fords, Howard and Hulbert.

Woodworth, Samuel. 1816. *The Champions of Freedom; or, The Mysterious Chief: A Romance of the Nineteenth Century, Founded on the Events of the*

War, Between the United States and Great Britain, Which Terminated in March, 1815. New York: C. N. Baldwin.

Woodworth, Samuel. 1824. *La Fayette; or, The Castle of Olmutz: A Drama in Three Acts.* New York: C. N. Baldwin.

Woodworth, Samuel. 1825. *The Forest Rose; or, American Farmers: A Pastoral Opera in Two Acts, Music by John Davies.* New York: Hopkins and Morris.

Woodworth, Samuel, and N. C. Bochsa. 1832. *I pity and Forgive: The Last Words of Gen Simon Bolivar Sung by Mr. Jones, the Poetry by S. Woodworth Esq. Music from Beethoven Arranged with Accompaniment for the Piano Forte by N. C. Bochsa, Respectfully Dedicated Silas E. Burrows, Esq.* New York: Firth and Hall.

Woodworth, Selim E. n.d. "Journal of a Voyage from New York to the South Pacific Ocean, on Board the American Brig *Margaret Oakley* of N.Y., 1834–35." Papers of Selim Edwin Woodworth, 1834–1947. Huntington Library. San Marino, Calif.

Woodworth, Selim E. n.d. "Log of Midshipman S. E. Woodworth 1838–9." Papers of Selim Edwin Woodworth, 1834–1947. Huntington Library. San Marino, Calif.

Woodworth, Selim E. n.d. Papers of Selim Edwin Woodworth, 1834–1947. Huntington Library. San Marino, Calif.

Wray, Leonard. 1848. *The Practical Sugar Planter.* London: Smith, Elder.

Wright, Robin K. 1987. "The Travelling Exhibition of Captain Samuel Hadlock, Jr.: Eskimos in Europe, 1822–1826." In *Indians and Europe: An Interdisciplinary Collection of Essays.* Ed. Christian Feest, 215–234. Aachen, Ger.: Herodot.

Index